CU00646403

Tuning In

THE OXFORD MUSIC / MEDIA SERIES

Daniel Goldmark, Series Editor

Tuning In: American Narrative Television Music
Ron Rodman

Tuning In

American Narrative Television Music

RON RODMAN

OXFORD
UNIVERSITY PRESS

2010

OXFORD
UNIVERSITY PRESS

Oxford University Press, Inc., publishes works that further
Oxford University's objective of excellence
in research, scholarship, and education.

Oxford   New York
Auckland   Cape Town   Dar es Salaam   Hong Kong   Karachi
Kuala Lumpur   Madrid   Melbourne   Mexico City   Nairobi
New Delhi   Shanghai   Taipei   Toronto

With offices in
Argentina   Austria   Brazil   Chile   Czech Republic   France   Greece
Guatemala   Hungary   Italy   Japan   Poland   Portugal   Singapore
South Korea   Switzerland   Thailand   Turkey   Ukraine   Vietnam

Copyright © 2010 by Oxford University Press, Inc.

Published by Oxford University Press, Inc.
198 Madison Avenue, New York, New York 10016

www.oup.com

Oxford is a registered trademark of Oxford University Press.

All rights reserved. No part of this publication may be reproduced,
stored in a retrieval system, or transmitted, in any form or by any means,
electronic, mechanical, photocopying, recording, or otherwise,
without the prior permission of Oxford University Press.

Library of Congress Cataloging-in-Publication Data
Rodman, Ron (Ronald Wayne)
Tuning In : American narrative television music / Ron Rodman.
p.   cm. — (The Oxford music/media series)
Includes bibliographical references and index.
ISBN 978-0-19-534024-2; 978-0-19-534025-9 (pbk.)
1. Television music—United States—History and criticism.   I. Title.
ML2080.R63 2009
781.5'460973—dc22   2009007222

This volume is published with generous support from the Lloyd Hibberd
Publication Endowment Fund of the American Musicological Society.

1   3   5   7   9   8   6   4   2
Printed in the United States of America
on acid free paper

To my wife, Mary Suzanne Rodman
"Who can turn the world on with her smile..."

Acknowledgments

When I began this project over ten years ago, information and primary sources were uncovered the old fashioned way—through visits to the special collections in libraries and by chancing to catch an old TV show or two on cable networks like TV Land and Nickelodeon. I also accessed books and articles of authors from media studies and communications departments, departments that have an extensive literature on television history, broadcast practice, aesthetics, and so on. Many of these works have made an impact on me, most notably (and obviously in this book) John Fiske's excellent book *Television Culture*, upon which, from a musical standpoint, some of this book is modeled. However, to date, little has been written on television music, at least from a scholarly standpoint. There were several helpful resources that got me started in a productive direction in this area. The first was Steven Westcott's *A Comprehensive Bibliography of Music for Film and TV* (1985), which includes an almost exhaustive listing of articles for music in television listed by decade of publication. The second was Jon Burlingame's *TV's Biggest Hits: The Story of Television Themes from "Dragnet" to "Friends"* (1996), a work that appeared just as my own interest in the area emerged. Focusing on TV theme songs, Burlingame's book is a treasure trove of information on television composers throughout TV history. To gather his information, Burlingame interviewed dozens of composers. Two other important resources were Philip Tagg's pioneering book *Kojak: Fifty Seconds of Television Music*, which appeared in 1979 but was republished in 2000, and Nicholas Cook's *Analyzing Musical Multimedia* (1998), another groundbreaking work that opened up the televisual musical repertoire to analysis. Though not a music book, Harry Castleman and Walter Podrizak's *Watching TV: Four Decades of American Television* (1982) also was useful in its year-by-year listing of programs from the early 1940s to 1985. Erik

Barnouw's works on the history of American television also have served as a springboard for my own work in TV music history.

As this book developed, so did accessibility of information on TV music. Thanks to the Internet, a plethora of information on both TV and movies is available on online databases, such as the Internet Movie Database (http://www. imdb.com), while many old programs and commercials mentioned in this book can now be viewed on YouTube and Hulu (http://www.hulu.com). Information on publication information for TV theme music was obtained through another very useful Web site, Classic TV Themes, at http://www.classicthemes.com. All of these resources have been very helpful to me in completing this book.

Despite the burgeoning technology, I wish to thank those who contributed and assisted this project in the good old-fashioned way. First, thanks to the good people at the UCLA Music Library Special Collections for their assistance over the years with the CBS scores and the Gilbert Collection. In California, it was my pleasure and good fortune to meet Gertrude (Trudy) Gilbert, wife of the late Hershel Burke Gilbert, who composed the music for *The Rifleman* series, and her daughter, Toby Bernstein. They are both very gracious people who granted permission for me to use Mr. Gilbert's music to illustrate my points. Thanks also to the librarians at the Wisconsin Center for Film and Theater Research, especially Ben Brewster, who helped me find photographs and gain access to the Harry Sosnik Collection—the publication rights to which (we discovered) are now owned by the center, as the Sosnik estate has been legally closed. Thanks also to Jonathan Belott at Hal Leonard Publishing, who went several extra miles in tracking down copyrights to many of the examples cited in this volume. Thanks also to the people at Oxford University Press for their encouragement and vision for this project, not to mention the invaluable assistance with editing this volume.

I also thank Elizabeth McKinsey, former dean of the college at Carleton College, who granted me a sabbatical for the project early on, and Scott Bierman, who as of summer 2009 is also a past dean, recently accepting the position as president of Beloit College. Both encouraged me and helped to produce this book by providing subvention funds from the Dean of the College's office. Also thanks to Lewis Weinberg and Tucker McNeil of the Carleton Public Events and Presentations Department, who assisted with video captures and the formatting of many of the examples. Thanks also go to Brent Kivell of Kivell Design of Northfield, Minnesota, for his help with scanning some of the facsimiles and for helping with the graphic design of many of the figures and examples in this book.

I have appreciated colleagues who have been very supportive of this project. Thanks to Erkki Pekkilä of the University of Helsinki, David Neumeyer of the University of Texas–Austin, and Robert Hatten of Indiana University, who served as role models and gave generous advice and encouragement early on, and to my colleagues at Carleton College in both the music and the cinema and media studies (CAMS) departments, especially Professors Carol Donelan and John Schott.

Above all, thanks and love to my beautiful wife, (Mary) Sue, who tolerated this whole project through months of my complaining and work time away from home. I have also appreciated the support of my two daughters, Regina and Catherine, whose questions about the status of the project became a long-standing joke and were always good for a few laughs. Also thanks for the love and support always of my beloved father and mother, Eugene and Juanita Rodman, both of whom, while not habitual TV watchers, are big fans of *The Andy Griffith Show* and *The Lawrence Welk Show*. Not coincidentally, both of these programs are mentioned in this book.

For permission to use the examples in this book I also acknowledge the following:

> Theme and Cue Music to *The Rifleman*. Copyright 1957 by Hershel Burke Gilbert. Used by permission of Toby G. Bernstein and Gertrude F. Gilbert, Trustees, The Gilbert Family Trust of 1989.
> Theme and Music to "Pride and Prejudice" from *Philco Television Playhouse*. Music by Harry Sosnik. Used by permission of the Wisconsin Center for Film and Theater Research.
> "Steel" Episode-Cues from *The Twilight Zone*. Music by Nathan van Cleave. Copyright 1963 by Aspenfair Music Inc. Copyright renewed. This arrangement copyright 2009 Aspenfair Music Inc. All rights administered by Sony/ATV Music Publishing LLC, 8 Music Square West, Nashville. International copyright secured. All rights reserved.
> Miller High Life Beer Commercial. Composer unknown. Used by permission of Miller-Coors Corp., Milwaukee, Wisconsin.
> *Gillette Look Sharp March*. Music by Mahlon Merrick. Copyright by Sunshine Music Co. (BMI). Used by permission of Gordon Music Co., Inc.
> *Dance of an Ostracized Imp*. Music by Frederic Curzon. Used by permission of Boosey and Hawkes.
> Themes from *Star Trek* "Shore Leave" episode (Planet, White Rabbit, Finnegan, Don Juan, Ruth, Medieval/Chivalry, Samurai, and Tiger motives) from the Paramount Television Series *Star Trek*. Music by Gerald Fried. Copyright 1966 by Bruin Music. Copyright renewed. This arrangement copyright 2008 by Bruin Music. All rights administered by Sony/ATV Publishing LLC, 8 Music Square West, Nashville, TN 37203. International copyright secured. All rights reserved.

Theme from *Star Trek* from the Paramount Television series *Star Trek*. Words by Gene Roddenberry. Music by Alexander Courage. Copyright 1966, 1970 by Bruin Music. Copyright renewed. This arrangement copyright 2008 by Bruin Music. All rights administered by Sony/ATV Publishing LLC, 8 Music Square West, Nashville, TN 37203. International copyright secured. All rights reserved.

Theme to *Leave It to Beaver*. Music by Dave Kahn. Lyrics by Melvyn Lenard and Mort Greene. Copyright 1958, renewed 1985 by Merlen Music (ASCAP). Used by permission of Gordon Music Co., Inc.

Theme to *Dragnet*. By Walter Schumann and Miklos Rozsa. Copyright 1953 (renewed) by Chappell & Co. and EMI Robbins Catalogue, Inc. All rights reserved. Used by permission of Alfred Publishing Co., Inc.

Theme to *M Squad*. Music by Count Basie. Copyright 1958, 1959 by Leeds Music. Used by permission of Gordon Music Co.

Adam-12 Theme. Music by Frank Comstock. Copyright 1968, 1974 by USI A Music Publishing. Copyright renewed. This arrangement copyright 2008 by USI A Music Publishing. All rights controlled and administered by Universal Music Corp. All rights reserved. Used by permission.

Hawaii Five-0 Theme. Music by Morton Stevens. Copyright 1969 by Sony/ATV Music Publishing LLC and Aspenfair Music. Copyright renewed. This arrangement copyright 2008 by Sony ATV Music Publishing LLC and Aspenfair Music. All rights administered by Sony-ATV Music Publishing LLC, 8 Music Square West, Nashville, TN 37203. International copyright secured. All rights reserved.

Hill Street Blues Theme. Music by Mike Post. Copyright 1981 by MTM Music, Inc. This arrangement copyright 2008 by MTM Music, Inc. All rights controlled and administered by TCF Music Publishing, Inc. All rights reserved. Used by permission.

Theme from *NYPD Blue*. Music by Mike Post. Copyright 1993, 1994 by Ear Bunky Music. This arrangement copyright 2008 by Ear Bunky Music. All rights controlled and administered by Fox Film Music Corp. All rights reserved. Used by permission.

Theme from *The X-Files* from the Twentieth Century Fox Television Series *The X-Files*. Music by Mark Snow. Copyright 1993, 1995 by TCF Music Publishing, Inc. This arrangement copyright 2008 by TCF Publishing, Inc. All rights reserved. Used by permission.

Twin Peaks Theme. Words and music by Angelo Badalamenti and David Lynch. Copyright 1990 by Anlon Music and O. K. Paul Music. All rights controlled and administered by Universal Music Corp. and Song of Universal, Inc. All rights reserved. Used by permission.

Contents

Contents

Tuning In

Introduction

What Were Musicians Saying about Television Music during the First Decade of Broadcasting?

The Pleasures of Television

Americans in the latter part of the twentieth century were infatuated with television. According to the A. C. Nielsen Co., in the year 2000 the average American watched more than 4 hours of TV each day—that's 28 hours per week or two months of nonstop TV watching per year. The portion of households possessing at least one television was 99 percent; 66 percent of U.S. homes had three or more TV sets, the same percentage that watched TV while eating dinner. In a 65-year life span, the average American will have spent 9 years glued to the tube (Herr n.d.). Yet it's a love-hate relationship: 49 percent of Americans say they watch too much TV, while many (including academics like myself) often claim that they "don't watch much TV" yet are able to quote TV characters and are up to date on the latest TV sports scores.

America's (and, for that matter, the world's) love affair with television stems, in part, from its convenience as an in-home appliance that offers multiple uses for various needs: TV is simultaneously an information conveyer, an entertainer, a baby-sitter, a source of companionship, a storyteller, a tool of commerce, and more. Much of the animus toward television comes from its perceived excesses (too much sex, too much violence), but more often it derives from the notion that TV is nothing but an electronic bundle of banal programming that serves only as interludes among a mind-numbing plethora of banal advertisements, all of which constitutes a colossal waste of time. Indeed, the famous May 9, 1961, speech by Federal Communications Commission chair Newton Minow to the National Association of Broadcasters contained the oft-quoted description of television as a "vast wasteland." Nielsen's statistics suggest that if the 250 billion hours per year that Americans watch television were translated into wage work at $5 per hour, $125 trillion (yes, *trillion*) would be earned. Additional dislike of television comes from the perception that it does not require the engagement of mental activity, as is necessary, for example, to read a book. Television viewing is widely regarded as a passive, voyeuristic pastime devoid of intellectual stimulation.

For all its banality, television is in many ways a mirror of our culture. Contrary to the popular notion that it is a brainless and passive activity, television's discursive realm is actually quite complex and multilayered. While I will not contradict psychological studies indicating that reading a book is more mentally beneficial than television watching, I would agree with such authors as John Fiske that television is probably not the totally mindless activity we have grown to believe. Fiske (1987) makes a compelling case for the "reading" of television texts, employing the term "reading" in the exact same sense as the reading of literary texts. Fiske (along with other media theorists) argues persuasively that television is a transmitter of values and cultural beliefs and that it communicates effectively because we, the viewers, are able to "read out" and decode these messages through an understanding of the language of television. Music, as one component of television, communicates both as a language in and of itself and in terms of the multiple roles it plays in TV programs and commercials. For the language of music to communicate through television it must be capable of producing meaning either as a text within itself or through the tacit agreement with its audience that music correlates with extramusical sources of meaning. This book considers both aspects of music as a conveyor of meaning in television.

Along with its industrial and commercial aspects, the history of television is rich with artistic innovation and activity, some of it impoverished but much of it innovative. Television is a medium that draws upon many elements of the visual and performing arts: from the theater, stagecraft, scriptwriting, dramaturgy, costume design, makeup, and acting; from the cinema, camera, lighting, and sound technology; from dance, choreography; and so on. And above all, for the purposes of this study, television draws upon *music*, sometimes lots of it. Just as Americans have been attracted to the theater, opera, the minstrel show, vaudeville, radio, and the cinema, they are also drawn to television because it is a musical medium. Television has provided artistic expression for numerous composers and performers in various genres, from classical, dramatic, jazz, country and western, to rock. Many musicians used television as a sideline for larger careers, but others, especially those in the late twentieth century, devoted their entire careers to television music. This rich history has yet to be explored. While this book is not an exhaustive history of television music, it does provide historical snapshots of some of the American composers who wrote music for television narratives.

Early Development

The complexity of television discourse did not develop in a vacuum. As a relative newcomer to the electronic media (video games and the Internet are younger, of course), television has been dependent (some would say parasitic) on the discursive practices of other media, especially its predecessors, live musical theater, the cinema, and radio, to convey messages and meanings. Despite the obvious commonalities of television and film (both are visual *and* audio mediums), television's arc of development in the early years resulted from its ties to the radio stations that pioneered television broadcasting in the 1930s and 1940s. Television was a novelty during these decades and the subject of many public exhibitions, but it was not until the 1950s that the new medium began to rival other forms of entertainment. Radio networks, such as the Radio Corporation of America (RCA, which owned the National Broadcasting Co. or NBC), General Electric (which came to own the Columbia Broadcasting System or CBS), and Westinghouse, initially provided limited studio space for television, but after World War II these parent companies embraced the new medium, devoting time and resources to the development of cameras and sets and implementing programming that was comparable to their radio counterparts.

By the early 1950s, film studios (rightly) saw television as a competitor and sought to ban (or at least slow down) its development. One of television's earliest critics, Darryl F. Zanuck, head of the 20th Century Fox movie studio, was quoted as saying in 1946 that television "won't be able to hold on to any market it captures after the first six months. People will soon get tired of staring at a plywood box every night" (Genova 2001). Within a few years after Zanuck uttered these famous words he had to eat them because by the mid-1950s movie studios were investing time, space, and money in the new medium, beginning with Warner Brothers studios, which produced adaptations of three films that became rotating television series in 1955.[1] Eventually Zanuck's own Fox studios made the transition to television (and even developed its own major television network in 1986).

The era of narrative television could be said to have begun with the broadcast of a theatrical play, *The Queen's Messenger*, in Schenectady, New York (headquarters of the General Electric Co.), on September 11, 1928. The play was a popular melodrama that was enjoying a long run on Broadway. The sound elements to the play were broadcast on WGY, the local radio station in Schenectady, while the pictures were broadcast by an experimental television station, W2XAD (making the broadcast a pioneer also in simulcasting). Three cameras were used, all motionless, each taking only close-up pictures. Two actors spoke their lines on camera while two others acted as hand models for close-ups. The broadcast of the "radio moving picture" was seen on a total of four, 41-line television sets all in Schenectady. The broadcast was a novelty, having no immediate impact other than to be viewed as an interesting experiment by General Electric technicians, but it foreshadowed the performance practices of early television, notably, the use of theatrical adaptations modified by radio, performances by stage and radio actors, live broadcasts from radio facilities, and the borrowing of directors experienced in stage or radio productions.

As television developed, programming in its early years borrowed heavily from the codes of radio, and these included musical codes. To a modern (post-1950) audience, many of these codes may seem redundant or peculiar. Since radio depended on sound through its three "sensory channels" (spoken language, sound effects, and music), it developed an elaborate use of these sound codes in its dramatic programming. Radio actors, sound effects technicians, and composer/musicians telegraphed their actions through dialogue (e.g., "Marcia, why are you walking out the front door?"), elaborate sound effects (e.g., door slams), and dramatic musical scores that borrowed heavily from theater and film. As with radio, early television soundtracks consisted of either live musicians performing along with the drama but in an adjacent studio (while the conductor frantically watched a television monitor) or canned music, that is, music that had been prerecorded, often for another purpose. Of course, it was less expensive to use prerecorded music than to hire live musicians. As television broadcasting matured, these sound codes were modified to adapt to the new visual medium. Not coincidentally, the change from radio-like sound codes to more cinematic sound codes came in the mid-1950s, when film studios began to take a more active interest in television programming.

The first television stations sprang up in the early 1930s. Some were owned and operated by electronics companies (the same companies that manufactured radio and television sets) while others were owned by the print media and the radio networks. In New York CBS and NBC both owned stations, as did the Jenkins Corp., founded by inventor Charles Francis Jenkins. Philadelphia had two stations, both owned by the Philco Radio Corp. In Chicago, there were five stations owned by radio networks as well as Zenith, Western Television, and the *Chicago Daily News*. The lone station in Los Angeles was owned by Don Lee Broadcasting.

Early American television imitated radio also in its administrative practices. Network executives determined that television, like radio, would be a "free" medium, that is, available to anyone who owned a television set. Revenue would be raised through on-air advertising, following the system adopted for radio in the 1920s. As many studies show, the commercial has become the primary mechanism for program sponsorship, for projecting an image of products and corporations (as well as the networks), and for generating revenue to cover operating costs. Of course, as Raymond Williams (1992) has pointed out, "free" in this context really means being controlled by corporations rather than by government through television's dependency on advertising revenues. Indeed, the history of television is filled with stories of networks bowing to the will of their advertisers.

Television programming also imitated radio by complying with the radio log schedule, a system that coordinated program placement, continuity, airtime availability, pricing, research, and demographic analysis (Hawes 1986: 13). While the scheduling of performances was long a practice for live theater and the cinema, it was essential for the shorter programs offered by both radio and television. According to Stuart Kaminsky (1985), it was radio that introduced the time slot, which established the hour as the standard measure of time and fragmented that hour into split-decimal time periods: 30 seconds, 1 minute, 5 minutes, 15 minutes, 30 minutes, 1 hour, 90 minutes, 2 hours. Television followed radio's practice of continuous programming, a concept that actually dates back to the early years of vaudeville.[2] Radio began as a medium that broadcasted discrete events: reporting the results of the election of President Warren G. Harding by KDKA in 1922 was the first such broadcast in the United States. Television followed suit in its early days by broadcasting programs mostly of political or sporting events with intervals of dead air in between. Just as radio filled up its time with news reports and commercials in the late 1920s, by the late 1940s television was doing the same thing.

A regular television program schedule was instituted by CBS on July 21, 1931. Although CBS president William S. Paley's main thrust was radio programming, he hired Edward Klauber and Paul Kesten to develop television. The first program had the unceremonious title of "Television Inaugural Broadcast." It featured New York mayor Jimmy Walker as well as performances by the Boswell Sisters, singer Kate Smith, and composer/pianist George Gershwin.[3] RCA affiliate NBC followed CBS's lead by installing a television station in the new Empire State Building in 1932 and began regular programming in 1935. Despite these initial successes, broadcast television was limited first by the Great Depression (when many people were unable or, given the dearth of programming that was available in that period, unwilling to purchase TV sets) and then by World War II. Only after the war did the golden age of television as a *mass* medium begin. Lasting roughly from the late 1940s to the

7

early 1960s, this early golden age was characterized by beefed-up programming, especially the live broadcasts of numerous original and classic dramas, the selling of TV sets on a massive scale, and corporate sponsorship of programs in the new medium.

By 1948, five radio networks had made the transition to television. NBC and CBS were the undisputed leaders, with the American Broadcasting Co. or ABC (which was the NBC–Blue radio network until its sale in 1943), Dumont, and Mutual also contending for viewers. The larger studio spaces for the radio networks were remodeled for television, and the creative forces of the networks grappled with the new visual medium. Experiments were conducted on building sets and developing makeup and costumes that would create appealing images when broadcast on the black-and-white television screen. Also, much of the experimentation involving television programming had to do with camera improvements, creating sharper images and more fluid camera movements, as well as the development of color TV sets and cameras. While much energy went into the development of the visual image, television producers found that radio sound technology was already highly developed and was well adapted to the new medium. By the postwar years, television had adopted the frequency modulation (FM) system, which provided much more clarity than its AM (amplitude modulation) counterpart. Now, the only problem was how to hide microphones and nondiegetic musicians (live musicians whose performance is not incorporated into the mise-en-scène, that is, it is heard by the audience but not by the actors) from the view of the audience.

Music and Early TV

While no mention is made of music being part of the broadcast of *The Queen's Messenger*, music was a part of earlier experiments done to develop a mechanical television camera. Charles Francis Jenkins, having developed the motion picture camera in the 1890s, set about to develop a television camera in 1923–1924. Jenkins put on some public demonstrations of a mechanical camera that used rotating disks with spiral perforations that produced a rapid scanning process. Pictures of these experiments show that his subjects were by and large *musical* subjects. One picture shows Jenkins photographing a woman playing the piano (see Barnouw 1990: 64). Other demonstrations were given on private television sets and on large screens in movie theaters, often with musical performers as subjects. In addition to its inaugural broadcast, in 1931, CBS logged its first tele musical on July 22. On August 27, it broadcast the first musical miniature comedy. Other musical firsts included the first musical variety series, *Half Hour on*

Broadway, and the first musical comedy series, *Ned Wayburn's Musical Comedy*, both broadcast in August of that year (Hawes 1986: 34).

Other stations followed. NBC began television broadcasting in 1935 and in 1939 was the first to broadcast an opera, an abbreviated presentation of *I Pagliacci*, a popular verismo opera by Ruggero Leoncavallo. The broadcast was heavily criticized by the press, with critics complaining that the singers were not sufficiently attractive, that they seemed to strain as they sang, and that the entire production was just inadequate for the tiny television screen (Hawes 1986: 90). These comments set a standard for the portrayal of musical performance on popular television that persists to this day.

Like television programming itself, music and musicians for television simply moved from their radio formats to the new television medium. Much music was broadcast live on television, especially as part of the musical variety shows that filled programming logs in the early years. For dramatic programs, however, much music was prerecorded or canned—often in foreign countries to keep costs down. The American Federation of Musicians did not quite know how to respond to the new medium, as before 1949, fearing exploitation from the networks, they sought to ban all live music on television. Then, in 1950, after an agreement on live music had been reached, the union, fearing a loss of jobs for American musicians, sought a ban on prerecorded music (Bowman 1949b and Chotzinoff 1949).

What Were Musicians Saying?

As television developed in the postwar years, the sky seemed to be the limit for the new medium, which offered a new home entertainment potential for the American public as well as a new outlet for musical expression. Paul Whiteman, the famous bandleader perhaps best known for commissioning and conducting the first performance of George Gershwin's *Rhapsody in Blue* in 1924, became music director for ABC in 1943 and kept that position into the 1960s. In the late 1940s Whiteman became one of the first musical celebrity spokesmen for television, often appearing in commercials for the early *Philco Television Playhouse* where he plugged the features of new Philco radios and high fidelity or hi-fi systems. Whiteman believed that television held great promise for the future of music. He noted the wide variety of programming suitable for the medium: live concerts, musical theater, sporting events, dramatic programs, news and current events. He even envisioned music lessons being given over the airwaves (thus making him an early proponent of distance learning) (Cooke 1949: 341). Whiteman hosted several dance music programs, including *The Paul Whiteman's*

Goodyear Revue (1949–1952), *On the Boardwalk with Paul Whiteman* (1954), and *America's Greatest Bands* (1955), all designed to introduce young people to big band music (and to promote his own projects).

At the same time that Whiteman was speculating on the future of music, others also began to tout the musical possibilities of television. The editor of *Etude* magazine, James Francis Cooke, in an article that appeared in the June 1949 issue of the magazine, for example, while asserting that TV had not done much to promote orchestral concerts (orchestras don't have eye appeal), was nonetheless enthusiastic about broadcasting opera and musical theater on the small screen. Noting that viewers were curious to see celebrity conductors like Arturo Toscanini perform on television, Cooke conceded that smaller chamber groups would come across much better on TV.[4] Cooke was enthusiastic also about the other educational potentials of television, citing Roy Marshall of the Franklin Institute of Philadelphia who engineered a broadcast of the institute's large telescope aimed at the moon! Nonetheless, Cooke claimed that adaptations of theatrical, chamber music, musical theater, and vaudeville would be better served on television.

Despite such innovative thinking, most musicians and music critics of the era took a more traditional view of music on television, that is, as an entertainment or narrative agent, taking on the roles it played on radio. Indeed, television's close association with radio (in the areas of administration, production, and programming) made early television look, or more accurately *sound*, very much like radio.

In addition to television music continuing to entertain audiences—live music was an inexpensive means of providing programming in the early years—musicians were also concerned about the quality of background music in television programs. Several articles published in the mid- to late 1940s clearly show that musicians were concerned about the quality of music in both radio and early television and about music fitting the mood and emotion of the radio or television narrative. There was tension also between the use of so-called library music, that is, prerecorded music, and music newly composed for radio and television. One article, by Rose Heylbut (1945), describes the development of background music on radio and television, focusing on an interview with Thomas Belviso, a composer and conductor who had been hired to take over as music director for both the radio and television divisions of NBC, and his associates Leo Kempinski and Morris Mamorsky.[5] Upon arriving at NBC, Belviso discovered that radio programs relied heavily on library music to express narrative moods and reportedly stated that for these programs, "mood and background music still leaned on the policy of dipping into familiar numbers for a bit of sad places, and a bit of gay tune in gay spots." Belviso's contention was that "music must either fit the drama exactly, or keep out of the drama" (Heylbut 1945: 493). Other composers commented on the need for music to be subservient to the drama or narrative. According to Kempinski, "Background music is actually an obbligato. It should never take attention away from the script itself—either for its goodness or its badness! If for any reason, the music outshines the story, it isn't good background music" (quoted in Heylbut 1945: 494).

Billy Nalle (1962: 121), an organist for daytime TV soaps (*Young Dr. Malone* [1958–1963] and *The Way of the World* [1955]) and a studio musician for several other programs, also wrote about the effect of music on a television narrative: "Music greatly helps both the writer and director in many ways. It gives tensile strength to the script and camera work. It can enrich and heighten the dramatic line. Further, not only does it encourage active participation on the part of the viewer, but also it gives a real 'lift' to those in the cast. Provision is made purposely for them to hear the musical score via studio speakers as they play their parts." Here Nalle describes the effect of music not only on a television audience but also on the actors. Playing music for actors was a practice held over from the era of silent films, when music was played for the mute actors to encourage them to emote.

Nalle also describes the practice of performing live musical accompaniments to television programs, especially as these accompaniments were combined with recorded music in a show. He mentions that his earliest use of this combination was for a *Studio One* show in 1952. The recorded music played was the *Ballade for Piano and Orchestra* by Fauré. The irony of the use of music in this broadcast was that some themes of the *Ballade* were used in scenes depicting a live piano performance while at other key points live piano music was used (presumably at points with *no* pianist depicted!).

Nalle's comments point to the complexity of live music accompanying live acting in early television. Harry Sosnik, a music director/composer (and successor to Whiteman as music director at ABC), described the process of synchronizing music with a drama:

> In the new science of composing music for television, the composer writes to a script in which he tries time the sequences calling for music as accurately as possible by himself, always making allowances for the visual stageplay between lines of dialog. In the script the scenes without audio are briefly described and what may look like a two-minute sequence on paper may turn out to be three or four minutes during the dress rehearsal.
>
> Since the dress rehearsal is the first complete run-though for cast and orchestra, and is held shortly before the telecast, it is obvious that the

music must be flexible enough so that entire sections can be added or taken out at a moment's notice. After the dress rehearsal, corrections are made. Then it is up to the conductor for the next run-through is the actual telecast and that is it.

The conductor and orchestra are in a different studio than the cast. He has a screen with no audio and the other ear for master control cues, a Script and his scores before him. From all this it is apparent that this medium will have to develop a highly specialized group of men as did the motion picture industry during it formative years.

Of course the ultimate answer to all the complicated problems is to eventually do shows of this type on film. (Sosnik 1949)

Sosnik's comments were written at a time when music was normally broadcast live along with a show and the conductor (much like a film composer) had to watch the video but also (unlike a film composer) provide musical cues timed exactly on the spot! Sosnik was prophetic also about TV shows being filmed, which became the practice in the 1950s, especially with popular programs like *Dragnet* and *I Love Lucy*.

While introducing the world to immediate mass broadcasting that was spatially removed from its audience, radio also provided immediacy to a vast audience across the United States. Early television programs were similar to both radio and the theater in that they were broadcast live. Despite the obvious drawbacks of potential miscues, dead air, and other mistakes, live performances were viewed favorably by producers and audiences alike. Sosnik reports that when Bing Crosby decided to prerecord his *Kraft Radio Broadcast* program in the 1950s, it was seen by some critics as a decline of the medium (Sosnik 1982: 100).

Despite its liveness, radio, along with the cinema, was an intermediate step in separating the performer from the audience. In live musical theater, performers onstage play to spectators seated in the audience. The resulting immediacy of interaction and feedback between performer and audience has leant itself to a certain dynamic for acting and spectatorship within the theater. With the advent of film, the audience was still physically present in the theater but viewed only the virtual presence of the actors on "pictures" that had been produced in studios months or even years before the viewing. The reproducibility of these pictures enabled them to be disseminated to many locations at once, thus turning film into a mass medium, somewhat on a par with newspapers and magazines.

Unlike film, on radio, performer and audience are separated not in time (except in the case of prerecording), but in space. Once it became possible for listeners to own receiving sets, radio became a seemingly free source of entertainment emanating from the households of the audience. Radio was thus conceived as a personal, rather than a communal, medium. Although early radio programs were broadcast live before a studio audience, the vast majority of listeners were in remote locations, usually the home. Television followed this pattern with the sale of television sets and the broadcasting of so-called free programming over the airwaves. TV imitated radio in its early years also by offering live programming from studios in New York and Chicago and later in Los Angeles.

Despite the appeal of live television, as film studios became more invested in television in the mid-1950s, more and more programs were filmed for later broadcast. Columnist Roger Bowman predicted as early as 1949 that television would need to film programs and prerecord music rather than rely on live music. In an article for *Film Music Notes*, he outlines a list of musical functions for "films in TV" or "spoken dramatic shows on films" (versus live shows and musical programs). As will be shown in chapter 4, Bowman's list of functions for television music predates Claudia Gorbman's (1987) list of musical functions for the cinema by nearly 40 years and already points to a developed theory of musical function in TV music as well as films.

Quality control was utmost in the minds of many musicians, as the low-budget production and quick turnaround for television programs often resulted in some highly inferior shows. Like the other writers discussed here, Bowman (1949a: 20) believed that music has the ability to rescue even a very bad narrative: "Music can bring to films an element of unreality, of fantasy, or overtones of super-reality not achievable otherwise. A weak scene can be made to click, a broken scene can be fused into a unified whole. Music can support the plastic quality of the drama with its impersonal texture. It must be subordinated to the drama so that it is not a distracting influence. It must achieve a blend with the story line that is plastically narrative—lyrical where it should be, but unobtrusive."

By the mid-1950s, some television composers had come to grips with the problem of limited budgets in producing high(er) quality scores. Tom Scott, a composer and folk musician who doubled as an actor on television, wrote in 1956 that low-budget shows had produced the most daring and successful original scores on television to date. He cited the program *Camera Three*, a long-running anthology series on CBS, as having broadcast several teleplays using a minimal score to great effect. Music in the episode "The Open Boat" was composed by Robert Herridge using only an accordion to signify the sea. Another *Camera Three* episode, "Dream of a Ridiculous Man," was scored for cello, accordion, and piano-celeste. In Scott's view, such minimal scoring for television was a strength, not a weakness, of the new medium, as it differentiated television from film and created a new form of dramatic expression. Scott's account reflects the development of television music as it moved away from massive film scores and toward the creation of its own language. Many television programs in the

1960s had smaller, condensed musical scores that may be considered *televisual* rather than cinematic.

Other TV music critics in the 1950s boasted of television's ability to draw high-quality music to its programming. In 1956, for example, Albert Elias cited the many musical contributions of such high-caliber contemporary composers as Norman Dello Joio, Paul Creston, George Antheil, William Schuman, and Henry Cowell, who had either created original scores for documentaries or used bits of preexisting music as theme music for other programs. One notable program, *The Twentieth Century* (1957–1966), was critically acclaimed for its excellent music, which featured a theme by Antheil and scores in many episodes by such renowned composers as Creston, Franz Waxman, Alan Hovhaness, Gail Kubik, and even the French composer Darius Milhaud.[6]

On with the Show

Analyzing music in television offers a new approach to music scholarship. Traditional music scholarship has operated on the assumption that every musical piece is essentially unique. The goal of musicology has been either to find and generalize the properties of uniqueness in a piece or to envisage a kind of signification in which everything—the sign, the code, the signified—is not replicable and every detail of the signifier is mapped on to the signified (Monelle 2000: 15). Semiotician Umberto Eco calls this process *ratio difficilis*, where a particular expressive element ("expression-token") is directly accorded its content because a corresponding expression type either does not exist or is identical to its content type (Eco 1979: 183). Eco recognizes that this is the primary process for finding significance in music. A Beethoven symphony is a unique artifact and, as such, is special, venerated, of high quality, and so on. The goal of traditional musicology and music theory has been to trace what makes these artifacts special and unique and thereby add them to the pantheon of what we call culture.

When examining or studying artifacts of popular culture, such as television music (or film music, or popular music), the process of *ratio difficilis* proves ineffective. Scholarship that tries to study pop culture in the same way we study "high" culture usually results in data that seemingly proves that pop culture is somehow lacking in quality. Indeed, scrutinizing a television score by William Lava in the same way that we would analyze a Beethoven symphony will likely reveal the former to be lacking in qualities borne out by musicological analysis. Most likely, the analysis will show that the TV score is in fact *not* unique, that it draws upon musical styles that persist in the audience's collective memory and perhaps even borrows material from many other musical sources that preceded it—including perhaps bits of a Beethoven symphony. While scholars may perceive this lack of uniqueness as a weakness in music, television producers and directors consider it a *strength* because this lack of uniqueness taps into a cultural familiarity with viewers. In other words, the music communicates and resonates with its audience. This volume, too, is less interested in the uniqueness of a musical score than in the music's ability to tap into the culture from which it sprang. The strength of a television score lies in its ability to convey, enhance, or expand the message that the other sensory channels (visual image, sound effects, dialogue, etc.) attempt to portray on the small screen. For music to accomplish this feat, it must express a musical language that is understood by and accessible to the recipients of that text—the viewers.

In our search for the signifying power of music within a narrative scenario or a visual image, then, we study music through the process that Eco calls *ratio facilis*, whereby an *expression token* is directly accorded an *expression type* and then linked to its content. This book analyzes a number of musical expression tokens (actual pieces of music composed for TV) and attempts to abstract them against a prevailing expression type, a *topos* that serves as a means of discourse that mediates meaning within culture. Topics are considered *types* because they have become habituated within a culture, and thus stylized, through the repetitive representation of related *tokens*. For example, when viewing a painting or piece of sculpture of the Virgin Mary, even though they both have unique characteristics, we nonetheless recognize each as a token representation of the generic Madonna type. Similarly, when we hear the fanfare flourish of horns in the theme music for the late 1950s–early 1960s western *The Rifleman*, we are likely to think of the generic topic of "the hero" because we have heard similar flourishes corresponding to "the hero" in other musical settings, such as heroic movies, heroic theater, and heroic pieces of concert music. Television relies heavily on familiar musical tokens that represent the more generic topics which evoke meaning for its audience.

This book begins with an attempt to frame a theory of television music based on preestablished habits and beliefs about musical types or topics. For this, I tap into semiotic theory, which, in my opinion, is the most comprehensive and inclusive framework in which to construct a theory of musical meaning. Umberto Eco (1979: 3) defined semiotics as "a unified approach to every phenomenon of signification and/or communication" that should be "able to explain every case of sign-function in terms of underlying systems of elements mutually correlated by one or more codes." According to Eco, the overarching philosophy of semiotics is that it can explain meaning universally, that is, in *all* areas of academic scholarship. While this may be an exaggeration, as a music theorist I find semiotic theory to be the most compelling way of communicating how musical structure aligns with television structure to produce meaning. Also, there have been numerous studies from film, television, media studies, and even musicology (many of them cited in this volume) that have employed semiotics as a tool. The semiotic theory that I espouse herein is decidedly structuralist (which many in media studies consider to be old hat). The essential point of this theory is that musical structures align with visual and other sonic structures to produce an aggregate meaning in a television text, what Roland Barthes, Michel Chion, and others have called *ancrage*. The association of musical meanings is brought out by the structure of the music, which associates or correlates with similar meanings that derive from the visual and sonic elements of a TV text. In addition, I use recent developments in cognitive theory (especially the work of Giles Fauconnier and Victor Turner) to reinforce my semiotic approach set out in chapter 1.

In chapter 2, I take up Charles Morris's ideas of "dimensions of the sign" and Gérard Genette's theories of narrative agency and develop the idea of the three semiotic spaces of television: the extradiegetic, the intradiegetic, and the diegetic. I investigate the narrative agency of television, specifically, how music functions in the role of narrator on a television program. In this chapter I also examine two anthology dramas, the *Philco Television Playhouse* and *The Twilight Zone*, to see how music functions as a narrating voice for both the television program and the network on which it airs. Whereas the music of the *Philco* show continued to use the narrating voice of radio, by the broadcast of the *Twilight Zone* episode 10 years later, TV music had become more cinematic or at least televisual.

Chapter 3 is a kind of station break in which I show how music serves as an agent of mediation and signification in the small texts commonly called commercials. Mediation is a key concept defining the interplay between music, images, dialogue, and song lyrics on television.

The second part of the book gets down to the business of defining the narrative and televisual functions of television music and how music functions both within a narrative program and outside the narrative to keep our attention on the programming. In chapter 4, I explore a small (but not the smallest) unit of televisual meaning, the leitmotif, and how it derived from the cinematic and the operatic leitmotif to operate as a televisual "ascriptor," that is, a unit that signifies in several different ways. Due to television's ephemerality, a leitmotif, whether heard as part of a program's theme music or repeated as intradiegetic music within the TV narrative, is an effective means of quickly delivering televisual meaning. In this chapter I investigate the use of leitmotifs in Gerald Fried's score to a 1966 *Star Trek* episode.

In chapter 5, I juxtapose theories of narrative structure with linear musical analysis borrowed (and heavily adapted) from Schenkerian music theory to describe how music shapes the temporal trajectory of television narratives. This chapter features the music of Hershel Burke Gilbert, who for his music to the western series *The Rifleman* used tonal areas, musical range, and timbre to allow the music to help shape the narrative arc of an episode.

Chapter 6 takes a look at music operating as music, that is, music presented not in the service of narrative, but as entertainment. In this chapter, using Roland Barthes's and Julia Kristeva's philosophical conceptions of pleasure as *plaisir* and *jouissance*, I view music as a form of televisual pleasure, a term that invites a closer look from a semiotic standpoint. The chapter briefly surveys the portrayal of musical performance on television and then focuses on three situation comedies produced by Desilu studios: *I Love Lucy*, *The Dick Van Dyke Show*, and *The Andy Griffith Show*.

The last section of the book deals with larger issues involving style and the development of musical trends. Chapter 7 takes a look at commercials produced approximately 20 to 30 years after those discussed in chapter 3, commercials in which the hard sell of the musical jingle has ceded its position to a new soft sell of musical style that attempts to identify demographic and psychographic groups being targeted by the advertising. It tells the tale of two vehicles, a luxury auto-mobile ad campaign in the United States in the 1990s set against a long-standing ad campaign for an American-made pickup truck. Chapter 8, using the police drama genre as a case study, examines the role of musical style in television theme music and how it evolved over a 40-year period. Finally, adapting theories of theatrical speech for the avant-garde theater by Michel Chion (1994), chapter 9 speculates on later developments in music and television narrative. The final chapter describes television as an interesting and unique blend of modernist and postmodernist traits in such programs as *Twin Peaks*, *The X-Files*, and *Northern Exposure*. These and other programs of the 1980s and 1990s reflect a new golden age of television in which the medium has matured beyond the influences of film and radio and become uniquely more televisual than cinematic.

The goal of this book is to convey a theory of how meaning and mediation occurred in television music in the 40-year period from 1949 to 1999. Lacking in this volume are a rigorous historical overview (though some history is included), hard-hitting cognitive science (what makes our brains think about music in this way?), and sociological demographic statistics, though I dabble in all three areas. Also lacking is an in-depth overview of the role of music videos and the MTV network, both of which arose during the scope of this study. The impact of MTV on television programming in the 1980s and 1990s cannot be minimized, and I incorporate this acknowledgment in analyzing the music to such MTV-influenced programs as *Miami Vice*, *NYPD Blue*, *Homicide*, and others. Apparently the topic of music videos is so important that it warrants a separate volume, and several have been written by capable authors, among them, E. Ann Kaplan (1987), Andrew Goodwin (1992), Steve Reiss and Neil Feineman (2000), and Carol Vernallis (2004).

I also make no claim that every TV genre receives extensive scrutiny here. I have chosen the genres discussed in this volume on the basis of the availability of the music as well as on my own enjoyment, as a viewer and an analyst, of both the genres and the music. As a result, many other genres warranting careful attention have admittedly been given short shrift in this volume, including the game show, the daytime soap opera, the hospital drama, news and documentary shows, and cartoons, each of which is undoubtedly a font of interesting material for further study.

And now, on with the show.

1

Toward an Associative Theory
of Television Music

Teens watching TV western, 1956 (Getty Images).

The term "television" encompasses a wide array of disciplinary fields and ideas and draws on centuries of technological, economic, social, theatrical, artistic, and musical developments in the Western world. Technologically, the development of the television machine can be traced through the discovery and harnessing of electricity, the development of the camera, the discovery of radio waves, the development of the cathode ray tube (whether by Vladimir Zworykin or Philo T. Farnsworth),[1] the transistor, magnetic tape recording, and digital audio and video technology. And this technological television apparatus broadcasts programming that reflects the economic, social, theatrical, and artistic values and norms of the society in which it operates. Artistically, the pictures and sounds transmitted on television are the result of centuries of theatrical and visual arts practices in Western civilization that can be traced back to theater in ancient Greece continuing through Shakespearian theater, European theater, American musical theater, vaudeville, the cinema, and television itself.

The two areas mentioned above—the technology of the television machine and the theatrical practices that were broadcast on television—reflect two facets of television as a semiotic and communication system. As part of a system, both the theatrical and technical aspects of television are dependent on each other for creating and conveying the televisual message to the audience. Then there is the audience itself, a third and essential element of television. Television relies on the audience to be both a receiver and an interpreter of the pictures and sounds it transmits. This audience must be able to understand and comprehend the other two facets, both the technical aspects of broadcasting and the theatrical and narrative conventions. Thus television can be envisioned as a tripartite phenomenon consisting of the physical television apparatus, the images and sounds that convey stories and information on the television screen, and the audience that interprets those images and sounds.

The advent of television in the 1930s and 1940s was an exciting, though not necessarily monumental, event in the history of American broadcasting. Americans were already somewhat media savvy by the 1940s, when television began to follow many of the broadcasting practices of radio and the cinema. The types of programming and program schedules found on radio were transferred nearly verbatim to television in its earliest years, so much so that television became virtually radio with pictures. Audiences were knowledgeable also of the narrative forms of the cinema and the theater (as well as radio), and many of these forms translated directly to the new medium. As a new generation of TV viewers emerged in the 1960s and 1970s, television came into its own as a unique medium with its own narrative genres and musical practices. Programming eventually became more and more televisual, that is, demonstrating a look and structure that began to differ significantly from the parent media.

Much of the success of television in the 1940s and 1950s lay in its nature as a home entertainment medium, a feature it shared with radio but not with cinema. Part of the novelty that television offered its viewers was moving-picture accompaniment to the sounds and music of radio. By the mid-1950s, television had made significant inroads in appealing to the movie-going public, so much so that movie studio executives became fearful that their dwindling revenues were due to audiences staying at home to watch television. Film studios fought back by producing large epic films in the new CinemaScope and Technicolor processes, using popular music, like jazz and rock, and creating larger-than-life film stars. Radio stations, in turn, abandoned the variety programming developed in the 1930s and resorted to format programming in order to seek larger, but demographically fragmented, audiences.

Even as television flourished visually in the 1950s, music remained an important component of programming. Music was easy and inexpensive to reproduce in the new medium, and, especially at its inception, television borrowed heavily from the earlier performing media of radio, musical theater, and the cinema. The musical variety programs constituting the bulk of early television programming looked and felt much like old vaudeville shows while sounding much like their predecessor radio shows.[2] As television programming developed, its own unique form of musical expression emerged, and music soon began to play a number of different roles on television: as entertainment (through, for example, the musical variety show and, in later years, the music video); as dramatic narrative (depicting moods, settings, and character traits); and, beyond these creative functions, as a functional mechanism used to sell products, identify networks and broadcasting stations, signal the beginning and ending of individual programs, and generally mark the passage of the temporal televisual flow.[3] Television music performs all of these functions in precise time spans ranging from a 5-second bumper to a 15- or 30-second commercial to a 30- or 60-minute dramatic program, time constraints that have resulted in further adaptation of musical practices to convey moods, ideas, and narrative situations in a highly efficient manner.

Because most TV texts are of these specified, brief durations, television conveys its message by relying heavily on verisimilitude, the filling in of missing portions of a narrative text by calling upon the textual knowledge of its audience, and repeating conventional references to previous performing practices (see Chatman 1978). Jonathan Culler (1975: 134) writes that "to read is essentially to take up or construct a reference," later invoking Todorov's notion of the *vraisemblable*, defined as "the relation of a particular text to another general and diffuse text which might be called 'public opinion'" (Culler 1975: 138–139). Television relies on this verisimilar relationship by borrowing narrative structures and formulae from film and theater, compressing them into new formulae,

21

and repeating them in program after program. In the resulting text, a great deal of narrative detail may be omitted, but usually there is enough for the audience to fill in and comprehend. For example, that a particular program is a hospital drama will be immediately evident by the presence of doctors, nurses, and patients on-screen, and the repeated viewing of the same characters week after week makes possible an elision in the character exposition part of the narrative, which allows more time for plot development.

While the ephemerality of TV texts requires televisual verisimilitude in order to communicate, television has also grown to rely on the combination of sound and image to convey meaning. If you have ever watched television with the sound turned off, you are aware of how fragmented and brief the images are. Indeed, according to Michel Chion (1994), the rapidity of visual editing is one of the distinctive traits of television in contrast to the cinema. Conversely, if you have listened to the sounds and music of television, you have noticed that these too are fragmentary. Yet put together, the sounds and images of television communicate by presenting images and sounds that are meaningful to an audience independent of the medium and then combining these images and sounds into a larger, more meaningful text.

The purpose of this book is to explore *how* images and sounds (in particular, music) combine to convey these meaningful messages to a TV audience. A great deal of the book is concerned with how autonomous musical structures produce meaningful messages as a result of the television audience's ability to interpret them as such. Music has been an effective communicator in television because TV composers and producers have consciously drawn upon popular musical traditions, a musical past that is known by TV viewers at any given time. This knowledge enables TV music to express or signify extramusical ideas and concepts, such as emotions, settings, character traits, objects, and more. TV audiences (in the United States and elsewhere) have developed a competency in decoding the meaningful messages expressed in the music through the very act of watching television. As a medium, television has masterfully used and manipulated what communications theorists call *codes*, that is, structures of meaning recognized by a given society. Through verisimilitude, audiences are able to translate these codes into meaningful televisual structures.

Television as a Communications Process

Television is considered a mass communication medium because it follows most standard schemas for communication.[4] In most of these schemas, an act of communication presupposes (1) a sender of information (addresser); (2) a receiver (or many receivers) of information (addressees); (3) a channel of communication between (1) and (2), that is, any structure that facilitates communication, from simple channels, such as a telephone wire, to more complex channels, such as language (verbal or gestural) and even customs, art norms, or the sum of cultural monuments (practices, artifacts, etc.); and (4) a message or text (Lotman 1976: 36).

Communications theorists have elaborated on this basic model of communication. For the purpose of this chapter, the communications model put forth by linguist Roman Jakobson in *The Framework of Language* (1980) is considered. In addition to outlining the elements of communication, Jakobson also describes the functions of each element (figure 1.1).

Like most communication models, Jakobson's is framed by the addresser and addressee, as the existence of sender and receiver is an essential aspect of the communicative act. However, Jakobson's model also considers the roles or functions played by other aspects of communication, such as the context of the communication and the social codes through which the communicative act is filtered. For example, one person (the addresser) may telephone a friend (the addressee) to invite him/her to the movies (the message). The addresser serves an *emotive*, or expressive, function by expressing the desire to go to the movies with a friend. Besides the content of the message, we may scrutinize the message itself for its *poetic* function or, as Jakobson explains, "the message for its own sake." In context, the message would you like to go to the movies? may be poetically scrutinized according to the rules of grammar and syntax, the elegance of its presentation, etc. The addressee is the receiver of information, functioning in what Jakobson calls the *conative* function. The telephone, with all its wires and electrical impulses, serves a *phatic* function as *contact*. The *context* and *code* deal with broader cultural issues: the context serves a referential function, as it addresses their relationship and the nature of relationships vis-à-vis their cultural

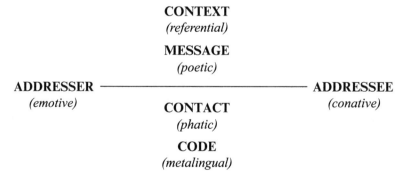

CONTEXT
(referential)

MESSAGE
(poetic)

ADDRESSER ———————————————————— **ADDRESSEE**
(emotive) *(conative)*

CONTACT
(phatic)

CODE
(metalingual)

Figure 1.1. Jakobson's (1980) Communication Model.

23

milieu. For example, is the addresser acting as friend or potential suitor in this act, and is following the codes appropriate to one of these roles? Codes serve a *metalingual* function, that is, they operate within the context of what can be mutually understood. This would include the understanding of language but also the type of jargon used in communication: for example, if the friends are casual acquaintances, they would operate within one set of linguistic codes, whereas if there is a potential romantic interest, a different set of communicative codes might be employed. Finally, as Jakobson points out, codes are not always linguistic; visual images and sounds often contain codes, too.

Television is a mass medium that communicates according to Jakobson's model but in a more complex way. First, we cannot refer to a single source as addresser or transmitter. Who is the transmitter in television? The actors/news anchorpersons whose actual likenesses we see on-screen or the producers or directors of programs who pull together all the actors, writers, camera operators, sound engineers, and others? According to Jakobson's model, all of these function as transmitters, as they all function within the emotive or expressive realm. The television apparatus is an amplification of the communications model: serving the phatic function of contact is everything from the transmitting tower that sends forth the electrical impulses to broadcast the images and sounds to the coaxial cable that also transmits these sounds and images to the colored pixels on-screen and the vibrating membranes of the speakers within the television set itself.

The message of television is another complex facet of television broadcasting. We may consider a simple example of a television anchorman broadcasting the news of a local fire. As receivers of the broadcast, we may certainly understand and scrutinize the message (if we are English speakers), but often the message is inflected by the anchor's tone of voice, facial expressions, body language, etc. While the message of the fire may be clear, we may also read other aspects of the message and detect a sense of pathos, tragedy, or relief based on *how* the message is broadcast.

The example of the news anchorman illustrates that television communicates through multiple channels (not to be confused with television network channels!). Christian Metz (1974a) has identified five sensory channels for the cinema, but these may also be applied to television. These channels (or contacts) are (1) visual, (usually) moving images, (2) written language, (3) spoken language, (4) sound effects, and (5) music. Television usually communicates by using more than one of these channels simultaneously. As the newscaster reports the burning house story viewers hear it both though the channel of spoken language, but also in the newscaster's serious facial expression. The tone, pitch, cadence, and volume of the newscaster's voice also may play a role in communication, illustrating nonverbal sound. In television, the visual contact is usually a constant, with spoken or written language, sound or music interspersed at strategic moments in a text. Plus, television usually does not present an unmediated image but refines it through camera lenses and angles, special lighting and editing—that is, through the technical apparatus of television.

Just as complex as the emotive or transmission function is the conative, or reception, function. Television broadcasts reach many different types of people, even within a single society, such as the United States. As a mass medium, television strives to communicate its messages to a homogeneous audience, using codes and contexts that are common to the widest audience possible. In fact, the audience is not homogenous but comes to the television text with a wide variety of experiences and biases as well as different intellectual, ethnic, and social backgrounds. The result is that receivers of television texts will perceive them in different ways. Although television tries to regulate its messages into common languages (or codes), audiences are polysemic, that is, at least some segment of the viewing audience will interpret texts differently from the preferred or intended meaning of television producers, what Umberto Eco (1979) has termed "aberrant readings."

The notion of multiple receivers implies the notion that the television receiver (i.e., the audience) is not a passive receptor of television images and sounds but instead must be able to actively read, or decode, the televisual messages in order for communication to occur. Jakobson's communication model assumes a single receiver, but in mass communications, such as television, the message likely reaches millions of people. Moreover, the presence of code in Jakobson's model implies a tacit agreement between sender and receiver whether that agreement means the understanding of a common language or participation in common systems of culture. Communication is thus not a one-way process, a path only from sender to receiver, but a two-way exchange between sender and receiver. Stuart Hall (1981) states that in any communicative event the receiver must not only receive a message but also read and decode the message. Communication is thus a continual process of encoding and decoding by both producer and receiver of a message. Furthermore, both parties must mutually agree upon these codes. If someone began speaking Lithuanian to an American who did not speak Lithuanian, communication would not take place, as the American is unable to decode the message. This type of miscommunication also occurs in the media and the arts, as when an untrained audience does not fully understand aspects of an art film or a piece of avant-garde music. Often, there is confusion as well in the context or code area, as will be shown later.

One of music's roles in television is to help shepherd the audience to the preferred or intended meaning of a text. Music does so by aligning itself with the images and sounds of television and through its ability to convey extramusical aspects, often signifying in more than one way.

Television as a Semiotic Process

By now it is becoming apparent that television is more than just a collection of images, sounds, and music. Jakobson's communication schema is not just about the act of communication from addressor to addressee but also entails much of the contexts and meaning of communication. Add to his model the complexity of a mass communications model with multiple components of each of its elements: multiple senders, channels, messages, codes, and receivers. Television texts merit closer examination of the message, context, and code and how producers and receivers of these messages negotiate meaning from them. In his book *Television Culture*, John Fiske (1987: 1) asserts that television is a cultural agent, a provoker and circulator of meanings. Television broadcasts pictures and sounds that are familiar to the culture of the viewer, but it manipulates these images in conveying stories or selling products in a familiar way. These images and sounds are replete with many potential meanings, but television attempts to corral these meanings into a singular preferred syntax. The process of television is largely a matter of manipulating the audience to form beliefs and values according to a dominant culture. Meaning in television lies within the provenance of the dominant culture, the culture that can be accessed by the largest number of viewers. These controlled meanings are shaped into a singular, more preferred meaning that performs the work of the dominant ideology.

In order to shape meaning, television must convey its message to its audience, but the audience must also be able to read and decode that message into meaningful units. This is the area wherein Jakobson's components of context and code lie and, along with that, the functions of "reference" and "metalingual," which go beyond a communications model and enter into the realm of a semiotic model.

The Codes of Television

Fiske (1987: 5) has constructed his own hierarchical schema for television communication, a model he calls the "codes of television" (figure 1.2). Fiske's schema is expressed through codes, which he (1987: 4) defines as "a rule-governed system of signs, whose rules and conventions are shared amongst members of a culture, and which generate and circulate meanings in and for that culture." The first level, "reality," consists of social codes of appearance, behavior, speech, and so on. These are codes that all members of culture encounter (or at least know exist) in every-day life. Even before these codes are broadcast on television, they are already encoded within our cultural system, in a common field of understanding. Examples include language (characters in American television speak English), dress (appropriate with the genre), gestures, expressions, and so forth. The reality codes are the physical world that serves as the raw material to construct television texts.

These social codes are then manipulated for presentation, or representation, on television by technical codes: camera angles, lighting effects, film editing, musical scoring, sound effects, etc. These technical codes are production

An event to be televised is already encoded
by *social codes* such as those of:

Level one:
"REALITY"

appearance, dress, make-up, environment, behavior, speech,
gesture, expression, sound, etc.

these are encoded electronically by
technical codes such as those of:

Level two:
REPRESENTATION

camera, lighting, editing, music, sound

which transmit the
conventional representational codes, which shape the
representations of, for example:
narrative, conflict, character, action, dialogue, setting, casting, etc.

Level three:
IDEOLOGY

which are organized into coherence and social acceptibility by
the *ideological codes*, such as those of:
individualism, patriarchy, race, class, materialism,
capitalism, etc.

Figure 1.2. Fiske's (1987) Codes of Television.

techniques that have been put in place through television productions (and before them, through cinematic and radio productions) over a period of time. As one of these technical codes, music is the subject of examination here, and how it interacts with other technical codes becomes important in the conveyance of televisual meaning.

The technical codes in turn animate the social codes into representational codes that depict a story, a fictive, or at least a televisual world that includes character types, actions, settings, dialogue, and narrative microstructures. Fiske maintains that even in nonfiction television genres representational codes still maintain a text's narrative or mythic quality, for example, the news anchorperson who conveys a voice-of-authority mythic persona through representation, that is, makeup, clothing, hairstyle, facial expression, and voice intonation.

Finally, these conventional representation codes are received conatively by the viewer and processed into ideological codes through which the viewer interprets the narrative according to prevalent ideological norms. In the 1980s, according to Fiske, the ideologies for the United States (and possibly much of Western Europe and elsewhere) were individualism, patriarchy, race, class, materialism, and capitalism.[5] American television is rife with ideological potential, whether considered as a commercial medium or as an arbiter of American values.

A Brief Analysis: Opening Credits of *The Rifleman*

An illustrative example of the multichannel communication and semiotic model of television can be seen in the opening scenes of a classic American western, *The Rifleman*, which aired on the ABC network in the years 1958–1963. The program starred actor Chuck Connors as Lucas McCain, a widower rancher who lived near the town of North Fork, New Mexico, during the late nineteenth century. Most of the episodes portrayed McCain as a highly moral father and town citizen who raised his son, Mark (Johnny Crawford), in an environment surrounded by outlaws, gamblers, and land cheats. In addition to being a rancher and father, McCain is also a famous gunman whose claim to fame is a customized Winchester rifle that can rapid fire in less than half a second (thus the name of the series). Nearly every episode contains at least one scene featuring the rapid firing of the rifle, the program's trademark.

One way to undertake an analysis of a television text is to use Fiske's codes of television to investigate how what viewers see and hear in a TV text (reality) conveys meaning (representation). We can then only speculate on the interpretations of an audience of the time and what ideologies that audience brought to the text. Syntactically, we begin with Metz's sensory channels: (1) visual images,

(2) written text, (3) human speech/language, (4) sound effects, and (5) music, which, though somewhat overly simplified, are useful categories in analyzing film and television texts. Much of the meaning in the music in the opening to *The Rifleman* is not derived only by images but also by many aspects of the broadcasted images and sounds. Each of these channels, including music, conveys its own set of codes, all of which carry potential interpretations. Within each of Metz's five sensory codes (image, written text, speech, sound effects, music) are many subcodes, all containing their own potential interpretations.[6]

In the opening credits to *The Rifleman*, we see a man from the waist down firing a rifle in rapid succession (figure 1.3.a). As the theme music sounds, the camera pans upward to the face of the man, who we see is actor Chuck Connors; he wears a whitish shirt and cowboy hat. In bold white type, the words "The Rifleman" are superimposed on-screen during the camera's tracking shot (figure 1.3.b). Connors then cocks the rifle by twirling it in his hand, and the rifle's sound is synchronized to fit the rhythm of the music. He then tosses the rifle into his other hand and reaches into his pocket to find bullets to reload it. As he does so, he looks directly into the camera ("direct address" of the camera), and the words "starring Chuck Connors" appear on-screen (figure 1.3.c) as the disembodied voice of the announcer reads them. The music ends with an ascending, full-orchestral flourish.

In this brief opening, all five sensory channels contribute to communicate a meaningful message. To begin the analysis, we can describe the elements of each sensory channel and what occurs in each:

1. Image: Chuck Connors in a cowboy outfit, on the streets of a town in the nineteenth-century American West, firing his rifle and then looking menacingly into the camera as he reloads. Among the many codes to consider here are the setting, Connors himself, and his accoutrements, namely, his cowboy costume, his Winchester rifle, and his actions.[7]
2. Sound: 10 rifle shots followed by a cocking sound (all amplified acoustically) to coincide with the image of the rifle cocking and synchronized to the music.
3. Written language: "The Rifleman" and "Starring Chuck Connors" superimposed over the images on-screen in a large white font reminiscent of nineteenth-century playbills.
4. Spoken language: the announcer's voice reading (and thus reinforcing) the written words on-screen.
5. Music: a theme song consisting of a motive played by horns then completed by strings and ending in a full-orchestral flourish.

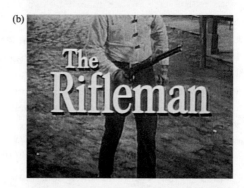

Figure 1.3. Opening Images to *The Rifleman*.

As in the openings to all television programs, these elements operate phatically; that is, they call attention to the contact of the text, as if to say, "You are watching the TV program *The Rifleman*," thereby directing the viewer from the flow of television broadcasting to the world of television *narrative*. These same elements also function poetically to provide information about the story of

Lucas McCain and the late-nineteenth-century western denizens of New Mexico. And though very few television viewers at that time actually lived in the American west, many had cultural knowledge of the Old West as portrayed in history books and novels as well as on film and in other TV shows (much of the latter fictionalized).

In the opening to *The Rifleman*, reality is portrayed through the syntax of a variety of the sign-vehicles listed above. The announcer speaks English. The actor appears in character: a tall, thin man dressed in jeans, a cowboy hat, boots, etc.; his facial expression, grim and somewhat menacing; his makeup, portraying a tanned and weathered face. The setting is a replica of a late-nineteenth-century town in the American West. The gunshots are loud and somewhat antique sounding—like an old Winchester rifle. The music also is loud and bold.

The technical codes include lighting to simulate daylight, as the surroundings are visible as if the action is taking place in daytime. The film stock is black and white, as it was for nearly all television shows at that time. The opening camera shot shows Connors from the waist down firing the rifle. The camera then tilts upward to reveal both his face (and thus his identity) and the rifle. It then zooms in for a close-up of his face. This camera motion emulates a mininarrative structure in that it foregrounds a narrative enigma—who is firing the rifle?—and ends with a resolution of that enigma—the rifleman. While reaching into his shirt pocket for bullets to reload his rifle, Connors stares into the camera, a somewhat threatening look on his face. In terms of sound effects, the gunshots and other rifle sounds are amplified by microphone to create a very loud, noisy opening. This is reinforced by the theme music, which also is loud and brash and characterized by a fanfare-like opening featuring timpani and French horns. A disembodied announcer's voice reads the titles appearing on-screen: "The Rifleman," followed by "starring Chuck Connors." The continuous visual images of the camera panning in and out on Connors are syntactically juxtaposed with the sounds of the rifle, music, and announcer so as not to interfere with each other.

On the representational level, the opening scene becomes a meaningful text through the combination of the elements of the different sensory channels with each element signifying a meaning in its own way. Connors's menacing stare is enigmatic, but the pairing of heroic-sounding music and his cowboy good looks portrays a good guy or cowboy hero. The appearance of Connors and the image of the rifle, in tandem with the gunshots and the loud music, also identify the text being watched/heard as *The Rifleman*, a particular TV cowboy series.

Finally, the representational codes of image and sound produce interpretations by the viewers. As Fiske states, television produces images and sounds with the hope of prompting a preferred meaning, but by the nature of signs and codes—especially in a mass medium such as television with a pluralistic viewing audience—the interpretations will be polysemic. The preferred meaning of the opening of *The Rifleman* is to announce that the program falls within the genre of the TV western. Within this genre is the recognition by the audience of the good-triumphs-over-evil theme, since McCain is a heroic figure who battles outlaws and land-cheats to protect his home, his son, and his town. Viewers watching in the late 1950s and early 1960s when the program originally aired would pick up on this theme and perhaps even see McCain's actions as patriotic, as the American Way, given the cold war tensions of the time. Viewers might also interpret the overwhelmingly male cast as containing a patriarchal ideology. Males in the show are both protagonists and antagonists. The opening demonstrates an ethos of male violence in solving problems and keeping the peace, an aspect of the program that may be construed as either positive or negative.

However, these preferred readings do not necessarily exhaust the potential meanings of the opening sequence of the show. A gendered reading, for example, might interpret the opening as a metaphor for male sexual violence, with the waist-down shot of the firing rifle symbolizing the phallus and the glare on Connors's face signifying patriarchal control of sexual potency and violence. A political interpretation could contend that Connors is the gregarious and self-sufficient American hero who sometimes has to take the law into his own hands and fight against the forces of evil (i.e., criminals) with his rifle and his gritty determination. Indeed, many of these readings derive from preexisting myths of America generally and the American west in particular.

These aberrant readings reveal Fiske's "ideology" category as an amplification of the Peircian interpretant and of Charles Morris's (1946) pragmatics dimension of the sign. The interpretant is the meaning of the object and resides in the mind of the perceiver (and usually is shared by an interpretive community) and instantiates or realizes the relationship of the sign-vehicle to the object. As a meaning, the interpretant is, in itself, another sign, whether it be a thought in a person's mind, a written translation, a sentence spoken, or anything else that is interpretative (Greenlee 1973: 26). Umberto Eco (1979) described the effect of the interpretant as "unlimited semiosis" as a way to define and test how signs operate as cultural units. In this extensive theory of semiotics, Eco notes how Charles Sanders Peirce's idea of the final interpretant may lead to establishing habits and beliefs in a cultural context. Eco's (1979: 69) notion of the interpretant is worth quoting here: "The object of representation can be nothing but a representation of which the first representation is the interpretant. But an endless series of representations, each representing the one behind it, may be conceived to have an absolute object as its limit. Peirce later calls this absolute object not an object but a *habit*, understood as the *final interpretant*." Thus, the notion of the interpretant creates the possibility of unlimited interpretations of a television text. Music goes a long way toward mitigating such open readings in television, as will be shown below.

The "Codes of Television Music"

As one of the sensory channels of television, music has the potential of being a semiotic system, that is, a system of signs that transmit meaning or signification to receivers.[8] While it is part of the discourse of television (and often only a small part of that discourse), music operates within Fiske's hierarchy and carries Morris's syntactical, semantic, and pragmatic properties (Morris 1946; see appendix A). As shown in *The Rifleman* analysis, music serves to shepherd preferred and intended meanings in television.

Following Fiske, a schema I call the "codes of television music" is illustrated in figure 1.4. In television, the musical elements of pitch and duration (i.e., notes and rhythms) are combined into familiar syntactical tonal and formal units that form the reality level of music. In television, as in film, these musical works are either recorded and engineered into a television film or performed live by a group of musicians offstage, the music amplified by microphones in the studio. The music played bonds with the images and sounds of the TV program and conveys some sort of representational meaning to the program. The conveyed meaning could be an emotion (love, hate, fear) or what Robert Hatten (1994: 290) has called "expressive genres," a term I borrow to mean the discursive expressive states organized within topical fields (heroic, pastoral, evil, tragic, comic, etc.). In addition, in electronic media of the twentieth century, music can signify through even more generic categories, such as musical style, which would include large (and perhaps crudely defined) musical categories, such as classical, jazz, rock, New Age, country and western, urban contemporary, and so on. As I show later, these generic musical style topics connote sociographic and demographic meanings as well as denoting specific settings and objects. These styles also connote somewhat ambiguous codes of social acceptability or deviance on TV, describing characters that are "cool," or wholesome, or socially deviant, and so on. Such signification through styles draws upon the viewer's social knowledge of musical style (usually transmitted through other media, like radio) and often taps into certain viewers' musical preferences that help attract them to a particular program. *The Rifleman* undoubtedly attracted (especially young) male viewers in part through the heroic, brash music of the series. Finally, music may simply serve as a representation of the TV show itself through correlation of music with the show in a week-to-week repetition.

An event to be televised/broadcast is already encoded
by social codes, such as those of:

Level one:
"REALITY"
> musical form, syntax, timbre combinations, expression,
> gestures, etc.

> these are encoded electronically by
> *technical codes*, such as those of:

Level two:
REPRESENTATION
> recording technology, sound design, underscoring, etc.,

> which transmit the
> *conventional musical representational codes*, which shape the
> representations of events and characters in a media text
> by paradigmatic codes (style topics) and
> by syntagmatic codes (musical structures)

Level three:
IDEOLOGY (OR INTERPRETATION)
> which are organized into coherence and social acceptability by
> the *ideological codes*, such as those of:
> individualism, patriarchy, race, class, materialism, capitalism, etc.
> (but also by *dramatic codes* of the heroic, tragedy, comedy, epic, etc.)
> or *social codes* of acceptability ("coolness," "wholesomeness," etc.).

Figure 1.4. The Codes of Television Music (after Fiske's [1987] Codes of Television).

While theorists have emphasized the role of music in conveying emotion in visual media, such as film and television, music can and does convey much more. In the music to the opening of *The Rifleman*, the theme music conveys discursive topics of the heroic and action but also represents the particular program itself (THIS is *The Rifleman*). Like images, music functions phatically and conatively as well as poetically, emotively, metalingually, etc. In this regard, a single piece of music can represent many facets of a program at once. Moreover, the actual musical work might convey many topics but would not necessarily exhaust or be exhausted by these particular meanings. In fact, these pieces function as musical tokens for these topical types.[9]

To illustrate how the codes of TV music work, I return to the opening of *The Rifleman*. The music for *The Rifleman* was composed by Herschel Burke Gilbert (1918–2003), a veteran film and television composer. Like many opening credit cues, the opening of *The Rifleman* is designed to announce the beginning of the program, thus serving Jakobson's "phatic" or what Philip Tagg (2000) has called an "appellative function," which summons viewers to the TV. The loud gunshots of the sound/image track are followed by timpani and French horns boldly announcing the beginning of the program (see example 1.1).

While the theme is an emotive expression of Gilbert's musical idea of the Rifleman character, it also represents the show itself: the week-by-week repetition of the theme music forms a phatic semiotic bond with the program to the point where when a viewer recalls the program, he or she also recognizes the theme music, and vice versa. This bond with the text is further reinforced by the disembodied voice of the announcer reading the words "The Rifleman" and "starring Chuck Connors."

In addition to the obvious phatic and emotive function of the music, music also functions poetically within a semiotic system to convey the narrative world of the program. Of note here is that the syntactical elements of the main title music reinforce the narrative subject of the show. These syntactical elements include pitch in the form of melody and harmony and temporality in the form of surface rhythm but also duration, pacing, form, timbre or use of instrumental color, and volume or loudness.

Analyzing the syntactical features of the theme music reveals that within the 17 seconds of the opening, music is played during the final 8 seconds. Gilbert's composition is 11 measures (with a 2/2 meter signature) consisting of two phrases with an extension on the second to end the excerpt. The first phrase features an arpeggiated melody played by the horns with jaunty, dotted rhythms. The second phrase develops the motivic ideas of the first, continuing a melodic

Example 1.1. Opening Theme to *The Rifleman.*

ascent to tonic, played by the entire orchestra to conclude the cue. The key is D major and, despite its brief duration, is tonally closed (i.e., it begins and ends) on D. The harmonic motion in the piece follows that of the harmonic system used by composers associated with the traditional Western European tonal system, Mozart, Haydn, Beethoven, and their successors. Indeed, much television music of the early period drew from the tradition of Western European art music, which included the functional tonal system. The endings of phrases are approached through the dominant chord, forming authentic cadences, and the piece ends with the traditional subdominant-dominant-tonic motion (IV–V–I). The melody also completes a pattern of ascent through the pitches of the tonic triad (D, F#, and A) and hovering around scale degree 3 (F#) before a final ascent to D at the end. The brief opening of the program is a conventional closed tonal form that can be represented by a Schenkerian diagram (see example 1.2).[10]

Reflecting the bipartite structure of the piece, the timbres used in the main title theme music also define the structure of the piece: the three horns (with timpani) in mm. 1–10 constitute the first part; the full orchestra in the pickup to measure 11 to measure 12, the second part. The timbral contrast highlights the two separate phrases, one introducing the *Rifleman* motive, the second a concluding melodic gesture. Also, the theme is loud (or intended to be loud, depending on how high or low the viewer's volume control is set). The loudness of the music imitates (or competes with) the rifle shots and creates another semiotic bond with the rifle as a sort of energetic interpretant[11] wherein loudness of the music is isomorphic with loudness of the rifle shots.

These syntactical, or reality, aspects of the opening music serve as sign-vehicles for the representational, or semantic, level of codes. Historically, music has been considered as both a nonrepresentational and a representational art form from various perspectives and at various times but as a representational form particularly from the perspective of dramatic music, such as opera or program music. Finding representational meaning through the codes of TV music model is to evaluate how

Example 1.2. Schenkerian Linear Reductive Graph of *Rifleman* Theme.

the musical elements of the reality level function to convey meaning to the listener. In the main title music of *The Rifleman*, these same elements of timbre, melodic gesture, and structure are examined for their *topical* implications, that is, discursive musical labels that trigger within the audience some idea of extramusical expression. Audience members are able to decode these musical meanings based on their own experiences and competencies with musical styles.

In search of expressive topics in the *Rifleman* theme I note that the opening motive outlines the D-major triad, beginning with the interval of a perfect fourth, A to D. This gesture can be considered bold and heroic, based on other preexisting pieces that have a heroic intent. The heroism of this melodic gesture is reinforced by the fact that it is played by French horns and timpani, two instruments historically associated with the heroic. The comparison of French horns to heroism is a cultural artifact that has its origins in European music dating back several hundred years.[12] The exact origins of this equation are vague (and outside the scope of this study), but one famous historical example is from Beethoven's Symphony No. 3, known as *Eroica* (Italian for "The Heroic") (example 1.3), composed in 1803, in which horns articulate the principal theme of the first movement and play important roles in the subsequent movements.

Other examples abound in classical literature, notably symphonic poems by Richard Strauss that depict heroes, such as *Ein Heldenleben, Till Eulenspiegel*, and *Don Juan*. Strauss's use of horns as heroic was emulated in the mid-twentieth century by many film composers, notably Erich Korngold in the early years of sound film and then later by such composers as Alex North, Miklos Rózsa, and John Williams.[13] From the use of the heroic horn in film, the path to television is evident. The identification of the music as a heroic topic is drawn from the syntactical aspects of the music (the outlining of the D-major triad in the horns) and from how this gesture fits with the audience's intertextual association of this musical gesture with other similar heroic gestures in music of the past, such as Beethoven, Strauss, Korngold, or even some of Gilbert's film music, especially that composed before *The Rifleman*.[14]

The second musical gesture in the *Rifleman* theme is the final flourish played by the full orchestra, including strings. The final flourish is a typical ending in tonal music with the subdominant and dominant chords resolving to the tonic chord.[15] The addition of the strings augments and brightens the texture, bringing

Example 1.3. Opening of Beethoven's Symphony No. 3 (*Eroica* or "The Heroic").

the theme to a rousing climax. The ascending motion of the melody might prompt a semantic, metaphorical reading of the music as climbing or striving and finally attaining the harmonic goal of the tonic chord. Ideologically, such a topic would correlate with the good-versus-evil theme of the genre, highlighting McCain's struggle and eventual victory over evildoers in each episode.

When the theme to *The Rifleman* is opened up to comparison with previous texts and the intertextual knowledge of the audience, other musical topics can be drawn from the main title theme. For example, the dotted note and repeated sixteenth note rhythms in the opening motive often have been identified with cowboy music. The connotation of the dotted rhythm with cowboys probably stems from cowboy songs that use such a rhythms ("Good-bye, Old Paint"), and transmission of these songs were codified by American composers, such as Virgil Thompson and especially Aaron Copland, who quoted cowboy songs in his ballet music to *Rodeo* and *Billy the Kid*.[16] The slowing of rhythm at the end of the opening credits shifts from the cowboyness of the theme to bring viewers to an exciting conclusion of the opening (and into the first commercial!).

Music can signify extramusical phenomena in at least two ways. First, music can sound like something it is imitating.[17] Such mimetic music has been composed to imitate bird calls, steam locomotives, babbling brooks, thunderstorms, airplanes, automobiles, and many other sounds.[18] Second, music can signify through convention or symbolically as a culturally agreed upon code.[19] Gilbert's theme to *The Rifleman* signifies in this way, as the music does not really *sound* like cowboys, or Lucas McCain, or Chuck Connors (whatever any of these may sound like). Rather, the theme harkens back to the conventions of cowboy and heroic music used by other composers, like Copland and Beethoven. Television music relies heavily on such symbolic signs (i.e., codes) for meaning.

Musical Correlation and Association

Music can also produce meaning through the symbolic sign as easily as invoking a certain style of music within a television text. Historically, extramusical connotations have been imparted by certain musical gestures or expressive genres, but television also uses musical styles for extramusical signification in its programs. For example, jazz music is often used to signify the city in programs with urban settings, while Coplanesque classical music, like Gilbert's, is used for westerns like *The Rifleman*. Bluegrass or country style music may be used for programs with rural themes. While style is a somewhat vague concept in music, it is one basis to create a discourse for television music: it creates categories that can be identified by audiences and compared with other like categories. These musical codes are based on the reality of everyday life or on the reality of our knowledge of the media. In the first case, the use of jazz for a TV show with an urban setting is a code, based on the fact that viewers in both the United States and many Western European cities can indeed hear a lot of jazz music in urban nightclubs, bars, concert halls, and so on. In the second case, the use of classical Coplanesque music in westerns also is a code, but one based more on media knowledge than on knowledge of the "real" world. We accept the music of *The Rifleman* because we may have seen western movies or other TV shows that use similar music. Fiske highlights these differences of codes, stating that codes correspond broadly to three key kinds of knowledge required by interpreters of a text, namely, knowledge of the world (social knowledge); knowledge of the medium and the genre (textual knowledge); and the relationship between the two (modality judgments) (Fiske 1990: 64–84).

In short, music operates in television through a process of association or correlation with other texts: either other musical works, which serve as syntactical objects of comparison, or through extramusical texts, such as images, words, or sounds through which a listener can draw common meanings. This model of correlation is found in other studies of music, such as that of J. Peter Burkholder (2006: 78–79), whose five-step associative model for music includes the following conative process: (1) recognizing familiar elements (in a piece of music), (2) recalling other music or schema that make use of those elements, (3) perceiving the (extramusical) associations that follow from the primary associations, (4) noticing what is new and how familiar elements are changed, and (5) interpreting what all this means. Recognizable in the *Rifleman* theme are the tonal design of the piece, the instrumentation, and the bold melodic gestures. These may recall some other musical texts that are similar, such as the Beethoven and Copland pieces mentioned earlier. Next, the extramusical interpretations of heroism from these previous pieces are aligned and then overlaid onto the TV theme. While viewers recognize that the derivation of these gestures conveys these musical attributes, they are also aware that the music is unique and that the outlines of the gestures are unique. The musical gestures of the theme music may be used as correlations for future TV theme music.

A second (and similar) associative model of musical correlation is by Gino Stefani, who describes the listener's musical competency as a process that is the musical equivalent to the literary verisimilitude described by Seymour Chatman and Jonathan Culler. Stefani (1987a: 7) has defined competence as "the ability to produce sense through music...the ability to realize either individual or social projects by means of music." Stefani (1987a: 8) described competencies in terms of a complex of codes, similar to Eco's definition:

> First, a code can be an additional correlation between a musical unit and a cultural context, both already constituted.
>
> Second, a code can be a structuring correlation between a field which is already constituted and another which is still informal and which therefore takes its structure from the first one.
>
> Third, a code can also be a correlating organization of two fields which are both still informal and which therefore structure themselves simultaneously.

When considering music and a TV genre, such as a western, as separate entities, one would think of putting a conventional musical style, such as movie music, with a standard narrative genre (the western) as a correlation, where the vocabularies of both genre and musical style have been well established (Stefani's first model). As a different style topic, such as jazz or rock, encroaches into the genre, one would view the change as an additional correlation, as the musical style topic has changed. However, a viewer who approaches the television text more holistically may view the change from a different perspective, perhaps as either a structuring correlation or a correlating organization. The music and images from *The Rifleman* form an additional correlation, as both musical style and image style are familiar to an audience. However, the correlations can be structuring or correlating as well, as both image and music are unique to this particular program. So, while viewers are familiar with the musical style and genre of the music, both of these are combined in a unique way to produce this particular TV show. This is the essence of television, relying on the familiar while trying to make the familiar unique.

In addition to the correlation of expressive genres within a style of music, like the Hollywood symphonic style, many musical correlations involving television entail extramusical associations of generic musical styles.[20] Hatten (1994: 289) defines correlation as the stylistic association between sound and meaning in music that is structured (kept coherent) by oppositions and mediated by markedness. While Hatten's context of style focuses on the music of Beethoven and deals in binary oppositions, audiences of film and television music draw upon a menu of styles and topics for meaning in a media text. Stylistically, listeners can follow the musical logic of a western with a theme like that of *The Rifleman*, which features a Romantic-style orchestra score, but might find a western with a jazz theme as odd because of their previous experiences and competencies, either in real life or with previous experience with the genre.[21] Other musical styles are used in other genres; jazz, for example, seemed to be acceptable for the genre of the detective show in the 1950s and 1960s but not for the police drama (as will be shown in chapter 8). However, using musical styles as signifiers was not widespread in television until the 1980s, with most TV composers sticking with the Hollywood symphonic style.

Television (and film) music signifies through topics, that is, correlations and connections of music with extramusical sources ranging from emotions to settings to objects. In addition to the main title of *The Rifleman* being recognized as heroic, based on its connection to other heroic music, the image of Chuck Connors in cowboy regalia, following Burkholder's third step, also is seen as heroic. In Burkholder's fourth step, Connors becomes the embodiment of the cowboy hero.[22] Burkholder's final step is the viewer's interpretation, or reading, which coincides with Fiske's interpretation stage. How does *The Rifleman*'s role of hero manifest itself?

Music and TV: An Interpretive Network Model of Correlation

Given the premise that music has the potential to signify on the representational level, how does it function when combined with the sensory channels of television? These collections of musical topics (discussed in more detail in chapter 2) can be employed to interpret the opening to the program, thereby paralleling Fiske's ideology level of codes. Indeed, music helps to facilitate a particular reading of the opening of the program. The cowboy music of the main title interprets Connors's glaring into the camera as heroic rather than villainous, intense rather than menacing. The discharging of the rifle is interpreted as peacemaking rather than as a threat. The closing gesture, after an ascent that requires some musical effort, is read as the goal of goodness and heroism attained. As music helps to portray Chuck Connors as an ethical hero, music also helps to define and reinforce the ideology of the program and of many westerns that include American themes of self-sufficiency and patriarchy, of ethical and moral behavior, but with the option of using force (the rifle) when necessary.

While the correlation of music and extramusical topics in the codes of television music model may be seen as hierarchical, the combination of music and visual image functions more as a network. The music in *The Rifleman* serves to announce the beginning of the program, but it also informs the audience about the narrative nature of the program through the presentation of a heroic musical topic. However, rarely does music act alone in doing the heavy lifting of signification within a TV show; rather, it combines with the other sensory channels to produce a meaning in the text. Heroic music accompanied by the image of the

41

ultramasculine Connors produced a correlation of the heroic. Loud music correlated with gunshots to signify action or violence. Music functions by combining or *correlating* with the other sensory channels to produce a preferred meaning. The correlation of music and visual images in film and television has been the subject of much study, notably by Claudia Gorbman (1987), Kathryn Kalinak (1992), Nicholas Cook (1998), Philip Tagg (2000), and Michel Chion (1994). These authors use different terms for the combined relationship of image and music, such as "ancrage" (Gorbman), "conformance" (Cook), and "synchresis" (Chion).

The process of how all sensory channels (image, sound, music, language) combine to create meaning in a television text suggests a network model of correlation that relies heavily on the viewer's ability to draw correlative meanings from all five sensory channels of the text. Correlations operate through two or more sensory channels on television that share a set of common attributes and that can be described as the "semantic field" (Eco) or as a "Generic Space" (Fauconnier and Turner), or as a "Reality" code (Fiske). Each sensory channel of television carries potential signifiers for interpretation within a semantic field. The image of Chuck Connors could convey him as hero or villain, certainly male, serious, earnest, and perhaps hostile. The music of the opening is loud (perhaps excessively so) and heroic. The gunshots are violent, loud, and may be interpreted as menacing or as a means of security. When all these channels are combined, the audience must draw out those attributes that conform to each other, in this case heroism and action. The viewer reads the opening of the show as heroic, based on these input cues and how the viewer can relate back to previous westerns. Such a model is illustrated in the Venn diagram in figure 1.5.

Here the interpretation is the result of the viewer's drawing out an intersection of the multiple sensory channels. For the opening of *The Rifleman*, interpretants are articulated from the visual images (the rifle, the town, Chuck Connors) with such descriptive words as "cowboy," "action," "hero," "menace," with others that might be added such as "violence," "determination," "maleness," and so on. The sounds from the screen are interpreted as "gunshots," "loud," with other terms like "violence," "action," and so on. The music overlaps many (but not necessarily all) of these terms, notably, "cowboy," "heroic," and "loud." These intersecting terms are reinforced by the large letters on-screen and by the announcer's loud voice.

While the text helps shepherd the viewer to select the preferred meaning, it is up to the viewer to pull these correlations from the text and interpret the text. This is the essence of Jakobson's conative function. In this case, the heroic and action descriptions are drawn out as an amalgam of the gunshots, Connors's appearance, and the loud, heroic character of the music. However, viewers also

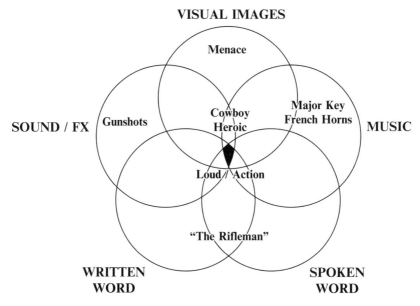

Figure 1.5. A Network Model of Signification in Television.

accept the signification of music and character as heroic because of their knowledge of the genre of the TV western. They know that the program will deal with issues of good guys versus bad guys and that probably there will be violence in the form of gunplay and fistfights, that the cast will be mostly male, that the protagonist will be a virtuous male and that the villain(s) will be criminal males and will be vanquished at the end of the episode. They also know that if any character appears at the beginning of the show, that person will be the hero and not the villain.[23] This textual knowledge thus contributes to facilitating meaning in television. Through a relationship he has called "motivation," Hatten (1994: 292) describes the systematic coordination of codes and conventions enabling "efficient acquisition" by listeners. In television, genre and an audience's understanding of genre are strong motivational forces for meaning.

From Network to Hierarchy

As compelling as the correlation network model is in describing the component parts of the television text, it does not fully describe the full signifying power of the text. The opening to *The Rifleman* does indeed consist of component parts, such as music, visual images (containing an actor in costume on a set with specific lighting, etc.), and sound effects, all of which do conjure up common (or conforming) interpretants. But to the viewer, there is a point where the discrete sensory channels of a TV program like the opening of *The Rifleman* are unified by the audience to become a monadic text. *The Rifleman* consists of some of the following attributes: it includes Chuck Connors as the star; it is set in the Old West town of North Fork; it was shot on grainy black-and-white film stock; it contains a musical score composed by Gilbert; it was produced by Four Star Television Productions, etc. In fact, it is the combination of these (and other) components that makes the program unique. To change one facet of the program is to create a different text altogether. This point is easily proved by taking the commutation test, in which some of the component parts of the original text are taken away. For example, if Strauss's "Blue Danube" waltz is substituted for Gilbert's theme music, the program takes on a very different character, quite different from the original. There is a point where the uniqueness of a text is measured by the specific signs attached to it. Lawrence Kramer (2002: 174) has called this phenomenon "mixture," a sort of "shared absorption" of all sensory channels within a mixed-media text.[24] Kramer makes the case for a mixed-media text, such as television, to be considered as a homogeneous semiotic entity. Likewise for film music, Claudia Gorbman (1987: 15–16) described the role of music and visual image as creating a unified text of meaning: "Image, sound effects, dialogue, and music-track are virtually inseparable during the viewing experience; they form a *combinatoire* of expression." Despite its difference from film music, television music is similar in this regard. *The Rifleman* is *The Rifleman* because it is a unique mixture of TV genre (western), narrative style, black-and-white TV production values, Gilbert's theme music, and (of course) Chuck Connors. So, while each sensory channel may be interpreted independently by the viewer, channels combine hierarchically to create the complex television texts.

A hierarchical network, such as a television show, can be shown using a blended space model used in cognitive science. Giles Fauconnier and Mark Turner (Fauconnier 1997 and Fauconnier and Turner 2002) would describe the visual and musical codes of the television text as "conceptual integration networks" in which two input spaces (in this case, a musical heroic space and a Chuck Connors cowboy hero space) are drawn from "generic space" (similar to Fiske's "reality" level), have matching qualities, and are thus paired in a "blended" space. This blended space produces an emergent structure, namely, *The Rifleman* with Chuck Connors as the cowboy hero. With television programs, however, there are at least five input spaces that draw from generic space, and these combine to create the unique television program. Although each channel works as a network (as shown above), the combination of these is essentially hierarchical.

An adaptation of Fauconnier and Turner's model for television is shown in figure 1.6.

In this model, there are at least five input spaces (and probably many more within the visual channel alone) corresponding to Metz's five sensory channels for cinema. Visual images, sound effects, dialogue, written text, and music all have their own expression and content planes (and interpretants), or generic spaces, but all combine hierarchically to create the content plane of the television text. The dotted lines show the projections and mappings of concepts from generic space through the filters of each sensory channel and onto the new, emergent blended space. Solid lines between input spaces show the conceptual connections between channels (in this case heroic and action). As shown in the graph, some concepts do not blend (dotted lines that terminate in input space), whereas some

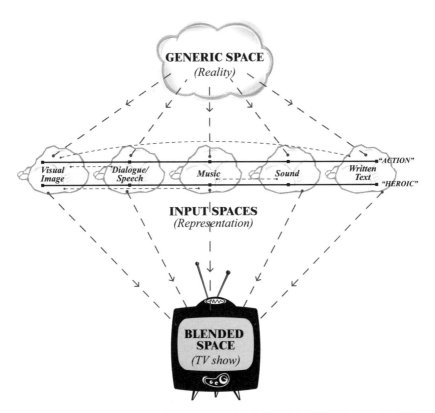

Figure 1.6. A Hierarchical Model of Signification in Television (after Fauconnier 1997 and Fauconnier and Turner 2002).

inferences may come from input space directly to the blend (someone who sees Lucas McCain but does not know that he is a character being portrayed by the actor Chuck Connors). Changes in one of these input spaces would affect the larger text and create a different text with potentially different semiotic values. If sinister music was being played during the opening of *The Rifleman*, for example, McCain would seem to be a villainous character rather than a hero, and this understanding would alter the way viewers interpret the program and essentially make it a different program—even if all the other parameters of the opening were the same.

Finally, the emergent, blended spaces are often aided by the viewer's knowledge of genre, television broadcasting practices, musical styles, and more.

Conclusion: Welcome to TV Land

Despite the often blanket simplistic description of television as a mass communications medium, it is actually a very complex semiotic system that relies heavily on cultural competency and a sophisticated reading/viewing process that can approach a text from both a network and a hierarchical perspective. The images and sounds that are broadcast on television are the result of habits and beliefs (i.e., codes) of a given culture that manifest themselves as semantic fields. These semantic fields are combined as correlations to produce tropes or additional correlations of new meaning in television texts. In the analysis of the opening to *The Rifleman*, it becomes apparent that the meaning imparted by music relies partially on musical traditions from previous musical texts to establish its own meaning; that is, music signifies through musical convention. However, music also signifies through iconicity (sounds like) and through combination and correlation with other sensory channels of television. The main title theme to *The Rifleman* relies on heroic musical gestures that, in turn, rely on a collective (or intersubjective) knowledge of musical topics, that is, a network of knowledge of repertoire, as in late-nineteenth-century orchestral music that conveys the heroic as well as Coplanesque type musical figures that convey cowboyness. But the music also correlates with the images of Chuck Connors, the western town, the sound of the gunshots, all of which invoke the semantic fields of the heroic and action in the program. Further, these sounds and images correlate with our knowledge, our verisimilitude of the TV cowboy genre. These significations are not exhausted, however, and other interpretations of the program are made possible by the main title. Is Lucas McCain's toughness and willingness to use a rifle a virtue for the American west? Does the overwhelmingly male cast aligned with the heroic music signify and actually promote a patriarchal male-dominated society? These and other questions get to the heart of Fiske's ideology or interpretive level of the text.

Besides its ability to convey meaning outside itself, to signify as semioticians like to say, music in television helps to demarcate television texts into discrete, hierarchical units. Fauconnier and Turner's conceptual integrative network models of blended space illustrate this concept well. Taking their metaphor of space, the next chapter continues by considering three structural spaces of television: an extradiegetic or broadcasting space, an intradiegetic or narrative space, and a diegetic or textual space. Music functions to define these spaces to convey meaning as well as to signal transitions between these various spaces.

Stay tuned.

2

"Hello Out There in TV Land"

Musical Agency in the Early Television Anthology Drama

"Pride and Prejudice," from the *Philco Television Playhouse*, airing January 23, 1949, and featuring actors Madge Evans (left) and John Baragrey (right) (Wisconsin Center for Film and Theater Research).

In the first chapter, television was considered as both a mass communications medium and a semiotic system in which images, sound, and music coalesce or correlate with each other to form a preferred meaning from a text. Besides being a communications medium, television is also a narrative medium—a *storyteller*—that presents many small narratives, both fictional and nonfictional. Television conveys these narratives in a unique way, and music plays a role in how these narratives are told. In this regard, music can be seen as a narrative agent that serves to support the process of storytelling in television. While music contributes to the conveyance of stories on television, it functions also to mediate the manifold narratives that crowd the airwaves during the broadcasting day. Music also transitions in and out of narratives, marks the beginnings and endings of narrative texts, and even helps to identify the nature of these texts through connotation and denotation. In this chapter, I identify these functions, focusing on music as a framing device for narratives.

Anthropologists such as Claude Lévi-Strauss (1970) have indicated that narrative or storytelling is a nearly universal aspect of human culture that spans all cultures in all times and spaces. From a semiotic perspective, Roland Barthes (1988: 79) describes the universality of narrative:

> Narrative is first and foremost a prodigious variety of genres, themselves distributed amongst different substances.... Able to be carried by articulated language, spoken or written, fixed or moving images, gestures and the ordered mixture of all these substances, narrative is present in myth, legend, fable, tale, novella, epic, history, tragedy, drama, comedy, mime, painting... stained glass windows, cinema, comics, news items, conversation.

To Barthes's list of narrative genres can be added television, with music as an important part of the narrative discourse.

As an analyzable object, narrative may be broken down into various component parts. Perhaps the most fundamental categories of narrative are (1) a narrative must have a *story* to tell; and (2) a narrative must have *someone* (or perhaps *something*) to tell the story. In other words, narrative contains both a story and a discourse.[1] In television, the "how," or the discourse of the story, is told (or rather, *shown*) through the representational codes enumerated by John Fiske. The lighting, camera angles, sound quality, and usually the music are components of televisual discourse and usually not part of the story itself.[2] Although they are not really part of the story of the television episode, discursive components such as music are part of the world or space of the television narrative, to paraphrase Jerrold Levinson (1996a).[3] The discursive parts of narrative serve to illuminate certain aspects of the narrative, often providing guides through which the viewer may watch or listen to a program, and also providing a tone or modality for how the narrative is told. The shot-reverse-shot camera angles help viewers focus on the characters and attend to what each may be saying. Certain types of lighting will produce a certain effect, such as dark or underkey lighting creating a mysterious or ominous setting to a set or natural light creating an effect of the great outdoors. As shown in my codes of television music model, music functions in both of these ways, as seen in the *Rifleman* opening. Through its discourse as theme music, the opening title theme announced the beginning of the show (the story) and conveyed viewers to certain aspects of the story: a cowboy show with a heroic character acting in action-packed situations. In these and other aspects, music serves fully as a narrative agent as part of the narrative discourse.

Narrative Agency in Television

In addition to story and discourse, a third component part of a narrative is the act of narrating itself. In a narrative, who is telling the story, or more explicitly, how is the story being told? The act of narrating entails the recounting of a series of narrative events and describing characters or settings, whether by oral, written, visual, and/or musical means. If there is no recounting of narrative events, that is, if there is no narrator, then there simply is no narrative or story. The focus on whom or what narrates a story and how that narration affects the tone, mood, and perspective of a story is referred to as *narrative agency*.[4]

In a medium like television, the multiple sensory channels (visuals and audio) open the possibility of stories being conveyed by more than a verbal storyteller. In fact, television, like cinema and the theater, may be seen as having *multiple* narrators. For example, for a narrative television program, the scriptwriter creates the story and thus serves the role of a traditional narrator. However, the scriptwriter is not directly involved in conveying the story (he or she usually does not read the script to the audience), so the actors who actually convey the lines of the story to the audience might also be considered as narrators. And, given that the producer hires the actors and production staff, and the director coordinates all aspects of production, might these people serve a role in the narration process? If so, the images, words, and sounds themselves convey narrative meanings on-screen, and each of these elements might be considered a form of narration.

The multiple narrators of television operate in two modalities, diegetic (narration of *telling*) and mimetic (narration of *showing*).[5] Traditionally, storytellers relate stories by orally transmitting them. In print media, someone has to tell the story by writing/typing/word processing words on a page. In film and television, however, narratives seldom have a speaking or writing narrator, and if they do, the narrator's role is minimal, usually used only to initiate the story line. Rather, in visual media like the cinema and television, the role of the diegetic narrator (the *tell*-er) is subsumed by the mimetic narrator (the *show*-er).[6] On television, the role of the diegetic narrator is greater, particularly in televisual texts of news broadcasts and commercials, where talking heads convey information about news stories or extol the virtues of a product being advertised. However, the role of mimesis—supplying the pictures that accompany the news story or the product—also functions as a narrator.

The model of multiple narrators on television must account for the multiplicity of producers of a television text. For example, the scriptwriter: is he or she a diegetic or mimetic narrator? Seymour Chatman (1990: 132–133) would consider this person and others involved with television production as either a *presenter* or an *implied author*:

> In cinema as in literature, the implied author is the agent intrinsic to the
> story whose responsibility is the overall design—including the decision
> to communicate it through one or more narrators. Cinematic narrators
> are transmitting agents of narratives, not their creators.
>
> In short, for films as for novels, we would do well to distinguish
> between a presenter of the story, the narrator (who is a component of
> the discourse), and the inventor of both the story and the discourse
> (including the narrator), that is the implied author.

For the fiction film, narration is usually mimetic, with the story often shown to the audience through nonhuman narrative agents but created by an implied author. The implied author for television is actually a group of *multiple* implied authors: the writer, the producer, the director, the music composer, the lighting designer, the costumer, and so on.

Such multiple narration in television is *synchronic*, meaning that multiple narrators, often both diegetic and mimetic, work together to gang up on viewers to narrate the story on television. This synchronic narration is evident in the opening to *The Rifleman*, where image, sound, and music combined to narrate a story of heroism and action.[7] Along with this synchronic narration, television also has a diachronic dimension in which multiple narrators tell different stories in fast-paced, consecutive time blocks unique to television and often referred to as flow. Before engaging the synchronic aspects of narrative, I will first consider this flow.

Televisual Time, Flow, and Narrative Agency

Since the early 1950s, American television has featured the continuous broadcasting of images and sounds, which Raymond Williams ([1974] 1992) termed "flow." Televisual flow has bathed the viewer in an uninterrupted stream of images and sounds continuously through time, 24 hours a day, 7 days a week, 365 days a year, for more than 30 years on U.S. television. Television log schedules, such as those that appear in newspapers, in publications like *TV Guide*, and even on cable and satellite TV networks, are palpable, written-down examples of flow. TV logs have a vertical dimension, which shows all TV programs broadcast at a given time, as well as a horizontal dimension, which illustrates programs as they appear through time. Such schedules do not include other aspects of televisual flow, such as commercials, newsbreaks, public service announcements, and the like.[8] Williams also conceives of flow as both "intratextual" and "intertextual," differentiated as flow within a single text and flow between texts. For example, a news broadcast typically operates in relating intratextual flow in which newscasters report on one story after another within the same newscast. Intertextual flow is exemplified by the progression of programming in a typical broadcast day, moving from programs to commercials to news breaks to station identifications to program promotions, to other programs. Williams analyzes flow in a somewhat unsuccessful attempt to find links between these two modes of flow and to find recurring elements that would produce textual closure between the televisual units.

Flow implies a continuous, temporally amorphous mass of sounds and images but, in fact, really consists of small, discrete hypertexts that are juxtaposed and concatenated through broadcasting time. The components of these texts differ in their style and substance: some are narrative programs; others are commercials, station identifications, public service announcements, news updates (from both national and local news broadcasters), and more, all of which have discrete (though often very brief) narrative beginnings, middles, and ends. Videographer David Antin noted that a half-hour of television flow time discloses a complex mélange of loosely related video chunks: "In a half hour you might see a succession of four complete, distinct and unrelated thirty-second presentations, followed by a twelve-minute half of a presentation, followed by a one-minute presentation, one thirty-second presentation and two ten-second presentations, followed by the second and concluding half presentation (twelve minutes long), followed by yet another four unrelated thirty second presentations" (Antin 1976; quoted in Fink 2005: 131).[9] Antin's architectonic conception of televisual time is more accurate than Williams's amorphous flow model, but Antin's (and Fink's) attempt to define a hierarchical "teleme" as the smallest unit of televisual meaning is not convincing, given that the components of flow are actually quite different depending on the space of agency in which a text operates.[10] Although it appears within Fiske's representational space of broadcasting, a station identification operates within a televisual space that is different from the final scene of a 30-minute narrative program, for example. Moreover, televisual time actually operates more as a menu of signs and codes in the context of a differentiated broadcasting flow rather than as a monolithic series of telemes. A commercial may convey a narrative beginning, middle, and end in 15 to 60 seconds (whereas a 30-minute program's narrative unfolds more leisurely) while a PSA that serves as a means of information for the viewer may rely on rhetorical, rather than narrative, models.

The Televisual Spaces of Flow: Some Useful Categories

From the perspective of narrativity and narrative agency, the context of flow can be seen to operate in three semiotic spaces, with each part representing a different narrative agency.[11] Borrowing Gérard Genette's (1980) categories of narrative agency in literature, television narrates in one of three spaces: extradiegetic, intradiegetic, and diegetic. By most definitions, including Genette's, diegesis is the "story world" of the narrative text; thus diegetic narrating is that which comes from the story world of the text itself. On television, diegetic narration would show characters or talking heads on-screen actually conveying the story to the audience. However, this conveyance may not necessarily be verbal but, rather, mimetic (showing), as done through Fiske's codes of acting, costume, makeup, setting, and so on. Often music is used diegetically for its mimetic qualities.

Extradiegetic space is the realm of television that narrates outside television's narrative programs. It consists of flow in its entirety, the programs, commercials, station identifications, news updates, broadcasting sign-offs, etc. The extradiegetic space is a sort of meta-narrator of television, ordering and coordinating the many small and large texts that make up the flow of television. Extradiegetic space is that of the log system of TV broadcasting, coordinated directly by producers and engineers of TV stations as well as by advertising companies and corporate sponsors that produce the commercials. This space corresponds roughly to Fiske's reality level of the codes of television. Music functions in this space but more often functions as a vehicle to transition in or out of extradiegetic space.

Intradiegetic space consists of the story world (including both the story and the discourse around the story) of a particular TV show, news story, and often of a particular commercial but consists of those aspects not within the actual story world itself, but those things that convey the tone or mood of the story. In this aspect, intradiegetic space conforms to Fiske's technical codes of television that include camera positions, lighting, film editing, sound reproduction, and musical underscoring. Intradiegetic space is like the author of a book as implied narrator who calls attention to certain traits of characters, describes settings, highlights certain details within a story, and sets the overall tone or mood of the story. Unlike some aspects of narrative, television music is often associated in this space (as was noted in chapter 1), as it calls attention to the characters, emotions, settings, and objects in the diegesis without actually being *in* the diegesis.

We can consider the three spaces as emanating from television in ways shown in the diagram in figure 2.1, with extradiegetic space being the outer, inclusive space; intradiegetic space including Chatman's narrative model of story and discourse; and diegetic space being story only.

Each of these spaces reflects differences in narrative agency. Extradiegetic spaces can be seen as being narrated by the operators of the technical apparatus

Figure 2.1. The Three Discursive Spaces of Television.

of television, engineers, producers, network executives, and the ubiquitous sponsors. Intradiegetic space has agency through the implied authors, including writers, producers, directors, costume designers, and musical composers of individual programs (though in U.S. television network executives and sponsors usually play a large role in the content and production of narratives).

Musical Functions in the Narrative Spaces

Music operates within each of the three televisual spaces and functions in different ways both between each space and within each space. Operating in extradiegetic space, some TV networks and studios use musical mottos to identify themselves, though these mottos tend to be less elaborate than themes and jingles but no less effective in creating a semiotic bond with the audience. One example of extradiegetic musical space is the three-bell tone motto in the ascending–descending melodic configuration of G–E–C that has identified the NBC network for decades. Another extradiegetic motto is the 18-second fanfare composed by Alfred Newman that identifies 20th Century Fox, first as a film company, then as a television studio, and then as a television network. These examples of mottos are used to identify specific televisual texts and institutions, and contribute to the extradiegetic flow of broadcasting.

Another use of music in the extradiegetic space is with the bumper (sometimes called an eyecatch or just a bump), which is a brief text occurring during commercial breaks in the middle of a program. Bumpers usually display a program's logo on-screen and are accompanied by music, usually a segment of theme music from the program. Bumpers function to remind the viewer that a program is in progress and will return after (still) more commercials. Bumpers began as a transitional device from a program to commercials (usually with an on-air announcer saying something like: "We'll be back right after these messages"), but in the 1980s and 1990s these evolved into the logo/theme song format without verbal narration.[12]

Roy Prendergast (1992) illustrates the bumper from the program *Dallas* (1978–1991; CBS), one of the most popular American television programs in the 1980s, achieving very high Nielsen ratings for most of its run. *Dallas* is the saga of a wealthy Texas oil family, the Ewings, and their various business and personal dealings with members of the family and their enemies. The program began as a miniseries but was upgraded to a recurring serial in 1979. As a serial (i.e., an ongoing story line where the plot is left hanging from week to week), each episode ended in some sort of crisis or surprise. One of the highlights of

American television in the 1980s was the answer to the question "Who shot J.R.?" (the villain of the series portrayed by actor Larry Hagman) after that character was shot before the summer hiatus of the show in 1980.

The music to *Dallas* was composed by Jerrold Immel, a veteran television composer whose scores drew the attention of *Dallas* producer Leonard Katzman.[13] Katzman was interested in a big score on the scope of the film *Giant* (1956; music by Dmitri Tiomkin) but also something more urban and current. In a three-bar bumper for the series, Immel restates a fragment of the main theme (example 2.1) which is reminiscent of the excitement of the theme: the loud dynamics, the motive from the theme music in the horns and trumpets, and a cowboy-like tag ending of sixteenth notes leading up to the cadence.[14]

The bumper from *Dallas* illustrates the fluid nature of music on the extradiegetic space of television. The bumper functions (phatically) primarily on the extradiegetic level: it calls attention to the flow of broadcasting, reminding viewers that the show, *Dallas*, will return after more commercials and newsbreaks, and so on. However, the use of the *Dallas* logo and the snippet of the theme song also calls attention to the intradiegetic space of the story world. The music conveys the diegesis of *Dallas* in the extradiegetic space of the broadcast apparatus, the network. The bumper tells the audience to stay tuned (to this network and view its revenue-producing advertisements) because the story world of *Dallas* is being broadcast here. Music can be seen to function in two spaces simultaneously or at least as a pivotal or transitional device between the extradiegetic and the intradiegetic. This double function is one marker of television music over its related music in film.

Intradiegetic music, often serving as a musical narrator of a particular story, helps present the discourse of television narratives but more generally is any music that conveys or narrates the tone, mood, or subject matter of the story. Intradiegetic music consists of the underscore or background music of television programs, following the narrative and narrating (mimetically) its narrative trajectory. Transitional musical devices, such as the theme music to a program (for example, Gilbert's theme to *The Rifleman*) as well as act-ins and act-outs, are so-called because the transition from space to space: act-ins from extradiegetic to intradiegetic spaces and act-outs from intradiegetic to the extradiegetic spaces.

Example 2.1. Excerpt of Bumper from *Dallas*
(Music by Jerrold Immel).

As has been shown, the theme music to *The Rifleman* identifies and denotes specific programs through weekly (or daily) repetition and correlates with association with a program. In this guise, theme music often signifies in identificative mode.[15] Theme music is also an important marker in highlighting the opening and closing of a program, acting as a sort of sonic frame or curtain by demarcating and separating the diegetic text from the extradiegetic televisual flow. Effective theme music draws and immerses the viewer into the story world of the program, functioning both phatically (calling attention to the show) and poetically and conatively (establishing the story world of the show from narrator to viewer), as Roman Jakobson would have it. The expressive power of the music through style topics accomplishes this initially, as was discussed with regard to the opening to the show *The Rifleman*. The theme of a program provides a sort of temporal frame or buffer, separating the flow of television discourse with the flow of a particular narrative. As poetic text, theme music is essentially intradiegetic and discursive, as it signifies aspects of the story world of the TV program, but it also functions extradiegetically as a transition from flow to story. In this regard, theme music exhibits traits of both intradiegetic and extradiegetic spaces. If such spaces could be quantified, it might be seen that theme music functions more in intradiegetic space while bumpers are more extradiegetic than intradiegetic. Like the frame of a painting, the frame of the theme music helps the viewer transition from the intertext to the intratext.

Intradiegetic music thus serves as temporal gatekeeper, announcing the beginnings and endings of programs, thus transitioning between intertexts and intratexts but also within intratexts. Other transitional intradiegetic musical devices that function in dual spaces are act-ins and act-outs. Like bumpers, they are amalgams of extradiegetic and intradiegetic music that function in a transitional way to move from the narrative to a commercial break and vice versa. From a narrative standpoint, they function to put the story on hold, pause, or reintroduce the story while the television discourse transitions to or from the extradiegetic realm of the televisual flow. In this regard they keep the viewer in suspense as to what will happen next in the story. In American television, these transitional devices are very brief, ranging from 3 seconds to as many as 15 seconds. The musical cues often accompany discursive practices of the image, act-ins usually accompanying establishing shots, which, as their name suggests, establish a scene or a continuation of a scene from before the commercial break. Act-outs often accompany a reaction shot (usually a long hold of the camera on one of the characters, thereby creating a stage wait designed to keep viewers in suspense and so tuned to the program. As Jane Feuer (1994: 557) has written, "This conventional manner of closing a scene...leaves a residue of emotional intensity just prior to a scene change or commercial break. It serves as a form of punctuation, signifying momentary closure, but it also carries meaning within the scene, a meaning connected to the intense interpersonal involvements each scene depicts."

Immel's act-out music for *Dallas* helps to magnify the intensity of the scenes and to keep viewers watching—even when the story is interrupted by commercials. His musical cues actually reveal a great deal of resourcefulness and creativity in expressing musical ideas in a very short period of time. The instrumentation of one act-out features a small ensemble of flute, alto flute, oboe, English horn, clarinet, bassoon, gut-string guitar, two horns, two trombones, harp, two (Yamaha DX7) synthesizers, four cellos, and bass.[16] This unusual combination of instruments is typical of television scoring, in which composers use the instruments available to them (and budgeted for them) but also exploit combinations of sounds unique to a particular program. The guitar and electric bass connote a sort of western-ness to the show, while the use of synthesizer is added to convey a sense of modernity.[17] The orchestral instruments add to the distinctive color of the music and convey the tradition of orchestral scoring for film and television.

Also innovative in Immel's act-out is his use of harmony. In the act-out, Immel basically pivots between a tonality of C minor and A-flat major. The clarinet, bassoon, and synthesizer enter with a melodic figure suggesting C minor, while horns and guitar suggest A-flat major. In the next bar, trombones, cellos, and basses switch from their C major centricity to A-flat. The result is a polychord (example 2.2) interlocking C minor and A-flat major (with a B-flat added). The chords played in the harp part reinforce this sense of polytonality, as the first chord is centered on C while the second is on A-flat. Such a harmony lends itself to an unstable, or suspended, feel, thus contributing to the suspense left at the end of the act.[18]

A final intradiegetic musical device is the bridge, a short piece of music that connects scene to scene within a program. Bridges are purely intradiegetic and serve to move the story along its narrative course. Most bridges are composed to wrap up a scene and convey a mood of expectation for the next scene.

Diegetic music is music that emanates directly from the story of a narrative, a term identical to that used for film music—music that both the characters and the audience can hear.[19] For television, diegetic music is also music that emanates from any television program, including singers and instrumentalists on musical variety programs as well as the special cases of music emanating from a

Example 2.2. Polychord in *Dallas* Bumper.

narrative television program. Diegetic music often narrates in a very special way, usually by signifying itself as music rather than correlating with a narrative object, especially in the musical variety show or music video. However, diegetic music has been used in other narrative situations (discussed in chapter 6).

How music functions on television does not always fall discretely within three spaces of television, as I have discussed with theme music, bumpers, and other transitions. Indeed, the ability of music to operate in several aspects is one reason it is so powerful in television. Moreover, these musical functions change over time as new codes of television are negotiated between viewer and producer. As in literature, narrational devices that are useful in conveying stories in one era of television may become redundant or arcane for a future generation. Such is the case with music found in the anthology dramas characteristic of early television. To illustrate the development and evolution of one aspect of television discourse, I will focus on two programs from the genre of the anthology series, one broadcast in 1949 and the second in 1963.

The Three Musical Spaces of Television in the Anthology Series

The anthology series was one of the earliest television genres, a genre that transitioned and adapted itself from its parent genre, radio. The anthology series is critically acclaimed as a high point in television, typifying the so-called golden age of television in the 1940s and 1950s. The genre reflected the vision of some producers, directors, and sponsors who wanted to make television a highbrow cultural medium by broadcasting serious plays by famous and upcoming playwrights. Many anthology series presented a different play each week, initially performed live and later filmed in studios. The popularity of the genre is evidenced by the proliferation of such programs in the 1950s, notably *The Kraft Television Theater* (1947–1958), *The Ford Television Theater* (1952–1957), *Playhouse 90* (1956–1961), *The Bell Telephone Hour* (1959–1968), *Producer's Showcase* (1954–1957), *Studio One* (1948–1958), *The U.S. Steel Hour* (1953–1963), and the *Philco Television Playhouse* (1948–1954), later the *Philco-Goodyear Playhouse*. The genre differs from others in that while a consistent host introduced the program each week, the episodes usually featured a different cast of characters, often combining theater veterans with up-and-coming young actors. These programs presented adaptations of Broadway stage plays, famous literary works condensed, and new teleplays written for the 30-, 60-, or 90-minute time slots. The anthology series was an especially effective and lucrative training ground for emerging playwrights, as the insatiable desire for new material to broadcast on television created a demand for more and more scripts. Among the most notable talents who arose from the anthology series was screenwriter Rod Serling, noted both for his work on *Playhouse 90* and later as creator of *The Twilight Zone* series.

Philco Television Playhouse

The *Philco Television Playhouse* debuted on NBC in October 1948 and ran for seven seasons. The program was developed to broadcast Broadway and Off Broadway plays as well as new plays and adaptations of classic literature. Despite ensuing complications over the legalities of broadcasting copyrighted plays on television and several legal battles that ensued, the show flourished. At that time, television programs were initially broadcast live in New York before a studio audience and simultaneously filmed on kinescopes for distribution to other network studios (by 1948, NBC had nine such studios across the country). Film studios, fearing competition from the new medium, threatened to sue over the rights to plays owned by studios even though these second-generation TV films were blurry kinescopes. Studios were okay with the one-time live broadcast in New York but argued that circulation of these filmed broadcasts infringed on their distribution rights.[20] Ultimately, *Philco Playhouse* avoided this legal problem by using new material not subject to restrictions based on copyright, such as contemporary works by up-and-coming playwrights or adaptations of classic literary works by Jane Austen, Charles Dickens, Shakespeare, and others. Also, *Philco* became remarkably rich in soliciting new material from emerging playwrights such as Paddy Chayefsky, Bob Arthur, J. P. Miller, David Shaw, and Reginald Rose. Thanks to *Philco* and other anthology series, television became a stepping-stone for many rising American playwrights.

Harry Sosnik and *Philco*

While the anthology series was providing new career opportunities for writers, it was also becoming one of the last bastions for live music in broadcasting.[21] The anthology series of the 1940s and 1950s was essentially an extension of both live theater performance and radio broadcasting from the 1930s and 1940s, with live acting accompanied by live music during the programs. Due to the similarity of television and radio broadcasting, TV studios hired music directors, composers, singers, and instrumentalists seasoned from radio to create music for the programs. Orchestra leader Harry Sosnik was hired as music director of the *Philco Television Playhouse* primarily because of his experience in radio as well as his skills as arranger and composer.

Sosnik was born in Chicago on July 13, 1906. He began his career as a dance band composer, arranger, and conductor, broadcasting and recording with many artists, Ethel Merman, Mel Tormé, and George Jessel, among others. Clarinetist Woody Herman reportedly spent time in Sosnik's big band before establishing his own Thundering Herd. One of the most popular big bands of the 1920s and 1930s, Sosnik's band was a featured act on radio broadcasts from hotel ballrooms. His radio career in the 1930s and 1940s as a composer-arranger-conductor overlapped those of noted vaudevillians Olsen and Johnson, Joe E. Brown, Gracie Fields, and Hildegarde. At the end of the 1930s, he also was working as an arranger-conductor for the American branch of Decca records. Sosnik moved into television in 1948, again serving as composer-arranger-conductor of music for both musical variety and dramatic programs. He is noted primarily for his work as a composer for the *Philco Television Playhouse* and other shows, such as *The Ford Show*, *Twenty-Five Years of Life*, *Your Hit Parade*, and *Playwrights '56*. He also arranged music and conducted the pit orchestra for several Emmy Awards shows in the 1950s and 1960s. Sosnik became musical director at the Ted Bates Advertising Agency in 1963 and, in 1970, vice president in charge of music for ABC-TV. He retired in 1976 but continued to compose as well as write and lecture on music and the electronic media.[22]

For the *Philco Television Playhouse*, Sosnik served as both composer and conductor of music, with duties similar to those of most music directors at the time. Sosnik would sketch his musical ideas for each program on letter-sized staff paper arranged in three staves and later copy parts for a small orchestra that performed live with the actors. According to Sosnik (and others), composing music for the television drama was a continual race against time. The pace of weekly programming meant that he had between two and three days each week to compose a completely new score. Sosnik would first wait for a copy of the script and watch the actors rehearse onstage in order to determine where musical cues were needed. He then set about composing a score for that broadcast, again within just a few days. Finally, he conducted the orchestra during each broadcast, with the actors performing on a studio stage in front of the cameras and the orchestra playing in the next room, Sosnik simultaneously conducting and watching a TV monitor to keep track of the action onstage. Sosnik was successful in large part due to having worked under similar constraints as a radio composer.

Sosnik's Music to the *Philco* Production of "Pride and Prejudice"

Producers of these early anthology series believed that a wide variety of sound was necessary to navigate the viewer away from the extradiegetic televisual flow toward the particular presentation in the time slot. The *Philco Television Playhouse*, like most programs in early television, retained many of its broadcasting practices from radio, such as the use of an announcer or host to introduce programs and live music. Since the anthology series featured a different story each week and different actors playing the characters, music, sound, and the host all were used to move the viewer away from the series itself and into the particular play of the week. Unlike a series or serial program led by a regular cast of characters, the anthology series had the double function of presenting a regular announcer/host but also introducing new characters and new narrative situations each week. This double transition leads from extradiegetic televisual flow to the intradiegetic space of the program to the diegetic space of the story in a sort of frame-within-a-frame format.

One example of how music functions this way can be found in Sosnik's score to "Pride and Prejudice," an adaptation of Jane Austen's novel that aired on *Philco* on January 23, 1949, and starred yeoman Broadway actors John Baragrey as Darcy and Madge Evans as Elizabeth. Sosnik's music for the episode consists of 26 cues, some of them drawn from stock or library (previously composed) music. The cues conform to the three-act play structure, with Sosnik composing extradiegetic introductions (or opening curtains) and finales to each act.[23] There are also several intradiegetic bridge cues and some indications for diegetic stock music performed during dance/party scenes. The introductory and finale cues, though taking the viewer from the diegetic to the extradiegetic realm of the teleplay, seem to function more intradiegetically, that is, as genuine finales to each act rather than as transitional devices as found in later television.

The first extradiegetic cue for the show is the theme of the program, the *Philco* theme. This "main title" or opening theme (example 2.3) is a brief but rich melody that establishes the program as a drama. Like the theme to *The Rifleman*, Sosnik's theme contains a fanfare topic, here illustrated by the ascending figure in the violins (rather than the horns as in the *Rifleman* theme). The upward motion of the melody is similar also to the yearning motives prevalent in nineteenth-century music by Wagner, Strauss, Tchaikovsky, Mahler (and others) and lends an air of expectation and anticipation to the theme. Measures 5 and 6 of the example feature some chromaticism, also characteristic of the post-Romantic style: measure 5 contains a secondary half-diminished 7th chord (viiø7/V) followed by a minor 7th chord on B-flat (iv7), resolving to C11th chord (V11 with b9) before resolving back to the tonic chord of F major. This chromatic harmonic vocabulary, which stems from post-Romantic music that was readily adopted in the scoring practices of Hollywood films of the 1930s through the 1950s, is used by Sosnik to signify the frame of the show as an extradiegetic piece of theater and becomes distinct from the intradiegetic music of the play itself.

After the host announces the episode of the week (in this case, "Pride and Prejudice"), it is introduced by new music. Sosnik cleverly begins the "opening

Example 2.3. Main Title or Opening Theme to the *Philco Television Playhouse* (Music by Harry Sosnik).

curtain" music (cue 2) with a reiteration of the *Philco* theme. As the credits roll, the opening theme gives way to a new theme, what Sosnik calls the "narration theme," a 24-four bar siciliano–type melody in 6/8 meter (example 2.4). The style of the theme can be described as pastoral, following the tradition of pastoral movements in classical music of the eighteenth and nineteenth centuries that employed 6/8 meter

Example 2.4. "Narration Theme" to *Philco* "Pride and Prejudice" Episode.

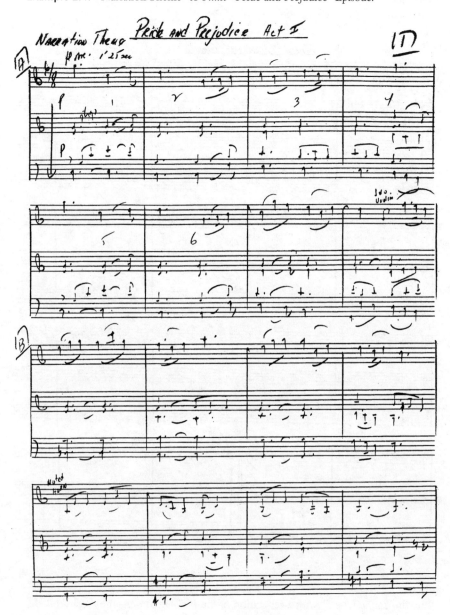

and smooth, diatonic melodic writing. The dotted eighth-sixteenth rhythm also is reminiscent of the siciliano, a gentle pastoral genre of the seventeenth and eighteenth centuries. The pastoral topic of the theme thus signifies the quiet, gentle mood of the play, romanticizes the setting, and identifies the play as a period piece. The theme is in C major, marking a motion away from the key of the main theme.

The narration theme is played seven times during the play, undoubtedly saving Sosnik much musical scoring time. However, the repetition also grounds the audience to the play, as the music becomes more and more familiar, becoming a leitmotif and correlating the play with the audience. This manifold repetition is a trait of TV music inherited from scoring narrative music on radio. Since radio broadcasts relied solely on sound parameters (spoken dialogue, sound effects, and music), repetition of musical motives was necessary to keep the audience engaged with the narrative. In this sense, musical repetition is similar to the bumper function of later extradiegetic television music, such as in the *Dallas* example.

The third intradiegetic motif is the "love theme" signifying the love between the characters Elizabeth and Darcy. This theme first is heard in the middle of act 1, recurs once in act 2, and in act 3 is played three times, including at the very end of the play. It is a simple 16-bar waltz with a diatonic melody and harmony (example 2.5). The waltz would have been recognized by an audience in 1949 (as well as today) as a musical topic connotative of elegance, in particular, an antique elegance thought to signify (and romanticizing) the nineteenth century. Like the narration theme, the love theme is in C major.

The only other intradiegetic cue is the "awkward theme," which occurs twice, in act 3. This theme depicts the awkwardness of the relationship between Darcy and Elizabeth. It is a staccato theme in 2/4 time played by an oboe (example 2.6). Unlike the other two themes, the "awkward theme" is not completely diatonic but uses chromaticism, primarily on the raised fourth and second scale degrees. While clearly in C major, the cue is marked by an extended pedal on the dominant. The final measure features a comical cadence of a G# minor 7th chord (a sort of misspelled German augmented 6th chord) to a C6/4 resolving to C in root position.[24]

The use of chromaticism in the "awkward theme" illustrates a differentiation between the musical cues within the intradiegetic realm of the play, which separate chromatic cues that serve as narrative commentary, from the diatonic cues that seek to portray the diegetic realm of the early nineteenth century. These chromatic intradiegetic transitions are stylistically different from the other cue music in that they use Hollywood-style idioms and clichés. Besides the "awkward theme," the "chatter bridge" (so-called because of the chattering of characters) in act 3 uses the technique of chord planing (parallel movement of chords in similar positions), a device used by such renowned composers as Debussy and Ravel and often employed by film composers in the 1940s and 1950s (example 2.7).

Example 2.5. "Love Theme" to *Philco* "Pride and Prejudice" Episode.

The parallel motion between the B major triad and the C major triads in measures 1–2 is reminiscent of the B–C motion in the "awkward theme." The bridge (which is marked "2" on the score) ends with a D7 chord moving to an Em7 to a Gr.+6 chord (in a wrong inversion), finally resolving to a D major triad

Example 2.6. "Awkward Theme" to *Philco* "Pride and Prejudice" Episode.

in 1st inversion (measures 5–6 in the example). While C is asserted as tonic at the beginning of the bridge, the presence of D at the last measure implies a half cadence in G (major or minor), setting up the dominant to C. Other iterations of the bridge in the play (marked "3" on the score) end on a surprise cadence on E-flat (measures 11–12 in the example).

Rather than use extradiegetic act-ins, Sosnik uses the "narration theme" to reintroduce the narrative after commercials. For act-outs, Sosnik uses the more theatrical term "finale" for his tag endings.[25] The finale to the third and final act of the play transitions from the "love theme" to the "tag," consisting of a melodic figure similar to the *Philco* theme. The chord progression of D minor to E minor to C to E-flat, finally cadencing on C, breaks from the eighteenth–nineteenth-

Example 2.7. "Chatter Bridge" to *Philco* "Pride and Prejudice" Episode.

century style topic of the intradiegetic music and transitions back to the Romantic style of the *Philco* theme (example 2.8).

The finale tag is the only use of extradiegetic transition music in the score. Other music that ends the acts, and thus transitions into commercial breaks, is

Example 2.8. "Tag" Finale to *Philco* "Pride and Prejudice" Episode.

labeled "finale" by Sosnik, indicating an intradiegetic function of truly concluding a teleplay act rather than transitioning into commercials. It should be noted that, by television standards, commercials for the program were quite long; on the *Philco* show, they were labeled "intermissions" and featured the host of the program advertising the sponsor's product. On this particular installation of *Philco*, the intermission consists of an interview with Paul Whiteman, the famous bandleader and then music advisor to the Philco Corp., who demonstrates the then-new 33 1/3 rpm record on the new Philco record player.[26]

In addition to the extradiegetic and intradiegetic music, Sosnik uses diegetic music in the form of three stock waltzes in the play. The first is "Sympathy," by Eduard Mezzacapo, a Venetian composer known for his gondola songs; the second is "Impassioned Dream," by J. Rosas; and the third is the popular song "A Toi," by Émile Waldteufel. This diegetic music is heard by characters and audience alike. These waltzes are used as diegetic music during ballroom scenes and are included both for their diegetic value (they could have actually been heard in the nineteenth century) and to save Sosnik time by not having to compose more original music. Diegetic music thus had both diegetic space and production value.

Narrative Agency and Music in "Pride and Prejudice"

Sosnik's music in the "Pride and Prejudice" episode demonstrates several different strategies of narrative agency. According to Genette, the narration of stories operates within five categories: order (which includes tense—past, present, etc.), duration, mood, frequency, and voice. Of these categories, Genette focuses on three as important in studying the relationships among all aspects of narrative discourse: tense and mood operate at the level of connections between story and narrative, and voice designates the connections between both narrating and narrative and narrating and story. Music has the ability to narrate in these areas within a television program, and it does so in "Pride and Prejudice." Sosnik's music in the *Philco* episode is one way in which the story is narrated; thus the music serves as a part of the narrative's discourse.

Reflecting Genette's category of duration, perhaps one of the most striking observations of the music of this episode is that some cues consist of complete pieces of music, that is, they have definite musical beginnings, middles, and endings, and can be ascertained as complete musical structures.[27] The "narration theme" is a 24 bar siciliano beginning and ending on C major with a brief modulation to the dominant. The "love theme" is a 16-bar waltz, also in C major consisting of a period with an antecedent-consequent phrase structure. In contrast to the complete pieces, other cues are incomplete fragments. These include the bridges and tags that vary in length from 4 to 16 measures but are marked by their lack of tonal closure and by their sometimes highly chromatic harmonic vocabulary. The incomplete cues also feature faster and brighter tempo markings and faster note values, like sixteenth notes. It can thus be concluded that Sosnik was interested in describing the characters and the setting of the episode in a relatively lengthy manner while relegating transitions and finales to minimal time periods. In this sense, the complete intradiegetic music connotes music of being while the shorter cues connote music of doing or action, even though this action is in the context of the program's production and not necessarily of the narrative itself. This dichotomy of length also affects the tone and voice of the narration. Musical time is lavished on the characters, especially the interaction between Elizabeth and Darcy, while transitions and endings of scenes are acquitted rapidly.

Sosnik's music also conveys a particular time period depicted through the opposition of diatonic versus chromatic passages. The "narration" and "love" themes are primarily diatonic while the bridges, tags, and finales contain chromaticism. The "chatter bridge" is a mixture of both, beginning diatonically and cadencing with the chromatic ending. The diatonic cues signify the simple, antiquated setting of Austen's story while the chromatic music is that which refers the viewer back into the extradiegetic space of 1949 television. Sosnik chooses stock diegetic music that is also diatonic, though not necessarily from the time period of the story. Still, these diatonic diegetic cues connote the time period of the story even though they are not quite historically correct.[28] Also, while the chromatic cues contain clear tonal/diatonic progressions from classical common harmonic practice, they also use progressions connotative of mid-twentieth-century techniques as well as popular Hollywood-style chord progressions with chromatic substitutions and chord planning, such as the comical cadence pointed out above. The different agencies that are brought out by the diatonic/chromatic duality reflects a complexity in the intradiegetic level of music, where diatonic music seeks to imitate the setting and traits of the characters (in past tense) while the chromatic music is a commentary on the narrative as a whole, in this case sentimental and mildly comical.

Musical narration of tense and mood can be found also in Sosnik's use of style topics. Sosnik's intradiegetic music in "Pride and Prejudice" purposefully shares many of the style characteristics of the diegetic music. Both types represent antique style types that signify elegance, such as the pastoral, the siciliano, and the waltz. The pastoral topic of the "narration theme" and the waltz topic of the "love theme," along with the diegetic waltzes, reflect the antique setting and the genteel nature of Austen's story. The "awkward theme" is a stock comic topic à la contemporary Hollywood that depicts the emotions of the characters. It plays on the competencies of 1949 viewers who would identify the style topic as comic, but it does not necessarily reflect an authentic comic musical gesture from the late eighteenth century.

Also with regard to tense, Sosnik's score to "Pride and Prejudice" contains the narrative agency of storytelling, beginning in the present and moving to the past, into a simpler, romantic story. While signifying a drama, Sosnik's score is not overly dramatic but rather conveys an elegant, sentimental, and sometimes comical voice. The oppositions of complete versus incomplete, diatonic versus chromatic, long versus brief, leisurely versus quick reveal a narrative agency of toggling back and forth from present to past, from extradiegetic to intradiegetic, and from the televisually real to the narratively imagined.

Multiple Narration and Overcoding

Sosnik's score is another reflection of early television's roots in radio. As a sonic medium, early radio depended solely on the parameters of sound to convey dramatic meaning to the audience. The primary source of narration was an actual narrator who read a story or described a scene verbally, using diegetic narration. However, radio dramas often attempted to be mimetic, with the actor's dialogue often functioning both to describe the narrative scene and further the action.

Sound effects and music were used to convey aspects of the narrative, and radio drama represented the heyday of the sound effects man and the musical composer.

Early television drama retained much of radio's mimetic practices. As Sosnik's score to the *Philco* episode shows, there is a significant amount of music for a 60-minute teleplay. By today's standards of television editing, Sosnik's score seems to be overly edited or, in a more semiotic sense, what Umberto Eco (1979: 133) calls "overcoded." Eco describes overcoding as a process of abduction, or hypothesis-making, where a new rule (grammatical, social, aesthetic, or otherwise) is proposed on the basis of a preestablished rule. The new rule operates within a narrower application of the older rule.[29] Adapting Eco's description, overcoding in television music can be considered as occurring when the broadcasting practices of television operate according to the practices of older media, such as radio, as in Sosnik's music to "Pride and Prejudice." For example, the "narration theme" is played seven times during the episode. Did TV viewers of 1949 need to hear the narration theme every time a new scene began, when visual images and voice-over narration were present? Here, Sosnik is falling back on his experience as a composer for *radio*, where such music *was* necessary in the absence of the visual image, thus overcoding the score for television. In early TV music, overcoding takes the form of redundancy—playing music where music was once needed for radio but perhaps is no longer needed for television.

Sosnik's music for *Philco* also demonstrates overcoding at the extradiegetic level. The *Philco* episode has *two* musical themes: the extradiegetic *Philco* theme and the intradiegetic "Pride and Prejudice" ("narration") theme. These two themes create a sort of double frame: one extradiegetic in the world of the *Philco Television Playhouse*, the virtual televisual playhouse visited weekly by viewers greeted by the host, who acts as usher, leading viewers to their seats; the other, an intradiegetic frame that introduces the story world of "Pride and Prejudice," establishing place and time through musical narration. As noted above, these frames are differentiated by their respective musical styles (determined by topics) and the diatonic/chromatic duality. While all this music is a nice part of the television program, all of it is really not necessary to establish the narrative. The double musical frame also is a holdover from radio, where music helped the listener transition into the narrative world. Sosnik's narration theme to "Pride and Prejudice" serves the same function.

The Twilight Zone

As television developed in the early 1950s, filmic codes began to exert more of an influence on television; as a result, musical scoring practices such as those used by Sosnik were attenuated, and overcoding was eliminated. An example of how music scoring in the anthology series developed can be found in the program *The Twilight Zone* (1959–1964), the flagship of the anthology series and critically acclaimed as one of the greatest series in television history. The program was created by Rod Serling, a writer who gained fame from his earlier work on the television programs *Playhouse 90* and *Kraft Television Theater*. Writing about the human condition within the genres of fantasy and science fiction, Serling often set his stories in imaginative locations (including distant planets) and created dramatic situations that included supernatural and apocalyptic events. The program actually transcends the genres of its narratives, however, by dealing with broad social issues as well as the environment, time, and space.[30]

By the late 1950s and early 1960s, programs were furnished musical scores not by a single composer, but by a stable of composers employed by the TV studios. Music for *The Twilight Zone* was provided by composers employed by CBS, but the program also reached out to some notable freelance composers, the most formidable being Bernard Herrmann. Herrmann, who by this time was considered to be one of the premier film composers in Hollywood, was hired to score the pilot episode and to compose the show's theme music. Herrmann subsequently composed seven scores for the series, including original theme music and music for some of the earliest episodes. Other series composers included Leith Stevens (1909–1970), William Lava (1911–1971), René Garriguenc (1908–1998), Fred Steiner (b. 1923), and Jerry Goldsmith (1929–2004). The largest number of scores by one composer was 12, by Nathan van Cleave (1910–1970).

One of van Cleave's scores accompanies the episode called "Steel," which aired on October 4, 1963. An adaptation of a short story by Richard Matheson, "Steel" centers on a down-and-out former boxer, "Steel" Kelly (portrayed by Lee Marvin), and his assistant, Pole (played by Joe Mantell). The year is 1974—then considered the distant future! Live boxing has been outlawed for a number of years, and only robots are allowed to be pugilists. Kelly and Pole manage an obsolete robot boxer, Battling Maxo, an outmoded B2 model robot in a continual state of disrepair. Battling Maxo is engaged to fight a new B7 model robot, the Maynard Flash, in Maynard, Kansas. During a test run, Battling Maxo falls apart, and in order to collect the purse, Kelly decides to disguise himself as the robot and fight the B7 himself. Kelly is beaten badly in the first round and collects only a portion of the purse promised but resolves to return to his home in Philadelphia and repair the robot for future bouts.

Although the story has the potential of being comical (boxing robots, etc.), the script and Marvin's acting instead portray a human-versus-machine theme, with a moving perspective of humanity that is both tragic and optimistic. The ideological message (to use Fiske's terminology) or the moral of the story is the indomitable spirit of humankind in the face of adversity—including humanity in an age of advancing technology. As Serling's closing monologue declares: "you can't out-punch machinery...[but] something else: that no matter what the future brings, man's capacity to rise to the occasion will remain unaltered. His potential for tenacity and optimism continues, as always, to outfight, out-point, and outlive any and all changes made by his society" (Zicree 1982: 380–381).

Van Cleave's jazz score uses an orchestra that includes an ensemble instrumentation of saxes, bass flute, trumpets (doubling flugel horns), trombones, electric guitar, bass and drum set and is augmented by violins and clarinet and bass clarinet along with other woodwinds and brass. By this time, jazz scores on television were not uncommon; others had been created for episodes of *The Twilight Zone* as well as for the programs *Peter Gunn* (theme music by Henry Mancini), *Seventy-Seven Sunset Strip* (theme music by Jerry Livingston; lyrics by Mack David), *M Squad* (theme music by Count Basie), and other programs of the late 1950s and early 1960s.[31] The use of jazz shows a predilection for composing in style topics to convey a semantic meaning.

For "Steel," van Cleave composed 22 cues for the 30-minute episode. Like Sosnik's score to "Pride and Prejudice," van Cleave's music utilizes a musical style topic that signifies the setting of the drama. The jazz topic evokes the urban culture of boxing (even though the setting for the play is in the small Kansas town of Maynard) and the big-city roots (Philadelphia) of Steel Kelly and Pole. Rather than a narration theme, as in Sosnik's Philco score, the music for this *Twilight Zone* episode immediately immerses the viewer in the narrative, with a musical opening cue accompanying the introductory scene of Kelly and Pole hauling the veiled robot off a bus. For the first cue, van Cleave composes an improvisatory bass flute part with rhythm section backup, but in the episode the flute player deviates little from the written score. Van Cleave's score uses the jazz idiom almost exclusively, with the exception of the "test run" scene cue, where the managers are testing the B2 robot's movements. The highly chromatic cue signifies mechanical music and is played by three violins with punctuations by exotic drums and a distorted electric guitar (example 2.9).

Example 2.9. "Test Run" Cue to *Twilight Zone* "Steel" Episode (Music by Nathan van Cleave).

Example 2.10. "Sports Item" Cue to *Twilight Zone* "Steel" Episode.

The consistency of the jazz style topic in the episode contrasts with Sosnik's bifurcated topics in the *Philco* episode. The music narrates more consistently within the story world of the show by insisting on Kelly's urban persona. By 1963, the conventions of television having been developed, music was no longer needed to announce bridges, tag endings, station breaks, and so on. Van Cleave's score does contain several transitional cues that mark transitions between the intradiegetic and extradiegetic spaces, but these are subtler, serving like finales wherein the music remains within the intradiegetic space of the story.

Unlike Sosnik's score, van Cleave's score to "Steel" does not rely heavily on leitmotifs, those recurring melodic gestures found in film. However, among the 22 cues, two themes do prominently recur. The first theme is the improvisatory figure played in varied form at points of narrative importance. The first occurrence of the theme is at the first cue, "the arrival." A variation occurs at the "go for broke" cue (no. 6), where Kelly decides to stand in for the robot in the boxing match. Finally, the theme recurs in the bass flute in the "now the bread" cue (no. 11), as Steel sends Pole to collect the purse after the match. The second leitmotif is a slow jazz, ballad-style fragment that functions almost as an extradiegetic transition, though it too is tied to narrative action. The first occurrence of the theme is during Serling's narration at the beginning of the episode, after the establishing "arrival" scene (cue no. 2, "Sports Item") (example 2.10).

The next occurrence of the theme occurs at cue 6 ("go for broke"), where it occurs after the first cue is played. The theme announces the closing of the scene and segues to commercial. Finally, the theme is played once again at the end of the program, at the "resurgent spirit" cue (no. 12), again accompanied by Serling's final narration.

Van Cleave's music to the *Twilight Zone* episode narrates effectively yet in a more subtle way than Sosnik's *Philco* score. The jazz-style topic conveys the story's modern, urban setting. The only non-jazz cue is the "test run" cue, when the boxing robot is seen for the first time, and the topic used for the cue is an iconic "mechanical music" cue. The *Twilight Zone* music also is framed but in a more subtle manner than Sosnik's. The slow bluesy melody that accompanies Serling's narration at the beginning of the episode is also found at the last scene, where it accompanies Serling's voice-over narration. The cue serves both an intradiegetic and extradiegetic function, remaining within the diegesis but also assisting the transition out of the story into the extradiegetic spaces.

Conclusion

In this overview of two anthology series from 1949 and 1963, I have shown how narrative agency evolved in television from the narrating agent of radio to that similar to film. Sosnik's score to "Pride and Prejudice" owes much to the overcoding practices of radio with multiple narration of the story from extradiegetic and intradiegetic aspects. By the *Twilight Zone* example of 1963, much of this overcoding practice had vanished, as television codes developed along more cinematic lines, relying on visual cues and the ability of the audience to detect beginnings and endings.

As a descendent of radio, early television imitated radio practices by retaining narrative agency based on sound. Programs like the *Philco Television Playhouse* contain two (or more) framing musical themes, one to frame the presentation of the program and one to frame the individual episode. These musical frames illustrate demarcation points for the extradiegetic flow and the intradiegetic teleplay or narrative. The *Twilight Zone* episode dispenses with a teleplay theme (while retaining its famous program theme here by Marius Constant) and launches into the "Steel" episode, relying on intradiegetic visual cues along with the jazz-style topic to frame the narrative.

Sosnik's "Pride and Prejudice" score, though overcoded, illustrates musical narrative agency in all three narrative spaces of television, the extradiegetic, the intradiegetic, and the diegetic. Van Cleave's *Twilight Zone* score is based primarily in the intradiegetic, relying on Serling's extradiegetic narration to get the viewer into and out of the intradiegetic televisual space. In this regard, van Cleave's score is more cinematic while Sosnik's is more radiophonic.

Having explored musical narration in the three spaces of television, I shall now investigate further the role of music in the process of narrative itself. Continue to stay tuned.

3

"And Now a Word from Our Sponsor"

Musical Structure and Mediation in Early
TV Commercials

Muriel Cigar commercial, featuring singer Edie Adams (Getty Images).

Although early television borrowed numerous broadcasting practices from radio, the decision to make TV a commercial medium was not a foregone conclusion. Erik Barnouw (1978) has chronicled the events and trends of early television in the postwar years, including debate over whether or not it would adopt the sponsor system of radio. Although radio enjoyed great prestige at the end of World War II, the broadcasting system was strapped financially from converting its studios and other technical resources to the new medium. The idea that television would pay for itself from the sale of TV sets first gave way to the broadcasting networks' paring the budgets of most of their radio operations, but over time, the lure of commercial dollars became too great to resist. The impulse toward commercialism was helped by the large-scale postwar demand for consumer goods, which prompted what Barnouw described as a "gold rush mentality" by the networks to make the transition from radio to television, and also to make television a sounding board for the advertising of these goods. This same mindset soon also permeated existing and newly founded advertising agencies, all seeking to develop the art of advertising in the new medium. By 1950, the 60-second commercial had become the norm, and the number, length, and stridency of ads were being regulated. The 60-second slot soon gave way to the 30-second slot as well as spots of briefer durations (Barnouw 1978: 81).

The development of TV commercials, like the development of television programming as a whole, is the story of greater elaboration on and embellishment of previous practice. Most sources cite a Bulova watch ad that aired on July 1, 1941, as the first American TV commercial, its broadcast having occurred several years before the postwar TV boom. The 10-second spot, which was broadcast during a Brooklyn Dodgers–Philadelphia Phillies baseball game on New York's WNBT, simply featured a clock face on camera with an inscription that read: "America Runs on Bulova Time" (Ulanoff 1977: 345).[1]

Postwar television commercials tended to be longer, with spokespersons using a hard-sell approach in describing and extolling the virtues of a product. These sales demonstrations were unregulated with regard to length and often appeared as short intermissions to live programming.[2] As these types of commercials became commonplace, advertisers sought more stimulating solutions to capture the attention of the viewing audience. Ad agencies began producing animated commercials and mini-narratives in which actors dramatized the need for, or benefit from, a product. By the mid-1970s, these mini-narrative commercials were the norm. Still other ads foregrounded visual and audio spectacles that seemed to take precedence over the product itself. This trend emphasized the need for sponsors to foreground the corporate image over visual placement of a product, and it became more prevalent in the late 1970s and continued on through the 1990s and beyond.[3]

The sponsor system adapted well from radio to television, and at first, networks sought sponsors who would underwrite entire programs. Many early television programs bore the name of their sponsors, such as the anthology dramas the *Philco Television Playhouse*, *The U.S. Steel Hour* (1953–1963), and *The Alcoa Hour* (1955–1957), as well as comedy and variety shows, such as *The Texaco Star Theatre* (aka *The Milton Berle Show*, 1948–1956), and *The Chesterfield Supper Club* (1948–1950). On these live, single-sponsor shows, the narrative or variety act would pause as the camera swiveled around and panned to the show's host or star stepping out of character and pitching the product. Shows broadcast on film featured similar ads, filmed commercial spots, as in the case of *I Love Lucy*, in which stars Lucille Ball and Desi Arnaz were shown smoking Philip Morris cigarettes while extolling the virtues of smoking. Direct sponsorship was especially well suited to the genre of the game show, wherein prizes were donated in exchange for on-air, commercial-type descriptions of each prize. On *The $64,000 Question* (1955–1958), for example, a Cadillac automobile was usually given away as a *consolation* prize. Such direct advertising became the norm on many games shows in the 1950s and 1960s, in particular, those airing during the day, when appliance manufacturers could cater to housewives interested in the newest home appliances. On many programs, these major sponsorships were augmented by satellite mini-sponsors that aired their own commercials (Barnouw 1978: 42), the voice-over narrator adding "and also brought to you by..." and naming the product as the alternate sponsor.

With the growth of commercial television, networks turned their backs on their own, self-sponsored programs, and many were discontinued. Television adaptations of long-running radio programs like CBS's *School of the Air* and *Columbia Workshop* were dropped in the 1950s as the financial lure of commercial television became too great to ignore. The NBC Orchestra (in its symphonic form), which was funded by General Motors during their radio broadcasting years, was laid off by the network after Arturo Toscanini retired on April 4, 1954. Other projects, such as the NBC Opera Unit that produced Menotti's *Amahl and the Night Visitors*, still regarded as a benchmark highlight of music on television, were mothballed. The disappearance of these educational and highbrow programs—performing on them was the aspiration of many musicians in the prewar years—prompted the development of the U.S. public television system, which continues to this day, though usually in a relatively poverty-stricken position when compared to its network (and now cable) counterparts.

In contrast to the fate of classical music and opera on television, the move to the commercial system in television was not all disadvantageous for music and musicians in the industry. Advertising agencies found themselves hiring musicians to provide music for the new medium, both for live programming and for commercials. So-called jingle houses formed as clearinghouses for composers to provide music for the new commercial formats, usually compiling libraries of music composed and recorded for use in television commercials. Like programs on narrative television, commercials used music in a variety of ways as advertisers sought to make their products appealing to the viewing public. The way in which this appeal was expressed varied with each ad and with how music interacted with the visual images and dialogue of the ad. In this chapter, I explore the structure of early television commercials and how music was used in them. This survey reveals that even in its early days, there were diverse genres of television commercials, including jingles, mini-dramas, testimonials, vignettes, and more. This chapter describes each of these advertising genres and how music interacts within them to produce meaning, just as it does in narrative television.

Structural Functions of Music in Commercials

Like its counterpart in narrative television, music functions in specific ways to convey meaning in commercials. How music functions in commercials has been a focus of interest in academic and business circles but usually for different reasons. While academics such as David Huron (1989), Nicholas Cook (1998), and myself (Rodman 1997) are interested in the semiotic qualities of music to convey meaning, business and practicing musicians also are interested in the effects of music, if only for the effect music has on commerce. The question that ad agencies ask is: does the music in an ad motivate an audience to buy its products? While the goals of these two respective areas are different, the observations on music in ads are remarkably similar. One compelling subject in both communities is what music should *do* in a commercial, or how music functions. Figure 3.1 lists functions of TV commercial music by two sources, a business how-to manual by Walt Woodward (1982) and an academic article by David Huron (1989).

Although these lists come from two difference perspectives, the functions are similar. Both recognize that music can create moods and feelings and can unify aspects of an ad. "Music can wed the visuals to the message, highlight the action, embellish the optical effects, and give an inexpensively and locally produced spot the feeling of being a Hollywood production" (Woodward 1982: 25). For advertising music to be entertaining, it needs to contain pleasurable aspects (see chapter 6), including catchy song lyrics, humor, or simply compelling music. Music in an ad arresting the viewer's attention harkens back to Philip Tagg's appellative function (and my conative) function of music. Woodward also stresses musical unity of the ad where music unifies all elements of the ad, while Huron stresses "structural continuity."

Woodward (1982)

1. arrests your attention
2. is entertaining
3. has strong visual component
4. has strong production values
5. is memorable
6. creates mood or feeling
7. contains strong advertising message
8. music appeals to musical tastes of the largest purchasing demographic
9. music unifies all elements of the ad
10. lyric is easily understandable

Huron (1989)

1. is entertaining
2. possesses structural continuity
3. is memorable
4. possesses a lyrical language
5. targets a specific demographic
6. establishes authority

Figure 3.1. Woodward's (1982) and Huron's (1989) Essential Elements of a "Good" Musical Commercial.

A subtle difference in viewpoint occurs with another of Woodward's tenets: "contains strong advertising message" is an important concept of early television advertising, wherein the product was kept in sight every instant of the ad. Woodward also advocated that music should appeal to the widest possible demographic, whereas Huron adhered to the belief that music should target a specific demographic. These differing points of view reflect a change in television advertising in the 1980s, a trait discussed in chapter 7.

Woodward's metaphor of musical television commercials being visual is an implicit semiotic trait. As he (1987:20) wrote: "Good music, whether it is music with lyrics, background music, or music to be used with a television announcer, paints a picture." He advised budding commercial composers to "close their eyes and paint a mental picture of what the lyric is describing." Here, he is implicitly referring to correlation, in which music and visual images corroborate to produce meaning. Above all, music should entertain with a lyrical language that simultaneously establishes an authorial voice and/or advocacy for a product while producing an artistic surface message that sugarcoats the appeal to buy a commodity with an aesthetic dimension of music.

Music in commercials relies on the same semiotic functions as those in narrative television, only the texts are compressed into 60-, 30-, or 15-second durations. As with television narratives, music in commercials signifies through correlation with the visual image and through style topics that are familiar to the viewer. Often, however, music must also interact with the dialogue and verbal texts of commercials, as words are the most direct means of relating information about a product. In Woodward's terms, music must unify all aspects of the ad.

This correlation with words, images, and music creates a more complex form of signification for products and services, which I call mediation.

The Structure of Musical Television Commercials

Despite their multiplicity and diversity of looks and presentations and products being advertised, early television commercials actually come in relatively few structures. In fact, some sources advocate that early television commercials fall into only two major genres: the testimonial and the mini-drama (see Geis 1982). The testimonial is noted for its authoritative voice-over or on-screen narrator, who uses various rhetorical devices to convince the viewer of the benefits of the product. The testimonial format is found in the majority of locally produced commercials (like local car dealerships) to show or demonstrate the qualities of a product (like cleaning products where demonstrations are fast and show effective results). The mini-drama is based on the social interaction of characters on-screen and falls into two subcategories: the interview and the mini-narrative. An interview is usually between two or more fictionalized characters on-screen with one character describing the product to the other, less-informed character. This interview may be in the form of a straight sales demonstration or could be fictionalized for entertainment value. These interviews tend to blend in with the mini-narrative, which is a slice-of-life vignette in which characters engage in normal activities in naturalistic settings (Geis 1982: 131).

The way music functions in commercials tends to cut across the two subgenres of testimonial and mini-drama, resulting in a sort of grid of musical commercials in four categories. These typologies are illustrated in figure 3.2. On the horizontal axis (or X axis) are Woodward's testimonial and mini-drama genres. The vertical axis (or Y axis) conveys the musical categories of constituent versus background music. Constituent music is music that is foregrounded in the commercial, that is, music intended to be heard consciously in the ad. Background music is music that is subordinated to the background, to accompany either the visual images and the dialogue between characters in a commercial or the voice-over of a narrator. Background music functions much like background music in film and television, where it sets the mood for a story but is not the focus of it.[4] Constituent music tends to provide the lyrical language of a commercial while background music tends to make a commercial more dramatic, as mentioned by Huron. Lyrical music is that foregrounded music that utilizes music's power as discourse. Dramatic music uses music in the same sense as narrative music, that is, to convey extramusical meanings.

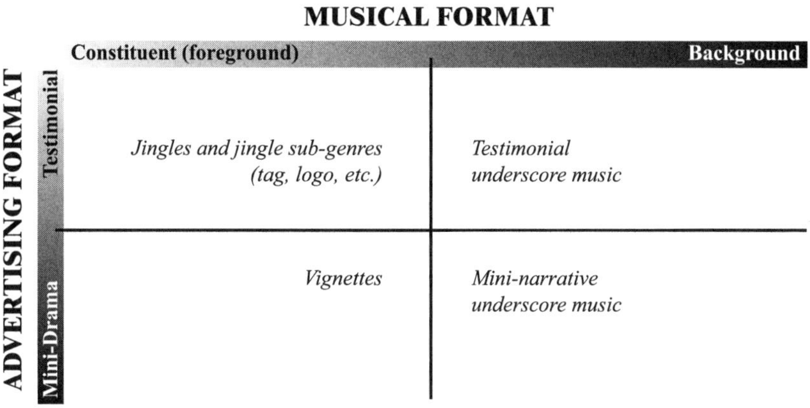

MUSICAL FORMAT

	Constituent (foreground)	Background
Testimonial	*Jingles and jingle sub-genres (tag, logo, etc.)*	*Testimonial underscore music*
Mini-Drama	*Vignettes*	*Mini-narrative underscore music*

ADVERTISING FORMAT

Figure 3.2. A Typology of Musical Commercials.

Figure 3.2 creates a typology of musical commercials in which the various functions of music can be assigned. On the upper left-hand side of the grid are commercials with foregrounded music in testimonial form. In this area are commercials with jingles, usually brief, catchy tunes with lyrics that include the name of the product being advertised. Because of the intimate semiotic relationship between music and lyrics, jingles are actually lyrical testimonials for products.

In the lower left-hand quadrant are commercials that exhibit traits of a mini-drama while using foregrounded music. In this quadrant are what I call vignettes or the lyricized slice-of-life ads that were very common in the 1950s and 1960s. A popular vignette commercial scenario of this time featured a couple (husband/wife, boy/girlfriend) or group of people (friends/family) at an event (party, dinner table, etc.) enjoying the product advertised. Other vignettes were abstract images that may have conveyed a narrative scenario accompanied by music. This type of commercial vignette predates the look of many music videos of the 1980s. Since music is foregrounded, often these commercials contain pre- or postsynchronized music tracks that function much like a film musical with supradiegetic music.[5] In fact, many of these musical mini-dramas are only thinly veiled testimonials, and many commercials of this era began as vignettes and lapsed into full-fledged musical testimonials with the product's jingle sung at the end of the ad.

The upper right-hand quadrant is the testimonial with background music. In these types of commercials music is underscored to a voice-over narrator. The narrator's testimonial is supported by music in the background, often setting the mood. Finally, the lower right-hand corner of the quadrant is a true mini-drama with a musical underscore that accompanies a brief story with a narrative beginning, middle, and end. Often, the story is someone demonstrating a need or a lack (in the Proppian sense) while another character reveals how to overcome that lack (by using the advertised product), after which both characters live happily ever after because of the use of the product. Such mini-narratives have included ads for household cleaning products, food, cigarettes, cosmetics, new cars, and medical products ranging from pain relievers to acne cream. These mini-narratives also often employ the format of the interview.

The Jingle

Much writing on musical advertising has dealt with jingles, the short musical tunes with lyrics that bond together to describe a product being advertised. Most effective jingles have a tag or hook, which is a smaller portion of the jingle that links directly to the product. The tag is usually placed at the end of the jingle but may be at the beginning or repeated throughout. Steve Karmen (1989), a longtime TV jingle composer, has identified the "logo," which is the musical portion of the tag but without the lyrics. Logos often are derived from jingles (especially as the jingle becomes familiar with the viewing audience) but are sometimes created independently. For example, the pitches G–E–C is the long-standing tag of the NBC network and is perhaps the most famous and enduring in television broadcasting that does not link with a lyric (except perhaps an imaginary intoning of the letters N–B–C).

Television jingles are direct descendants of those first used on radio. The first musical advertising jingle was heard on the air in 1929, when a barbershop quartet sang a song about the breakfast cereal Wheaties on a Minneapolis radio station.[6] The ad caught on, and many more jingles were developed for products ranging from soft drinks ("Pepsi Cola hits the spot") (see Booth 1990), to other breakfast cereals ("Snap! Crackle! Pop! Rice Krispies!") to gasoline ("You can trust your car to the man who wears the Star"). By the 1940s, jingles had become a staple of radio advertising. Their effectiveness was due to radio's proclivity for overcoding sounds as well as repetition, through which music and lyrics in a jingle became inextricably linked semiotically.

Jingles were effective also in early television advertising. Jingles have the ability to lyricize a product, that is, create a mood realm in which the product is associated. In this respect, jingles function as ascriptors through which the jingle forms a semiotic denotative bond with the product while at the same time signifying a connotative mood in bas-relief in which the product is placed. The overall effect cited by Woodward and other practitioners is that the product is made to look less serious or effective. Mark Booth (1990) has viewed the jingle as a form of "lyrical proverb" that serves only to reinforce a buyer's already made decision to purchase an item or to positively reinforce the buyer's purchase.

Jingles on radio are considered successful if they boost the popularity of a product over a long period of time. One such case is with the jingle for Pepsodent toothpaste. In an anecdote about his association with comedian Bob Hope, Bob Mills (1998) wrote about Hope's radio sponsorship by Pepsodent:

> Following glowing reviews in Broadway's "Big Broadcast of 1938," the Pepsodent toothpaste company offered Bob his own radio show to replace their sponsorship of the popular *Amos 'n' Andy*.... The show, which debuted on September 27, 1938, had all the earmarks of a hit, but unexpectedly got off to a rocky start. It took ten or twelve weeks of tinkering with the format before Hope was satisfied with the laughs he was getting from the studio audience (the show would remain on the air for 20 years).
>
> Since radio was still in its infancy, there was as yet no reliable method of measuring listenership. If the live audience appeared to enjoy the show, it was considered a success. Later, the Hooper Ratings, an audience sampling system similar to today's Nielsen's, would be used to set advertising rates. But when Hope began his show, the Hoopers were still in their experimental stages and he was forced to wonder from week-to-week how he and his on-air gang were doing. Whenever he approached executives at Pepsodent's ad agency, all he would get was, "Don't worry about it, Bob. You're doing great. Just keep doing what you've been doing." He got the strange feeling they weren't leveling with him.
>
> One day, after the show had been on for almost a year, he was approached by a man on the golf course who had been playing in the foursome ahead of him. "Bob, I want to thank you," said the man. Hope, thinking he was just another fan, returned the compliment and moved on. "No," continued the man. "I want to thank you for making me a millionaire." Of course, Hope had no idea what he was talking about.
>
> It seems that the man had run a small cardboard box factory that he'd inherited from his father. It was a modest business servicing many clients—including Pepsodent. "About six months ago," explained the man, "Pepsodent doubled their orders, then a week later, tripled them. Eventually, I dropped all my other customers and provided boxes for Pepsodent exclusively. My company became so successful; I ended up selling it for a million dollars. Thanks, Bob." Hope was stunned. No one

at Pepsodent had mentioned such a large increase in their production of toothpaste. Completely by accident, Hope had stumbled onto an audience gauge as accurate as the Hooper Ratings would later become.

Hope smiled wryly as he concluded his story. We all sat mesmerized. "Well?" one of us asked, "what did you do then?" "Let's just say," said Bob, "when contract renewal time came along, I negotiated one of the biggest goddamned raises in the history of radio."

The persuasive power of the mass media to sell products couldn't have been driven home more forcefully and Bob Hope never forgot the lesson he learned from it. Over the ensuing years, he would make sure that his name became aligned with major sponsors whose products he would hawk enthusiastically in countless TV commercials—a practice that some Hollywood stars of Hope's magnitude considered somehow degrading to their "art."

Part of Pepsodent's association with Hope's radio program was its tag: "You'll wonder where the yellow went / when you brush your teeth with Pepsodent." The words alone could not sustain a campaign of the stature mentioned by Mills's reminiscence. But, when augmented with music, the jingle was successful, due in large part to its simplicity.[7]

The form and function of jingles on early television were not developed by a musician, but by Rosser Reeves, chairman of the board of the Ted Bates Ad Agency in New York. Reeves rose through the ranks at Bates, beginning in 1940 as a copywriter and working his way up to chairman of the board in 1955. As head of Ted Bates, Reeves steered the agency toward the new medium of television and made it one of the premier producers of TV commercials in the 1950s and 1960s. As board chair, he was committed to making ads that were simple, direct, and focused around the repetition of what he called the "unique selling proposition" or "U.S.P."[8] Reeves believed that television ads had to state one primary reason why a particular product should be bought or was better than its competitors and that these reasons should take the form of slogans or, when music was added, jingles. Many of his slogans enjoyed great longevity, such as the one for M&M candies that "melt in your mouth, not in your hand." Reeves argued that advertising campaigns should remain constant with only a single slogan for each product.[9] Often the extreme repetition of his TV spots annoyed viewers, but sales of the products he advertised almost always rose. He was particularly famous for his ad for Anacin (a headache medicine) that ran successfully for more than 10 years, and though it was reported to be grating and annoying by many viewers, sales for Anacin tripled during the period that Reeves's ad ran, proving that his ends justified his means.

Reeves believed that music in television commercials was a most effective way to highlight the U.S.P., especially in jingle form. In an intraoffice memo published on September 11, 1950, Reeves described 10 traits of the musical jingle. His list is shown in figure 3.3. As evidenced by his list, Reeves believed strongly in setting words to music in a straightforward manner. He believed that ads should primarily communicate the slogan of a campaign, and he often shunned excessive artistry and creativity. However, he did believe that music had an effective role to play in advertising.

Reeves hired composer Harry Sosnik to help compose music for clients at Bates in 1963, just after he retired as music director at ABC.[10] That same year, he wrote an unpublished article describing the process of jingle composing, adapting many of Reeves's ideas of simplicity and efficacy of the lyrics. Sosnik states that the first part of the process is laying out the lyrics so that the title appears first. The jingle should take an A–A–B–A form so that the name of the product would be heard three times within the A section. The title and the remainder of the lyrics (the copy) are then laid out to form the U.S.P., which is imperative to the jingle composer. Once the U.S.P. is laid out, the next step is to scan the lyrics to find where the accented syllables are. Sosnik also describes the process of choosing an appropriate style of music in which to set the commercial. He (1963: 1) wrote: "There are any number of styles from which the professional musician must decide to use *one*. His decision is determined by the product and the type of audience he is desirous of reaching. To illustrate, his choice might be a march form, childlike, swing, blues, sweet ballad, strong masculine, pretty feminine as well as many other styles. The composers should have all of these techniques at his command." This off-the-cuff list of styles was intended to correlate with targeted sociographic and psychographic groups of the time. Sosnik's styles include topics that would target demographic groups (march, swing, ballad) as well as appeal to both men and women ("strong masculine" and "pretty feminine"), all placed within the context of 1960s American culture and television's attempt to play to those stereotypes.

1. The length of the jingle must not exceed 13 seconds.
2. The jingle must carry the whole U.S.P (unique selling proposition).
3. The jingle must carry the name of the product.
4. In cases of a new product, the jingle must carry "new product identification," that is, identify what the product is.
5. The lyric must be set to a melody.
6. This melody must be a new melody.
7. This new melody must be singable.
8. This new singable melody must be written so that it is singable by one voice.
9. A musical gimmick is often effective, like repetition of words, or extension of words ("Good, Good, Good" and "So-o-o-o-o-o-o Good").
10. No fake scansion, i.e., words must fit music following proper, natural accents.

Figure 3.3. Reeves's (1950) Guidelines for Music Jingles in Television Advertising.

Sosnik's final step in composing the jingle is putting words and music together. The scansion of words and music is of paramount importance, and words and music must match perfectly. "When the music is heard, it automatically brings to mind the words...and vice versa."[11] Sosnik's goal is to have a jingle that is a hit like a popular song, only in advertising a hit jingle is where a spoken or written U.S.P. combines with a *musical* U.S.P.

An interesting example of Sosnik's theory of jingle composing put into practice can be seen in his campaign for Viceroy cigarettes. Cigarette companies constituted one of the largest corporate sponsors of American television in the 1950s and 1960s, when thousands of their commercials were broadcast on the major networks. Indeed, cigarette companies sponsored many of the most popular shows of early television, with Philip Morris sponsoring *I Love Lucy*, Camel cigarettes sponsoring *Topper* (1953–1955) and *You'll Never Get Rich/The Phil Silvers Show* (1955–1959), and Winston sponsoring *The Beverly Hillbillies* (1962–1971) and *The Flintstones* (1960–1966).[12] In addition, Lucky Strikes sponsored *The Jack Benny Show* and *Your Hit Parade* while Newport sponsored *The Joey Bishop Show* and Kent *The Dick Van Dyke Show*. Jack Webb smoked Chesterfields for his *Dragnet* sponsor.[13]

Sosnik's cigarette campaign for Ted Bates was produced when cigarette advertising was in its heyday.[14] His manuscript score (dated November 11, 1963) shows him following Reeves's advice. The tag line for the product is "Viceroy's got the taste that's right." While not placed at the beginning as preferred, it is placed at the end of the A sections. Lyricist Jeremy Gury completed the U.S.P., which extolled the virtues of the "deep weave filter" and a taste that is "not too strong, not too light," that is, somewhere in the middle.

Sosnik seems to speculate on the appropriate style of music to be used in the ad, as at the top left of the manuscript (example 3.1), he lists musical styles possible for the jingle and crosses out "march," "waltz," "polka," and others that are unintelligible. The score itself conveys a sort of pop/jazz style, a topic used in ads throughout the 1950s and early 1960s, especially in commercials aimed toward adults.[15] The extended jazz-style chords in the keyboard part and the syncopated rhythms of the B section point to the jazz style. The A section features a singable, diatonic melody accompanied by relatively simple diatonic chords (with some added jazzy color tones). The B section extols the "deep weave" filter with a more chromatic melody and more chromatic chords, such as the inverted minor 7th chords in measures 9 and 11. The diatonic melody returns later to reprise the tag: "Viceroy's got the taste that's right" (not shown in the example). The final A section repeats the opening material, only up a step to G major, providing a tonal lift to the jingle.

Sosnik's jingle fits the template for both the commercial and music U.S.P. that he and Reeves established. The commercial U.S.P. is included in the lyrics.

Example 3.1. Jingle for Cigarette Commercial (Music by Harry Sosnik).

The tag is sung three times, and all lyrics are set syllabically in the texture; thus the scansion of the text is well-suited, although an apparent correction to "and the taste that's right" seems to distort on the repetition of "taste that's, taste that's right." The jazz topic also makes the speed or tempo in which the ad is sung flexible: a slow tempo results in a slow swing for a one–minute ad while a faster tempo results in an upbeat jazz piece for a 30-second ad.[16]

In contrast to Sosnik's jingle, which may have represented a failed campaign as the ad apparently never made it to the airwaves, an enormously popular jingle at the dawn of the TV era was the "Look Sharp" jingle for Gillette razor blades. The Gillette Razor Company got its start in 1901 when founder King Gillette invented the disposable carbon steel safety razor blade. The blade was an almost overnight sensation, and the company became profitable almost immediately. A series of good marketing and product development decisions kept the company profitable for decades after its inception. The company received product endorsements from major league baseball players as early as 1910 and began sponsoring broadcasts of boxing matches on radio in 1935. It entered the world of television in 1944 with broadcasts of boxing matches. The company advertised in newspapers and on the radio in the 1930s and 1940s and developed the "Look Sharp, Feel Sharp, Be Sharp" slogan for a trade publication in 1945 (McKibben 1998:50). During the postwar boom, the Gillette Company assessed the efficacy of marketing its product on television. The company continued its advertising niche in sports programming, sponsoring telecasts of the World Series beginning in 1951. For the 1952 series, the company unveiled a new jingle, a driving march composed by Mahlon Merrick, the musical composer and conductor of *The Jack Benny Program* (1950–1965).[17] The march (example 3.2) was so popular that it became the theme song to the Gillette-sponsored *Cavalcade of Sports* (1944–1960).[18]

The Gillette jingle is a march, a common feature in American sporting events, especially associated with college football games. The march has a college fight song rhythmic drive to it, marked by the syncopated figures on the downbeats of measures 1, 3, and 5. The sequential repetition of the syncopated rhythmic motif contains a threefold repetition to reinforce the U.S.P. of the lyrics: "To look sharp every time you shave / To feel sharp and be on the ball / To be sharp, use Gillette Blue Blades / It's the quickest, slickest shave of all!" The use of the march topic

Example 3.2. "Gillette Look Sharp" Jingle for Gillette Razor Blades (Music by Mahlon Merrick).

conforms to the use of marching bands and marches at some (but not all) American sporting events. Marching bands were certainly a part of college and some professional football games at the time but were less associated with baseball, basketball, and boxing. However, due to their association with football, marches and marching bands create a topic that signifies all types of sporting events, and more importantly, link male sports fans to Gillette razor blades.

Jingle Subgenres

As the jingle reached its heyday in the 1960s and 1970s, it became more sophisticated structurally. In a retrospective of his own career as the self-professed King of Jingles, composer Steve Karmen (1989) listed five types of musical commercials: (1) the jingle, (2) the tag or hook, (3) the logo, (4) background scores, and (5) the donut. Actually, these are subcategories or constituent musical procedures of a jingle rather than different genres. The jingle is the complete song (albeit brief) with the union of music and lyrics, such as Sosnik's cigarette song. The tag, or hook, is the key line of the jingle, often used at the beginning and/or the end of the jingle, and is what Karmen has called "the sponsor's audio banner." The tag/hook should be the most memorable words/tune of the jingle that sum up a campaign, which the viewer (hopefully) remembers. The logo is the tag without the lyrics, but also is sometimes a newly created tune that provides (through repetition) a mnemonic of a product. Finally, the donut is a jingle with a hole left in the middle of the spot for a voice-over description of the product. Usually, background music based on the jingle continues through the voice-over segment as underscore, and then the jingle with lyrics sounds again as the voiced-over concludes. Often this process is repeated with multiple voice-overs, creating double or even triple donuts.

Pseudo-Jingles

In addition to the popular and successful jingles, other early commercials used the basic precepts of the jingle to present products, but the tags were usually not catchy enough to achieve jingle status. These commercials simply wanted to lyricize a product without too much repetition. Though perhaps less effective than jingles, these pseudo-jingles would attract attention to a product through lyricizing the ad, thus placing it in a particular mood realm. Pseudo-jingles were especially common on daytime TV of the 1950s and 1960s, when the desire to lyricize a product was strong. Pseudo-jingles were prevalent in ads for such products as baby food, children's toys, and cleaning products, especially laundry detergent. One example of a pseudo-jingle is an advertisement for Tide laundry detergent that aired in the 1960s. The ad shows a woman on a beach hanging her laundry on a clothesline. As she does so, an arpeggio of violins plays followed by the following musical gesture directly out of a Hollywood romance. As the woman inspects her clean laundry, an angelic wordless chorus can be heard, another borrowing from Hollywood cliché. The ad is a donut with other musical style topics mixed in, namely, a lush string orchestra and wordless angelic chorus. The motto ("the cleanest clean under the sun") is repeated throughout, and the ad ends with a more final musical ending (with V–I cadence). Despite the repetition of the motto phrase and the intertextual borrowing of Hollywood musical topics, the musical slogan, while lyrical, is easily forgotten.

Another variation of the jingle was to take a preexisting piece of music, like a popular or folk song, and set it to lyrics. Producers were compelled to use this format, in which memorability/familiarity was built into the tune, thus making brand recognition easier to achieve. One successful advertising campaign that used a pop song set to jingle lyrics was for Pepsi Cola in 1961; these commercials featured singer Connie Francis singing "Now it's Pepsi, for those who think young" to the tune of "Makin' Whoopee," a popular song by Walter Donaldson. A slightly different musical emphasis was found in another successful campaign for Lark cigarettes in which the slogan "Have a Lark, Have a Lark, Have a Lark Today!" is sung to the finale of Rossini's "William Tell Overture." Pall Mall cigarettes featured a version of the folk tune "Sweet Betsy from Pike" set to words extolling the flavor of the cigarettes, while an attractive couple in formal wear waltzed around a balcony between smokes. A particularly popular jingle in the 1960s featured singer Edie Adams who advertised Muriel Cigars (a still photo of one of her commercials appears at the opening to this chapter). Adams sang a jingle to the Cy Coleman/Dorothy Fields tune "Hey, Big Spender," only instead of singing the lyrics: "spend a little *time* with me," Adams sang, "spend a little *dime* on me," musically incorporating the price of the cigar, part of the U.S.P.[19] Adams added a spoken motto for the product in a sultry, Mae West impersonation, intoning: "Why don't you pick me up and smoke me sometime?" These jingles led to a more pervasive use of popular music in commercials in the 1970s, 1980s, and 1990s. Commercials from these decades are discussed in chapter 7.

Vignettes

Often, jingles were incorporated into mini-narrative scenarios in commercials. A form of ad that foregrounded music while showing scenes of people enjoying the product in some sort of fictionalized narrative situation I call the vignette. Vignettes

Example 3.3. Jingle for Miller High Life Beer
(Composer Unknown).

featured characters in a small slice-of-life situation involving the product. Common themes for vignettes would be scenes of a family enjoying dinner, workers at a workplace, or people at a social event with a musical jingle foregrounding the product advertised. Although containing at least the potential for a narrative (featuring characters, setting, etc.), vignettes are usually thinly veiled testimonials and often lapse into jingles that focus on the product. A common theme in these early commercials was one character who is dissatisfied with a certain product, like the taste of a cigarette or the performance of laundry detergent, and another character who demonstrated how the product being advertised was better.

One particular example of a vignette is a commercial for Miller High Life beer that aired in the late 1950s. Like many other adult commercials for beer, wine, cigarettes, and so on, the ad features adults at a house party. A voice-over narrator lip-synchs the dialogue of the characters while a jazz combo plays non-diegetically on the sound track. As the Miller High Life beer is poured for the guests, voice-over singers perform the Miller jingle (example 3.3).

The ad begins with foregrounded party music with a narrator furnishing the dialogue for the mute characters. The jingle takes more and more of the nondiegetic sound, as the visuals focus exclusively on images of the beer that accompany the tag of the jingle.

Testimonial with Musical Underscore

Some early television commercials featured testimonials accompanied by music. Images in such ads focused on the product itself and not on a story line. An ad for peanut butter that aired in the mid-1950s illustrates this type of commercial (figure 3.4). It features abstract images of animated figures representing peanut butter consumers and the product itself. A voice-over narrator reads a script that recounts the history of peanut butter, citing its pros and cons, specifically the pros of the brand being advertised. The abstract stick figures are shown discovering peanut butter for the first time and then, after encountering the drawbacks of the old-style product,

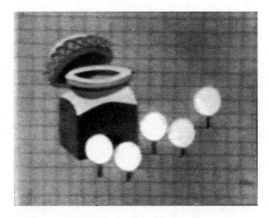

Figure 3.4. Peanut Butter Commercial.

coming upon the new improved brand. The voice-over text is modulated in such a way that the musical underscore can be heard during pauses in the text. The music is light and upbeat and complements the simple animated images.

The music for the ad is taken from the "Dance of an Ostracized Imp" by English composer Frederic Curzon (1899–1973), a popular composer of so-called light classical music in theater and concert halls who also composed pieces for film and radio. Curzon's "Dance," with its light and bouncy Prokofiev-sounding score, is an interesting choice for the peanut butter commercial. The three-part form of the music coincides with the three-part structure of the ad. The first part of the music introduces the ad with pizzicato strings (with a I–viio4/3/iii–ii 4/3–V7 chord progression) as the narrator recalls the history of peanut butter. Images of little stick figures gather round the crock of peanut butter accompanied by the opening musical motive (A) played by violins, clarinet, and flute in G major (example 3.4).

The B section begins as the narrator describes the drawbacks of early peanut butter as being "oily and sticky," "hard to digest," "doesn't taste like peanuts," and so on. The music shifts to a motive in E minor played by a solo oboe (example 3.5). The accompanying chords outline a German augmented sixth chord and a V/V chord resolving to a V chord in E minor.

The final section is a musical reprise of the A section in the original key with the narrator describing the advent of the brand-name peanut butter in 1933 (curiously, he never mentions the brand by name, relying instead on the visual image of the jar). The narration seems to end abruptly with the line "It had practically nothing in common with the old style product," as pizzicato strings play a final cadence (V–I).

Example 3.4. Section A of "Dance of an Ostracized Imp" (Music by Frederic Curzon).

Moderato *(tempo giusto)*

Despite its curious aspects (including not specifically mentioning the product or U.S.P.), the ad is a tightly knit structure with visual images, narration, and music all working together. Visually, the flanking (A) sections feature peanut butter, first in a crock and later in a jar with the brand's label. The middle (B) section is marked by more abstract designs representing "oiliness" and "stickiness." The narration divides into the positive segments of the A sections and the negative/critical drawbacks segment of the B section. The music reflects this dichotomy, as A sections are played in the up-beat G major key while the B section is in the more dour (but only slightly so) key of E minor.

The peanut butter commercial reveals a quite sophisticated approach to 1950s television advertising. The ad may be seen as an example of "undercoding," uncommon in 1950s programming. The brand name is never stated by the narrator, relying instead on the visual image of the product in the last part of the ad. Moreover, the text infers quality but does not explicitly state that the brand name is better, only that it looks, smells, and tastes "different" and that it has

Example 3.5. Section B of "Dance of an Ostracized Imp" (Music by Frederic Curzon).

"practically nothing in common" with older, oily, sticky peanut butter. Curzon's musical score is elegant (at least by televisual standards), connoting a style of light, contemporary classical music, potentially attempting to target a well-educated middle- to upper-class audience.

Mini-Narratives

Mini-narratives, that is, commercials with beginning-middle-ending archetypes accompanied by underscored nondiegetic music, are rare in early television, only gaining in popularity from the 1970s onward. However, there are a few examples from early television, especially in children's television. One such example is an ad for PF Flyers, a brand of children's sneaker. The voice-over narrator recounts the story of a boy who, walking along the waterfront in Hong Kong, encounters a dog with a PF Flyers decoder ring in its mouth. Hidden in the ring's secret compartment is a distress note written by an unnamed scientist (played by character actor Olan Soule), who is being held captive next to a ticking time bomb. The boy springs into action, running and jumping (in his sneakers) and arriving just in the nick of time to save the scientist from imminent destruction—all in 42 seconds and including an inset testimonial from the narrator describing the shoes.

The music in the ad relies heavily on Hollywood clichés and stereotypes. The ad opens with a gong and a stereotypical Chinese motive of parallel fourths (example 3.6a). The boy discovering the distress note is accompanied by a diminished 7th chord played by violins in tremolo, all hearkening back to techniques found in nineteenth-century melodrama and silent films (example 3.6b). The final scene has a consonant, concluding gesture played by strings and woodwinds (example 3.6c).

Example 3.6. Music to PF Flyers Commercial (Composer Unknown). *(A)* "Chinese" Motif; *(B)* "Suspense" Tremolo; *(C)* Concluding Gesture.

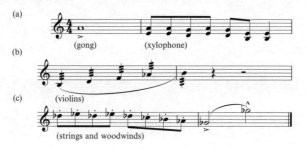

Mediation of Music and Visuals in TV Commercials

In his analysis of music videos of the 1990s, Nicholas Cook (1998: 151) has theorized on structural oppositions between sound, music, and images and intuitively observed that lyrics in a song (whether a jingle or a pop song) seem to belong to the *music*, whereas any dialogue in video belongs more to the *image*: "The division of the video into music, words, and pictures cuts across the video's functional categories; while the words of the song belong with the music, the diegetic dialogue with which the video begins belongs with the pictures.... Diegetic narrative and song, then, function as superordinate structures within which individual media are subsumed; one might think of them as constituting parallel hierarchies." Another way to interpret Cook's remarks is to put them in the perspective of Metz's sensory channels, wherein the relationship of lyrics (sung words) and music runs parallel and perhaps competes with the on-screen images and dialogue (which Cook considers the narrative agents). Song lyrics and music are conventionally paired within the preexisting texts of popular music (i.e., songs) while image and dialogue are part of the preexisting texts of the theater, film, and television (i.e., narratives).

Cook's suggestion that music and lyrics are novelties to television is somewhat at odds with his contention elsewhere that music aids viewers to find meaning in television commercials: "Music, then, does not just project meaning in the commercials; it is a *source* of meaning" (22; emphasis added). Another way of approaching the relationship of words, music, lyrics, and images is to consider how each parameter serves to mediate another. The common *Webster's* definition of "mediation" is "the interposing between elements for the purpose of effecting a reconciliation or agreement." In the case of music and television, I use "mediation" to refer to the interposing of a certain televisual element or sensory channel to connect with one or more disparate elements to create a unified, meaningful text. Mediation is another way of considering correlation. For example, I have noted how the music and visual images within the main title music of *The Rifleman* correlated due to the similarity of extramusical codes conjured up in overlapping semantic fields. In fact, the music to *The Rifleman* mediated the image, enabling (at least most) viewers to interpret the image of Chuck Connors as hero rather than male chauvinist villain. Each parameter on television, though different and operating within parallel spaces, has the potential of interposing itself to connect other parameters for overall meaning.

The mediation between music, image, lyrics, and dialogue suggests (somewhat loosely) the structure of Greimas's "semiotic square."[20] A Greimasian square for TV commercials would look something like figure 3.5. In this square, the terms for music and lyrics are complementary, as are the images and the

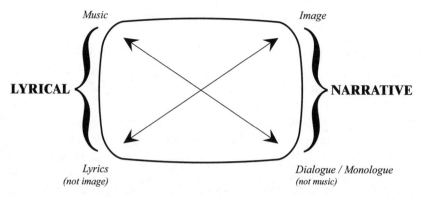

Figure 3.5. Semiotic Square of TV Commercials (after Greimas 1987).

monologue/dialogue. I have labeled the complementarities of music/lyrics and image/dialogue as "lyrical" and "narrative" (Cook's superordinate parallel universes), respectively. A conventional reading of the square would put the music/image and lyrics/dialogue as contrarieties and the music/dialogue and image/lyrics terms as contradictions.[21] Such relationships have been intuited by film and television composers, as music and image are indeed considered contrary by composers and film theorists who have expressed how music and image often compete against each other, thus necessitating that music be unobtrusive. Likewise, musical lyrics and dialogue are often considered contrary, a contrariety that is highlighted in film and stage musicals where dialogue transforms into lyrics as a musical number begins.[22] The contradictory terms of the square also can be noted, wherein the music/monologue and image/lyrics pairs are very uncomplementary. Music and the spoken word are very different, as are visual images and song lyrics, each pair existing on different planes. More to the point, song lyrics rely on music, not images, for meaning, whereas the spoken word relies on language, not music, for meaning. These relationships seem even more distant than the contrary relationships and thus may be noted as contradictions.

Given this rather perfunctory reading of TV parameters in relationship to the semiotic square, it can also be viewed in a manner slightly different from Greimas's binary contradictory and contrary oppositions. For musical television commercials, this would involve considering the relationship illustrated in the square as terms that function to mediate and facilitate the other components of the commercial. Here, one term of the square would serve to interpose itself to bring a contrary term and a contradictory term into a threefold symbiotic relationship. A visual conception of these mediating elements of music and image in TV commercials is illustrated in figure 3.6.

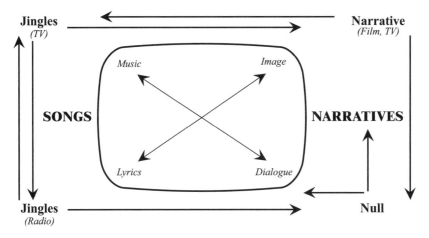

Figure 3.6. Mediation of Elements in TV Commercials.

As can be seen in the upper left-hand corner of the figure, music mediates between lyrics and image in the jingle, wherein image is ancillary to the jingle's format as a commercial pop song while lyrics are extraneous to an ordinary television text (i.e., a text with images, dialogue, and perhaps underscore music only). Music, then, becomes a sort of linchpin that holds lyrics about a product together with images of it. Similarly, in a commercial narrative image mediates between two competing sound sources, dialogue and music (as shown in the upper right-hand corner). Here, image is the term that provides continuity to the ad, whereas music and dialogue might alternate in order to stay out of the way of the viewer's perception. The other two combinations (bottom left- and bottom right-hand corners) are less well suited to television: the music-lyric-dialogue combination (bottom left) and the image-dialogue-lyric combine (bottom right). In the music-lyric-dialogue combination the lyric is the mediating term, which is actually well suited for (and exploited in) radio commercial spots, wherein lyrics tie music and dialogue without having an image. The image-dialogue-lyric combination also is not possible, as lyrics require music for expression. Such a combination is labeled "null," a scenario that is allowed (and common) in Greimas's structure (Greimas 1987: xvi).[23]

The mediation relationship of the jingle is basically about adding images to a popular song, as in a music video. Images are extraneous to the song, but adding them creates a new semiotic bond, one that is tertiary rather than binary. Such a bond could be deemed unusual or unique to film and television, especially in comparison to normal song texts. It could also be said that such a mediation relationship is marked.[24] Markedness is another way to structure oppositions, only under this description, oppositions are asymmetrical; that is, a marked term is more narrowly defined and distributed than its unmarked counterpart. As shown in the semiotic square, the jingle is marked in that it combines the complementary music and lyrics with their contrary image. An unmarked commercial would be one in which an announcer provides a verbal sales pitch on the product advertised. In music, an unmarked element would be a song with music and lyrics. In other words, a marked television event is one in which three elements of the square are operative, with one element mediating the other two. Given that figure 3.7 deals explicitly with all television texts, four structures of commercials can be derived from the terms articulated within its square. In Greimas's system, this is usually found in the links between terms around the perimeter of the square. These emergent structures are labeled between terms in figure 3.7.

Jingles fall on the side of the square where music mediates the lyrics and the image. Vignettes fall on the side of the square where music mediates as in a jingle, but they may also rely on the images to mediate the music and dialogue/monologue. The Miller High Life beer ad mentioned in this chapter utilizes both types of mediation, as the ad begins as a mini-narrative and ends as a jingle. All musical underscores are located in the part of the square where image mediates between music and dialogue/monologue, the difference being that in a mini-narrative the dialogue may consist of characters on-screen rather than just the voice-over narrator (although the PF Flyers ad featured the narrator). Finally, the image must be accounted for on TV, and mediation between music, lyrics, and dialogue is not found on TV but is common in radio. Such a relationship reveals just how powerful image is on television in spite of the nickname given to early television as radio with pictures.

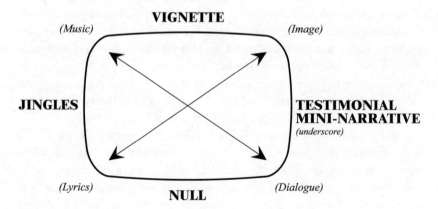

Figure 3.7. Structures of TV Commercials.

Conclusion

Mediation is another way to conceive the correlation of music and image on television and is an especially compelling model when considering television commercials. Music is composed or chosen based on styles of music that will be appealing to a certain targeted demographic for a product, but it is also a link, a mediator, to the images on the screen, connecting images and lyrics in a three-fold semiotic. Thus music has been effective in television advertising because of the manner in which music links the artistic text of the ad (as demonstrated in the semiotic square above). Music mediates the image with lyrics in the jingle, whereas image mediates music and dialogue in the mini-narrative. In television commercials, as in television texts in general, it is apparent that the most operative terms are the image and the music, with each serving either as mediator or as an object of mediation with the other term of the square.

Stay tuned.

4

"Beam Me Up, Scottie!"

Leitmotifs, Musical Topos, and Ascription in the Sci-Fi Drama

Cast of *Star Trek*. From left: Captain Kirk (William Shatner), Dr. McCoy (DeForest Kelley), and Mr. Spock (Leonard Nimoy) (Getty Images).

TV Music/Film Music

As has been discussed in previous chapters, radio greatly influenced the style and structure of early television programs. In fact, much programming in television of the late 1940s and early 1950s involved direct transfers and adaptations of radio programs. Radio dramas like *The Lone Ranger* and *Dick Tracy*, variety shows like *The Original Amateur Hour,* and game shows like *Break the Bank* made relatively smooth transitions to television as early as 1948. As programs made the transition to television, so did radio personalities, among them, Milton Berle, Ed Sullivan, Jack Benny, Fred Allen, and Edward R. Murrow, to name just a few, who appeared as guests or hosted new television programs, lending credibility (and corporate sponsorship) to the new medium. Joining these radio actors were radio musicians who also made the transition to television; some of them, like Bing Crosby, Perry Como, Dinah Shore, and the Dorsey brothers, became TV stars while others, such as Nelson Riddle, David Rose, and Harry Sosnik, became TV studio musicians.

Television's early affinity with radio and the live theater seemed to bypass the seemingly more symbiotic relationship that television had with the cinema. Despite the similarities of TV with film in broadcasting edited images with amplified sound, early television did not draw upon production practices of the cinema to a great extent, but rather relied on the live theater and a sort of radio-with-pictures format, complete with the fixed program time slots and corporate sponsorship system of its parent medium. In the late 1940s and early 1950s, as television emerged as a more pervasive medium with wide-ranging broadcasting, film studios rightly viewed television as a rival medium, with television drawing audiences away from movie theaters toward less expensive home entertainment. As the 1950s progressed, however, movie studios increasingly grew to regard television less as a rival and more as a new source of commercial potential. By the mid-1950s, many film studios took a if-you-can't-beat 'em-join- 'em position by establishing subsidiary studios to create television programs and by making deals with television networks to sell programming. These new studio-produced programs resembled movies, complete with the cinematic codes of production and reception.

The debut of the program *I Love Lucy* in October 1951 revolutionized the production values of television programming. Speculating that television may indeed have a future, Lucille Ball and her husband, Desi Arnaz, sought funding to produce a comedy series based on the CBS radio program *My Favorite Husband* (1947–1951), which had featured Ball and Richard Denning. Ball and Arnaz were driven to make the project a reality and even organized a multicity vaudeville-style tour to promote the new series. Executives at the CBS network were initially reluctant to fund the series—believing that a television audience would not accept the mixed marriage of Ball and the Cuban-born Arnaz—but as a result of the success of the tour finally demurred and decided to produce a pilot for the new series.[1] What made *I Love Lucy* innovative for television was that each episode of the series was filmed for broadcast instead of broadcast live onstage, as was the case with many other programs. Ball and Arnaz's plan was to film the pilot and all the episodes, as filming made it possible to distribute the program to multiple TV stations. Filming the show also had the fringe benefit of making the program archivable, portable, and of high visual quality. In addition, it gave the couple the rights to the show, as they stated on their contracts that they would retain physical ownership of the filmed episodes. Much of the success of the program was due to the comic talents of the couple (and sidekicks Vivian Vance and William Frawley) as well as to the great music (which will be explored in chapter 6), but the visual quality of the filmed episodes also helped confirm its success. The first program was filmed on September 8, 1951, and by February 1952, the program was at the top of the Nielsen ratings, where it remained for four of the six years of the series. Within months of its initial airing, another program, the police drama *Dragnet*, also made its appearance on TV on film.[2]

The growing success of Desilu studios and the filming and distribution of television programs eventually caught the attention of the major U.S. film studios. Originally aloof and often antagonistic toward television, film executives began to see the economic potential of television production. In 1954, Warner Bros. studios made the first move by making a deal with ABC to produce a series for the network, a short program called *Behind the Camera*, which became a vehicle for Warner to publicize its film stars in 10-minute segments at the end of other TV programs. By the 1955–1956 season, the studio was producing three television shows that were billed together as *Warner Bros. Presents*: *Casablanca*, *Kings Row*, and *Cheyenne*, all loosely based on old Warner Bros. films. The first two series were eventually dropped, as was *Behind the Camera*, but the *Cheyenne* series, a western starring Clint Walker, became a success. The popularity of the series led to the production of other Warner westerns, such as *Maverick* (1957–1962), *Sugarfoot* (1957–1961), *Colt 45* (1957–1960), and *Lawman* (1958–1962). Every one of these series was produced on film.

The success of the telefilm led other studios to jump into TV production. MGM and Twentieth Century Fox entered the business in 1955–1956. Columbia Pictures operated through a subsidiary studio called Screen Gems that produced such filmed series as *Ford Theater* (which began as a staged anthology series in 1952 but appeared on film beginning in 1955), *The Adventures of Rin Tin Tin* (1955–1959), *Captain Midnight* (1955–1958), and *Father Knows Best*

(1955–1960). Other, smaller production companies filmed a spate of westerns, including *The Life and Legend of Wyatt Earp* (1955–1961), *Gunsmoke* (1955–1975), *Tales of the Texas Rangers* (1955–1959), and *Death Valley Days* (1952–1975). Also during the 1955–1956 season, United Artists was in negotiations to purchase Ziv, a radio-television syndicate that produced the filmed series *Highway Patrol*, *Boston Blackie* (1951–1953), *Sea Hunt* (1958–1961), and *World of Giants* (1959), and ended up eventually buying the studio. MCA, operating through Revue Productions, was preparing to purchase the Universal Studios lot for television filming. By the 1960s and 1970s, MCA had become the largest production company in the television industry, becoming the 26th largest industrial company in California and the major employer of freelance television music composers and music support staff (Faulkner 2003: 50).

As the film studios appropriated television programming, they poured money, equipment, and studio space into television productions. As a result, many television programs began to look more and more like miniature movies. Eventually, the locus of television production moved from the live broadcast studios of New York to the film studios of Los Angeles. Although their television shows were never on a par with their major film productions, film studios devoted more space to television, and B movie sets and costumes were recycled for use in new TV series. Live broadcasting was never completely replaced, especially by local television stations, but filmed programs had a look that was reminiscent of film.

As television programs came to look like their cinematic counterparts, there was also a need for the programs to *sound* like movies. While the very earliest composers for television, like Harry Sosnik, gained their experience through radio and the Broadway stage, many of the second generation of television composers in the mid-1950s were seasoned film composers. These composers carried with them the skills of composing for films, which often included a musical vocabulary steeped in the nineteenth-century, post-Romantic Hollywood symphonic style, with chromatic chords and long, sweeping themes played by large orchestras. The more successful composers in television learned to adapt to the strict time frames and tighter budgets allotted by the film studios. The large, sweeping musical gestures of the cinema gave way to recycled stock scores in which theme music for programs served as points of musical reference. Also, smaller chamber ensembles for television programs often replaced the large symphonic-sized orchestras of films. More creative and adaptive composers found that the smaller financial resources were suitable and actually enabled greater creativity. Bernard Herrmann, the venerated composer of such important films as *Citizen Kane* and many of the Hitchcock movies of the 1950s and 1960s, displayed remarkable ingenuity and detail with television scores. Herrmann contributed music to the TV shows *Have Gun Will Travel*

(1957–1963), *The Alfred Hitchcock Hour* (1963–1965), *The Twilight Zone, Studio One*, and a host of others. He composed the original theme to *The Twilight Zone* and produced scores to several early episodes. Herrmann's meticulous vision for television music is evident in the *Twilight Zone* episode "Little Girl Lost"; the score includes the use of five bass flutes, and he actually specifies on the manuscript the distance the instruments are to be played from the microphone during recording.[3]

Of the new breed of film-cum-TV composers, it was the B movie composers who seemed to thrive most in the new medium. Many of these lesser known composers were accustomed to dealing with small budgets, small performing forces, and severe time constraints. For its first season, Warner's western *Cheyenne* was scored by William Lava and Leith Stevens. Lava was a veteran B movie composer for Republic serials and westerns of the 1930s and 1940s, whereas Stevens composed and conducted for CBS radio in the 1940s as well as composing B movie scores for various studios (Burlingame 1996: 22). Both Lava and Stevens went on to have successful careers in the 1950s and 1960s as part of the stable of composers at CBS-TV. At Warner, David Buttolph scored the *Maverick* series, having come from a similar career as a B movie composer at Twentieth Century Fox in the 1940s.

As television gained in popularity in the 1950s, it attracted many A film composers eager to try their hands at the new medium. Along with Herrmann, by the late 1950s and early 1960s, such famous or soon-to-be-famous film composers as Elmer Bernstein, Leonard Rosenman, Henry Mancini, and Jerry Goldsmith all worked in television while also working on films. Mancini, who composed music for the films *The Pink Panther* and *Breakfast at Tiffany's*, is noted also for composing the jazz-themed, 1960s detective series *Peter Gunn*. Rosenman contributed to such shows as *Combat!, The Alfred Hitchcock Hour, The Twilight Zone*, and *Marcus Welby, M.D.*, and he won Emmy Awards for the television films *Sybil* (1976) and *Friendly Fire* (1979) while at the same time winning Oscars for *Barry Lyndon* (1975) and *Bound for Glory* (1976). Goldsmith represented another breed of TV composer, starting out as a TV studio conductor for the show *Climax!* (1954–1958) and eventually working his way into composing, beginning with his theme music to the spy series *The Man from U.N.C.L.E.* (1964–1968). From his television experience, he went on to compose for both film and television through the 1990s. John Williams's career followed a similar trajectory: he began his career as a copyist for television shows but later broke into composing by producing scores for episodes of *M Squad, Playhouse 90* (1956–1961), and *Tales of Wells Fargo* (1957–1962). By the 1960s, Williams was working as head composer for Irwin Allen's sci-fi programs *Lost in Space* (1965–1968) and *The Time Tunnel* (1966–1967).

How Television Programs Are Not Films

As film studios became more involved in television production, television programs began to look and sound more and more like films. Visually, film studio–produced television programs moved away from the live staged-theater approach to production, adapting technical codes of film: the 180-degree rule, the eyeline match, the shot-reverse shot camera technique (made possible by the three-camera technique), the cinematic codes of makeup, lighting, costume, and the fourth wall (the imaginary boundary between the stage and the audience), among others. Shows produced by film studios also embraced the sonic codes of film, from film-style sound engineering to the use of music. Thanks to radio, sound technology was fairly advanced by the advent of television; however, most television sets at the time had small speakers with less-than-faithful sound reproduction. In practice, early television composers wrote cues much as they did for narrative film: music was used to signal transitions in the narrative, to signify emotion, and to identify characters through musical leitmotifs.

Despite similarities, television offered new challenges to production that differed from film. First, television programs were generally much shorter than films, with time spans of 24 minutes for a 30-minute program or 49 minutes for a 60-minute program. These brief durations made generic narrative formulas a necessity. Moreover, these brief narratives were continually interrupted by commercials and station identification announcements. Such discontinuities created the necessity to build in devices for continually attracting the attention of the audience. To keep viewers watching, television shows drew upon familiar conventions (codes) that were both external and internal to a program. External codes include the regularity of the broadcasting schedule, in which a program resides in a particular weekly time slot and airs on a particular network (TV channel). More internal codes for a show include the characters and plots and their recurrence from week to week (or day to day in soap operas, game shows, and news programs). The attenuated narrative structure of television programs has also led to reliance on conventional narrative genres, formulaic plotlines, and familiar musical styles. This reliance on formulas is one reason that television is often considered a banal medium.

Television also differs from film in its production values. Film music scholar and composer Roy Prendergast (1992: 274) has noted that editing and cutting in images are more frequent in television than in film, and thus the editorial pacing of television is usually faster. Cinema theorist Michel Chion (1994) has added that television more than film often uses diverse forms of editing, including freeze frame, stop action, slow and fast motion, and so on. Chion lists four characteristics of video as contrasted to the cinema, and these can be summarized as two basic ideas: the first deals with the speed of editing (reflecting Prendergast's ideas); the second, with the environment of audience reception. Television frequently plays with the speed of movement on-screen. As Chion has suggested, in this respect television has affinity with dance, since both television and dancers can arrest a pose or speed up or slow down movements. Also, while television frequently employs techniques to control the speed of images, cinema rarely does.[4] Chion also uses the metaphor of weight to differentiate between film and television, at least in terms of audience reception. He calls cinema "heavy" because moviegoing elicits a gravity of spectatorship akin to that of live theater. Television, conversely, is "light," as it is usually viewed in the home. Also, movie cameras are large, heavy, hard-to-move pieces of equipment, whereas video cameras are portable and light. This "lightness" of video production on television means that aspects of video must be "weighed down," by redundancies on the screen: repetitions of images, dialogue that describes images, and music that also serves as a commentary for images on-screen (Chion 1994: 162–163).[5]

Music plays a role in weighing down television's lightness as a medium. Jane Feuer (1992) has suggested that television music relies on musical styles that are intelligible to an audience, both as entertainment and as conveying meanings to narrative genres. The intelligibility of television music is the result of direct borrowing from both film and radio. Television borrows not only the genres of its predecessor media but also the musical styles of these genres. This is why popular music has been used far more than classical music in television variety shows, as early TV audiences were already familiar as well as comfortable with the ritual of the variety show. Television composers tapped into this familiarity by composing in a menu of popular music styles: Tin Pan Alley–style songs and jazz heard on radio and in nightclubs and the so-called Hollywood symphonic style that imitated cinema music of the time.[6]

Even though much narrative television imitated the cinema, television texts are marked by the broadcast slot schedule that divides texts into very short durations continually interrupted by other texts within the televisual flow. As a result, given the ephemerality of the broadcast schedule, many music critics and theorists are skeptical about music's ability to express anything in television. Prendergast (1992: 276) has bemoaned the plight of music in the television, writing, "Music moves through time and, because of this, needs a certain amount of it to express something. Even if we leave thematic statement aside and consider only musical color, the ten to twelve seconds allowed for music in the television version is little time indeed." The typical classical film cue is often measured in minutes, or at least many seconds, rather than the few seconds for a television cue. As a result, musical ideas in a television cue cannot be developed in the symphonic sense, that is, with an elaborate unfolding of musical ideas over time.

Prendergast's second critique of television music is that the main purpose of television is to sell products and make profits. Here, Prendergast identifies the very core and conflict of television that makes it the quintessential postmodern medium. Television is a continual dichotomy between the artistic text and the consumer text where the two are in conflict but at the same time inextricably linked. While much of television's resources have been used to sell products, so-called good television (see Feuer 1984, Coe 1991) also attracts consumers when certain programs are perceived as good artistic/dramatic texts. While it is difficult to separate the economics of television from its artistic text, television programming may be read for its artistic merit and its ability to express meaning. Prendergast's argument that film is somehow less commercial than television rings hollow in an industry that seeks audience approval within a capitalistic system and often measures success by the amount of money made at the box office. One could argue that both television and film rely on some sort of adver-tising for success. The difference is that a television program appeals to a sponsor while a film's success lies in its marketability to the public.

Another marked difference between television music and film music is that music for a particular television narrative often consists of fragments of pieces from other episodes, studio library music, or even music from films. For exam-ple, in the sci-fi series *Lost in Space* (1965–1968), music for many episodes con-sisted of a pastiche of cues from the Twentieth Century Fox film studios library.[7] The music was chosen and edited by the music supervisor, in this case, Lionel Newman. Other programs, like the western *Gunsmoke* (1955–1975), featured a single composer from the stable of CBS composers, who would compose origi-nal music while also recycling preexisting music for the series. This latter prac-tice was common for the series *Star Trek* (see Bond 1999).

In spite of the ephemerality and fragmentation of the TV schedule, music can and does convey meaning on television, but not always in a cinematic way; rather, it relies on the expressive codes formulated by theater, radio, film, and other television programs, all adapted for television and mediated by a viewing audience competent at decoding these expressive elements. At its worst, televi-sion music is overly ephemeral and banal with little sense of expression or devel-opment. However, at its best, television music can and does act as an agent of signification for characters, settings, emotions, and narrative time in an efficient, convincing, and sometimes clever manner. Repetition is at the foreground of musical signification on television, whether through the week-to-week repeat-ing of a program's theme music or the repetition of the theme as a leitmotif throughout a single episode. Musical cues beyond a particular program's theme music must rely heavily on musical conventions that are meaningful to the audi-ence, whether these conventions are gestures or musical styles.

How Television Programs Are Like Movies

While different in the ways enumerated above, narrative television programs are like movies in many ways. The most obvious property that both share is that cinema and television are multisensory media using images, sound, dialogue, and music. Like film, television conveys its message through the combination of visual images, sound, words (both written and aural), and music. Another important attribute is that, like film, the format most often chosen for television over its history has been narrative, that is, the telling of stories and the perpetuation of myths. Although television has been a source of information, education, and current events, a significant percentage of its programming in the 1950s and 1960s was in some way narrative and reflected established genres, such as the western, the situation comedy (or sitcom), the police drama, the soap opera, the sci-fi drama, the hospital drama, and others (see Castleman and Podrizak 1982). As a narrative medium, television has borrowed extensively from the narrative structures of film in order to produce its own stories. One of the musical elements that television has borrowed from film is the musical leitmotif.

A leitmotif is a musical figure (a chord, a melodic gesture, a phrase) that, through repetition in a narrative text (like an opera, film, or television program), becomes identified with a character, an idea, or a situation.[8] The earliest film composers borrowed the leitmotif from the Wagnerian operatic tradition for use in silent films. A 1910 editorial in *Moving Picture World* expressed the hope that "just as Wagner fitted his music to the emotions, expressed by words in his operas, so in course of time, no doubt, the same thing will be done with regard to the moving picture" (quoted in Paulin 2000: 66). In 1911, critic W. Stephen Bush wrote in the magazine *Moving Picture World*: "Every man or woman in charge of music of a moving picture theater is, consciously or unconsciously, a disciple of Richard Wagner." By the mid-1920s, symphony conductor Ernö Rapée asserted that "it was Richard Wagner who established the fundamental principles of the music drama of today and it is his work which typifies to the greatest extent and in the minutest detail the accompanying of action with music" (Rapée 1925; as quoted in Kalinak 1992: 63). Rapée put his theoretical words to practical use by publishing catalogs of musical pieces to be played during silent films, categorizing them according to mood, emotion, setting, character, and so on, all to be used as cinematic leitmotifs (see Rapée 1924 and 1925).

The practice of using operatic-style leitmotifs in silent film also thrived in sound film, where composers used the device to convey characters and settings. Kathryn Kalinak (1992: 28), in discussing the musical practice of film composer

110

Erich Korngold in the 1930s, wrote that "the leitmotif served as both a point of identification and as an embodiment of that which it accompanied, delineating important narrative elements such as character or situation." Claudia Gorbman also has traced the use of the Wagnerian leitmotif in early sound film. According to Gorbman (1987: 27), in film, a motif is a (musical) theme "whose recurrences remain specifically directed and unchanged in their diegetic associations." Gorbman asserts that Wagner's reason for the textual (word) labeling of the motif is for denotative purposes—to make certain that the audience gets the connection between musical gesture and narrative character, object, event, or location. It is notable, though, that Wagner did not always indicate this textual origin by labeling his leitmotifs, and this has resulted in later scholars using many different labels for leitmotifs. When a motif is adapted for film, Gorbman believes that it is unnecessary to label its linguistic origin, as film employs mnemonic devices unique to the medium, such as the mimetic visual aspects of framing, especially the close-up, camera angles, and so forth. As another means of representation, music also provides a nonverbal mimetic and a mnemonic device for signification.

Commentary on the cinematic legacy of the leitmotif on television is evident as early as 1949, when television critic Roger Bowman wrote an article for *Film Music Notes* in which he described the functions of music in television. Bowman's brief article was probably not intended as a composition manual for would-be TV composers but, rather, as a descriptive list of musical functions used by television composers at that time. Bowman predicted the trend in television of broadcasting more narrative programs on film, and he anticipated the trend of Desilu and other studios to film programs for broadcasting rather than present live performances. Bowman's list of functions of music for television films is given in figure 4.1.

Bowman's list anticipates the three generic areas, or functional spaces, of television music. The extradiegetic space is represented in items 1, 8, and 10, which illustrate music's function as navigator through the televisual flow (introducing programs and transitioning from program to program, or program to commercial). Intradiegetic space is reflected in items 2, 3, 4, 5, 6, 7, 9, and 11, wherein music serves as an agent within the story of a program (identifying characters and imitating extramusical sounds while also recalling past events, predicting future events, conveying the thoughts and feelings of characters, and transitioning from scene to scene).

Bowman's mention of Wagnerian leitmotifs seems to reflect his perception of television as a cinematic-style medium. However, the ephemerality of TV programs restricts the use of musical (and other) leitmotifs to brief, highly coded ones that are repetitive and thus convey aspects of the story line easily to the audience.

1. The theme: identifying the program as a whole.

2. The Wagnerian leitmotifs, or "character themes," heralding or accentuating the approach or presence of a character by use of a theme identified with him.

3. Recalling past events by repeating music identified with those happenings.

4. Predicting future events by suggestive themes.

5. Imitating sounds, actions, or characteristics, in musical caricature.

6. Building action, or indicating time, place, or unseen action.

7. Providing a transition from scene to scene, place to place, thought to thought, period to period.

8. Suggesting a blackout or a slow fade-out.

9. Showing subjectively the inner thoughts, feelings, and meanings of a character or a scene.

10. Achieving montage effects with two or more themes or types of music played contrapuntally for special effects or distortions, as in Prokofieff's Lieutenant Kije music.

11. Use of music to annotate dialogue. Parallel annotation may weaken dialogue unless skillfully used as stylized sound effect.

Figure 4.1. Functions of Television Music (from Bowman 1949).

Often televisual leitmotifs are built upon the musical material that is used in the theme music, thus creating an economical package of signification. Here, the role of theme music expands, serving a plurisituational significance in the narrative of the program. In a program like *The Rifleman*, for example, the melodic outline of the theme is used as a leitmotif in the narrative situations of the program to identify the character of Lucas McCain while the heroic nature of the theme also helps to signify the McCain character as the heroic protagonist of the series. Because of repetition of television narratives in a series, the leitmotif principle and the repetition of the theme music from week to week go hand in hand with the series, and thus the recurrence of the leitmotif is a built-in feature of the program.

Leitmotifs as Ascriptors

Bowman's mention of musical leitmotifs indicates that early television had appropriated from film what film had appropriated from opera. However, because television wasn't (and isn't) film, television composers adapted the notion of the leitmotif to suit the ephemeral musical functions of television. Though different in some ways, televisual musical leitmotifs retain the properties of their predecessors in opera and film as *denotative signifiers*, that is, as units of musical meaning within dramatic narratives. Musical leitmotifs may be seen as units of music that draw upon, or correlate with, other semantic fields for extramusical meanings. Most often, meaning is drawn from the association of musical themes with some aspects of the narrative, characters, settings, situations (love, action, tension, etc.), as seen in J. Peter Burkholder's (2006) and Gino Stefani's (1987) associative models (as shown in chapter 1). Frequent repetition of the music and the character (for example) in a film or television narrative mutually reinforce the association of the two and imbue both the character and the music with meaning.

Both the leitmotifs and the objects they represent are paradigms in the Sausurrian sense, that is, categorical units of meaning that may be exchanged for others to change the meaning of a text.[9] As paradigms, leitmotifs act as categorical objects that can be selected, exchanged, or substituted by a composer, producer, or director to convey different meanings to the audience. For example, the theme to *The Rifleman* is a paradigmatic leitmotif, as contrasted with any other TV theme, all of which exist in the same category of theme music but differ in the musical content and therefore the meaning conveyed. In a similar vein, Justin London (2000) has compared musical leitmotifs with proper names (citing philosopher Saul Kripke), claiming that leitmotifs, like proper names, have no fixed semantic quality but instead refer to someone/something specifically in a film through conventionalized association and through the specific context of the film. In this regard, leitmotifs act like proper names: just as the name John can apply to millions of people and not one specifically, one can refer to a particular John who is a friend or family member. Television themes are specific denotative leitmotifs in that they identify a specific character and/or program (like a proper name attached to a familiar person) through repetition week after week. As was noted earlier, Lucas McCain refers specifically to Chuck Connors's character in *The Rifleman* and not, say, to Luke Skywalker (or George Lucas?) in the film *Star Wars*. The distinction is understood due to the association of the name and the image of the character.

Claudia Gorbman (1987: 26–27) also emphasized the nature of the cinematic leitmotif as a denotative sign: "A theme [leitmotif] can be extremely economical: having absorbed the diegetic associations of its first occurrence, its very repetition can subsequently recall that filmic context." She goes on to write that motifs can have a fixed reference within a film or may accumulate meaning or could vary meaning, playing a part in film's dynamic evolution. Finally, she mentions two kinds of leitmotifs: motifs that are arbitrarily assigned to a character or situation and that accrue meaning through repetition (corroborating Noske's and London's theses) and motifs that are assigned to characters or situations that have some intertextual reference. The first kind of motif operates exclusively within the narrative realm of the film, whereas the second straddles the narrative and the intertextual, or referential, dimensions of the sign. This latter type is both denotative and connotative while the former is denotative only.

Writing about opera, Frits Noske (1977) called leitmotifs "corroborative signs" that link music with the words of the libretto and thus also link music with the story line and characters of a drama. Noske claims that leitmotifs are of value as semio-dramatic tools, as they make psychological connections between music and character that may go overlooked. Here, Noske implies that leitmotifs have two functions: indicating and describing. Noske points out the denotative aspects of leitmotifs in opera and film and how, through this denotation, they cement the relationship between music and image through repeated association in a filmic or televisual text. However, he goes further by stating that leitmotifs are connotative as well as denotative because they signify through intertextual signs. Since leit-motifs are musical and music is expressive of, or signifying of, moods and emotions, musical leitmotifs have the potential of carrying a dual signifying capacity. In short, leitmotifs carry denotative properties, wherein they name characters or label situations, but they also connote other aspects of the televisual realm. Bowman refers to the expressive power of motifs with his comment about "musical caricature." Gorbman (1987: 84) is more explicit in citing the power of "connotative cueing" of leitmotifs, wherein music "anchors" the image by expressing moods and depicting the moral/class/ethnic values of characters.

To illustrate Noske's and Gorbman's points, I refer to the theme song to the popular 1950s program *Leave It to Beaver* (1957–1963). The show's theme song, entitled "The Toy Parade," was composed by Dave Kahn with lyrics by Melvyn Leonard and Mort Greene (see example 4.1). The song falls under a stylistic label often referred to as light music, that is, music for the concert hall that was performed by pops orchestras, especially in the United States and the United Kingdom from the 1930s through the 1980s.[10] However, when the song is used as a theme song on a program like *Leave It to Beaver*, it obtains properties as a denotative signifier of the program. Although in the concert hall the song may be a generic piece of light concert music, it becomes a denotative signifier (like a proper name) when put in the context of the popular TV show.

Example 4.1. "The Toy Parade" (*Leave It to Beaver* Theme) (Music by Dave Kahn).

As part of the show, the song takes on the semantic field of the program, which is identified by the childhood antics of the protagonist, Theodore "Beaver" Cleaver (portrayed by child actor Jerry Mathers), but that also permeates to signify the squeaky clean, white middle-class mores of the family in small-town America in the 1950s. The song connotes the impish quality of the Beaver character through the muted trumpet and his childhood innocence through the romping long-short rhythmic patterns of the piece's compound meter.[11] As a signifier that is tied to the program, the theme takes on the other characteristics of the program and thus becomes a sign for these. The music has become a signifier for the ideal white, suburban family of the 1950s and has also been used to lampoon this ideal in subsequent television shows.[12] The theme reflects Gorbman's idea of dramatic "economy" in that viewers know that the theme denotes the Beaver character but also that it connotes such topics as adolescence, mischievousness, and comedy as well as American white suburbia of the 1950s.

The dual signifying capacity of television leitmotifs for denotation and connotation is an extension of what Charles Morris (1946) has termed "ascription." Morris distinguishes five modes of signifying for language as three major "pragmasemantic" modes, which consist of designative (statements), appraisive (valuations), and prescriptive (imperatives), and two less important modes, the identificative (locators in time and space) and the formative (contextual functions, such as conjunctions, quantifiers and other function words, and punctuation marks) (see Morris 1946: 351). In articulating these modes of signifying, Morris realizes that statements can and often do signify through more than one of these modes. Some statements contain an identificative mode of signifying with another mode. For example, the statement "this is a fine deer" identifies a perceived deer, but it also signifies in appraisive (and designative) mode. Morris (1956: 345) has called such multiple-mode sign complexes "ascriptors," defined as "sign complexes (or combination of sign complexes) in which something is signified in the identificative mode and signifying in some other mode."

As musical statements, leitmotifs function in much the same way as Morris's ascriptors. When combined with visual images, leitmotifs carry not only the denotative signifiers to identify characters or situations but also the connotative signifiers. These connotations tend to signify what Robert Hatten (1994) has called "expressive genres," defined as musical structures that are capable of conveying extramusical expressive states through an overarching topical field.[13] The use of the heroic connotation in the theme to *The Rifleman* has been noted. *The Rifleman* theme identified (denoted) the show and designated it as a western by drawing from the Coplanesque quality of the score. Moreover, the theme appraised the Lucas McCain character through the connotated expressive genre of the heroic. The theme music is thus a plurisituational leitmotif, or an ascriptor, denoting that *this* theme represents *this* character/show while also, through the musical expressive genre, connoting traits of the character or situation, that is, that *this* theme connotes that *this* character is good. Likewise, in the *Leave It to Beaver* theme, the music identifies the show but also designates it as part of an expressive genre of juvenile comedy.

Television composers rely on the ascriptive ability of leitmotifs to identify, designate, valuate, and prescribe images and situations in a television narrative. Television themes function in the identificative mode by identifying the program that is to follow or precede the music. The weekly (daily in syndication) repetition of television programs creates this identificative correlation between music and program. The ascriptive value of television themes serves as designator by defining the particular genre of the program, whether a comedy, western, action series, drama, news program, and so on. Theme music can also designate the location or time period of the narrative through the correlation of music to stylistic conventions. For example, TV westerns often use certain musical clichés, such as guitars, harmonicas, and banjos to indicate the nineteenth-century American West, or Coplanesque orchestrations, as in Gilbert's theme to *The Rifleman*. Theme music can also designate (or connote) expressive genres of comedy, tragedy, pathos, romance, suspense, or other such traits of a program. For example, along with identifying the program, Alexander Courage's theme to the sci-fi series *Star Trek* conveys the heroism of the crew of the USS *Enterprise* along with a sort of 1960s campiness, first through the fanfare at the beginning of the theme and then through the beguine rhythms of the middle portion of the theme. The designative mode of signifying thus acts primarily within the narrative realm of television.

Leitmotifs in television dramas tend to differ from their counterparts in film by degree rather than nature. Due to the ephemerality of the television text, leitmotifs tend to be more economical and draw more from the competencies of the audience to express meaning. Where a two-hour film has sufficient diegetic space to develop its modes of signification between music and drama, a 30-minute television program must rely on repetition of a limited number of musical leitmotifs for signification. The ascriptive nature of the leitmotif is important for its signifying potential in television, providing multiple modes of signification in a very short period of time.

Leitmotifs as Style Topics

In addition to their denotative properties, leitmotifs are often expressive of emotion, and film and television composers frequently use this emotional quality as an additional designative, even appraisative, quality. Morris holds that discourse on emotion is usually more referential than truly emotive.[14] As a behaviorist, Morris reflects that if a statement is made about an emotion, but no emotion was felt, then the emotion is referential rather than truly emotional. Likewise, Peter Kivy (1984) has discussed emotion in music in much the same way, viewing emotional music as being "expressive of" an emotion rather than arousing an emotion from a listener. These theories gel with the discussion in chapter 1, where music was considered as being primarily referential in its mode of signifying (especially on television) while allowing for the possibility that it may also be appraisative or emotive.[15] This referential function of music on television goes beyond merely signifying emotion; it also encompasses other traits of narrative, which I (like Hatten) call expressive genres, an area that includes such obvious emotions as love, fear, and anger but also less tangible human traits, such as heroism and villainy, as well as the narrative traits of tragedy, comedy, suspense, and mystery, among others.

The ability of leitmotifs to convey expressive genres and thus to connote extramusical traits, such as emotion, is one of the great semiotic powers of music in film or television. However, when formulating an expressive discursive field for television music, one must revert to Morris's realm of reference to describe the various modes of signification, as reference implies knowledge of the viewer. One way to accomplish this is to refer to musical signification in terms of style topics. Topics (from the Greek *topos*) are defined as traditional musical formulae passed from one generation to the next (Noske 1977: 319). In this sense, topics are very much like Eco's codes, where sign-vehicles are conventionalized by habituation, and describe how the semantic aspects of the sign are influenced by the pragmatic. Musical style topics have been identified also for eighteenth-century classical music by Leonard Ratner (1980), Kofi Agawu (1991), Raymond Monelle (2000, 2006), Eero Tarasti (1994), and others.[16] Musical topics may be thought of as the point where the nonreferential structure of music engages a referential component of the listener. In this sense, they are isotopies or sets of semantic paradigms whose redundancy guarantees the coherence and analyzability of any text or sign complex (Tarasti 1994: 6). The syntactical aspects (notes and rhythms) of a leitmotif make up the sign-vehicle of the leitmotif, and these coalesce into the twofold object: the denotative leitmotif along with the connotative style topic. The topic is subject to interpretation (through a potentially unlimited number of interpretants), but because of its correlation with the visual objects on the screen, and because of its alliance with the indexicality (a "pointing to") of an extramusical object or idea, the number of interpretations is limited. These correlations reinforce Fiske's notion of preferred readings on television. Conversely, while the number of interpretations of a musical topic may be limited by correlation to image on film or TV, because they are symbols that point to a nonmusical universe, topics are ideological types represented by a potentially infinite number of musical tokens. The world of topic, like its parent world of the sign, is potentially open such that one cannot specify the total number of topics current in a particular musical style. Since musical style topics are open signs, their component parts may vary greatly. Some style topics may consist of a single melodic gesture; others may involve a specific combination of instruments/timbres and still others a more extensive combination of musical parameters. Also, since topics are referential, their origins must come from the cultures in which they exist. As shown below, the referential basis for many musical style topics on television is extroversive and intertextual, originating in other electronic media, such as radio and music video.

To summarize, musical topics have two important aspects: (1) they link music to nonmusical concepts/ideas/objects, and (2) this link must be recognized by the culture in which it is produced. Topics are more a system of labels for discourse than actual signs of content. Topics are therefore open signs that rely heavily on interpretation from the culture viewing/hearing these signs.[17]

Musical Topics in Twentieth-Century Cinema

Although the focus of much topic theory has been on eighteenth-century music (by Ratner, Agawu, Monelle, and Tarasti, among others, as noted above), the use of topics continued into the nineteenth and throughout the twentieth century, especially in film and, later, on television. Musical topics for eighteenth-century art music composers were meant to convey or represent life experiences, such as the military (march), the hunt, and country or pastoral life (pastorale). Other topics were meant to evoke affective or emotional states (sensible style, etc.), and still others signified specific musical styles (*galant*, learned style, etc.). Thus, the concept of topics for the eighteenth century is rather broad, referring to musical styles (music referring to itself) as well as extramusical aspects of culture.

Conventions such as topics have persisted in music since the eighteenth century, especially in dramatic music, such as opera, lieder, and theater music. With the advent of film in the 1890s, musical accompaniments were devised for films (which had no sound) for various reasons: to cover the noise of the film projector (and quite often the audience!) and to lend a sense of drama to the film.[18] As the practice of composing for film became conventionalized, catalogs of topical musical cues were published containing both preexisting and newly composed music. One such collection, the *Encyclopaedia of Music for Motion Pictures* (1925) by Ernö Rapée, contained preexisting musical pieces cataloged by such topics as "love scene," "chase," "sinister," "aeroplane," and so forth. In fact, Rapée's

1. Places
  a. Countries/States/Ethnicities
    African
    Algerian
    Irish
    Spanish
    California
    Indiana, etc.
  b. Generic places
    The Sea
    Carnival
    College
    Jungle
    Tavern, etc.
2. Objects
  a. Inanimate
    Aeroplane
    Bagpipes
    Clocks
    Dolls
    Taxi, etc.
  b.1 animate (real)
    Bees
    Birds
    Butterflies
    Cats
    Dogs
    Lovers
    Children, etc.
  b.2 animate (mythical and romanticized)
    Fairies
    Ghosts
    Witches
    Pirates
    Indians, etc.
3. Actions
  a. Narrative action
    Battle
    Drinking
    Hunting
    Military
    Hurry, etc.
  b. Dances
    Antiques dances
    Ballet
    Bolero
    Cakewalk
    Fox trots
    Tango, etc.

4. Emotions
    Agitato
    Appassionata
    Comic
    Dramatic
    Eccentric
    Mysteriosos
    Fear
    Furiosos
    Happy/content
    Love
    Tension
    Tragic
    Savage
    Sinister
    Sentimental, etc.
5. Events
  a. Social events
    Christmas
    Election
    Halloween
    Weddings
    Bullfight
    Coronation
    Duel
    Beaten army, etc.
  b. Natural events
    Spring
    Storm
    Fire, etc.
6. Intramusical
  a. By genre
    Ballads
    Fanfares
    Hymn
    Opera
    Marches
    Overtures
    Processional, etc.
  b. By tempo
    Allegro
    Andante
    Maestoso
    Presto, etc.

Figure 4.2. Musical Topic Genres for Film (based on Rapée 1924, 1925).

encyclopedia illustrates an early-twentieth-century theory of topos. Like lists of topics for eighteenth-century music (see Ratner 1980 in particular), Rapée's topics are listed without regard to the object of the topic (the list is alphabetical). Rapée's listing suggests six generic categories of topics based on the nature of the objects they signify. These categories are illustrated in figure 4.2.[19]

Rapée's list illustrates how music signifies both intra- and extramusical objects as part of the cinematic system in the early 1920s and how music retains the potential for signification in film and video up to the present time. Rapée's categories are not always discrete, as many of them overlap. For example, the dance topic "bolero" would also have been used to signify a "Spanish" topic and not just the dance. (In fact, Rapée cites numerous cross-listings of this nature.) This categorization of topics shows that when linked to film, music conveys not only emotion (though the emotion category is quite extensive) but objects and actions as well. To put it in Peircian semiotic terms, topics generate not only emotional interpretants but also energetic (at least vicariously) and logical interpretants. In terms of language, music serves not only as adjective and adverb but as noun and verb as well.

The use of Rapée's generic musical topics persisted into sound film. Many studios kept libraries of generic cues that were produced by composers and used for low-budget B movies. Studios kept such libraries of topic music in order to keep production costs low. These scores consisted of generic cues that would evoke the mood of a scene. Titles such as "love scene," "chase," or "combat" were common. More recently, Annahid Kassabian (2001: 17) discussed music library businesses that rent topical music to low-budget video production companies that index musical cues by mood, geography, time, genre, structural function, and action. Such libraries reveal a continuation of practices that date back many centuries as well as provide concrete artifacts of topic theory for music.

Musical Topics for TV

More evidence that composers were thinking topically when composing for television is found in Marlin Skiles's how-to manual for composers, *Music Scoring for TV and Motion Pictures* (1976). In this manual, Skiles delineates various "mood categories," such as "drama," "mystery," "romance," "humor," "scenic," "science fiction," "horror," and so on, and differentiates each not by musical gesture, but by timbre and register. For the "scenic" or pastoral mood, for example, Skiles recommends nine different instruments: flute (middle and high register), horn (middle and high register), trumpet (middle register), clarinet (middle register), English horn (middle register), oboe (middle and high register), violins (high register), harp (middle and high register), and piano (middle and high register) (Skiles 1976: 70; as listed in Lerner 2001: 484). Such correlation between musical topics and timbre and range is unique in the literature and deserves further study.

Linda Scott (1990) has classified music for TV commercials in a way similar to Skiles's list of topics. Scott references music as a functioning element in multimedia texts through: (1) bipolar meaning of consonance and dissonance, (2) representing motion, (3) pacing through rhythm and repetition, (4) serving as a narrative agent, (5) representing location, (6) structuring time, (7) forging identifications (similar to Kassabian's), and (8) creating an "ethos." In short, Scott's categories indicate that music is able to signify place, time, motion, stasis, and ethos. Using a linguistic analogy, music can be noun, verb, or adjective, depending on it usage.

Style topics are useful in television to promote and support the preferred meanings of a text. As paradigmatic structures, topics rely on the realization of a musical score in the context of the other four sensory channels of television to create a textual syntax. The musical style topic is a sign that is tied to some aspect of culture and dependent on the listener's competency with the music in that culture. Kassabian (2001) has called this "affiliating identifications," which depends on an audience's competency with histories outside the film scene (compiled scores). Barthes (1988) also stated that much of cinematic (or televisual) meaning comes from outside the text—literally from the mind of the viewer, complete with the life experiences of the viewer in the cultural context and semantic field. Television composers worked with a knowledge of style topics, though not always with a conscious, formalized idea of what those topics were or how they might be categorized. What follows is an analysis of a television program that utilized leitmotifs as style topics in a very cinematic way. By tracing these leitmotifs, I show how these serve as ascriptors and propel the narrative while engaging the viewer.

The "Shore Leave" Episode from *Star Trek*

The influence of film on television is evident in many TV shows of the 1950s and 1960s. In particular, cinematic-like leitmotifs were used in many dramatic shows during this time. One program that relied heavily on leitmotifs was the science fiction drama series *Star Trek* (1966–1969). Despite its humble beginnings, *Star Trek* has reached near mythic status in the history of television. The program began with two pilot episodes produced for the series, neither of which aired initially. NBC grudgingly allowed the show to run in 1966. By 1969, after three seasons, the show was canceled by executives at NBC because it perennially lost money through production costs, ran into difficulty finding sponsors, and was just considered too cerebral by the network executives. However, in subsequent syndication, the series became a cult success and led to the production of four spin-off TV series (the fourth, *Enterprise*, debuting in 2002) and ten full-feature *Star Trek* films. In addition, *Star Trek* conventions, Web sites, books, recordings, magazines, pseudo-degrees from Star Fleet Academy, language courses in Vulcan and Klingon, and e-mail chat rooms have attracted Trekkies for decades.

During the program's original run, no fewer than eight composers, all veteran television composers, contributed music to the series. At the request of Gene Roddenberry, the show's executive producer, Alexander Courage composed the theme music (with Roddenberry contributing the seldom-heard lyrics). Other composers for the show included Wilbur Hatch (who served as musical consultant), Sol Kaplan, Fred Steiner, Joseph Mullendore, Gerald Fried (who will be considered below), George Duning, and Jerry Fielding.

As Jeff Bond (1999) has pointed out, the program was typical for television at that time in that a single episode of the program would contain a combination of newly composed music for that episode along with music from previous episodes or even music from other television programs as a means of relieving time and budget constraints. The recycling of previously used material (already referred to as library music) saved time for composers who had to produce a score on a very tight schedule, and it also saved money for the studio, as money spent on composing, copying parts, and recording time would not be needed with music that was already in the can.

During the first season of the series, one episode in particular stands out for its outstanding musical score: Gerald Fried's score to the episode "Shore Leave," which aired on December 29, 1966. The episode was Fried's first contribution to the series, and the recording for the episode was completed on December 2, 1966.[20] Fried, a Juilliard graduate, found his way into film composing through a friendship with the legendary film director Stanley Kubrick, scoring Kubrick's student film *The Day of the Fight* and subsequently the director's first theatrical films, *Killer's Kiss*, *The Killing*, and *Paths of Glory*. As with many composers at the time, Fried remained active as a film composer while also composing music for popular television programs. In addition to *Star Trek*, his works for television in the 1960s and 1970s include the programs *The Man from U.N.C.L.E.*, *Gilligan's Island* (1964–1967), and the epic miniseries *Roots* (1977), for which he won an Emmy.

In "Shore Leave," Fried was faced with supplying a score for a somewhat complex story line with multiple characters. The story revolves around the crew of the USS *Enterprise* as they search for an appropriate place to spend an interplanetary shore leave. They discover an ideal planet with an idyllic peaceful outdoor setting, fresh air, sunshine, and beautiful flora. The peace and quiet of the planet is disrupted by fantastic characters that appear before the various crew members: first a large white rabbit (similar to that found in Lewis Carroll's *Alice's Adventures in Wonderland*) appears to the spaceship's doctor, McCoy (DeForest Kelley). A Don Juan–type character appears to Yeoman Barrows (Emily Banks) and assaults her, tearing her tunic. A ferocious tiger and a World War II fighter plane appear to two crewpersons, Angela Teller and Esteban Rodriguez (Barbara Baldavin and Perry Lopez, nonregulars on the series). And a samurai warrior appears to the ubiquitous Lieutenant Sulu (George Takei). Characters from his personal past also appear to Captain Kirk (William Shatner), including Ruth, a former lover, and Finnegan, an Irish bully from Kirk's days at Star Fleet Academy. Kirk and Spock (Leonard Nimoy) later hypothesize that all the characters and objects that appear are figments of the crew's imagination, either as memories of their respective pasts or as parts of their individual fantasies. Later, it is revealed that unseen inhabitants of the planet are able to read the thoughts of the crew and manufacture these thoughts into objects, animals, and even humans in an underground assembly plant. At the end of the episode the caretaker of the planet explains that the planet is really a highly sophisticated amusement park designed to entertain his race. The benign alien invites the crew to enjoy the planet, provided they take the necessary precautions.

In accounting for all of these characters and objects in the episode, Fried's score to "Shore Leave" is a classic example of cinematic leitmotifs transferred to television narrative. It is extensive by the standards of television; of the episode's 49 minutes of story time, there are 35 cues constituting nearly 36 minutes of music. However, it is a mixed score comprising 20 minutes of original music by Fried and motifs from other episodes (Bond 1999: 19). The amount of music in this score is in marked contrast to the nearly 2 to 3 minutes of music found in most 30-minute situation comedies of the era. Like many cinematic scores, Fried's music serves two purposes: first, it identifies characters and their traits through the leitmotif, and second, it helps to move the story through narrative time. Paradigmatically, the leitmotifs in "Shore Leave" are ascriptors, having the double function of identifying and designating the characters and objects while also signifying the traits of these characters in designative and appraisative modes of signifying through topics and expressive genres. Fried's leitmotifs for "Shore Leave" are illustrated in example 4.2.

Fried employs many different style topics to designate the characters and objects of the episode. Typical of Hollywood-style film scoring, these topics are not always authentic. For example, the motif accompanying the samurai character is not authentic Japanese music, nor is Finnegan's music authentically Irish. Rather, these musical cues are drawn from topics used in vaudeville and earlier American (and perhaps Western European) sound film that then connected with the

123

Example 4.2. Leitmotifs in "Shore Leave" Episode of *Star Trek* (Music by Gerald Fried).

intersubjective semantic field of an American audience in the 1960s; the viewers would thus understand and interpret the topics through their previous encounters with similar topics in American film and musical theater (even as many also would recognize these topics as inauthentic). This is the musical verisimilitude of film and television, where meaning relies on the negotiated meanings of previous texts more than on authentic texts that may or may not be known by the viewer. Here, musical authenticity usually has little place in signification: had authentic Japanese music been played at the samurai's appearance, for example, most viewers would probably not have interpreted it as Japanese. But Fried's samurai theme draws upon conventions of American musical theater, film, and other TV shows that, though inauthentic, would be interpreted as Japanese.

The two *Star Trek* motifs, listed here as "main title" and "main title fanfare," were used week after week in the series and thus became leitmotivic through weekly repetition.[21] The viewer recognizes these motifs as signatures (or signals) of the program, and these themes serve to structure the program in discursive space, announcing the beginning and ending of the program along with transitions to and from commercial breaks. As ascriptors, these leitmotifs situate the viewer within the program (we know we are watching a *Star Trek* episode when we hear these motifs), designates the program and characters therein along with the genre (we are watching a science fiction genre story and can therefore expect fantastic things to occur as part of the story). In other words, these motifs provide a point of narrative stability or reference within each episode and help to structure the narrative (as will be shown below). Moreover, these leitmotifs are ascriptors of a different kind in that they signify not only within two modes of signification (identificative and designative) but also within two semiotic spaces of television, the extradiegetic and the intradiegetic.

The remaining leitmotifs are unique to the "Shore Leave" episode (or at least were originally composed for that episode). An introductory theme, which I have labeled the "planet" motif sounds first, played by woodwinds and accompanied by images of the idyllic landscape of the planet paradise. The comical mood of the "White Rabbit" motif is expressed through chromatic melodic leaps played by the oboe and bassoon, the latter traditionally considered a comic instrument; the former, a pastoral instrument (Skiles 1976). "Finnegan's" motif with its lilting 6/8 meter and modal pitch inflections (complete with lowered seventh scale degree) is reminiscent of an Irish jig and thus can be perceived as Irish music or at least Irish music as an American audience in 1966 would have understood it theatrically. The jig is transformed from a lilting motif played by the oboe to a fast, brawling theme played by strings and xylophone during the fight scene between Kirk and Finnegan. The "Don Juan" motif is intended to evoke a Renaissance lute song, portraying Don Juan as a character from antiquity. The "medieval/chivalry" motif is a melodic transformation of the "planet" motif and is essentially a fanfare with dotted rhythms, first played by violins when associated with Yeoman Barrows and her relationship with McCoy and later by trumpets when associated with the appearance of the Black Knight. The "tiger" motif is played by clarinets accompanied by bongo drums, the latter often used in films to signify the jungle and more generically the exotic. The clarinets play in their very low register in parallel fourths, an effect that is meant to sound primitive and menacing. A similar effect was used in films, especially films that dealt with indigenous peoples of the African jungle or the American west.[22]

Other motifs include the "samurai" motif, which is a modal theme with percussion, especially percussion instruments associated with the Orient, for example, gongs and chimes. Finally, "Ruth's" motif is a sweet, conjunct melody played in high flutes and strings and signifying feminine beauty and the love affair between Ruth and Kirk. The descending motion of the first part of the theme is reminiscent of the eighteenth-century "sigh" motif and is followed by the wider ascending leap of a perfect fourth, recalling "ecstasy" motifs of the nineteenth century in music of Mahler, Wagner, and Richard Strauss. They all function as ascriptors in that they locate and designate characters and objects while also appraising these designations through Hollywood musical clichés of love, savagery, the exotic, chivalry, and the comic.

Besides the leitmotifs within the narrative program, television theme songs are also leitmotifs that both identify the television program and often signify within the narrative text. Theme music serves the dual function of navigating the viewer through the extradiegetic space of the televisual flow, by announcing the beginning of the program called *Star Trek*, and also inviting the viewer into the narrative space, or story world, of the program. The theme to *Star Trek* is a leitmotif for the entire story world of the program, the USS *Enterprise*, Captain Kirk, the entire crew, space travel at warp speed, aliens—all of it. In addition to its role in the extradiegetic space, Fried utilizes the *Star Trek* theme song in imaginative ways in the episode. The theme in a minor key portrays the panic of Kirk and McCoy in response to hearing gunshots (which actually come from Sulu, as he test fires the twentieth-century, .38 Special he has found on the planet). The playing of this theme allows various interpretations: the panic of Kirk and McCoy, a sign of danger for the *Enterprise* crew, and /or the diegetic act of running by Kirk and McCoy. The plurality of meaning in the theme raises the question of what is signified through the theme song of a television program. Does the theme refer to the *Enterprise*? Kirk, the captain and protagonist? The crew? In fact, because the theme music is ascriptive, it signifies all of these things. The theme is essentially another leitmotif that can be brought in to further the narrative.

While Fried's score to "Shore Leave" provides a good example of how the cinematic practice of using the leitmotif can be adapted for television, it should be noted that most television programs do not always use leitmotifs in this way. Production costs and the amount of time needed to produce such a heavily crafted score make it impossible to produce scores by composers of Fried's caliber on a regular basis. However, leitmotifs are used in most television programs in a special way—through a program's theme music. Whereas cinematic or operatic leitmotifs play out over the course of a two-hour movie or a three-hour opera, television themes play out on a week-to-week (or day-to-day in syndication) basis. Themes signify the program for audiences as they are repeated weekly throughout the television season—and continue through re-re-runs and syndication. Furthermore, these themes are introduced as "memory-motifs," according to Wagner's theory, since they are performed during the opening credits where the program's title and/or logo are displayed. As has been noted, in the case of *The Rifleman*, an announcer read the words "the Rifleman" as the words flashed on the screen and the theme played.

The Pacing of Narrative through Style Topics and Expressive Genres in "Shore Leave"

Fried's leitmotifs for the episode are ascriptors, as they signify in more than one mode of signification. The leitmotifs identify or denote the various traits of the characters/objects they represent through topics (e.g., Finnegan is Irish, Don Juan is a character from the Renaissance, etc.), but depending on how Fried composes the leitmotifs and the context in which they appear, they also shape the trajectory of the narrative, through what Hatten has called "expressive generic schemas."[23] This treatment of motifs sets up an additional layer of connotative topics, all of which deal explicitly with the trajectory of the narrative or help to move the story along. Although both functions of the leitmotifs are intradiegetic, the layers represent two layers of the intradiegesis, the denotative serving an identificative function and the connotative a designative function.

Figure 4.3 illustrates the deployment of leitmotifs for the "Shore Leave" episode. Actual leitmotifs are shown in bold, while nonrecurring cues also are included. Of the 35 cues for the episode, 26 include some iteration of a leitmotif. Listed below the motifs are both the denotative and connotative topics. While the denotative topics are somewhat self-explanatory, the connotative topics are interpreted according to how they accrue to propel the narrative of the episode. The "heroic" topics are those that involve the recurrence of the *Star Trek* main title theme and the weekly "standard orbit" theme. These are the week-to-week musical recurrences (composed by Fred Steiner and Alexander Courage) that contribute a sense of stability or a narrative point of reference to each episode (see Bond 1999: 41). I call the topic "heroic" in the same sense that I labeled the theme to *The Rifleman* "heroic": the program projects a heroic ethos of the triumph of good over evil. Other connotative topics are "fantasy" the "comic," "danger/suspense," and "romance."

Fried aligns the connotative music topics to help shape the narrative. The teaser (the narrative segment before the main title opening) consists of three cues beginning with an embellished "standard orbit" cue and continuing with the "planet" and the "White Rabbit" motifs. The three connotative topics are heroic (Star Trek), fantasy (planet), and comic (White Rabbit), respectively. While the appearance of the White Rabbit presents the narrative enigma, the musical topic

Cue	1	2	3	4	5	6
Motif	**"Standard Orbit"**	**"Planet"**	**White Rabbit //**	**Main Title Theme**	**Orbit #2**	**"Laughing"**
Topic	Heroic (stable)	Fantasy	Comic //	Heroic	Heroic	Comic
Cue	7	8	9	10	11	
Motif	Pistol (Main Theme)	Tremolo	**Rabbit**	**Finnegan**	**Don Juan**	
Topic	Danger	Mystery/Suspense	Comic/Suspense	Irish/Comic	Renaissance/Fantasy	
Cue	12	13	14	15	16	17
Motif	Chase	**Ruth //**	**Orbit**	Stinger	**Chivalry/Knight**	**Tiger**
Topic	Action	Romance//	Heroic	Suspense	Fantasy	Exotic/Danger
Cue	18	19	20	21	22	23
Motif	**Knight //**	**Orbit**	**Planet**	**Samurai**	**Tiger+Planet+Knight**	Murky Chords
Topic	Fantasy//	Heroic	Fantasy	Exotic/Danger	Exotic/Danger	Suspense
Cue	24	25	26	27	28	29
Motif	**Planet** (dissonant)	**WWII Airplane** (<planet)	Stinger	Stingers//	**Finnegan**	**Finnegan**
Topic	Distorted	Danger/Suspense		//	Comic/Chase/Irish	
Cue	30		31	32	33	
Motif	**Tiger/Airplane/Samurai/Knight/Don Juan //**		**Planet**	"Sexy" Music (McCoy Returns)	**Ruth //**	
Topic	Danger/Suspense/Exotic, etc. //		Fantasy (restored)	Comic	Romance //	
Cue	34	35				
Motif	**Orbit**	**Main Title Theme**				
Topic	Heroic	Comic–Heroic				

Figure 4.3. Deployment of Leitmotifs in the "Shore Leave" Episode.

indicates that the episode will not be overly serious, due to the comic topic. After the main title, the episode begins an overall expressive trajectory from comic to danger/suspense. Cue 7 (the appearance of the .38 Special) is accompanied by a sinister version of the *Star Trek* theme in low bassoons and timpani. The "danger" topic is replaced by a "mystery" topic at cue 8 with the appearance of the antenna accompanied by horns playing an enigmatic tone cluster. The suspense is interrupted by two more comic cues, the "White Rabbit" theme and the "Finnegan" Irish jig theme. The "Don Juan" theme at cue 11 begins a trajectory toward Romantic interest, first involving Yeoman Barrows and McCoy, which culminates at cue 16 with the "chivalry" motif and with Kirk accompanied by the "Ruth" motif at cue 13.

The deployment of connotative musical topics creates an overall narrative trajectory of increasing instability or suspense and danger, a trajectory that is common for a mystery story. However, the overall motion of stability/instability is frequently interrupted by comic topics (the White Rabbit, Finnegan) and by romantic topics of the various love interests (McCoy/Barrows, an idealized romance illustrated by the "chivalry" theme, and Kirk's memory of romance illustrated by the "Ruth" motif). Moreover, the main trajectory of stability/instability is realized musically in two ways: first, with the occurrence of "danger" motifs, such as the "tiger," "samurai," and the "World War II fighter airplane"; and second, through the harmonic and melodic distortion of the "planet" motif that begins at cue 20 and continues through cues 22 and 24–26. Only when the motif is returned to its original form with the appearance of the "caretaker" at cue 31 is the narrative enigma resolved.

The narrative trajectory described is illustrated in figure 4.4. The diagram lists three primary layers of narratives, all of which reappear or are resolved at the end. The main narrative thread is the stability-fantasy-suspense-stability topics that resolve with the reappearance of the "planet" motif with the caretaker and, ultimately, with the return of the "standard orbit" theme and return to the ship at the epilogue. The comic topics begin with McCoy's vision of the White Rabbit and return with the reappearance of McCoy with two "chorus girls from Riegel" after his apparent death (thus reassuring viewers that he is quite healthy). Finally, the romantic topics are introduced by the three couples (McCoy/Barrows, Teller/Rodriguez, Kirk/Ruth) and distorted through the dangers each couple faces (the tiger, the black knight, Finnegan). Two of the three topics are resolved as Kirk returns to the image of Ruth for one last fling while Barrows chides McCoy to give up the chorus girls (which also is reinforced by the musical comic topic).

In addition to the deployment of topics, the musical leitmotifs of the episode are paced temporally in an imaginative way. In one scene, McCoy and Yeoman Barrows wander through the forest, and as they do, they fantasize about the

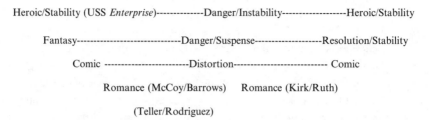

Heroic/Stability (USS *Enterprise*)--------------Danger/Instability-------------------Heroic/Stability

Fantasy-------------------------------Danger/Suspense--------------------Resolution/Stability

Comic ------------------------Distortion--------------------------- Comic

Romance (McCoy/Barrows)   Romance (Kirk/Ruth)

(Teller/Rodriguez)

Figure 4.4. Narrative Trajectory of "Shore Leave" Episode based on Musical Leitmotifs.

Middle Ages, and their thoughts result in the appearance of a fifteenth-century Burgundian dress. McCoy convinces Barrows to put it on, as the "chivalry" motif is played softly by the strings. As the scene continues, a contrasting theme is played followed by the beginning portion of the theme, resulting in an a-b-a structure common in concert music and used effectively here to prolong the scene while providing a degree of musical variety. Another scene, the fight between Kirk and Finnegan, is the lengthiest segment in the episode: 4 minutes and 30 seconds before the commercial break and continuing on for 3 minutes after the break. Here, Fried reworks the "Finnegan" theme with several variations with different instrumentations, tempi, and other musical devices. The variations on the theme function to highlight the scene and to slow down the narrative and prolong the well-choreographed fight. Fried's score also has places that speed up the narrative pacing of the episode. Just before the narrative denouement, or resolution, of the enigma, all of the menacing characters and objects reappear to members of the *Enterprise* crew (at 42:35) accompanied by their leitmotifs. Fried rapidly juxtaposes the five leitmotifs of the tiger, the samurai, the World War II fighter plane, Don Juan, and the knight bringing the scene to a chaotic climax in 80 seconds. The chaos is resolved with the appearance of the planet's caretaker, who assures the crew that all is well.

The musical leitmotifs used in the "Shore Leave" episode create an overarching expressive genre of security–danger/suspense–resolution or stability–instability–stability in which the story begins with a stable situation, continues with the presentation of an enigma, and leads to an ultimate resolution of that enigma. Such a narrative trajectory is common in narrative macrostructures and especially in television plotlines (to be explored in greater depth in the next chapter). This overarching expressive genre is interpolated with comic and romantic topics, illustrated by music accompanying the White Rabbit, Finnegan, McCoy's chorus girls, and Kirk's old flame, Ruth. The interpolation of these secondary expressive genres lends a narrative richness to the episode while expanding the appeal of the story to a broad viewing audience.

Conclusion

Television has borrowed heavily from the cinema in its narrative genres and in its discourse. However, it has also adapted these techniques to make itself a more efficient medium. The use of music in television is also heavily indebted to film, especially in the use of cinematic style leitmotifs. Leitmotifs are also ascriptors, as they carry with them not only the denotative signifiers to identify characters or situations but also the connotative signifiers of topics. The use of a "heroic" topic has been described in terms of its use in the theme to *The Rifleman*. So, leitmotifs operate as a kind of textual twofer by identifying a character or situation (denotation) while also carrying a style topic that will inform the viewer about the character or situation's traits (connotation). Gorbman's notion that leitmotifs can function in more than one dimension of signification is important for use in television. Leitmotifs usually denote (*this* theme represents *this* character, etc.), but they also can simultaneously connote characteristics of a character or situation (*this* theme connotes that *this* character is good or evil or tragic, etc.). The leitmotif thus becomes a plurisituational sign; that is, it signifies in more than one way. Moreover, television has the added advantage over film of utilizing its theme music not only to signify the narrative action, but also to consistently remind the viewer of the program they are watching. Fried's imaginative use of the *Star Trek* theme is also plurisituational, both within the storyline of the episode and in the extradiegetic space of television.

By using style topics that are familiar to American television audiences of the 1960s, Gerald Fried crafted an effective score for the *Star Trek* episode. Using music from both the theme and from commonly accepted musical topics, Fried's score proves that televisual leitmotifs can signify effectively and efficiently, adding narrative weight to a program, and compensating for the hyperephemerality of television texts.

Stay tuned for more!

5

"Go for Your Guns"

Narrative Syntax and Musical Functions in the TV Western

The Rifleman. Chuck Connors, right, with a young Johnny Crawford (Courtesy of the Gilbert Family Trust of 1989).

As television adapted the technical codes of cinema in the 1950s, such as camera positions, lighting, sets, costumes, makeup, and sound, it also adopted many of the narrative codes of film. Television dramas, especially those that aired in one-hour time slots, took on story lines that resembled feature films with a narrative arc that, along with character development, included the establishment, the disruption, and the reinstatement of narrative situations and settings. Following the lead of television writers and producers, composers also adapted techniques of film scoring to television and in many cases, such as Harry Sosnik's music for the *Philco Television Playhouse* (discussed in chapter 2), moved away from the radio music model. Chapter 4 demonstrated how television dramas, such as *Star Trek*, used the cinematic leitmotif in effective ways to denote characters and settings of the sci-fi drama while also conveying expressive genres suited to the story line of the drama. The use of leitmotifs is only one of the ways that music functions in a television narrative. Leitmotifs are paradigmatic, or synchronic, categorical signifiers in television, where they denote/connote characters, settings, and expressive traits of a story, but music for film and television also possesses syntagmatic, or diachronic, properties that help navigate narratives through their respective temporal trajectories. Having already revealed some of the ways music signifies characters in a narrative (chapter 4), here I investigate how music contributes to the unfolding of television stories over narrative time. After a brief review of some theories of narrative structure (and how these may apply to television), I investigate how the deployment of music in a television narrative reinforces, complements, and mediates its temporal structure while also pacing and otherwise advancing the narrative through its course. Aware that music is inevitably part of the discourse of television narrative, I will focus also on aspects of the story itself: the what of televisual narrative as well as how music assists the trajectory of that narrative. Toward this end, I will reconsider the "Shore Leave" episode of the original *Star Trek* series (described in chapter 4) and return also to the 1950s–1960s western *The Rifleman* (discussed in chapter 1) and consider the musical narrative structure of an episode from that series.

Some Theories of Narrative Syntax

For a story to be a story, it must have *characters* of some sort who exist in some setting, who *do* something (or to whom something is done) with these actions unfolding in *narrative time*. Seymour Chatman (1978: 25) has listed the first of these two fundamental components as "existents" and "events," as a sort of subject and predicate of the grammar and syntax of a narrative story.[1] Chapters 1 and 4 investigated the notion of character and more specifically how music signifies TV characters through the televisual leitmotif. As was demonstrated in those chapters, music is an efficient signifier, often signifying both denotatively and connotatively as ascriptors through the leitmotif. Existents and their corresponding musical leitmotifs represent the synchronic components of narrative. However, existents that are also characters must also *do* something (or have something done to them) in a manner that is recognizable to the readers of a narrative through narrative diachronic space.[2] Some scholars have investigated how existents and events are deployed through a story, or narrative space, and how recurring patterns of events and existents create a fundamental structure for narrative. In particular, Vladimir Propp and Tzvetan Todorov have observed structural features common to many types of narratives and how the accumulation of these common features becomes coded as meaningful patterns that are formed and negotiated by the habits and beliefs of author and audience alike, thereby contributing to the formation of generalized macrostructures. Such coding of narrative macrostructures serves television well, as TV relies on these narrative macrostructures to produce meaningful stories that can be negotiated by its audience in the short allotment of time given to programs.

Existents/Actors/Actants

Chapter 4 explored the naming or denotative properties of the musical leitmotif and how the leitmotif has become a staple for musical signification of film and television narrative. This denotative function operates on both extradiegetic and intradiegetic levels. On the extradiegetic level, theme songs function as leitmotifs identifying the program that is about to air or has just finished airing. These serve also as framing devices for the televisual flow. As was discussed in chapter 3, commercial jingles function in a similar way, that is, to identify the product with which they are associated. Leitmotifs function within the narrative realm as well, denoting the characters of the program while also often connoting their attributes as ascriptors (in the *Star Trek* "Shore Leave" episode, Captain Kirk = hero; Finnegan = impish villain; Ruth = beautiful lover, etc.).[3]

In terms of narrative structure, Algirdas Greimas has referred to leitmotifs in a film and television drama as "musical existents" or "actants" that reference characters, settings, and emotional states within a television narrative.[4] While also denoting specific actors in a drama, leitmotifs serve generically and connotatively as paradigmatic actants signifying such expressive genres as the heroic, the tragic, and the comedic. The theme to *The Rifleman* is one example; the timbre of the horns and the outline of the D major chord connote a heroic actant while the particular musical gesture of the theme denotes a specific actor, in this case, Chuck Connors as Lucas McCain or the show itself. A TV theme comprises a particular arrangement of notes and rhythms, which becomes a token that the composer uses to signify a type of heroic topos found in narrative.[5] Leitmotifs are paradigmatic in that they establish categories of actorial meaning operative in a particular narrative. These categories were defined in the previous chapter. This chapter will now explore the deployment of these categories through narrative time and space.

Narrative Events

While an infinite number of stories is theoretically possible, in practice most stories, and particularly stories broadcast on film and television, fall into predictable patterns. Within these patterns are archetypal characters and events that occur in many narratives. Vladimir Propp's (1968) analysis of narrative macrostructures in Russian fairy tales is an important contribution in constructing these archetypes, as he defines generic character types (hero, villain, princess, helper, etc.) who go through a chain of narrative events (or functions), usually in the form of a quest involving departing from home, battling a villain (sometimes a false hero), rescuing a princess and/or helper, and returning home.[6]

Narrative action is considered also by Seymour Chatman (1978, 1990), who states that events in a narrative rely on several causal functions. First, events must be sequential and present some sort of causality or, in the absence of causality, at least be contiguous.[7] Second, as all details and actions usually cannot be portrayed in all narratives, the narrative must be conveyed in such a way that the reader/viewer is able to fill in the gaps and make the narrative seem more natural as a coherent whole, even when that whole is at odds with real-world experiences. This notion of verisimilitude is important in the discursive side of television narrative. Verisimilitude is similar to Fiske's idea of representational codes, wherein codes are created that both producers and consumers of television texts negotiate in order to mediate narrative. Third, narratives function through hierarchies that must be recognizable to audiences. This hierarchy of events is a causal chain consisting of kernels, or the primary events that move the narrative through its course, while ancillary, or minor, plot events form satellites around these kernels. Chatman's diagram of this narrative hierarchy is illustrated as figure 5.1 (Chatman 1978: 53–56).

Chatman's chain of narrative kernels implies Aristotle's requirement for narrative that it have a beginning, middle, and end. Kernels bear the narrative load, expressing the vital events of the narrative course. Satellites add a quality or color to narrative by illuminating character traits through events or by providing suspense or surprise in a narrative. Suspense is created by providing anticipatory

begin

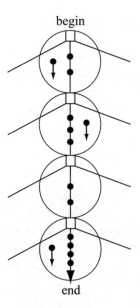

end

Figure 5.1. Chatman's (1978) Narrative Course.

satellites, which often provide the audience a foreshadowing of narrative events that may follow.[8]

Another theory that emphasizes time and causality as basic dimensions of narrative is that of Tzvetan Todorov (1977), who fuses Chatman's ideas of existents and events by emphasizing the implications of events upon the existents in a story or by augmenting the modalities of "being" and "doing" with the more sophisticated modalities of "becoming" and "knowing." In Todorov's model (1977: 111), a narrative begins with a state of equilibrium or social harmony that is disrupted by some action, either by a force of nature or a villain.[9] The narrative follows the course of this disequilibrium and invents a quest to gain a new, enhanced or more stable state of equilibrium. Todorov's narrative trajectory can be summarized as follows:[10]

1. a state of equilibrium at the outset
2. a disruption of the equilibrium by some action
3. a recognition that there has been a disruption
4. an attempt to repair the disruption
5. a reinstatement of the equilibrium

Todorov's model represents a trope of Propp's model of narrative structure, albeit streamlined into 5 functions from Propp's 31. Todorov's model also further differs from Propp's in that Todorov notes a return to equilibrium only at the denouement and not following a transformative event, such as proposed by Propp. Todorov's reinstatement of narrative equilibrium is often not much different from the original state, whereas Propp's hero usually returns in an improved narrative state. Todorov's narrative arc is thus a better fit for TV, as the narrative situation needs to return to a state of normalcy so that another disruption can occur on next week's show.

Like Todorov's model, that of Claude Bremond (1970; see figure 5.2) proposes a cyclical model for narrative syntax, with four phases beginning with either a state of deficiency or a satisfactory state and moving through different phases. Bremond's model, like Todorov's, is especially well suited to television narrative.

The final theory to be considered here is the "five narrative codes" model of Roland Barthes (1974), which combines synchronic and diachronic codes of narrative. Barthes illustrates his model in a detailed analysis of *Sarrasine*, a novella by Balzac, in which he examines narrative structures above the level of the sentence. Barthes posits five narrative codes, three of which, the semic, symbolic, and referential, involve actants (and are thus paradigmatic) and two of which, the proarietic and hermeneutic, deal with events or narrative trajectory, and are thus syntagmatic (Barthes 1974: 18–20).

The semic code constructs the meaning of a character, object, or setting. Semes are basic units of meaning in a text and are repeatedly attached to something (like a character or situation) in a narrative. In a sense, semes, or "lexies" in Barthes's terminology, act as name providers for a character or situation. As was discussed in chapter 4, leitmotifs are kinds of musical semes, or "musemes" as Philip Tagg (2000) would have it, as they act like musical denotators for

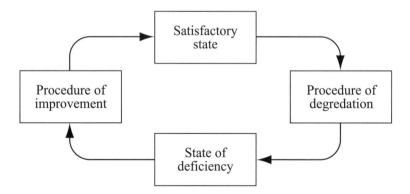

Figure 5.2. Bremond's (1970) Model of Narrative Structure.

characters. Along these same lines, semic codes are those that develop a figure, or cultural stereotype common to many narratives, into which a character, a figure with individual attributes, may fit. Semic codes can work through speech, clothing, gestures, action, and other parameters. Chuck Connors with his cowboy clothes and rifle certainly exemplifies the semic code of cowboy hero for television westerns in the 1950s.

Barthes's "symbolic" code organizes fundamental binary oppositions that are important within a particular culture. In television narrative, these would include: good/evil, male/female, nature/culture, individual/group, and so on. The "referential" code is that through which the text refers outside of itself. Often, this reaching out refers to reality; however, in television narrative it more likely refers to the reaching out to cultural knowledge or intertextual competence of the viewer. Referential musical codes often involve topics and expressive genres conveyed and understood by a television audience. The intertextual nature of the referential codes is of paramount importance in getting viewers to understand television texts. Verisimilitude, or the filling in of blanks on the part of the viewer, also plays a large part in realizing the referential codes on television.

Musical gestures such as the leitmotif adhere to all three of Barthes's paradigmatic narrative codes. Leitmotifs are referential and topical, and thus they signify through all codes simultaneously (and are thus ascriptors). For example, the "Ruth" leitmotif in the "Shore Leave" *Star Trek* episode (see chapter 4) is semic in its association with Ruth, Kirk's youthful sweetheart, and it is symbolic also in signifying the opposition male/female (the high flute and conjunct melody signifying femaleness). It is also referential, as it resembles (musically) the ballads and motifs in classical art music and popular songs through its slow tempo, harmonic rhythm, and high tessitura of the flute, thus projecting a style topic of love ballad.

Barthes's remaining two codes describe the diachronic aspects of narrative. These are codes of action and are classified by Barthes as the proairetic and the hermeneutic. These are irreversible codes, that is, they invoke notions of time, such as the causality of an action and its continuance and completion, or, a before and after scenario. The proairetic code is the "code of sequences of actions," which deals primarily with the structure of narrative based on an intertextual understanding of a particular narrative through similar actions in other narratives, ideas implicit in Propp's and Chatman's theories. Narrative experience is an aggregation of details arranged in these generic categories of actions. In television narrative these include falling in love, a perilous mission, a theft and recovery, a murder and its solution, an absence and reunion, and other scenarios, depending on the genre (see Fiske 1987: 143). Proairetic codes assume a sort of master narrative structure in which everyone within a culture can, through verisimilitude, understand and follow temporally just by filling in details.

Finally, the hermeneutic code is that which sets and resolves the enigmas of the narrative and is motivated by the desire for closure and truth. This code controls the pace and style of the narrative by controlling the flow of information, eventually resolving the narrative with a revelation of the "truth" in Barthes's terms. This revelation of the truth is the denouement or resolution of the narrative enigma. Barthes suggests that this code works through 10 morphemes that may occur in any order or in any combination. These morphemes are thematization, proposal of the enigma, formulation of the enigma, request for an answer, snare, equivocation, jamming, suspended answer, partial answer, and disclosure (Barthes 1974: 257). For Barthes, the hermeneutic codes often delay the narrative by keeping enigmas open, but they also articulate the closure of narrative through the resolution of enigmas. The proposal, suspension, and solution of enigmas within a narrative constitute a hermeneutic sentence that spans the entire story. The hermeneutic sentence is comparable to Todorov's and Bremond's narrative arc of disequilibrium-equilibrium.

Narrative Structures in Television

The narrative models of Barthes and Bremond/Todorov adapt well to television narrative. From situation comedies to westerns to science fiction to police dramas, all narrative television series maintain a status quo of narrative equilibrium from week to week. Fiske has attributed the popularity of this narrative model to a unique sense of time in television. In arguing that television narratives are "producerly" texts interpreted by the viewers as well as by the actors and writers, he (Fiske 1987: 145) wrote: "In a series, the future may not be part of the diegetic world of the narrative, but it is inscribed into the institution of television itself: the characters may not act as though they will be back with us next week, but we, the viewers, know that they will. The sense of the future, of the existence of as yet unwritten events, is a specifically televisual characteristic, and one that works to resist narrative closure." So, even though the characters seem to be acting in real time, the audience knows that little is at stake and that the same program will air next week, with a similar narrative structure. Thus, while television narratives are influenced by their counterparts in the cinema, TV has developed its own distinctive narrative structures.

Sarah Kozloff (1992) has compared television programs and commercials with Propp's characters and functions. Television narratives are usually brief, and she has found that many do not exactly correspond with Propp's model but, rather, utilize fragments of the model for their own storytelling purposes. For example, in a television series, the hero remains constant while villains and often (figurative) princesses appear anew each episode. In addition, some TV programs do not feature a false hero. Kozloff concluded that Propp's narrative theories reveal that stories are governed by a set of unwritten rules acquired by all storytellers and receivers and that American television narrative is plugged into these rules, much like audiences are for fairy tales. For example, the original series *Star Trek* varies somewhat from a typical Proppian structure but nonetheless displays certain traits: the program has a hero (Kirk), villains (usually aliens or unexplained supernatural forces), and often a princess, that is, a female lead character with a romantic interest. Helpers include members of the crew, most notably the main co-stars: Spock (Leonard Nimoy), Dr. McCoy (DeForest Kelley), Scottie (James Doohan), and often the starship *Enterprise* itself. Further, Kirk and crew go out on a quest (a trek) each week to explore a new part of the galaxy. Their return home is usually back to the *Enterprise* and the routine of running the ship.

A second point wherein television narrative may differ from its cinematic counterpart is that, while most theories of narrative emphasize causality and linearity in events, some television narratives are less likely than film to contain stories based on linearity and resolution. Rick Altman has pointed out that television narrative often relies more on characters and topics: "Whereas the level of audience attention to a given Hollywood film scene may be roughly dependent on the importance of that scene for resolving the plot's dilemmas, attention to a given *Dallas* scene depends instead on the topic and characters present. In recognition of this difference, we might say that classical Hollywood narrative is in large part goal-driven, while attention to American television narrative is heavily menu-driven" (Altman; quoted in Feuer 1986: 101–102). Altman's comments on the show *Dallas* reflect the narrative traits of the serial rather than the TV series. Jane Feuer (1986) has argued that television has developed a distinctive form of narrative through the two genres of the serial and the series. In the serial (most commonly illustrated on television by the soap opera), story lines may never reach a point of closure, since an original state of narrative equilibrium is absent and thus has no point from which to begin.[11] While the television serial does indeed avoid narrative resolution, the television series differs from the serial in that a narrative state of equilibrium is established, and the disequilibrium is resolved each week (or each day in syndication). However, unlike many films (and plays, novels, etc.) television series story lines often return to the *original* narrative state rather than achieving an enhanced state. As Mike Eaton (1981) has pointed out, in situation comedies a comic narrative may be resolved each week, but the situation never is. Syntagmatic chains of events may reach closure, but the paradigmatic oppositions of character and situation can never do so (see also Fiske 1987: 145). In this regard, series narratives on television tend to more closely follow a cyclical model, like Bremond's, than a utopian Marxist model, like that of Todorov.

Music and Narrative Events

Music has been a vehicle for narrative genres for many centuries, first in theater, then in opera, later in musical theater, and still later on film (both silent and sound) and television. Music's ability to accompany such narratives as plays and screenplays and its referential aspects have led to speculation that music itself has narrative traits. Many musical works in the Western European musical canon are described as program pieces, that is, music with an underlying extramusical narrative that runs through them. Program music has been in existence for centuries and was particularly popular in the eighteenth and nineteenth centuries. Such music has ranged from describing and representing very explicit events (such as various battle pieces) to embodying natural phenomena like flowing rivers, rainstorms, chirping birds, and more. Whether Haydn's "Representation of Chaos" in his oratorio *The Creation* or Beethoven's *Pastoral* Symphony or tone poems by Franz Liszt or symphonic poems by Richard Strauss, program music often operates through a set of iconic or sounds-like gestures to convey a story. Programmatic music demonstrates how musical gestures can correlate with extramusical narratives and provide musical representations of that narrative.[12]

Besides the iconic, sounds-like properties of music to convey extramusical ideas, musical structure has been often been compared to narrative. Anthony Newcomb (1987) has formulated the analogy of musical forms with narrative macrostructures (such as that by Propp) in which listeners follow the trajectory of the music based on their knowledge of conventional musical forms common to certain genres of music. This process is similar to what Paul Ricoeur (1980: 174) has called "following a story," that is, matching successions of musical events against known configurations in order both to forge an understanding of what one has heard and to make predictions of possible continuations. While Newcomb compared musical forms with narrative macrostructures (e.g., sonata form is like a story), the narrative properties of music extend also to the more obvious examples of program pieces that convey a story. Iconic musical sounds (like running water, gunfire, etc.) help cue audience members, who are already following the musical story, to paraphrase Ricoeur.

For music to take on narrative properties it must be seen (or heard) as having the same properties as narrative; in other words, it must have existents, events, and narrative space.[13] In the last chapter, I discussed how musical gestures become de facto existents through their function as leitmotifs in opera, film, and television dramas and through their correlation with characters and situations in these media. However, in addition to a collection of referential motifs, many pieces imitate the narrative *trajectory*, or temporal process, that often relates the entire story. The referential functions of musical leitmotifs adapt to narrative very well and have been a staple for musical expression in film and television. The succession of motifs is one way music has been compared with narrative in film and television. However, other musical processes also are capable of conveying narrative trajectory. For example, some theorists have noted that the action of tonal music, first to state a home key, then to migrate to a different key, and finally to return to the home key through the dominant, is a similar structural action to the narrative quest, that is, the departure and return home of the hero. Heinrich Schenker ([1935] 1979: 5) has noted the comparison of music with a narrative, or at least a dramatic, trajectory: "In the art of music, as in life, motion toward the goal encounters obstacles, reverses, disappointments, and involves great distances, detours, expansions, interpolations, and, in short, retardations of all kinds. Therein lies the source of all artistic delaying, from which the creative mind can derive content that is ever new. Thus we hear in the middleground and foreground an almost dramatic course of events."

The action of establishing a tonal center, moving away from that center, and returning to it creates a beginning, middle, and end of a musical piece and imitates the temporal sense of narrative. Kofi Agawu (1991, 1999) has written that much eighteenth-century music is based on a beginning-middle-end paradigm that certainly resembles the large-scale structure of narratives. Others, like Scott Burnham (1995) and Robert Hatten (1994), have read narrative processes that work themselves out musically (in the works of Beethoven in particular) in trajectories resembling a quest or other emotional narrative scenarios that move from tragedy to triumph.

Finnish musicologist Eero Tarasti also has described music as having the narrative attributes of inchoative, medial, and conclusive properties similar to narrative. However, Tarasti's focus on narrative is more specific to the modalities of "being" and "doing," adopting Greimasian semiotic theory for music and taking Greimas's model of modalities a step further to establish a theory of musical narrativity:

> Music evidently does not consist of presenting only one passion, one
> state of mind: music in particular is a temporal continuum of several
> passions, and a composition may contain several passions successively and
> even in a precisely planned order. Where ordering of passions occurs—
> where the listener is led to experience a given series of emotional
> states—we are approaching a still more complex series of events, which
> we might call narrativity. (Tarasti 1994: 73)[14]

While implicitly referring to Morris's notion of "ascription," Tarasti focused primarily on the parallel between narrative structure and musical structure. Music has parallels to narrative because it is temporally and spatially consistent with other narrative genres. For example, music, like a play, has a temporal dimension (its running time) as well as a spatial dimension, here meaning the performing forces, such as a symphony orchestra, string quartet, brass band, rock group, and so on. Moreover, in musical narratives, themes and motives operate much like musical actors in an anthropomorphic sense and are deployed in various guises throughout a piece. Tarasti then analyzes pieces of music that have narrative qualities wherein musical motives move through the time and space of a piece, thereby manifesting the modalities of "being" and "doing" and other like modalities, such as "wanting," "willing," and "knowing."

First to be considered are Tarasti's two basic modalities of "being" and "doing," simplifying these for television music to resemble Chatman's "referencing" and "action" functions. So, for musical narrative, the reference is to musical *existents* (e.g., leitmotifs) and musical *actions*. As has been shown in relation to the "Shore Leave" *Star Trek* episode, leitmotifs in TV music function as signifying agents for characters and objects. Being a narrative medium, music can contribute also to the generative course or trajectory of a television narrative. This course contains three structures and processes necessary for narrativity: temporal, actorial, and spatial. While Tarasti defined these categories "intratextually," or within the confines of music itself, they can be applied also to the intradiegetic music of television and how it interacts with the narrative on-screen.

The temporal aspect of musical narrativity means simply that music must have a time span in which to operate. Temporality in narrative has a double meaning, what many writers refer to as "story" time versus "narrative" time or the time taken up within the actual diegesis of the action versus the time it takes to tell the story. Here we consider the latter, though story time contains interesting musical effects to mark the passage of time within a story. In narrative time, temporal articulation involves how music moves through time and includes a comparison of the elements in a musical process, perhaps considering the basic aspects of rhythm, tempo, and harmonic rhythm but also encompassing the larger issues of proportion, pacing, and framing. The "actorial" articulation is the distinction of motives and themes (musical actors) and their distribution through a piece (Tarasti 1994: 48). The basic modalities of "being" and "doing" emerge from these articulations, with "being" as a state of rest, stability, and consonance; "doing," as musical action, event, dynamism, and dissonance.[15] Musical actants for film and television music are the leitmotifs that denote characters and objects by correlation with those visual objects and the style topics that become expressive genres connoting commonly held beliefs and ideas (codes) among the dominant viewing culture.

Finally, the spatial aspects consist of the texture and tonality of a piece of music (often metaphorically referred to as registral and tonal space, respectively). According to Richard Littlefield and David Neumeyer (1992: 39), "Narrativity, of a verbal or musical text, requires goal-directed motion, a transformation of the initial situation during the course of actions, and logical or causal entailment between beginning and end, all under the control of a 'deep structure' or *combinatoire*, a set of organizing functions that controls a textual surface." The deep structure to which they refer is the motion of much tonal music to first establish a tonic harmony, then move (eventually) to the dominant, and finally to return to tonic at the end of a piece. Television music may imitate narrative through some goal-directed motion that establishes a deep structure or hierarchy of musical kernels and satellites. This structure can be detected through the musical spaces of the leitmotif (actorial) and through tonal, textural, and other temporal events that proceed through the narrative.

Musical Narrative and Television

While Tarasti's primary concern is narrativity in Western European classical music, his theories have applicability for narrativity in television music. Television music is often temporally and spatially disjointed, and musical actants are rarely developed as rigorously as they might be in a symphonic work or even in a film score. However, the discontinuity of musical space in television does not necessarily mean that television music cannot possess narrative qualities. Although TV music is discursive and thus (usually) not a part of the diegesis (unless it is on-screen, as in a musical), it can also reflect and amplify narrative time and space. This reflection and amplification of narrative can be understood as part of music's own narrative properties. Music reflects and amplifies television narrative through existent and event space, reflecting the Barthesian narrative codes. Existent space is presented primarily through the musical motives, which include the theme music to a program, while event space is often a combination of the deployment of motives along with a program's tonal design.

On a more modest level from that of many symphonic pieces, the "Shore Leave" episode of *Star Trek* shows that music can pace the narrative trajectory through the concatenation of motifs. In addition to referencing the characters of a narrative, the deployment of motifs in the episode is an effective narrative device that serves to distribute the expressive states throughout the narrative; stability, comedy, suspense, romance, and the restoration of stability appear at different times in the story to maintain Barthes's proairetic and hermeneutic functions of narrative. Unlike a piece of program music (which, like most concert music is continuous), TV music is most often discontinuous, fragmented, and brief. As was noted in previous chapters, this has been the primary critique of television music: it just does not possess the time needed for sufficient musical expression, that is, to get the tonal structure of a composition (with its requisite themes and tonal design) under way. Despite these limitations, television music can and does serve a narrative function both paradigmatically (through leitmotifs) and syntagmatically (through its temporal deployment) by mediating with the image in television dramas. Moreover, the ascriptive properties of music (now seen in terms of the "symbolic" and "referential" codes) signify through the modalities of characters and events/actions (being and doing) of narratives. This type of musical signification also conforms to Barthes's notion of the hermeneutic code, wherein music signifies aspects of the narrative itself and operates within the deeper structure of the narrative in highlighting the establishment or resolution of narrative enigmas.[16]

Music in narratives like film and television often follow a format of certain broad, overarching functions in a narrative, following the idea of beginning-middle-end. In this sense, musical cues can function to steer the TV show through its narrative course or, in Barthes's terms, to function in the proairetic code. However, television narrative is different from literary or filmic narrative in that narrative is continuously interrupted by station breaks and commercials. The transition functions of theme music, act-ins, and act-outs serve primarily as extradiegetic agents moving the program out of the narrative space and into broadcasting/commercial space. However, in a sense, this extradiegetic function may be considered proairetic in that music controls the pacing of narrative through framing and through transitions in and out of narrative space while also signaling inchoative, medial, and concluding portions of a program. Such functions are listed in figure 5.3 and reflect the musical and narrative traits of beginning, middle, and end.

Beginning:
> Framing from extradiegetic flow to intradiegetic and diegetic realms of TV show (theme music, teasers, etc.)

Middle:
> Transitions to commercial breaks (intradiegetic to extradiegetic; e.g., stage wait, act-in, act-out, etc.)

End:
> Framing and transition from intradiegetic to extradiegetic (epilogues, end credits, etc.)

Figure 5.3. Extradiegetic Musical Functions in Narrative.

145

Nested within the extradiegetic functions of music are intradiegetic narrative functions that help the story of a TV show through its narrative course.[17] These functions are usually intradiegetic functions of a television program's underscore but may sometimes be found as diegetic music. These proairetic functions, combined with the hermeneutic functions, are illustrated in figure 5.4.

Narrative beginnings are not explicitly listed in Barthes's model but are necessary for the establishment of narrative trajectory. Narratives must establish characters and situations in order to develop the proper trajectory in order to arrive at denouement. Once weekly characters and settings are established within a TV program, expository scenes usually are minimal. In a series like *Star Trek*, one establishing shot of the starship *Enterprise* is sufficient to get the narrative started on its trajectory.

In contrast to beginnings, most television programs contain a great deal of narrative middle as part of the commercial ploy of television is to keep viewers watching or to stay tuned while they watch commercials during the extradiegetic portions of a program. Musically, narrative middles may contain smaller, nested submiddles, or satellites, as evidenced in the "Shore Leave" *Star Trek* episode, for example, by Dr. McCoy's romantic interlude with Yeoman Barrows and the Rodriguez/Teller romance. Music's proairetic function in narrative middles is to transition from scene to scene. Its hermeneutic function is to

1. Beginning:

　　Presentational/Expository—introducing the setting and characters of the teleplay.

2. Middle:

　　a. Hermeneutic Continuations

　　　　1. build up to climax

　　　　2. suspense

　　　　3. narrative realization of enigma ("ah, you're the one who did it!")

　　　　4. emotional realizations ("I love you!")

　　b. Proairetic Continuations (Transitions)

　　　　1. scene to scene

　　　　2. actions ("doing") music accompanying travel within a story (e.g., cowboys riding horses, car chases, fight scenes, etc.)

3. End

　　a. Hermeneutic: Denouement—climax and resolution of narrative

　　b. Proairetic: Recapitulatory—reestablishment of status quo; epilogue

Figure 5.4. Narrative (Intradiegetic) Musical Functions.

maintain the suspension of the enigma or disruption. Music in the hermeneutic code also may help the narrative, through pacing and dynamic construction, build toward climax and thereby realize the characters' thoughts or emotions. In this regard, music often accompanies scenes in which lead characters come to certain realizations about an aspect of the plot (solving some mystery or enigma, such as who committed a crime) or to a heretofore unknown aspect of their emotions (such as falling in love).

Narrative endings are often both proairetic and hermeneutic, as they wrap up the plot, often by resolving the narrative enigma. However, plots may resolve an enigma earlier and play out the remainder of the drama. In TV dramas, a reprise of a program's theme song is usually used for the transition of a program back into the extradiegetic flow while some sort of newly composed climax music is used to finish the narrative course of the program.

In the "Shore Leave" episode, the musical leitmotifs are paced temporally in an imaginative way, thus helping to pace the narrative action. The McCoy/ Barrows scene contains a musical a-b-a structure that is used effectively to prolong the scene hermeneutically while also achieving a degree of musical variety. The fight scene between Kirk and Finnegan is the lengthiest segment in the episode: four-and-a-half minutes before the commercial break and continuing for three minutes thereafter. Here Gerald Fried reworks the "Finnegan" theme with several variations in different orchestrations, tempi, and other musical devices. The variations on the theme function to highlight the fight scene and actually serve to slow the narrative down and prolong the well-choreographed scene. Fried's score also has places that speed up the narrative pacing of the episode. Just before the narrative denouement, or resolution of the enigma, all of the menacing characters and objects reappear to the *Enterprise* crew (at 42:35) accompanied by their leitmotifs. Fried rapidly juxtaposes the five leitmotifs of the tiger, the samurai, the World War II fighter plane, Don Juan, and the knight, bringing the scene to a chaotic climax in one minute and twenty seconds. The chaos is resolved with the appearance of the planet's caretaker, who assures the crew that all is well.

Musical Narrative in *The Rifleman*

To illustrate the ability of music to function temporally in a television narrative, I now return to the TV western *The Rifleman* for a closer look at the narrative structure of an episode. The western was a highly developed genre in both film and television by the 1950s and is often considered a uniquely American narrative genre. Precursors of the TV western appeared in Wild West shows of the late nineteenth century, and these transferred to silent film and, later, to sound film. The adventures of cowboys Tom Mix, Ken Maynard and Hoot Gibson, Hopalong Cassidy, Clayton Moore (the Lone Ranger), Roy Rogers and Dale Evans, Gene Autry, and others were staples for film serials and radio programs from the 1920s to the 1950s. The genre was attractive for television, as it carried the possibility of several different simple but highly developed plot macrostructures, but was also relatively inexpensive to produce, as usually only a handful of sets were needed (either newly built or reused from older serials or films) and were used over and over again during the series.

In the 1950s, television westerns featuring heroes who win the girl and defeat the always darkly clad bad guys presented reassuring images to Americans who faced the perceived threat of the Cold War. However, the television western soon transcended the simple narratives of cowboys, bandits, and Indians. The genre provides a number of narrative possibilities, though John Cawelti (1999: 19) cites seven basic plot types: the Union Pacific story (centering on the railroads, telegraph lines, or wagon trains), the ranch story, the empire story (a much larger ranch!), the revenge story, the cavalry and Indians story, the outlaw story, and the marshal story. As noted in previous chapters, the western was among the first genres that large movie studios transferred to television, with Warner's development of *Cheyenne*, *Sugarfoot*, and *Maverick* series for television.

The Rifleman (1958–1963) was one of the many westerns that aired on American television during the late 1950s and early 1960s. The series was part of a new subgenre of western that emerged in the late 1950s and early 1960s, what Gary Yoggy (1995) has termed the "domestic" or "family" western. These Westerns featured family groups, especially families with single parents, who sought to protect members of their family and/or property from week to week, as typified in programs like *Bonanza* (1959–1973), *The Big Valley* (1965–1969), *The Virginian* (1962–1971), and *The High Chaparral* (1967–1971). *The Rifleman* added nuance to the family western, as it focused on a widower father, Lucas McCain (Chuck Connors), and his son, Mark (Johnny Crawford), and their lives on their ranch outside of the town of North Fork, New Mexico. Many of the episodes deal with McCain trying to raise his son in an environment surrounded by outlaws, gamblers, and land cheats. Nearly every episode contains some kind of moral or ethical lesson for the youngster. In addition to being a rancher and a father, McCain is also a famous gunman whose claim to fame is a customized Winchester rifle that can rapid fire a volley of bullets in less than half a second (thus the name of the series). Nearly every episode contains at least one scene featuring the rapid firing of the rifle—a visual leitmotif for the program.

The series was created by Sam Peckinpah, who at the time was just beginning his career as a director and writer and who later would direct ultraviolent films, such as *The Wild Bunch* (1969) and *Straw Dogs* (1971). Reportedly, the series began after Peckinpah wrote a script for an episode of *Gunsmoke* (1955–1975) that was turned down. After reworking the script, Peckinpah submitted it to Dick Powell, then head of Four Star Films, who decided to use it on the *Zane Grey Theatre* (1956–1961), a combination western and anthology series he produced. Peckinpah's episode, with the reworked title, "The Sharpshooter," aired on March 7, 1958. Powell liked the episode, and the studio decided to pitch the scenario as a series. The ABC network picked it up in the fall of 1958. Connors, a former baseball player with the Chicago Cubs and Brooklyn/Los Angeles Dodgers, was hired in the title role, with Crawford, a former *Mickey Mouse Club* Mouseketeer, cast in the role of the son.

The music for *The Rifleman* was composed by Herschel Burke Gilbert (1918–2003), a veteran film and television composer. Gilbert graduated from Juilliard as a violist but began his career as an arranger for the Harry James Dance Band in the 1940s. His early film music works include a few brief cues in *It's a Wonderful Life* (1947), and later he received two Oscar nominations for scores to *The Thief* (1952) and *Carmen Jones* (1954) and for a song in *The Moon Is Blue* (1953). He began composing for television in 1951, working on freelance assignments that resulted in music for the programs *Death Valley Days*, *Sky King*, *Kit Carson*, and *Four Star Playhouse*. His association with Four Star productions resulted in his appointment as music director for the studio, a position he held for five years.[18] As director, he supervised the scoring for *Dick Powell's Zane Grey Theater*, *Johnny Ringo*, *The Detectives*, *Yancy Derringer*, *Burke's Law*, *The Big Valley*, and other series.

In 1958, Gilbert was asked to score music for *The Rifleman*. In order to side-step the constraints of the American Federation of Musicians union, Gilbert went to Munich, Germany, where he recorded 90 minutes worth of musical cues to be recombined and replayed within the entire series. What made Gilbert's scoring different from other library music at the time is that all the music he recorded in Munich was produced specifically for the particular series (while not necessarily for a particular episode) instead of for the general music library of the studio. Gilbert took the cues and edited them himself for use in each episode.[19] These cues were recycled from episode to episode, accompanied by other music inserted from his other TV and film music.

"Outlaw's Inheritance" Episode

Like many narrative TV shows, the story lines for *The Rifleman* series follow the narrative macrostructures mentioned by Cawelti. However, episodes also conform to narrative structures of Propp and others. McCain is the hero; his son is sometimes the helper and sometimes the figurative Proppian princess who is in peril and subsequently rescued (the series cast is overwhelmingly male). The marshal of North Fork, Micah Torrence, is a friend and sometime helper.[20] As in many westerns and other weekly dramas, new villains are brought in with each episode. McCain's rifle is his magic sword. The series also conforms to Todorov's and Bremond's models of equilibrium/disruption/ return to equilibrium. As in nearly all series, each episode begins with an expository scene (the teaser) that establishes the satisfactory status quo state, after which a disruption (usually a villain with an agenda) is introduced, and for the remainder of the episode McCain seeks a solution to the disruption (almost always involving his Winchester rifle) followed by a return to the satisfactory state.

One episode of *The Rifleman* that exhibits a rather sophisticated narrative structure is the "Outlaw's Inheritance" episode, which aired on June 16, 1959, at the end of the show's first season. The episode contains a dual plot, one of the possible variations listed by Propp (1968: 93). The first plot concerns the appearance of Dave Stafford, a con man who is hired by a Samuel Britton, a businessman of a rival town to North Fork, to sabotage North Fork's bid for a rail spur that would be an economic boon for the town. Stafford and Britton together form a sort of villain complex in the episode in which Britton serves as true villain (who has a financial stake in the outcome of the rail spur location) while Stafford, as a con man, plays the false hero role in Propp's narrative model. Stafford's assignment is to disrupt North Fork's efforts to send an emissary to convince the railroad to choose North Fork as the site for the rail spur and thus ensure that Center City, the rival town where Britton has a financial stake as a landowner, is awarded the new rail line. Acting as a false hero, Stafford goes to North Fork and gains the friendship and trust of its denizens in order to get them to elect him to go to Yuma to represent the town at the bidding meeting with the railroad company. His efforts are initially foiled as the town elects McCain to go to Yuma instead.

A second plot of the episode concerns a sum of money that McCain is to inherit, reportedly from an outlaw, Wade Joyner, who he claims to have never met. When the town learns that McCain is receiving money from an infamous outlaw, the town council becomes worried about McCain's ability to represent them at the railroad meeting. This situation is fortuitous for Stafford, who convinces the town businessmen to allow him to go in McCain's place. McCain subsequently recalls that he met the outlaw during a storm and put him up at his ranch for the night—not realizing who he was. For this act of kindness he was rewarded with a $500 inheritance from the outlaw at his death. Once

McCain recalls this incident (in a similar storm scene), he feels vindicated. The next morning as Stafford visits the ranch to pick up the survey documents, McCain states that, with his recollection of events, he is now qualified to go to the railroad meeting. Stafford becomes frantic in seeing his plan disintegrate and draws his pistol on McCain. McCain admonishes him to put the gun away, then wields his rifle and fires a volley into a chair next to Stafford. Stafford surrenders by handing his pistol to McCain and confesses to his scheme with Britton.

The final scene shows Britton getting on the stagecoach for Yuma only to find McCain, instead of Stafford, waiting for him inside. Britton is nonplussed but tries not to show his exasperation. The coach drives off with McCain and Britton, leaving the well-wishers, Mark, and Marshal Torrence waving farewell.

Temporal Structure of Narrative and Music

The "Outlaw's Inheritance" episode is structured in eight scenes with an additional prologue and epilogue along with the opening and closing credits.[21] The summary of scenes is shown in figure 5.5.

The running time of each scene in column 2 shows an ebb and flow of narrative temporal space. This episode contains two expository scenes in the prologue and scene 1. The prologue introduces the multiple villains: Britton, the wealthy landowner from Central City, and Stafford, the hired confidence man. The episode begins in media res, with Stafford riding through the snow-covered mountains to meet Britton. The riding scene dissolves to Stafford entering Britton's house, where they plan the conspiracy to prevent North Fork from obtaining the valued rail spur to town. The second exposition is scene 1 featuring Lucas and Mark greeting the new morning at their ranch. Mark predicts spring rains by testing the wind. The ensuing rain proves integral to the first narrative enigma resolution.

These two expository scenes together take up only about three minutes of program time. Lengthier scenes are those that involve posing and resolving the narrative enigma: Scene 3 (3:19) is set in the Madera House Hotel, where McCain's character is called into question due to the mysterious inheritance he receives from Wade Joyner, a notorious gunfighter. Scene 6 also is set in Madera House, where Lucas and Mark are spending the night due to a rainstorm (foreshadowed in scene 1) that prevents them from going home. Here, after a conversation with Stafford, McCain realizes that he met Joyner years ago when he took him into his home during a similar rainstorm. Scene 8 (3:35) is set back at McCain's ranch, where he realizes Stafford's plan to subvert the rail spur plans and fires his rifle to convince Stafford to surrender.

Scene	Time	Description	(Propp Function)
Expository			
Prologue	1:15	Britton and Stafford (villains) meet; disruption established.	(V)
Opening Credits	0:13	Connors fires his rifle on the town street; glares into camera.	
Expository			
Scene 1	1:40	McCain and Mark at Ranch, foreshadowing "spring storm"; Stafford reappears as "false hero."	
Continuation			
Scene 2	1:32	Town hall meeting; McCain chosen to represent town in meeting with railroad company in Yuma; Stafford defeated.	(IV, IX)
Scene 3	3:19	Madera House Hotel; lawyer enters to inform McCain of his $500 inheritance from Wade Joyner, a notorious outlaw; Business leaders speculate on McCain's knowledge of the outlaw; Stafford plants seed of doubt on McCain's character.	(VI, VII, IX)
Scene 4	2:12	Street; fistfight; McCain's character further called into question; McCain denies knowledge of Joiner, gets into fight.	(XII)
Scene 5	2:43	Bank; meeting with business leaders, who ask McCain to withdraw from meeting and ask Stafford to go instead; McCain acquiesces in disgust.	(VII, XII)
Scene 6	4:05	Hotel room; storm at night, McCain meets with Stafford, recalls meeting with Joiner in a storm like this one; resolves first enigma.	(XIV, XV)
Scene 7	2:23	Hotel, street, bank; Britton arrives on the scene to reinforce the McCain scandal with business leaders, replants seed of doubt; Marshal Torrence wants to stay with McCain out of loyalty.	(XX)
Denouement			
Scene 8	3:35	Ranch; Stafford meets McCain to get documents; Mark brings letter with Joyner's inheritance; McCain claims that the letter explains the situation and tries to meet with business leaders in town; Stafford stops him, and McCain responds by firing rifle as a warning; Stafford surrenders.	(XVI, XVIII)
Epilogue	0:43	Britton meets stagecoach for Yuma with business leaders; McCain appears in the coach and taunts Britton, who pleads ignorance of the plot against McCain.	(XIX, XXVII, XXVIII, XI)
Closing Credits	0:42	Rifleman theme played over bas-relief of Connors with rifle.	

Figure 5.5. Synopsis of Scenes from "Outlaw's Inheritance" Episode (*The Rifleman*).

Briefer scenes are primarily those involving transitions or actions, like the obligatory fistfight (embedded in scene 4). The scene may be seen as a satellite in that it does nothing to propel the narrative, but it does establish the derision shown McCain by the townspeople for allegedly receiving stolen money and consorting with an outlaw. Also, the introduction of minor characters, such as Marcus Trimble (Dabbs Greer), the lawyer who informs McCain of his inheritance, takes up little narrative time.

While Gilbert's music for the episode is drawn from the library of cues recorded for the entire series, it closely fits the episode's narrative (if, at times, in an overly dramatic way) to present the uniform cast of characters and the conventional narrative formulas. The series is rich in musical cues; in this episode, of the approximately 24 minutes and 30 seconds of narrative time, 12 minutes and 30 seconds contain music.

Overall, the musical underscore of the episode serves both the extradiegetic and intradiegetic functions of framing and transition while also highlighting Todorov's and Bremond's models of equilibrium in through tonal and motivic means. The music also reflects Propp's character functions of hero and villain. The temporal deployment of musical cues is illustrated in figure 5.6.

Musical cues (shaded in the diagram) serve as transitions between scenes 1 and 2, 2 and 3, 3 and 4, 5 and 6 (although this represents a commercial break), and 7 and 8. Moreover, when not used proairetically as transitions, music is used as frame: every scene begins with a musical cue, though not all scenes end with one. The temporality of music can also be seen as framing. Figure 5.6 shows the duration of each musical cue in relation to the real time of the episode. The example shows that music is concentrated at the beginning (including the theme) and at the end, the denouement (scene 8), the epilogue, and the closing theme. Music thus serves as an intradiegetic frame to the episode. In addition to its use in the normal opening and closing credits, music helps to introduce the episode (and the program) as well as bring the episode to a conclusion. Once the story has been introduced, music cues are relatively evenly spaced throughout the remainder of the scenes. Only in scene 6—in the hotel room where McCain finally recalls his encounter with the outlaw Wade Joyner—is less music to be found.

Following Tarasti's requirements that musical narratives contain sufficient actorial, temporal, and spatial dimensions in order to be considered narratives, the following analysis traces these dimensions to describe how musical narrative devices reinforce the narrative structure of the TV episode. Moreover, the analysis shows how these dimensions also reinforce the narrative modalities of "being" and "doing" (or "referencing" and "action") and how music affects the Todorov/Bremond model of long-range structure.

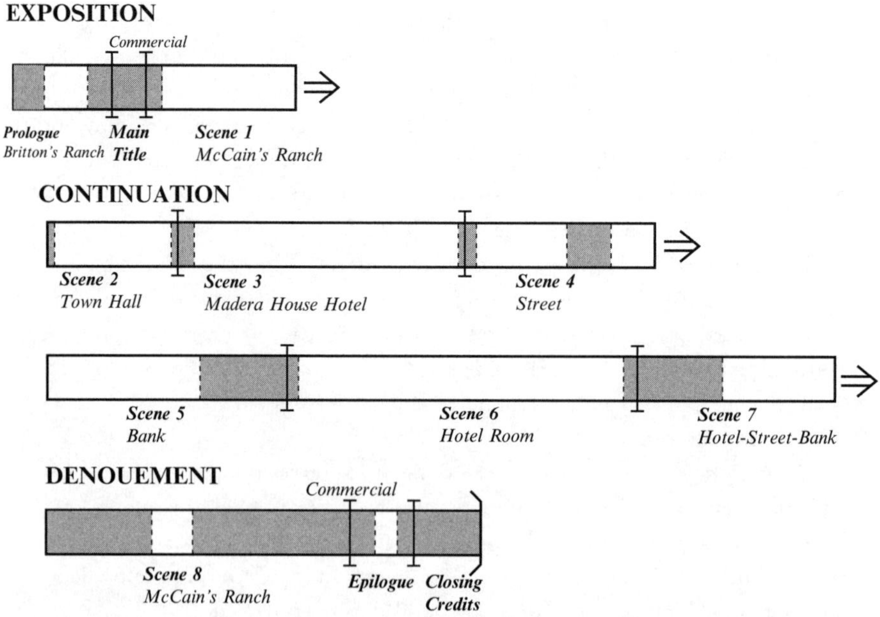

EXPOSITION

CONTINUATION

DENOUEMENT

Figure 5.6. Deployment of Musical Cues in "Outlaw's Inheritance" Episode (*The Rifleman*).

Music Actants: Leitmotifs

The "Outlaw's Inheritance" episode contains six identifiable musical motifs that are repeated and vary throughout the program. Most of the score consists of cues that quote variations of the main theme. The theme serves as the primary leitmotif of the program, identifying the program and its star, Chuck Connors. In addition to its denotative nature, it also contains at least two connotative style topics, the heroic and the pastoral (discussed in chapter 1).

The main theme and its variations in the program may be considered semic motifs, denoting the musical actors and operating primarily through a modality of "being." However, this main theme motif is altered a great deal in the score and is frequently played in a minor key by muted horns. There is a great deal of repetition and redundancy of this primary motif.[22] The theme is manipulated in several ways; it is fragmented and played in different keys (including a conversion from major key to minor key) and with different timbres (see example 5.1).[23] The shift of the main motif to the minor key signifies the Todorovian model of disequilibrium or Propp's functions of "testing the hero."

Other motifs include two "suspense" motives. One motif is a cue that is actually labeled "Mark's fear" (see example 5.2). It is a variation on "Mark's theme,"

Example 5.1. Variations of *Rifleman* Main Theme. *(A)* Major key version; *(B)* minor key version.

(a)

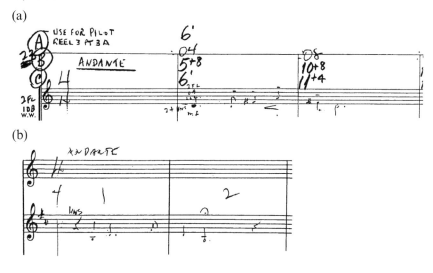

(b)

Example 5.2. "Mark's Fear" Motif.

which is not found in this episode. Usually the motif conjured up Mark's dilemma (when captured by a villain or lost), but in this episode it highlights complications in the villains' plot.[24]

Gilbert's label for another suspense motive is "dramatic build" and is reminiscent of the eighteenth-century affectation for a "sigh" with a melodic descent (see example 5.3). "Suspense" motives might be considered as having "becoming" modalities ("might be" or "perhaps shall be"); these reinforce the narrative enigma by suspending action and offering a choice on possible consequences. In the fight scene, will McCain prevail, or will he be defeated? In the episode as a whole, will the villains Stafford and Britton succeed, or will McCain prevail? These narrative options are left open by the suspended action created by the music.

Example 5.3. "Dramatic Build" Motif. Copyright 1957 by Hershel Burke Gilbert.

Example 5.4. "Spur the Horses" Motif. Copyright 1957 by Hershel Burke Gilbert.

There are also two motives of "doing" or "action" in the episode. The prologue features the dissonant "spur the horses" galloping motif played in horns and accompanied by timpani, which accompanies the scene of Stafford riding through the high country on his way to meet Britton (see example 5.4). This motif is played again as Mark rides to the ranch to deliver the mail to his father. The other motif is a "fight" motif that appears only during McCain's brawl with the town drunks in scene 4.

Other than the "Rifleman" motif, most motifs do not signify any specific individual, though some vaguely refer to the villains. In spite of their generic qualities, they can nonetheless be seen as possessing the modalities of "being" or "doing." In this regard, the motifs are differentiated as actants and actors in the same way that actors are: just as actors may leave a TV series and appear in others as different characters (actants), so-called production musical motives appear in other episodes (or other programs or films).[25]

Finally, the "Rifleman" leitmotif is used to move the story along both proairetically and hermeneutically throughout the episode. The proairetic usage of the theme is structural and helps get the narrative going. In this capacity, the theme helps establish the beginning, middle, and end of the narrative. At the beginning, a fragment of the main theme is heard in the flute in scene 1, here used as an exposition of the characters in the episode.[26] Scene 1 shows McCain and his son at their ranch, with McCain quizzing his son on his ability to predict the weather. The theme is played again with muted horns as a transition to scene 2, the town meeting scene, this time in B minor. The muted horns in minor key sound ominous, signaling the foreshadowing of the disruption in McCain's life. The theme is used also as a transition into scene 4. The theme is played as a conclusion to the episode in the epilogue, as narrative equilibrium is restored due to the defeat of Stafford.

The *Rifleman* theme is also used hermeneutically to reinforce the narrative enigma and its resolution. In scene 3, the lawyer enters the hotel and inquires about Lucas McCain. At the mention of McCain's name, the theme is played in the somber B minor key and is embellished through a repetition in E minor and then repeated in B minor. This prolonged iteration of the theme signifies the beginning of McCain's test with the townspeople of North Fork over Stafford's confidence game.

The theme is played in a similar fashion in scene 4 as the town drunks taunt McCain, resulting in a fistfight. In scene 5, the theme is played in its original D major guise as McCain acquiesces to the business community's wish that he withdraw from consideration as town representative at the railroad meeting. Ironically, the theme is also played in G minor in the same scene as Stafford protests McCain's withdrawal, falsely claiming that he "would feel like a Judas taking over." The theme is played in G minor in scene 7 as Britton questions the business leaders about McCain's ability to represent the town in light of the scandal. It is played again in scene 8, the denouement, as McCain learns of Stafford's true intentions and fires his rifle warning him to drop the con game. Noteworthy here is that the "Rifleman" motif refers only to McCain, whether he is on-screen or not, and helps to maintain the viewer's focus on the hero's travails and ultimate triumph.

Musical Events: Tonality and Texture

Besides serving to reference characters and situations in the narrative, Gilbert's music to the "Outlaw's Inheritance" episode serves a function of moving the narrative through its course. The deployment of motifs in the episode contributes to the pacing of the narrative through narrative temporal space. Scene 8 contains nearly every motif from the episode, and these are recapitulated in a buildup to the climax. The recurrence of these musical motifs is similar to what occurs in the "Shore Leave" *Star Trek* episode, where a rapid juxtaposition of motifs in time helps to create a sense of climax. The deployment of music in the *Rifleman* episode creates a musical hermeneutic that builds to the peak of the narrative disruption/disequilibrium (culminating in scene 5) and then builds again to the denouement (scene 8). Such pacing of musical cues creates the narrative schema of a double climax or, in musical terms, a double crescendo, reflecting the narrative trajectory to disequilibrium and to climax and denouement. Of interest in the temporal dimension is how music paces the narrative. As shown in figure 5.6, after the lengthy use of music in the prologue and opening credits, there is little music in the first two scenes (except as transitions). Musical cues get longer as the narrative enigma and McCain's testing become apparent in scene 3. After the fistfight scene, musical cues are absent in scene 6. Finally, as the episode prepares for, and reaches, its denouement, musical cues once again become longer and longer, until music plays continuously through scene 8 and the epilogue.

In addition to temporal space, music helps move the narrative trajectory along through Tarasti's third requirement for narrative, the spatial dimension, which I take here to mean the tonal and registral space that music occupies while accompanying the narrative. Here, I broaden the term to include these aspects while also considering dynamics and other aspects of texture. The first to be considered here is tonal space.[27] The deployment of tonal areas in a TV narrative can reflect its shape and trajectory. The reader will please indulge me here, as I present a scene-by-scene tonal analysis of the episode through musical graphs illustrating the linear motion of the music through each scene. Although these graphs resemble Schenker graphs, they are meant to illustrate how tonal space works through the deployment of themes and key areas.[28] These graphs are reductions of the salient elements of the surface music going on in the scene, with open note heads referring to the tonal center(s) in each cue; stemmed filled-in note heads represent important pitches (inchoative, final, or important melodic goal tones) while unstemmed note heads represent connecting notes to important pitches. Slurs are drawn to show connections, either prolongations of tonal areas or motion from one musical event to another.

The prologue to "Outlaw's Inheritance" features the two villains, Stafford and Britton, as they hatch a plan to get a rail spur built to Britton's hometown, Center City. The prologue opens with Gilbert's "spur the horses" motive, as Stafford rides on horseback to Britton's ranch. The horns play a descending line from the major third Eb-G to the dissonant diminished fourth, C#-G. As Stafford enters the house, Britton lays out his plan while the "Mark's fear" motive is played by the horns, suggesting the key of E major, but the A-flat tremolos in the basses create tonal tension. This tension is resolved with a horn call motive, B-F#, with basses playing a B. The scene ends with a dissonant cadence (see example 5.5) with a bitonal G major triad in the upper strings and an Ab-Eb dyad in the bass instruments. This cadence establishes the narrative enigma and is resolved later in the episode, as will be shown below. The E-flat to G motion in the upper voice at the cadence is also a melodic parallel to the opening interval played by the horns.

After the opening credits (which establish the key of D major), scene 1 begins with McCain and Mark stepping outside the door of their ranch house. A flute plays McCain's theme in D major. This tonal center continues that established in the opening credits, providing a sense of a home key for the episode. No other music is heard in the scene until a stinger on B that transitions to scene 2, the town hall meeting where McCain is chosen to represent North Fork in the bid for the rail spur. McCain's theme is played in B minor, as Stafford's presence creates a sense of conflict and suspense. No other music is played in the scene until a stinger D#-E is played in the upper strings, as Mark shouts his joy at the prospect of getting a sarsaparilla. The pitch E transitions as a third of the C-sharp minor chord that plays at the beginning of the next scene.

Example 5.5. Linear Reduction of the Prologue

Scene 3 opens in the Madera House Hotel in North Fork, where Stafford is playing poker with other men of the town. Marcus Trimble, an itinerant lawyer, enters inquiring as to the whereabouts of McCain, who according to Trimble, is to inherit $500 from a deceased outlaw. Seeing his chance to throw doubt on McCain's character and substitute himself for McCain to bid for the rail spur, Stafford tries to slander McCain by mentioning the ramifications of having an associate of an outlaw represent North Fork. The local businessmen begin to wonder about McCain's dealings with the outlaw and call a meeting of all local business owners. Stafford's deceptive speech is accompanied by McCain's theme in B minor, prolonged through E minor and returning to B minor (see example 5.6). The tonal center shifts to G as the poker game breaks up. Even though McCain is not on-screen, the theme refers to him and establishes the problem of clearing his good name.

Scene 4 shows McCain as he confronts the local businessmen about his association with the outlaw. As McCain rides to town with Mark in his buckboard, the "Rifleman" motif plays in G minor. An inverted form of the motif in A follows, creating a harmonic tension over the G tremolos in the basses (see example 5.7).

Example 5.6. Linear Reduction of Scenes 1–3.

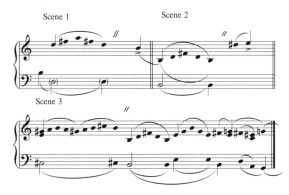

Example 5.7. Linear Reduction of Scene 4.

As McCain walks through town, he is taunted by two town drunks. McCain rebuffs them verbally, but the conflict escalates and the fight scene ensues. McCain's taunting is accompanied by the "Rifleman" motif in B minor, and the fight scene contains another bitonal cue, with a G minor outline in the strings over an A pedal in the bass. The scene resolves in A, with strings ascending to E over the A pedal.

In Scene 5, McCain confronts the local businessmen, who tell him that he is not suitable to represent North Fork in the bid for the rail spur. They announce that they will send Stafford (the con man, whom they don't suspect) instead. During the scene, the "Rifleman" motif is played in D major and G minor, then inverted in A, all over an A pedal in the basses (see example 5.8). A dissonant C/F-sharp tritone stinger accompanies the announcement that Stafford will represent the town. The stinger is prolonged through an upper-voice motion to E.

Music resumes in scene 7, where Stafford and Britton seek to reinforce their positions by further deceiving the locals about McCain. The F#/C stinger from scene 5 sounds at the sight of the two villains and gives way to a descending motive in G. After another stinger the "Mark's fear" motif is played in B. The scene ends again in the bank, with cues outlining harmonies in D major, G minor, and A similar to those in scene 5 (see example 5.9).

Scene 6 resolves the first narrative enigma, the matter of McCain's inheritance that must be resolved in order to solve the second narrative problem of

Example 5.8. Linear Reduction of Scene 5.

Stafford (villain)
gains upper hand.

Example 5.9. Linear Reduction of Scene 7.

Scene 7

exposing Stafford as a con man employed by Britton. While scene 6 uses no music (other than transitioning in and out of the scene), scene 8, the resolution of the second narrative problem, is rife with musical cues. The scene opens with Stafford at McCain's ranch, where he has gone to pick up survey maps for the trip to Yuma. The "Mark's fear" motif plays in C-sharp minor and again in B minor as McCain and Stafford discuss the transaction. The "spur the horses" motif (in G) suddenly breaks through the soundtrack, and the image cuts to Mark riding his horse to the ranch to deliver a letter to his father. The letter is the inheritance money from Wade Joyner along with a note describing his visit. McCain feels vindicated by the note and suggests going to town with Stafford to settle the matter with the townspeople. Stafford's uneasiness at the prospect that his plan will be foiled is accompanied by building musical motifs, first a descending motif over the dissonant F#–C tritone followed by the McCain theme in B minor. McCain discerns Stafford's plan and fires his rifle as a warning for him to give up his gun. Stafford acquiesces quietly, and the scene ends with the "button" motif with the G major triad (see example 5.10).

The epilogue begins with the McCain theme in B minor but ends with the McCain motif in D major. The epilogue segues immediately to the closing credits, also in D major. In contrast to the excitement of the opening credits, the end credits provide a more subdued closing frame. The credits (written text) scroll over a sculpted bas-relief of Chuck Connors with his rifle extended. During the closing, we hear the theme in its entirety for the first time, played by strings. Horns enter later in the theme but in a more subdued texture, surrounded by strings. Accompanying the melody is a woodblock, beating out a rhythm, an iconic sign of the hoof beats of horses, again identifying the program as a western. The calming closing is also reassurance to the viewer that the Todorovian narrative equilibrium has been restored (at least until next week!).

Example 5.10. Linear Reduction of Scene 8.

The textural contrast between opening and closing is symbolic of each week's narrative. The exciting opening represents the action (and violence) of the weekly episodes while the closing is representative of the moral, ethical, and peaceful life of McCain and his son.

Besides including references to the *Rifleman* theme and the tonal areas in which it is played, other scenes in the episode contribute to the narrative arc through other tonal areas that may be interpreted for their narrative significa- tion. The reductive graph in example 5.11 illustrates the key areas used in the episode and attempts to present the cues as a unified musical narrative. The graph breaks down the episode into essential tonal and registral elements in a two-part reduction. Beams connecting the bass notes on the graph denote three primary keys in the episode that have narrative connotations. The beams on the upper notes represent the registral connection of these notes and are discussed along with the role of register in the episode. The bar lines indicate scene divi- sions, whereas the double bars indicate commercial breaks.[29] The key of G may be called the intradiegetic and proairetic key because it establishes narrative time and space in the episode. The key signals the opening of the narrative, the pos- ing of the first narrative enigma (the villains plotting to gain the rail spur away from North Fork), and its ultimate resolution (the defeat of Stafford in scene 8 just before the third commercial break). G is also heard at several other points in the episode: at the beginning of scene 4 as McCain acts to preserve his good name and at the beginning of the denouement in scene 8. In particular, the "cadence" motif at the end of the prologue (the G major triad over the Ab–Eb dyad) serves as a foreshadowing of the ultimate resolution of the story, which is accompanied by the "button" motif at the end of scene 8 (see example 5.12). The incomplete resolution of the opening cadence (the A-flat/G chord) is finally resolved to the consonant G major chord at the end. (Both of these areas are marked by brackets on the graph).[30]

B minor is the primary hermeneutic key in the episode in that it prolongs the narrative through suspense. Music in B minor sounds during scenes of conflict

Example 5.11. Linear Graph of Keys and Ranges Keys in "Outlaw's Inheritance" Episode.

164

Example 5.12. *(A)* "Cadence" Motif; *(B)* Final Cadence Motif. Copyright 1957 by Hershel Burke Gilbert.

and drama. B minor is heard in scenes 2, 3, 4, 7, and 8 and at the beginning of the epilogue, accompanying scenes where the narrative outcome is in doubt. Finally, D major may be considered the extradiegetic key: it is the key of the opening and closing credits and also the beginning of scene 1 (coming right out of a commercial break) and the end of the epilogue (going right into the closing credits). D major serves as an extradiegetic frame for the episode that includes the transitional music of the opening and closing credits but that also encroaches intradiegetically into the opening of scene 1 and the end of the epilogue. In short, D major is the key of the program, G major the key of the episode, and B minor the prolonging "narrative suspense" key.

The role of extradiegetic framing is illustrated through the placement of commercials in the episode. D major is heard both going into the first commercial break and coming out of the last commercial break. The commercial break at the midpoint of the episode consists of a dissonant F-sharp half-diminished seventh with C in the bass. After the break, scene 6 features virtually no music (there is a very brief horn motif in B minor at the opening). Scene 7 reiterates the F-sharp half diminished 7th chord (this time with F-sharp in the bass by a large-scale voice exchange, illustrated by the arrows on the graph), resolving to the proairetic key of G. The reappearance of G thus reestablishes the resumption of intradiegetic/narrative space for the episode.

The reduction of the upper voices on the graph illustrates how range or tessitura helps to shape narrative space. Gilbert uses primarily two ranges: the low horn/timpani/bass range and the high strings/tutti range. As shown in example 5.11, Gilbert manipulates range where the overall form is a motion from low to high leaving important areas of the narrative with a sort of musical left-hanging effect, which may be thought of as another hermeneutic device. The prologue illustrates this process in microcosm, where the range of the music continually rises to the high G of the "cadence" motif. The opening credits establish a high register on D. After scene 1, the range is consistently lower, utilizing the horn/timpani motifs. With the exception of a few high stingers, Gilbert maintains the low register. The register moves upward in scene 5, climaxing right before the commercial break. Finally, scene 8 reveals two ascents (to prolong the suspense), culminating on the "button" motif signaling the final cadence and resolution of the narrative enigma. Scene 6 serves as a musical respite (or "interruption" in Schenkerian terms) for the episode by sitting within the voice exchange of the tritone C–F#, which ends scene 5 and resumes in scene 7. Overall, scenes seem to begin in low registers and end on high ones, thus providing a musical hermeneutic code that keeps the viewer watching.

Musical range also reflects the coded responses to highness or lowness of a musical sound. Peter Kivy (1989) has traced the history of low musical sounds as representing villainy or evil, noting the various uses of high and low registers in classical opera. Of note is the fact that the high = good, low = evil symbolic dichotomy has persisted through film music.[31] Scenes of suspense in the episode tend to begin in low ranges, especially in the "Rifleman" motif with muted horns. Most of the interior scenes of the episode are accompanied by horns, basses, and timpani—representing medium and low registers. These scenes contribute to the hermeneutic code and represent the unfolding of the narrative disruption. The low registers also coincide most often with the villains. High textures are associated with McCain, his son, or the ranch but also with climaxes or tension in the narrative. Two high stingers occur as a reaction to Mark's enthusiasm. The graph also shows how each scene ends on a high note for a suspenseful effect. The ubiquitous horns are considered medium though sometimes they are played in both their low registers (for an ominous effect) and their high registers (for a dramatic, suspenseful effect). Gilbert also prefers the muted horn effect to lend a sense of suspense.

In addition to tonality and register, musical texture, timbre, and volume can be read as signifiers in television narrative. Texture is normally defined according to the relationship of parts: as monophonic (one part playing alone), homophonic (one predominant melody with accompaniment), or polyphonic (many independent parts playing at once). Texture may also be taken to mean the density of parts playing at any one time. Gilbert's music for *The Rifleman* tends to be simple but with a multilayered texture. Scenes of high drama and conflict feature bitonal areas in which wind instruments play in one key while the timpani may suggest another key, creating a tonal tension that ultimately is resolved. Musical textures also thicken in a few spots, notably in the prologue where the full orchestra is used. This scene is counterbalanced by the epilogue, which builds to full orchestra at the conclusion. Other areas of full orchestra include the fight in scene 4 and the narrative denouement in scene 8.

Timbre also may be considered important in musical signification in this episode. The role of the French horn in *The Rifleman* and its signifying capability as a heroic and pastoral instrument have already been examined. Gilbert's propensity to use horns overshadows much of the score. However, the points where strings come in make their appearance so much stronger due to their scarcity elsewhere in the score.

Volume may be the most iconic and most natural response to music, as loudness indicates action or violence while softness signifies intimacy or stability. The opening theme to *The Rifleman* is loud, succeeding the 10 rifle shots and the announcer's voice practically bellowing the name of the program. This boisterous opening fulfills Tagg's appellative function, with the sheer volume of the opening distinguishing itself from the extradiegetic televisual flow and capturing the viewer's attention, even if the viewer is out of the room. The volume, the brassiness of the theme, the gunshots all signify action and, to some extent, violence.[32] In this regard, the assertion of authors Rick Altman and Michel Chion that television is primarily a sound medium or radio with pictures seems correct.

Conclusion

Music in television narratives is disjointed and discontinuous, so its narrative properties may seem suspect. However, television narratives are also discontinuous, continually interrupted by commercial breaks, yet, television audiences can "connect the dots" in these narrative structures through verisimilitude. It is my contention in this chapter that TV audiences also connect these dots through musical narrativity. Gilbert's music to *The Rifleman* is a good example of narrativity in television music in the late 1950s–early 1960s. The scoring is extremely efficient—not only in terms of production (90 minutes for an entire five-year series) but also semiotically. The music featured on the program illustrates musical existents and events through the modalities of "being" (*être*) and music of "doing" (*faire*) as enumerated by Tarasti and Greimas, functioning through temporal, actorial, and spatial dimensions of the narrative.

Music of being is represented in the one, sole leitmotif in *The Rifleman*. The leitmotif signifies Lucas McCain, the main character, and is thus derived from the operatic and cinematic practice of leitmotif. When the "Rifleman" leitmotif is played throughout an episode, it reminds the audience of Lucas McCain, even when he is not on-screen. As the leitmotif is repeated week after week (or possibly day after day in syndication), it signifies itself as a narrative agent within the episode while also signifying the program itself, reminding the audience that this is the show called *The Rifleman*. Further, the leitmotif came to signify its star, Chuck Connors, as the theme accompanied him on his many guest appearances on celebrity talk shows. The leitmotif thus has a triple articulation: at the intradiegetic level of the narrative, at the extradiegetic level of the program, and at the intertextual level of Connors's celebrity.

In *The Rifleman*, the opening and closing theme music of the program provides an extradiegetic temporal frame as beginning and end of the episode, but the music provides a tonal frame as well. Both themes are in D major, offering a sort of tonal closure (Patrick McCreless's requirements for both Schenker's fundamental structure and Barthes's hermeneutic sentence) or extradiegetic tonal frame for the program. A more intradiegetic frame may be seen in G major that opens and closes the narrative portion of the show, thus providing a proairetic function. In the interior scenes of the episode, other references to the *Rifleman* theme are played in B minor. This minor form of the theme is played in scenes 2, 3, 4, 5, and 7 as well as the epilogue. These cues, signifying drama and pathos to the narrative, remain identifiable as the *Rifleman* theme. B minor can thus be seen as the episode's hermeneutic key, the key that keeps the enigma alive. The minor version of the *Rifleman* theme is often expanded in the episode (and in the series) to include a sequence from B minor to E minor, and sometimes returning back to B minor, thus embellishing or prolonging the B minor key area through its subdominant.[33] However, as B minor is the relative minor of the extradiegetic key of D, eventually this key must resolve to the home key and bring the narrative equilibrium back so that a new episode can air next week. These three key areas provide the deep structure or kernels of musical narrative for the episode while other keys are ancillary satellites.

Overall, Gilbert's music to *The Rifleman* represents a televisual illustration of the modalities of "being" and "doing" in a television narrative. Leitmotifs represent musical actants while the deployment of these motifs represents events. Beyond the actorial aspects of the leitmotifs with their tonal associations, musical time and space contribute to the narrative arc of the episode. Musical cues are concentrated at the beginning and end of the episode, where they help usher in the narrative disruption as well as the resolution. Music serves the proairetic function as extradiegetic cues transition between scenes (and in and out of commercials). Musical space also includes texture, with thicker orchestral textures representing narrative climaxes and low register instruments representing suspense. While leitmotifs remain the most palpable musically narrative device, the aspects of musical time and space also lend themselves to musical narrativity.

And now for something completely different.

6

Tube of Pleasure, Tube of Bliss

Television Music as (Not So) Drastic Experience

Singers Perry Como (left) and Dinah Shore (Wisconsin Center for Film and Theater Research).

Thus far I have explored the signifying power of music in narrative television texts—what music *does* and how it operates in a complex visual narrative. Now it is time to stop and ask why music is so prevalent in television and why TV producers rely on it so heavily to convey aspects of narrative. One answer is that music functioned so effectively in its predecessor media, that is, film and radio, that it became integral in conveying the narratives in the new medium. Following filmic practices, music complements the visual images of television, heightens the narrative aspects of programs, sets the moods, identifies genres, and even helps to carry the narrative along its temporal course. In radio, music has always been a staple of narrative programming (e.g., story line series popular in the 1930s and 1940s) as well as music programming. Music also followed its role in radio by acting as a navigator through the continuous flow of broadcast space, as well as helping to sell the sponsors' products.

Perhaps a more fundamental answer as to why music is used so extensively in television (as well as film and radio) is not what music *does* but what music *is*: music is essentially an artistic medium that is *pleasurable* to the viewing audience. The pleasures of music on television are apparent through its ubiquitous presence on the variety shows, dramatic series, and commercials since television's inception. But how does one describe or define pleasure, especially in the context of television music? And are there different kinds of pleasure in television? Television is generally regarded as a recreational or pleasurable medium. It provides pleasure as a provider of information and as a recreational, escapist form of entertainment, through the broadcast of fictional narratives and real-life sporting events. It also provides a contact with the world (or at least a mediated world) for the isolated in society.

Of course, the notion of televisual pleasure is subjective. Indeed, the types of televisual pleasure mentioned above are substantially different from one another. While some viewers are pleased by television's capacity to instantaneously deliver news and information on current events or sporting events, others find TV's escapist aspects to be a source of pleasure. The former type of pleasure seemingly lies in the intellect of the viewer, the desire to know, to learn, to be informed, whereas the latter form elicits the imagination of the viewer, the desire to dream of improbabilities, to imagine the exotic or the antique, and to draw out metaphors between the real and the imagined. Music has always been an integral part of television and is usually considered a pleasurable art form as well. So, just how does music enhance the experience of pleasure on television?

Theorizing Pleasure

Outside of research in brain function and cognitive psychology, pleasure is usually not considered an area of academic scrutiny, yet there is a long tradition of theorizing on pleasure, particularly in the field of philosophy. Kant's ideas differentiating between the mind and body, or thinking and feeling, led to the foundation of an aesthetic in which the mind was considered the site of the highest form of pleasure. For Kant, the pleasures of the senses (body) were tyrannical; only in the contemplation of the aesthetic could people be free to experience a higher form of mental pleasure. Bodily sensuousness, the perception of the senses, is natural and therefore low. The body is an area of experience that escapes and threatens "pure taste," and thus taste, or high pleasure, can come about only through social training and discipline.[1] After Kant, the school of Bloomsbury art criticism coined the term "aesthetic pleasure" as a sort of pleasure of the mind, meaning that the highest faculty of consciousness partakes of a hypothetically universal set of values. Critic and philosopher Clive Bell stated that the pleasure of the mind "transports us from the world of man's activity to a world of aesthetic exaltation" (quoted in Watney 1983: 76–77). Needless to say, for Romantics in the nineteenth century, the point was that aesthetic pleasure was for the cultivated mind and thus reserved for the elite class.

The dichotomy of pleasures of the mind versus pleasures of the body was developed for literary criticism in the twentieth century in the work of Roland Barthes. Barthes's pamphlet *Le Plaisir du texte* (1973) is a clever collection of fragments and aphorisms (chapters are arranged in alphabetical order) in which he stages the question "what do we enjoy in the [literary] text?" The "text" is defined as a lifeless collection of symbols that come alive in the creation of it by the writer and in the reading of it by the reader.[2] Borrowing terminology from Julia Kristeva, Barthes develops an ideological polarity to distinguish between two types of pleasure derived from reading and decoding literary texts. The first is *plaisir*, a type of pleasure that is cultural in origin; the second, *jouissance* (commonly translated as bliss or ecstasy), defined as the pleasure of the body: the pleasure experienced through heightened sensualities that relate it directly to human nature rather than to culture. While *plaisir* corresponds to Kant's pleasure of the mind (aesthetics), unlike Kant, Barthes considers it a mundane pleasure that is essentially confirming of one's sense of identity within a culture. This type of pleasure is located in the reader who seeks to situate the text within the confines of known culture. *Jouissance* derives from the writer who experiences pleasure through the sheer act of writing, regardless of the cultural context. However, as John Fiske (1987) has asserted, it can also apply to the reader who detaches from the cultural constraints of a work only to take pleasure in the writing itself. *Plaisir* has connotations to the cultural, mundane, and cerebral; *jouissance*, the sensual, the sublime, and physical. In terms of literary texts, Barthes (1973: 14) defines the text of pleasure (*plaisir*) as "the text that contents, fills, grants euphoria: the text that comes from culture and does not break with it." Conversely, the text of bliss (*jouissance*) is "the text that imposes a state of loss, the text that dis-comforts...unsettles the reader's historical, cultural, psychological assumptions, the consistency of his tastes, values, memories, and brings a crises his relation with language."

I would interpret Barthes's dual-modality of pleasure semiotically: that *plaisir* is the result of interpreting the *signifieds* of a text (the conventionally ascribed semiotic process) and that *jouissance* is produced largely from the engagement of the physical *signifiers* of the text. In literature, *jouissance* might be experienced as a reader taking pleasure in the sound of the words—especially poetry—regard-less of their meanings while *plaisir* might be experienced by the reader conjoin-ing those words with meaningful associations from a cultural context. *Jouissance* escapes the control of culture and of meaning by distancing the signified and thus foregrounding the signifier by enunciation of the text. Kristeva calls the process by which *jouissance* is obtained *signifiance*, where meaning is not derived from the symbolic, or culturally mediated world, but rather through the more primal semiotic world of the *chora* and recesses of the Freudian developmental phases.[3] Borrowing from Kristeva, Barthes (1988: 10) has written that *signifiance* arises "when the text is read (or written) as a moving play of signifiers, without any possible reference to one or some fixed signifieds." For Kristeva, *signifiance* is a process in the course of which the subject of the text escapes the logic of the *ego-cogito* and engages in other logics, struggles with meaning, and is decon-structed or lost. Semiotically, this is the realm of emotional or energetic inter-pretants abandoning the logical.[4]

Fiske (1989) has described pleasures in a way similar to Barthes, albeit in a more Marxist way. Fiske describes pleasures as twofold, but his categorizations are popular pleasures versus hegemonic ones, that is, pleasures that arise from social allegiances formed by subordinated people versus the pleasures of power to subjugate subordinates (or subjugate the self). With popular pleasures (such as television), there are two subcategories: productive pleasures and evasive plea-sures. Productive pleasures are of the mind; evasive pleasures, of the body. Fiske states that theorists on the left (Bakhtin and Barthes) tend to find positive values in the pleasures of the body while those on the right (Kant and Schopenhauer) find the body a source of false or inferior pleasure. The struggle over the mean-ings of the body and the validation of its pleasures is a power struggle in which class, gender, and race form completely intersecting axes (Fiske 1989: 50). Fiske demonstrated this political view of pleasure in the example of the romance novel, suggesting that an American housewife who buys a romance novel may derive pleasure from having her husband disapprove of her reading it (presumably as opposed to cooking, cleaning, etc.). Also, the act of reading is evasive: she loses herself in the book, thereby evading the ideology of an American middle-class conception of femininity that centers on family, not self. This loss is character-istic of *jouissance* and enables her to avoid the forces that subjugate her and in turn produces a sense of empowerment and an energy otherwise repressed (Fiske 1989: 55).

Fiske's dichotomy of productive versus evasive pleasures may be adapted to the roles television plays for the viewer. As has been discussed, television func-tions in various ways for various audiences: it may provide information (news, weather, educational programming), it may keep us company (voices and col-ored lights), it may entertain or provide escape from the pressures or realities of everyday life. "Entertain" may be taken to mean evading or escaping the hum-drum routine of everyday life, that is, to enter into an imaginary world of plea-sure. The informative side of television has been viewed by many as productive but the entertainment side as evasive, leading to value judgments that the infor-mative side is valuable and useful, whereas the evasive side is part of the banal or so-called vast wasteland of television.

Music as Gnostic/Drastic

So far, music has been viewed as a narrative agent and thus as a means of generat-ing and conveying meaning, one of the productive pleasures of music on televi-sion. Since its beginning, however, television has been filled with programs in which music carries no narrative meaning but rather is foregrounded as perfor-mance, that is, music qua music. Here I will consider music as a source of, as well as a conduit into, a different kind of televisual pleasure, escapist or evasive plea-sure. The use of music on TV defines some televisual genres, such as the musical variety show and the music video, but is vital also to popular genres like the comedy variety show and the talk show, where music is an essentially escapist or evasive form of pleasure, one focusing on the body/voice of the entertainer.

In arguing for a pleasure-centric study of music, Carolyn Abbate (2004), fol-lowing Vladimir Jankélévitch, has distinguished two types of musical experience: the "gnostic," or the disembodied abstraction that is the work, the intellectual, supra-audible, mediated (i.e., interpreted) meaning of music; and the "drastic," or the actually made and experienced sounding event—the sensuous, audible, immediate experience that has a powerful physical and spiritual (pleasurable) impact on the listener. For the television audience, the gnostic experience of music comes from viewing television music as a hermeneutic, narrative artifact subject to extramusical interpretation. In spite of its preeminent function as a narrative/commercial (and thus gnostic) agent, even television music exists in time essentially as a material acoustical phenomenon, and creating and listening to music is a drastic, physical experience: "Composing music, playing it, and singing it; or even hearing it in recreating it—are these not three modes of doing, three attitudes that are drastic, not gnostic, not of the hermeneutic order of knowledge?" (Jankélévitch 2003; quoted in Abbate 2004: 505). Listening to music, then, even television music, is a drastic experience with physical ties to bodily pleasure. As Gino Stefani (1987b: 23–24) has written, "a singing voice corresponds to the principle of pleasure, as the talking voice does to the principle of reality." Drawing upon psychophonic research he adds that the singing voice is thought of as "being continuous, flowing, relaxed and free from resistance…similar to the movement of flying. Flying and dreaming: the longing to escape, the pleasure of escape from harsh reality…musical melody becomes a symbol of the same profound things involved in the flying-dream." It is notable that most musical entertainers on television were, and still are, vocalists.[5]

Plaisir/Jouissance and Television Music

In addition to the tripartite narrative spaces of television (extradiegetic, intradiegetic, and diegetic), music on television can be considered within the duality of foreground versus background. Thus far, this book has dealt extensively with music as background, where music serves as reference or signifier for a television narrative or a sponsor's product. As background, music is primarily a text of *plaisir*, wherein the viewer derives pleasure from the interaction of the musical score and the narrative. A viewer derives pleasure from a hermeneutic interpretation of a well-crafted musical underscore that draws upon the semiotic conventions of narrative and televisual codes. This pleasure is cultural in origin and relies upon the viewer's competency of television/cinematic codes. The viewer finds pleasure in the support and signification music provides the narrative and how music builds suspense, portrays emotion, or denotes characters or commercial products. Viewers may take pleasure also in inventive, satiric, or ironic uses of music as played against established conventions. This type of pleasure is possible because of the viewer's familiarity with the codes of television production and broadcasting. The musical text of *plaisir* in television is thus a gnostic pleasure in which the listener derives pleasure from a hermeneutic reading of the music.

Television music also has the potential to be a drastic experience, to elicit *jouissance*, especially when music is foregrounded, that is, when it is the raison d'être of a TV program. While one can take pleasure in well-crafted background music, viewers might experience a more visceral experience while listening to Toscanini conduct the NBC Symphony Orchestra on television in the 1940s or Perry Como sing on the *Kraft Music Hall* of the 1950s or the Beatles perform on

175

The Ed Sullivan Show in 1964 or while watching/listening to a U2 video on MTV in the 1980s. This foregrounded music is heard as a play of signifiers, detached from culture, where listeners delight in the sounds produced by the artist and not the representational aspects that music may convey. These sensual, corporeal qualities, which tend to be escapist, are what make many viewers watch music programs on television. To paraphrase Barthes (1988), representational, culturally based television music can be called the "pheno-song" as a text of *plaisir*, where pleasure is derived from the listener's ability to tie the music to cultural signifiers, such as interpretation, performance practice, historical context, and so on. On the other side of the duality is the "geno-song," the foregrounded text of *jouissance*, where the listener is detached from the signified and revels only in the sound of the voice, the signifier. Such experiences of *jouissance* are common among listeners of music all over the world. One need only look around to notice closed-eyed audience members at an orchestra concert or head-banging rock aficionados listening to popular music on their Walkmans (then) and iPods (now).[6]

Finally, Barthes has attributed the genotextual appeal of music to the grain of a singer's voice, that particular combination of timbres, melodic shapes, chord progressions, and other aspects of musical performance that are pleasurable to the listener. Like Barthes and Abbate, Richard Middleton (1990) has summarized these dualities as "grain" versus "sense" in popular music, wherein music may signify through *plaisir* but acts as its own signifier in *jouissance*. This dialectic, also viewed as expression versus content, highlights two functions of music in television. Television music that is phenotextual or narrative-based conforms to preexisting narrative codes of film and television and enables an audience familiar with those codes to read the TV text and its music—thus becoming also a text of *plaisir*, the cultivated, culturally based form of pleasure. Music as music on TV, found in the musical variety show or music video, is genotextual, focusing on the grain of a particular artist's voice or instrument. While still adhering to certain televisual codes, it is closer to *jouissance*, or *signifiance*, of the grain of the voice. But is music on television capable of *jouissance*, the sort of visceral bliss described by Barthes? The remainder of the chapter investigates this possibility by focusing on the musical genres of the musical variety show, and what I call the sitcom minimusical.

The Grain of the Voice: Perry Como and Andy Williams

Hundreds of programs that foreground the grain of a musician's sound have aired on television through the musical variety show. This genre was instantly popular on television for both producers and audiences: for producers, it was a relatively inexpensive way to fill airtime, as musical shows did not need elaborate sets or writers to write scripts; for viewers, the musical variety show enabled them to see, in the comfort of their own living rooms, images of the musicians they had previously heard on the radio or seen on film in movie theaters or performing live in clubs. Moreover, the artists who were popular during the early years of television were those who adapted well from radio. Singers and other musicians who were sensitive to the technological limits of the radio and television microphones tended to be more successful than their live stage counterparts at making the transition.

The development of recorded sound and the microphone revolutionized the transmission of music for radio and sound film. Singers known as crooners supplanted the earlier generation of theatrical/opera singers because their softer, more intimate sound was well suited to the early TV microphone. By the early years of television, the transition was nearly complete.[7] Radio musicians including Tommy Dorsey (*Stage Show* [1954–1956]), Bing Crosby, Frank Sinatra, Perry Como (*The Perry Como Show/Perry Como's Kraft Music Hall* [1948–1963]), Dean Martin (*The Colgate Comedy Hour* [1950–1955], *Startime* [1959–1960], *The Dean Martin Show* [1965–1974]), Andy Williams (*The Andy Williams Show* [1962–1967]) all hosted a television musical variety show at one time or another.

Perhaps the first televisual superstar musician was Perry Como. Como began his professional singing career in the 1940s with the Ted Weems Band. After that band broke up, Como was offered the job of co-host with Jo Stafford on the NBC radio program *The Chesterfield Supper Club*. The program transferred to television in the late 1940s and launched Como's career as a TV star. In 1950, Como signed with CBS, where he hosted his own program for five seasons. In 1955 he went back to NBC and starred in the weekly *Perry Como Show*, later titled *Perry Como's Kraft Music Hall*. He remained with NBC until 1963. Como's singing style conformed to the easy-listening, popular musical genre of the time and influenced a generation of lounge singers. Como's style was conducive also to the popular Tin Pan Alley–era songs and Broadway show tunes that he covered well. Como was also noted for his Christmas specials, beginning with his first, on Christmas Eve 1948. After the show became *Perry Como's Kraft Musical Hall* it grew even more popular, largely due to Como's relaxed manner as host. He talked to members of the studio audience, eventually wore cardigan sweaters rather than suits, and sang in relaxed positions. The more intimate manner in which music was presented on Como's show was in sharp contrast to the spectacles of musical theater and the film musical, and for years to come it helped to define the more casual presentation of music on television.

Following Como's legacy was singer Andy Williams, who hosted one of the more successful musical variety shows on television, which ran from 1962 to 1971 on NBC. Like Como, Williams began as a childhood singer with his brothers in his Iowa hometown, later making his way to radio in Des Moines and eventually to Chicago and Cincinnati. The Williams Brothers eventually caught the attention of crooning king Bing Crosby, who included them on his mammoth 1944 hit single "Swinging on a Star." With Crosby's help, the Williams Brothers appeared in the film musicals *Janie* (1944), *Kansas City Kitty* (1944), *Something in the Wind* (1947), and *The Ladies' Man* (1947). In 1947 they joined singer-personality Kay Thompson's eclectic nightclub act and stayed with the popular show until it disbanded in 1951. Thereafter Andy was the only Williams brother who ventured out to the East Coast to seek a solo singing career (Brumburgh 2008).

Williams's career received a major boost when he was offered regular singing duties on Steve Allen's *Tonight* show (1953), a very early television talk show and predecessor to shows of the same name featuring Jack Paar (1957–1962), Johnny Carson (1962–1992), Jay Leno (1992–2009), and Conan O'Brien (2009–). His appearances on the program led to Williams's first recording contract, with Cadence Records in 1956, and his first album. In 1962, Williams made a lucrative label change to Columbia Records, which produced the pop hit "Can't Get Used to Losing You" and led to a project with Henry Mancini, which inspired Williams's signature song, "Moon River," Mancini's Oscar-winning tune from the popular Audrey Hepburn film *Breakfast at Tiffany's* (1961).

With his success as a recording artist, Williams was ready to host his own variety show, and *The Andy Williams Show* debuted in 1962. Williams's crooning style and easygoing demeanor (much like Como's) made him a natural in front of the TV camera, and his duets with such singing legends as Ella Fitzgerald, Judy Garland, Peggy Lee, and a host of others were popular with audiences at the time. The program was noted also for discovering new talent, including the Osmond Brothers, who went on to host their own television variety show in 1972. Before concluding its run in 1971, the show won three Emmy Awards for best musical/variety series and Williams himself picked up a couple of nominations as best performer.

Como's and Williams's programs were typical of musical variety shows in the 1950s and 1960s, respectively—shows that foregrounded music as sung by these performers along with their musical guest performers. Regular viewers liked the grain of these particular voices. However, whether or not these programs were drastic experiences for the audience—that is, whether or not the audience felt *jouissance* from listening to their singing—is difficult to measure. In fact, observing these programs and their production practices reveals that any potential *jouissance* emanating from a performer was highly restrained by the technical limitations of television. However, performers like Como and Williams also demonstrated an artistic restraint through their on-screen personas and their respective crooning styles, and this restraint seemed to resonate with TV audiences more than the more flamboyant performers. It may be that beginning in and continuing past the 1950s, television producers have felt the need to adhere to strict social mores and to the wishes of conservative corporate sponsors by not offending anyone with excessive displays of televisual pleasure. Thus, the history of musical performance on TV is full of examples of producers, and even

(a)

(b)

Figure 6.1. TV Mitigates against Musical Geno-songs, as Demonstrated in Performances by Perry Como (*A*) and Andy Williams (*B*) (Getty Images).

performers themselves, attempting to restrain excessive displays of musical *jouis-sance*. How TV mitigates against musical geno-songs can be seen in performances by Como and Williams (see figure 6.1). The performances of both entertainers show that their singing is pleasurable if highly restrained.

In a clip of his program from the mid-1950s, Como is dressed in coat and tie and stands in front of a curtain singing the song "Till the End of Time" (by Ted Mossman and Buddy Kaye) (figure 6.1a). Due to the tight camera shot, his gestures are limited to folding and unfolding his hands. Como occasionally makes eye contact with the camera, but he also looks away, presumably at cue cards with the lyrics of the song. His facial expression is pleasant but somewhat stoic, reflecting his image as a detached crooner. His soft, mellow voice is well suited to the microphone and is pleasurable to listen to, but his demeanor is stiff and detached, mitigating any sense of musical *jouissance*.

Williams's presence on camera approximately 10 years later is markedly different from Como's. Williams appears in a medium-long shot surrounded by dancers (figure 6.1b). He is casually dressed in a turtleneck sweater and slacks. As he sings he makes eye contact with and smiles at members of the live studio audience as well as the camera. His gestures are more animated but still limited mostly to his arms waving out to the side of his body. At the end of the song, he stretches out his arms, a convention used by many live singers as a song reaches toward crescendo.

Clearly, Williams demonstrates more pleasure, more *jouissance*, in his singing than Como does. This is partly due to each singer's stage persona: Como is known as the restrained, detached crooner with the velvety voice while Williams tends to exude more energy and appears more outgoing and emotive. However exuberant Williams may appear, though, he is still highly restrained, both by the presence of the dancers who take up a great deal of the mise-en-scène and by the limited frame of the camera—a frame he fills very well but cannot extend beyond.[8] Any pleasure conveyed by these two performers is highly mediated by the technical codes of television, including few camera angles as well as minimal costuming and stark stage settings. The viewer may well enjoy the grain of each singer's voice, but the small TV speakers of the time did not project the singer's true voice—another reason why microphone-friendly crooners tended to come across better than the big broad voices of theater.

Apparently, the American viewing audience enjoyed such programs in the early years of television, evidenced by their successful multiyear runs. But any pleasure of the text is highly restrained through the limitations of the camera and electronic reproduction of sound. Here, as in TV narrative, the audience must rely on verisimilitude, but in this instance it is a sort of audio verisimilitude, where they must imagine or "fill in" the grain of the artist's true voice from the electronically reproduced voice they actually hear. The result of such verisimilitude leads the viewer/listener from a potential *jouissance* to a culturally based and moderated, mediated *plaisir*, forced to imagine the sound not only of their favorite singers, but also of their favorite Tin Pan Alley and Broadway songs performed on these programs. *Perry Como's Kraft Music Hall* and *The Andy Williams Show*, along with dozens of other like programs in the 1950s and 1960s, provided phenotexts, or mild escapist pleasure for viewers, but not the genotexts of *jouissance* described by Barthes. Musical variety shows functioned as large-scale advertisements for these singers, encouraging viewers to derive even more musical pleasure (perhaps *jouissance*) by purchasing a record (and enjoying increased fidelity of sound on their hi-fi and nascent stereo phonograph) while they may only imagine a drastic musical experience by hearing the songs on television.

Restrained jouissance was not only in the provenance of the viewer. A musical program that exhibited a high degree of highly restrained *jouissance* from a musical perspective was *The Lawrence Welk Show* (figure 6.2). Born to immigrant

Figure 6.2. Lawrence Welk (The Wisconsin Center for Film and Theater Research).

parents in North Dakota and raised on a farm, Welk began his life as a musician when his father bought him a $400 mail-order accordion. Welk played with several bands in nearby Aberdeen, South Dakota, and eventually toured with the vaudeville troupe the Peerless Entertainers. His experience in vaudeville was valuable, as he learned the merits of variety and versatility—elements that later helped him succeed on television. After the group broke up in 1927, Welk and three other former members managed to line up a 30-minute radio broadcast on WNAX in Aberdeen. Listener response was tremendous, and he was offered a one-week contract, which ended up stretching out to three years. After leaving the station (where he also served as station manager), Welk toured the Northern Plains states with his own big band, later returning to WNAX for another three-year engagement. In 1940 Welk began a nine-year association with the Trianon Ballroom in Chicago and afterward returned to touring the country.

Welk's television career began in 1951. While traveling from northern California to a date in Texas, Welk stopped to visit the manager of the Aragon Ballroom in Los Angeles. The ballroom was then on hard times and Welk offered to skip his Texas engagement and play at the Aragon for four weeks at union scale and a 50-50 split of the gate. The local television station (KTLA) had been broadcasting a weekly program from the ballroom for some time, and Welk's band was immediately successful on the show, and the station committed to the full four weeks. After fulfilling his commitments on the road, Welk returned to the Aragon, where he continued to broadcast his show for 10 years, until 1961, when he moved to the Hollywood Palladium. The local program was picked up by the ABC network in 1955 and in the early years was known as *The Dodge Dancing Party*. It became one of the top-rated programs on the network until it was canceled in 1970, not because of sagging popularity but because sponsors considered it too old-fashioned. The cancellation did not faze Welk, who continued producing the program in syndication for 11 more years. Yet another syndicated retrospective version is still being broadcast on PBS stations, and a stage version also continues to this day at the Welk Resort Center and Champagne Theatre in Branson, Missouri.

The Lawrence Welk Show consisted of a variety of songs played by Welk's band and sung by different singers, with each scene having sets and costumes befitting the mood of the song. The show also featured dance numbers in which Welk and members of the cast danced with people in the live studio audience. Like the musical variety programs hosted by Como and Williams, *The Lawrence Welk Show* exemplified the restrained *jouissance* of television music. On the air for 27 years (1955–1982), the show's success has been attributed by most critics to its easy-listening format, what Welk himself referred to as "champagne music," and to its stable ("family") of wholesome musicians, singers, and dancers. Although

Welk was never considered to be one of the great big band leaders of the era, his show enjoyed unparalleled longevity because of its light, nonoffensive ethos and Welk's skill at providing his audiences with what they wanted, a restrained *jouissance* characteristic of music on television.

These early musical variety shows were derivatives of radio and, as such, took on many of the characteristics of their radio predecessors. Perry Como's early unease in front of the camera as well as Welk's wooden posture were tell-tale signs that each was more comfortable in a sound world than a visual world (though prior to his television show, Welk was a band leader who each week had performed in front of live audiences). Andy Williams's more relaxed demeanor in the 1970s is evidence of television musicians becoming more comfortable in front of the camera as the decades progressed. Williams's more emotive performance was nonetheless mitigated by the fact that the television was an appliance in the home and that any *jouissance* of performance would be restrained.

Other Evasive Pleasures: (Almost) Escaping Racism/Sexism in Television

The genotextual escapism of television music in the early years was constrained by TV broadcasting and production practices as well as the artists themselves. Moreover, programs were subject to popular ratings dictated by the mores of the American television public and corporate sponsors. These demo/sociographic factors led to additional constraints on who performed on American television in the 1950s and 1960s. These cultural constraints were especially evident with regard to race and gender. The overwhelming majority of musical entertainers on early television were white and male (the big stars including Bing Crosby, Perry Como, Andy Williams, Dean Martin, and Danny Kaye). Yet several African American entertainers, in spite of overwhelming odds, did advance to the small screen. Nat "King" Cole, Louis Armstrong, Lena Horne, Johnny Mathis, Sammy Davis Jr., and Harry Belafonte were popular TV personas in the 1960s, making regular appearances on the big variety shows, including Ed Sullivan's *Toast of the Town* (1948–1971), *The Colgate Comedy Hour* (1950–1955), *The Tonight Show* (1953–), *Rowan and Martin's Laugh-In* (1968–1973), *The Hollywood Palace* (1964–1970), *The Mike Douglas Show* (1961–1982), and *The Dick Cavett Show* (1968–1972). Only Nat "King" Cole, however, attempted to produce and host his own program.[9]

The *Nat King Cole Show* aired on television in November 1956, just as the postwar American civil rights movement was getting organized. The show originally aired without a sponsor, but NBC agreed to pay for initial production costs, assuming that once advertisers saw the show and its sophisticated production values a national sponsor would emerge. A sponsor was never found, however, reportedly because many national companies did not want to upset their white customers in the South. In the 1956 season, the show ran for 15 minutes; the segment was expanded to 30 minutes in 1957. Although NBC agreed to fund the show until a sponsor could be found, Cole, disappointed with ratings and the lack of sponsorship, canceled the show himself in its second season.[10] He was quoted as saying of the doomed series, "Madison Avenue is afraid of the dark." Eartha Kitt, one of the show's featured guest stars, was quoted years later as saying, "I think it was too early to show ourselves off as intelligent people," referring to the stereotypical portrayal of blacks as inferior on such programs as *The Amos 'n' Andy Show*, *The Beulah Show*, and *The Jack Benny Program*, the last of which featured Eddie Anderson playing Benny's manservant, Rochester (Watson n.d.). It was not until 1966 that another African American artist, singer/dancer Sammy Davis Jr., hosted a musical comedy (*The Sammy Davis Jr. Show*). The show was a midseason replacement and ran only 15 episodes. The female singer Leslie Uggams fared better a few years later, when she hosted a musical comedy variety series on American television, *The Leslie Uggams Show* in 1969.[11]

Cole's program was indeed sophisticated in comparison to similar programs of the era. Like Como, Cole exuded a benign, soft-spoken persona onstage. He sang the requisite Broadway and Tin Pan Alley tunes, but the show was innovative in that it featured Cole not just as a crooner but also in his original role as jazz pianist, playing and singing with jazz notables Oscar Peterson, Ella Fitzgerald, Peggy Lee, and Mel Tormé as well as singers Pearl Bailey, Mahalia Jackson, Sammy Davis Jr., Tony Bennett, and Harry Belafonte. Despite the high caliber of music on the program, the race barrier was apparently too great to overcome in 1956 (Castleman and Podrazik 1982: 120–121).

Female artists fared no better than their male African American counterparts in early television. Of the many female singers who were active at the time (Lena Horne, Rosemary Clooney, Judy Garland, Ethel Merman, Kate Smith, Kay Starr, and numerous others), the only woman singers to host their own TV shows in the early years of TV were Dinah Shore and Judy Garland. Shore was a former big band performer who began her career as a vocalist with Xavier Cugat's orchestra in the 1930s and 1940s. In 1950 she made a guest appearance on Bob Hope's first NBC television special and was later signed to do a weekly show. It premiered in 1951 as *The Dinah Shore Show*. After Chevrolet picked up sponsorship in 1956, the name was changed to *Dinah Shore's Chevy Show*. It was assigned a Sunday evening time slot, where it ran for the next five years. Like Perry Como, Shore succeeded largely through her conservative vocal choices and middlebrow sensibilities. She was noted for her famed signature theme song, the catchy Chevrolet jingle, "See the USA in Your Chevrolet," accompanied by her closing gesture of a sweeping smooch to the audience. After *Dinah Shore's Chevy Show* ended, she went on to host three daytime television programs, *Dinah's Place* (1970 to 1974), the 90-minute talk show *Dinah!* (1974 to 1980), and *Dinah and Friends* (1979 to 1984). Her last television program, *A Conversation with Dinah*, aired in 1991 on cable TV's the Nashville Network. Shore died in 1994.

The Judy Garland Show did not fare as well as Shore's, and was canceled after only one season. In spite of her superstar status and immense popularity with fans, Garland's show ran into production problems (including the turnover of three producers in the 26 episodes of the series), a rocky relationship with the CBS network, and a time slot that ran against the popular western *Bonanza*, on NBC.

The evasive pleasures derived from watching these African American and female artists on television were mitigated by limitations placed on them by producers. NBC took a chance on Nat "King" Cole, but he was never able to find a sponsor. Shore achieved greater success on television, winning Emmy Awards for best female singer (1954–1955), best female personality (1956–1957), and best actress in a musical or variety series (1959). However, *Dinah Shore's Chevy Show* rarely entered the top 20 ratings, in part because it was on against CBS's *General Electric Theater* hosted by Ronald Reagan, which regularly won the Sunday time slot (Reagan also had a better lead-in with *The Ed Sullivan Show*). Garland, too, was nominated for four Emmys, but these were for her 1962 television special, and not her series in 1963–1964.

So, although black and women artists were viewed by American audiences on television, their exposure was highly restrained, an evasive pleasure dominated by a hegemonic one in which minority and women performers were passed over for white male hosts. For whatever reason, American television audiences in the 1950s and 1960s were complacent with the restrained phenotexts of white male performers. These mores would change in the 1960s and beyond with the advent of more programs starring African American and female hosts.

From Music-on-Television to Music Television

As the era of Tin Pan Alley crooners waned in the 1960s, it was supplanted by the era of rock 'n' roll, and television programming slowly, but eventually, followed the trend. Elvis Presley may be seen as inaugurating the era of rock on TV. In 1956, Elvis made his network television debut with the first of six appearances on *Stage Show*, a weekly variety program produced by Jackie Gleason and hosted by

Tommy and Jimmy Dorsey, two big band legends from the 1930s and 1940s. Presley followed these with two appearances on *The Milton Berle Show*, the second of which included a performance of "Hound Dog" that was so provocative for the times that it caused a national scandal. According to Marc Weingarten (2000: 28), the performance was a far cry from any that had been seen on TV to date:.

> The attire was a bit more casual this time—checked jacket and a mildly radical two-tone shirt—and so was the performance. With the band bashing out a suitably gutbucket arrangement unsweetened by Harry James's arrangements, Elvis worked the crowd masterfully—punctuating lines with a firm grasp of the mike stand, then engaging in a crowd-pleasing stunt straight out of *Minsky's Burlesque*.
>
> Elvis's second Berle appearance was unlike anything he had previously attempted on television—an uninhibited, no-holds-barred showstopper that radiated considerable sexual heat. Even today, the "Hound Dog" performance looks a little dangerous—you can almost picture the nervous suits at NBC's standards and practices department with their twitchy fingers on the "Please Stand By" button.

Presley's appearance on Berle's show as well as *The Steve Allen Show* led to multiple appearances on *The Ed Sullivan Show*.[12] When Elvis made his third appearance in January of 1957, Ed Sullivan surprised Elvis by telling him on camera that his show had never had a better experience with a name act, and he said, "I wanted to say to Elvis and the country that this is a real decent, fine boy."[13] It was on this very same Sullivan appearance that Elvis was shown on camera from the waist up only, one of early television history's most memorable moments.

Gleason, Allen, and (initially) Sullivan all wanted nothing to do with Presley, viewing him as a vulgar hayseed. Yet Sullivan recognized the popularity that Presley generated and had him on the show numerous times. Unlike the on-camera performances of Como and Williams, Presley's seemed to convey Barthesian *jouissance*, the sensual losing of one's self in the grain of Presley's voice. This *jouissance* is, arguably, a trait of rock 'n' roll and one that always made television producers of the 1950s through the 1970s uncomfortable. TV ignored rock at first, later came to tolerate it, then sought to tame it (see chapter 8), and finally embraced it in the 1980s by creating the MTV generation.

Presley was not the only performer to blaze the trail for rock 'n' roll on television. *American Bandstand* premiered on October 6, 1952, long before the Elvis phenomenon. The show was originally hosted by disc jockeys Lee Stewart and Bob Horn as a local music show in Philadelphia. In 1956, after a scandal had resulted in the firing of both DJs, Dick Clark was hired as host. Under Clark's tutelage, the program's popularity grew, it was bought by ABC, and ran nationally for 31 seasons. As Weingarten (2000: 41) has written, "From 1957 to 1980—before MTV and cable—every sea change in rock style was transmitted to million of kids through *Bandstand*." Although the show introduced millions of American teenagers to new trends in music, dance, and fashion, it never conveyed the energy or *jouissance* of Elvis's performances. Most of the artists who appeared on *Bandstand* lip-synched to their current hit records in a casual button-down way while teenagers danced unobtrusively around them.

In the 1960s, other television programs followed *Bandstand*'s lead. One such show was *Shindig* (1964–1966), a rock variety show broadcast on ABC and hosted by DJ Jimmy O'Neill. The program, which debuted on September 16, 1964, featured all sorts of performers who were popular at the time, from R & B artists to soul divas to folk singers. The program was produced in a progressive visual style with stage lighting schemes that changed in midsong and continuous

Figure 6.3. The Blossoms on *Shindig* circa 1964
(The Wisconsin Center for Film and Theater Research).

jump cuts that coincided with chord changes and lyrics. The show also featured a house band, The Shindogs, and The Shindiggers, a troupe of female go-go dancers, and regular appearances by the Blossoms, Phil Spector's favorite backup group (figure 6.3).

In 1965, NBC countered with *Hullaballoo* (1965–1966), a similar but somewhat more restrained show hosted by mainstream (by Hollywood standards) pop celebrities, such as Frankie Avalon and Annette Funicello. Meanwhile, *American Bandstand* faced competition from *The Lloyd Thaxton Show* (1961–1968), half of which was about current pop hits and half of which was a humorous lampoon on the rock dance show format featuring lip-synching contests between members of the studio audience. Finally the original *Soul Train* debuted on the airwaves in 1971 as a *Bandstand* type show that featured black artists. By that time, rock artists had found their way on to musical variety shows that had once been the exclusive domain of crooners. Rock musicians first appeared on such musical variety programs as the *Tonight Show* and *The Hollywood Palace* in the late 1960s. New variety shows were soon developed to showcase this new generation of musical talent. Comedy shows like *Rowan and Martin's Laugh-In* (1968–1973) as well as *The Smothers Brothers Show* (1967–1970) and *The Sonny and Cher Comedy Hour* (1971–1974) regularly hosted rock performers. NBC's *Saturday Night Live*, which began in 1975 and continues to this day, features a rock band every week, and late-night talk shows, such as *The Late Show with David Letterman, Late Night with Conan O'Brien,* and *The Tonight Show with Jay Leno* (and now *The Tonight Show with Conan O'Brien*), often feature rock groups. Indeed, the era of the music video can be traced to these early musical variety shows where music is foregrounded.

The popularity of rock music and situation comedies in the 1960s resulted in a new concept for music on television in 1966. Spurred by the popularity of the Beatles, who had their own historic American debut on *The Ed Sullivan Show* on February 9, 1964, and movie box office successes in *A Hard Day's Night* (1964) and *Help!* (1965), NBC executives developed a show that would piggyback on the success of the British invasion. Two Hollywood insiders, Bert Schneider and Bob Rafelson, sought to create a group of made-for-TV Beatles who could sell records and also have teen pinup appeal. Schneider and Rafelson conceived of an unconventional weekly situation comedy format influenced by the Beatles movies and British TV commercials and characterized by rapid-fire pacing and arch visual allusions. The producers hired four charismatic and photogenic actors (only one of whom was an actual musician) through a casting call ad in *Daily Variety*, and *The Monkees* was born.

The Monkees has been viewed as the television industry's jaded and cynical view of pop music. Only one member of the Monkees was a practicing musician (Michael Nesmith), while the others (Mickey Dolenz, Davy Jones, Peter Tork) were good-looking actors to front the show. The songs performed were composed mostly by hired songwriters Tommy Boyce and Bobby Hart. Indeed the history of the show is fraught with conflict between the Hollywood imaginary and the real—complete with the band members' struggle to achieve artistic legitimacy. The artistic integrity of the performers notwithstanding, *The Monkees* may be viewed as a different direction for musical expression in television music. Like *Shindig*, the program conveys a sort of *jouissance de technologie*, not through the artists losing themselves in the music à la Elvis or through the mass hysteria of fans, but rather through the play of signifiers of the technical apparatus accompanying the music that the Monkees performed. Each episode of *The Monkees* was rife with disjunct narratives, rapid jump cuts, and a bricolage of visual styles that included silent movie intertitle placards, fast-motion action sequences, and scenes of unrelated vignettes leapfrogging over one another in a seemingly arbitrary pattern. As Weingarten states: "It was Schneider and Rafelson's intention to infuse American network television with a jolt of the formal experimentation that could be found in films like Michelangelo Antonioni's *Blowup* and John Schlesinger's *Darling*" (Weingarten 2000: 114). *Jouissance* does not come from the artists or the fans, but from the producer and director who use bricolage and collage techniques borrowed from art films of the 1960s.

The Monkees demonstrates yet another distinctive type of television music. When Elvis and the Beatles appeared on variety shows, they always performed live (diegetically). In contrast, when the Monkees performed their weekly song on their show, they appeared to be singing diegetically, but the jump cuts and interpolated and unrelated action scenes progressed without any variation in the song's performance. So, is their music diegetic, intradiegetic, or extradiegetic? In some scenes the performers are seen singing and playing, but in others they are seen running, jumping, or doing other things while the music plays on without them. The music thus takes on another dimension of performance, similar to that of the film musical—a type of music called supradiegetic.[14] Supradiegetic music transcends the live performance of the diegetic but functions differently from the intradiegetic. In its imitation of the film musical, *The Monkees* can be seen as attempting to create televisual genotexts.

By defining and building a television audience for rock music, programs like *Bandstand*, *Shindig*, and *Hullaballoo* paved the way for the premiere of Music TV (MTV) in 1981. This audience was boosted by rock artists appearing on variety shows like *The Ed Sullivan Show* and later on talk shows such as *The Tonight Show* and especially by their prominent role on *Saturday Night Live*. With the advent of cable television and the fragmentation of the television audience, MTV was positioned to present the new concept of the music video, which depicted performing artists lip-synching to a prerecorded music track while video producers indulged in their own videographic *jouissance*. Such video production values can also be traced back to the cinematic soundies of the 1930s and 1940s to the art films of the 1960s and also (and somewhat more modestly) to the program *The Monkees*.

The Television Minimusical

Cinematic *Jouissance: Singin' in the Rain* (1953)

The production codes for *The Monkees* illustrate yet again television's willingness to borrow from other media for its own expression. While the visual collages of the show foreground the influence of art film, the songs performed during the show borrowed from the Beatles feature films specifically but also from the genre of the film musical generally. Rick Altman (1987a: 62–63) has considered in great detail the relationship between music and sound in the film musical, defining three categories of sound: the diegetic track, or the "realistic" causal relationship of sound and image; the music track, the off-screen music that is common to nonmusical narrative film (what I have called intradiegetic music), and diegetic music, that is, music sung on the screen but postsynchronized in the sound studio. In describing diegetic music, Altman calls attention to the process of transitioning film sound from synchronous to postsynchronous through what he calls the "audio dissolve." The audio dissolve is a key feature of the film musical in that it not only demonstrates the transitioning of production values of synchronous to postsynchronous sound but also functions in two ways that affect the narrative. First, the diegetic musical number in audio dissolve temporarily suspends the narrative just as the musical number or opera aria suspends narrative in the stage musical and opera, respectively. This narrative suspension results in a sort of narrative netherworld wherein music and dance transport images and sound to a sort of fantasy-like state similar to a dream, the state Altman calls "supradiegetic" music.

A second, and contrasting perspective of supradiegetic music was offered by Patricia Mellencamp (1977), who described the musical number in a film musical as a "spectacle" that, though placed at the service of the spectator, does not carry the viewer into a realm of narrative fantasy but actually brings the narrative into the "here and now" of the audience. For example, when viewers see Gene Kelly singing and dancing to the theme song in the famous scene of the film *Singin' in the Rain* (1953), they are watching Gene Kelly the superstar of the 1950s and not Don Lockwood, the character he portrays. Moreover, viewers today are probably as drawn to watching the film as audiences were in 1952 because it *is* Gene Kelly on-screen and not an unknown actor. Thus Kelly's celebrity subverts the story of the film with the discourse of the visual. Similarly, supradiegetic music subverts narrative for escape or evasion, wherein the narrative pauses so that viewers can hear the grain of the actor's voice. It is a point at which phenotext gives way to genotext. In fact, it is a filmic representation of *signifiance*, wherein the narrative *plaisir*, or culturally based enjoyment of the text's social conventions, dissolves into *jouissance*, the pleasure that shatters, dissipates, and lets loose that cultural identity. Kelly's *dance de jouissance* calls attention to the autoerotic: both his body and feet are in focus and soaked with rain; he dances suggestively with his umbrella, hugs the lamppost, and tips his hat at the store window display of a busty woman wearing a swimsuit and flanked by obelisks, not to mention the way he stomps through puddles in the street. The audio dissolve music violates cinematic verisimilitude, its *plaisir*—viewers do not see the orchestra, and Kelly's dancing and gestures are exaggerated and implicitly sexual (as the scowl of the police officer at the end of the scene indicates). The narrative is temporarily lost, ruptured, and dissipated in expressive *jouissance*. Viewers watch and listen to Kelly as spectacle (after Mellencamp) but also experience the disruption of the narrative trajectory of the film through the unfettered display of the human body and voice.

The TV Minimusical and Desilu Studios: *I Love Lucy*

Early in television's history, the conception and formation of new types of television programs perhaps unwittingly borrowed production techniques not only from film but also from the genre of the film musical. The situation comedy was one of those genres that drew upon the conventions of the film musical. The program *I Love Lucy* (1951–1957) established many of the characteristics of the situation comedy but also exhibited traits of film musicals by casting Desi Arnaz as Lucille Ball's husband as well as a bandleader whose group appeared regularly on the program (figure 6.4). With this built-in musical apparatus, the show exploited not only Ball's comedic talents but also Arnaz's musical talents—and the grain of his voice. Music was a regular feature of the show but somehow always related to the story line. Arnaz's TV music never reached the status of genotext as Gene Kelly's performances did on film. The grounding of music within the narrative anchored the show as phenotext, wherein music serves at the pleasure of the narrative in a sort of *plaisir* mitigating against visceral *jouissance*.

As was discussed earlier, *I Love Lucy* was the brainchild of Desi Arnaz and Lucille Ball, the husband-and-wife stars of Hollywood B movies. Lucille Ball had come into her own as a film actress by the mid-1940s and was a costar in

Figure 6.4. Lucille Ball and Desi Arnaz (The Wisconsin
Center for Film and Theater Research).

the hit radio comedy show *My Favorite Husband*, and believed a television adaptation of the radio show would be successful. One of the song and dance routines that Lucy and Desi performed during the touring stage show that they used to drum up publicity for the new TV show was a revival of Norman Henderson's "Cuban Pete," from Arnaz's 1946 film of the same title with Ethel Smith. The lyrics to the song were rewritten to include a stanza by "Sally Sweet," which featured one of Ball's comic personas, the "floozy." The number was very popular with audiences and was recycled for the TV show later.

The first episode of *I Love Lucy* premiered in October 1951. The situation of the comedy was the story of a Cuban immigrant bandleader, Ricky Ricardo, and his stay-at-home wife, Lucy. The story lines centered on Lucy's antics and the inevitable fallout that resulted. One of the continuing story lines of the program was Lucy's ambition to break into show business and her comically bad attempts at singing and dancing that continually met with Ricky's disapproval.

Indeed, Lucy's failures in this area reflect the dominant ideology of America in the 1950s, when women were expected to be stay-at-home moms. Yet despite the shortcomings of both characters—Lucy's ineptitude and Ricky's short temper—most programs ended with a reconciliation between the two.

Along with Ball's comedic talents as Lucy, the program featured Arnaz's realizations of Ricky's bandleader persona, with Desi singing onstage at the Tropicana, his fictional New York nightclub, accompanied by the onstage Desi Arnaz Orchestra (conducted by CBS composer/conductor Wilbur Hatch). As a bandleader, Arnaz was expected to sing and dance on the program, but the writers and director Jess Oppenheimer decided he should do so only if it furthered the story line. The result was many fine musical numbers featuring Ball and Arnaz, all in some way tied to the plot. As in the show film musicals of the 1930s, Ricky's nightclub and big band acts were always part of the mise-en-scène with the band playing live as the show was filmed on a Desilu sound stage. Such presentations usually began with Arnaz singing a popular song and Lucy subsequently crashing the performance with an inept singing and/or dancing performance. In one episode, however, Ball and Arnaz film their famous "Cuban Pete" number from the vaudeville show, and Lucy does a comic rendition of the song in her "Sally Sweet" persona, a performance that Ricky actually supports.

The "Cuban Pete" musical number is actually the culmination of the story line. Ricky grants Lucy permission to perform in the number for his nightclub act but only if she loses enough weight to fit into the costume, which is designed to fit another actress. Through much effort, Lucy loses the weight and subdues the other actress, locking her in a broom closet at the nightclub. She performs the number admirably but is so malnourished at the end that she is taken to the hospital. The epilogue to the episode shows Lucy on a stretcher talking to her friend and confidant, Ethel Mertz (Vivian Vance). As she is taken to the hospital, Lucy gestures for Ethel to open a nearby closet door, where the actual dancer for the Cuban Pete number is bound and gagged.

Sensibilities of the 1950s aside, the musical number is placed in the realm of diegetic music but as musical phenotext. The number is entertaining (Lucy and Desi are seen and heard onscreen) but does not really transport the narrative into a supradiegetic realm; in fact, it is the culmination of the episode. Rather than suspending the narrative in a fantasy-like genotext, as with Kelly's number in *Singin' in the Rain*, the "Cuban Pete" number is narrative phenotext, resolving the story line.

The success of *I Love Lucy* led to the creation of Desilu studios, founded and jointly run by Ball and Arnaz for almost two decades. The studio would create and produce many television programs of different genres, but the minimusical formula was behind some of the most memorable. Other Desilu programs used music the same way—as diegetic pheno-songs rather then supradiegetic geno-songs.

Reflexive TV: *The Dick Van Dyke Show*

Another Desilu sitcom that occasionally became a minimusical is *The Dick Van Dyke Show*, which aired from 1961 to 1965, with reruns in syndication virtually ever since. The show was the brainchild of writer-comedian Carl Reiner, who conceived of the comedy show as a satire of his experiences as writer and player on Sid Caesar's real-life *Your Show of Shows* (1950–1954). Van Dyke plays Rob Petrie, the head writer for the "Alan Brady Show" (Brady was portrayed by Reiner himself), a musical comedy variety show based in New York City. Episodes of the program alternated between Petrie's professional life at the office with his writing staff (played by vaudevillians Morey Amsterdam and Rose Marie, the latter of whom gained a modicum of fame as a childhood singing star in Warner Bros. film soundies), and his home life with his wife Laura (a very young Mary Tyler Moore), son, Ritchie (child actor Larry Mathews), and various neighbors. Because of Van Dyke's talent as a Broadway star and Moore's singing and dancing ability, the program regularly used them in musical numbers. Like *I Love Lucy*, when musical numbers were used on an episode, they were usually integrated into the plot as a show–within–a–show format. Either the writers were performing themselves or were auditioning a new talent for the Alan Brady show.

One notable musical scene is part of an episode in which the writing staff is rehearsing with a young Vic Damone for his appearance on the "Alan Brady Show." Damone portrays a young, up-and-coming star (as he actually was in the 1960s), and his good looks arouse the attention of co-writer Sally Rogers (Marie). The scene opens with an establishing scene of the door of the writers' office with piano music playing inside. A cut then shows Damone singing Rogers and Hart's song "The Most Beautiful Girl in the World," complete with the show's music composer Earle Hagen's big band arrangement. Damone's performance is postsynchronized (or perhaps presynchronized), and unlike Desi Arnaz's performance in *I Love Lucy*, the viewer does not see the band but rather Van Dyke and Rose Marie pantomiming playing the spinet piano in their office, with Van Dyke and Marie awkwardly trading off playing as Marie dances with Damone. The piano anchors the musical number in the diegesis, lending at least a degree of realism, and the song is also a calculated narrative device to enhance Damone's voice and physical appeal to Sally Rogers (Marie), the perennial bachelorette looking for a husband. The musical number seeks to enhance the narrative: through music we hope that Sally and Damone will unite as a couple. However, like the film musical, the number also interrupts the narrative trajectory. The piano is not a convincing anchor for Hagen's arrangement, and the addition of postsynchronized, canned applause at the end of the song lends an aura of a live (diegetic) performance, which pulls the piece even farther away from the writers' office and also away from a supradiegetic realm of escapist fantasy. The episode becomes a virtual variety show—on film with an imaginary studio audience.

Other episodes of the *Dick Van Dyke Show* utilized music to a great extent, most often in formats where the team of writers performed in various venues (in Rob and Laura's house, in nightclubs, in flashbacks to Rob's days in the army, or even on the "Alan Brady Show" itself). Some musical episodes poked fun at current musical trends, such as episode 24, in which Randy Eisenbauer portrayed a Chubby Checker–like singer performing the Twizzle, a spoof on

Figure 6.5. "I Am a Fine Musician" number from *The Dick Van Dyke Show*. From left: Mary Tyler Moore, Dick Van Dyke, Morey Amsterdam, and Rose Marie (The Wisconsin Center for Film and Theater Research).

the Twist, the contemporary dance craze. A later episode featured the real-life singing duo of Chad and Jeremy as part of the British invasion craze. Some episodes, however, featured music in a more fantastic realm. In one such episode during the first season, the Cole Porter song "You're the Top" was featured as part of a dream sequence in which Rob, while asleep on an airplane, feels guilty about being absent for his son's school musical. The episode makes it clear though that the fantastic sequence is *only* a dream. Yet another example of live performance occurred during the third season, in the episode called "The Alan Brady Show Presents," in which characters Rob, Buddy, Sally, and Laura present a Christmas show in which they sing and dance à la Broadway, presumably to be aired on television as part of "The Alan Brady Show." One particularly fine number in the episode featured the four actors in band uniforms singing "I Am a Fine Musician" and pantomiming performing musical band instruments: piccolo, trombone, tuba, and trumpet (figure 6.5).

In spite of the musical talent and Hagen's masterful jazz arrangements, music on the show was restrained to the phenotextual show-within-a-show format. Van Dyke's and Moore's singing and dancing talents were assets to the program, but they always took a back seat to the comedic situation narrative.

"That's Gooood Music": *The Andy Griffith Show*

Another Desilu sitcom that on occasion became a minimusical is *The Andy Griffith Show*, which ran on CBS from 1960 to 1968. The program starred Andrew (Andy) Griffith, at the time an emerging Broadway and film star from North Carolina. After graduating with a degree in music from the University of North Carolina, Griffith found his way first into regional theater and, later, the Broadway stage. Griffith was engaged by Desilu Studios after a successful Broadway run in the play *No Time for Sergeants*, which was made into a film in 1958. After acting in a Broadway version of *Destry*, Griffith told his agent at the William Morris Agency that he was ready to try roles in television. Coincidentally, at that same time, producer Sheldon Leonard was considering making an episode of *The Danny Thomas Show* that would feature a small-town sheriff. He met Griffith, and the two hit it off. The pilot, featuring Thomas speeding through a small southern town and Griffith arresting him, was successful enough for Thomas and Leonard to produce *The Andy Griffith Show* as a series.[15]

Leonard decided to fill the series with characters that would fit in with Griffith's rural style of humor. The show was set in the town of Mayberry, which was modeled after Griffith's hometown of Mount Airy, and featured stories related to Griffith's actual hometown experiences. Griffith portrays Sheriff Andy Taylor, very possibly fashioned after Mount Airy's sheriff at the time, Sam Patterson. Griffith even took the name of an early music group he sang with and incorporated it into the show. The Darlings were transformed from an actual folk singing group to a fictional backwoods family of musicians portrayed by the actual bluegrass group, the Dillards.

The Andy Griffith Show had narrative reasons for foregrounding music, as Sheriff Taylor often strummed his guitar on the front porch of his home or sang hymns in church on Sunday morning or joined the community choir with this sidekick, Deputy Barney Fife (Don Knotts). Also, like the *Dick Van Dyke Show*, some episodes contained talent search story lines in which new singers were discovered. The most famous of these is perhaps Jim Nabors, who played the naive but lovable Gomer Pyle character and who occasionally sang on the program—thus launching his career as a singer. However, perhaps the most imaginative use of music on the program was the perennial appearance of The Darlings, the backwoods family led by the father, Briscoe (Denver Pyle), and Charlene, the love-infatuated daughter (Margaret Ann Peterson). The "boys" of the family were the members of the actual popular bluegrass revival group the Dillards. According to one account of the program (Kelly 1981: 51–52), Griffith enjoyed bluegrass music and personally arranged to have the Dillards on the show "to provide an atmosphere of genuine country music." The Dillards were perhaps the most popular bluegrass group of the early 1960s, their performances infusing old bluegrass standards with folk and even rock elements and adding instrumental virtuosity. Their first appearance on *The Andy Griffith Show* was in March 1963 in an episode in which they had limited exposure (and did not even play a complete song).

In the "Mountain Wedding" episode that aired on April 29, 1963, however, the Dillards appeared and performed several pieces (figure 6.6). The episode centered around the Darling family visiting Mayberry and seeking advice from the sheriff on how to rid themselves of a neighboring pest, Ernest T. Bass (Howard Morris), who had affections for Charlene Darling. While "staking out" Ernest T. in the Darling cabin, Andy suggests that the family play the folk standard "Dooley," one of the Dillards' signature pieces. The song effectively pauses the narrative and highlights the talents of the Dillards while never leaving the diegesis of the Darlings' cabin in the mountains.

The Darlings also sing other numbers diegetically during the episode, including the 1888 protestant hymn "Leaning on the Everlasting Arms" (music by Anthony Showalter) during the wedding ceremony between Charlene and her fiancée, Dudley "Dud" Wash (Hoke Howell).[16]

The *Andy Griffith* example is unique in several respects. First, the music played by the Dillards is not the standard Tin Pan Alley fare of the *Lucy* and *Van Dyke* offerings but, rather, bluegrass, folk, or country standards. Second, the appearance

Figure 6.6. The Darlings (the Dillards) from *The Andy Griffith Show*. From left: Dean Webb (mandolin), Doug Dillard (banjo), Rodney Dillard (guitar).

of the Darlings is not really a show-within-a-show. Even though the Dillards were actual professional musicians, they are not portrayed as such on the program, but instead as a hillbilly family. To compensate for these televisual variances (and possibly to avoid conflicts between the actors' and musicians' unions), the Darlings (or at least the Dillards portion of the Darlings) are portrayed on-screen as almost purely musical beings; they speak no lines, relying on their father to speak for them. The boys (Rodney and Doug Dillard, Mitch Jayne, and Dean Webb) are always carrying their instruments—banjo, mandolin, guitar, and bass—around with them. And right before they are about to perform a song, the viewing audience is usually cued into it by the banter of the actors. Before one musical number, for example, Briscoe makes the proclamation, "If you have time to breathe, you have time for music," and the boys are asked to play songs with humorous faux titles, such as "Don't Hit Your Grandma with a Great Big Stick." Indeed, the Darlings' portrayal on *The Andy Griffith Show* is akin to Altman's subgenre of the "folk musical," in which the music enhances the utopian atmosphere of small-town southern life as conveyed through other narrative aspects of the show.[17] However, despite virtuosic (and postsynchronized) performances by the Dillards, their musicianship is reduced to a mere diversion—a pleasant musical *plaisir* but not a drastic supradiegetic bluegrass experience—due to the show's need for a strong link between musical performance and the comic rendering of narrative action.

The Desilu television minimusicals differ from their cinematic counterparts in several fundamental ways. First, musical numbers are portrayed as diegetic

198

music, even though they are postsynchronized (*I Love Lucy*, however, was recorded live on the sound stage). Attempts are made to hide the postsynchronization (Van Dyke's piano and the Dillards lip-synching). Second, music functions as both first- and second-order signifier: it enhances the narrative while featuring familiar musical celebrities. The musical number is thus an integral part of the narrative (as an existent) but is also entertainment or spectacle by popular artist and song (and thus a narrative satellite). In this regard, these mini-musicals helped to introduce and promote new talent as well as showcase the talents of the regulars, thus establishing a foothold in both the real and fictive worlds. Third, unlike films like *Singin' in the Rain*, there is no dreamlike fantasy of supradiegesis: no rain-soaked set, only the nightclub, writers' office, or backwoods cabin (the last setting does seem quite fanciful though). As Oppenheimer stated in the *I Love Lucy* context, music can be present in the sitcom, but it must tie in with the plot of the show. These Desilu examples demonstrate that TV music that is anchored to the plot or narrative of a program serves as phenotext in order to help make sense of the narrative world of the program.

Conclusion

As a musical system of information, television has redefined the experience of pleasure produced by its predecessor mediums of cinema and radio. Televisual pleasure is not the elevated, elite aesthetic pleasure of the mind as defined by Clive Bell of the Bloomsbury school of art criticism. But neither is it the heightened, sensual pleasure of the body, the *jouissance* of Barthesian thought. Rather, televisual pleasure is democratic and commodified, conforming to the *plaisir* or pleasant cultural expectations of most viewers. Musical pleasures are restrained on television, limited by the narrative expectations of genre as well as the social mores of the American viewer watching at the time. In other words, television continually seeks to undermine the nature of music making as a drastic experience, either by containing musical expression (Como is preferred over Elvis) or by making it hermeneutic by submerging it within a narrative structure, as in the Desilu sitcoms surveyed here. Musical *jouissance* such as that demonstrated by Gene Kelly (and others) in 1950s and 1960s cinema was simply not amenable to television, where more low-key, familiar faces were preferred. Both audiences and TV producers were apparently uncomfortable watching overt displays of expression (e.g., Elvis) or entertainers who were not culturally like them (e.g., Nat "King" Cole), and thus artists like Perry Como and programs like *I Love Lucy*, *Dick Van Dyke*, and *The Andy Griffith Show*, which masked any *jouissance* of musical expression, flourished on American TV in the 1950s and 1960s.

This comfortable arrangement would soon be rocked, however, by the advent of rock 'n' roll and its challenge to the status quo. Though initially uncomfortable with the mores of rock music and afraid it would not be accepted by sponsors and audiences, TV producers eventually found the economic potential too great to ignore. As nonconformists, rock musicians are averse to the safe, sanitary *plaisir* afforded by television and display musical expression with a great deal of *jouissance*. In their early performances on television, artists like Elvis Presley and the Beatles were asked to tone down their acts, a request that was often accepted with disdain by the artists (the Rolling Stones agreed to sing "Let's spend *some time* together" rather than "Let's spend *the night* together" on *The Ed Sullivan Show* in 1967—complete with Mick Jagger rolling his eyes during the verse). The *jouissance* of rock could not be tied down for long, though, and on-air expressions of musical *jouissance* soon cropped up, for instance, The Who's performance on *The Smothers Brothers Comedy Hour* in 1967, when they concluded their song by smashing their guitars and drum set onstage.

These constant checks and balances of genotext with phenotext on musical TV represent what anthropologist Victor Turner (1986) has called the "liminoid," wherein the liminal rituals of musical expression are subsumed into a technological culture through social and broadcasting codes.[18] The liminoid nature of music on television reflects a causal relationship between film and television; television takes conventions of film and due to the constraints of time and money, tends to transform cinematic fantasy into televisual habit. This relationship is but one explanation for the criticism of television as a bland, banal medium. Musical expression is subject to this same transformation from liminal to liminoid. Music adds a modicum of pleasure to television programming, but the pleasure derived from musical spectacle is restrained by the ritual of television programming and the constraints on that programming due to social mores and corporate sponsorship. In the television musical, genotextual pleasure and fantasy are eschewed for the phenotextual familiar and comfortable. Scenes like Gene Kelly's drastic cinematic musical *jouissance* are rare in television programming in the 1950s, substituted for the not-so-drastic performances of more comfortable-to-watch artists like Perry Como, Andy Williams, Arthur Godfrey, and Pat Boone. But phenotext and genotext are culturally mutable, as music videos of the 1980s and 1990s illustrate, and for a while, rock artists and television producers were able to reach a compromise on acceptable musically expressive behavior, undoubtedly sharing the common goal of making money. Of course, with the advent of cable TV and MTV in the 1980s, these rules changed significantly.

Stay tuned for more.

7

"And Now Another Word from Our Sponsor"

Strategies of Occultation and Imbuement in Musical Commercials

Magazine ad for Chevrolet truck "Like a Rock" campaign (GM Media Archives).

Television was embraced by the American public in a relatively short period of time and by the early 1950s had become a major player in the media market. In 1950, 9 percent of U.S. families owned television sets; by 1952, the number had increased to 72 percent. By 1975, the number of families that owned a set had risen to 97 percent (Ulanoff 1977: 345). Along with its popularity as a source of entertainment, the potential of television to sell goods and services also was quickly realized. As early as 1952, television had surpassed radio as an advertising vehicle, and by 1955 it was outpacing the entire output of America's print media for advertising dollars. In 1949, the total expenditure for TV advertising was $57.8 million or about 3 percent of total national advertising expenditures for the year. By 1974, expenditures for TV advertising were well over $4.8 billion or more than 18 percent of the total spent on advertising in the United States (Ulanoff 1977: 345–346).

Manufacturers increasingly looked to television to advertise their consumer goods in the glutted U.S. market of the post–World War II economic boom. However, the one-sponsor system, which imitated its radio predecessor, was expensive and restricted to only the largest, wealthiest companies at the time. Under this sponsorship arrangement, many TV shows were underwritten by a single sponsor, which often lent its company name to the program. Examples from the 1940s through the 1960s include the *Texaco Star Theater*, *Gillette Cavalcade of Sports*, *The Alcoa [Aluminum] Hour*, *The Philco Television Playhouse* (later the *Goodyear Television Playhouse*), *Lux Video Theater*, *Schlitz Playhouse of Stars*, *Kraft Music Hall*, and others. As the sole advertiser of a program, sponsors had free rein, and commercials were lengthy, often containing demonstrations of products between acts of the program. One *Philco* program (see chapter 2) from 1948 featured a lengthy presentation by bandleader Paul Whiteman touting the fidelity of the new Philco hi-fi system with its then-new, long-playing 33 1/3 rpm records. During its "intermissions," *The Kraft Music Hall* usually featured a narrator describing cooking demonstrations of recipes using Kraft food products.

Although the one-sponsor system provided financial stability, the potential existed for the sponsor to exert control over the content of programs if it suited the sponsor's interest. One such intervention led to the breakdown of the one-sponsor system in 1959 following a scandal in which the sponsor rigged the outcome of the NBC game show *Twenty-One*.[1] The incident caused NBC to accelerate toward an alternative advertising model, the magazine model, which featured multiple sponsors who purchased smaller slices of airtime. The magazine model proved beneficial to both smaller potential sponsors and the networks: more sponsors could afford to advertise on television while the networks could set prices based on the length of ads and the popularity of certain programs as well as determine when ads would air during the broadcast day. The magazine model also changed the nature of extradiegetic space in television. As Robert Fink (2005: 130) has stated, the new model was flexible, that is, it maximized the value of broadcast time but also regimented and formalized television broadcasting into discrete minitexts of flow that persist to the present. Eventually the magazine model of advertising prevailed: in 1955, three out of four TV programs had a single large corporate sponsor; by 1965, only one in eight did.

At about the same time the transition to the magazine concept was occurring, a creative revolution in advertising also was taking place, with advertisers seeking more creative and unorthodox ways to produce commercials.[2] The Rosser Reeves U.S.P. testimonial approach to TV advertising was dropped as sponsors began to emphasize style and image rather than the product itself. The move away from the Reeves U.S.P. model reflects a theory of marketing by Richard Tedlow (1990), wherein advertising in any medium develops in three phases. In phase one, a product is marketed to a local community. As the product is consumed and the company makes money and tries to expand, marketing moves into phase two, during which a product is marketed to a larger regional or even national community. For this larger market, the product or company must appeal to as wide a group as possible, positioning itself as unique or at least a viable alternative to other products. Tedlow's phase three occurs when a product saturates the larger market and thus begins to target certain segments of the population, thereby presenting an image of selectivity.

In its earliest years, television broadcasting was limited to a series of locally operated stations, and its advertising was directed toward marketing goods and services to those audiences, as in Tedlow's phase one. In the 1950s and 1960s, as networks began to reach nationwide audiences, television advertising entered phase two, focusing on product brands that were capable of national (and international) distribution and thus were advertised nationally, with each brand competing for dominance. Successful examples of such marketing were Coca-Cola, Procter and Gamble domestic products, the big three automakers (Ford, General Motors, and Chrysler), and Kellogg's breakfast cereals. By the 1980s and 1990s, however, some, but not all, advertising had entered the phase three scenario in which ads began to target more select demographic groups. While certain product ads have always aired during particular programs—ads for toys and breakfast cereals airing on Saturday morning children's television, laundry detergent and household cleaning products airing during daytime soap operas—by the early 1990s, many advertisers were beginning to market products based on other types of selectivity.[3]

The shift from a product-based advertising targeting strategy to one that is demographic/sociographically based led to more attention being paid to the style and content of commercials. Hal Himmelstein (1984: 53) has cited numerous advertising firms that began to consider commercials as artistic texts and thus to highly value individual creativity.[4] As commercials became texts with high production values, the act of selling the product shifted from a hard sell to a soft sell strategy. As has been noted, early TV commercials usually featured talking heads extolling the virtues of a product, but as this type of testimonial commercial became commonplace, advertisers sought more dramatic solutions to capture the viewing audience's attention and imagination. TV commercials increasingly adapted such filmic techniques as the montage to mix attractive visual images of the product and people enjoying it, thereby shifting the emphasis of the TV spot from describing the product to providing a feeling for the product or identifying a target demographic group for it. Consequently, TV commercials came to foreground the spectacle of visual images and sound over the former primary focus of commodity exchange.

Music in television ads played a large role in the shift from testimonial to artistic text (or from a phase two to a phase three marketing strategy). Music in early TV ads was mostly restricted to the Reeves/Sosnik approach of supporting the U.S.P. through a jingle or a narrative underscore that used a number of musical styles: light music (a style of music popular at the time, exemplified by the popularity of such ensembles as the Boston Pops Orchestra, 101 Strings, or Mantovani's Orchestra), jazz (especially big band but also bebop, etc.), classical, and folk. The ascriptive value of music made it useful in identifying a product and simultaneously conveying a mood for the product. By the 1960s, with the development and growing popularity of format radio, which identified and exploited the musical tastes of diverse American audiences, especially those in the baby boom generation, advertisers came to recognize the ascriptive power of music to target specific audiences and correlate these demographics with their products. From the 1960s onward, music began to be used in advertising to intentionally identify with and appeal to certain demographic (age, socioeconomic group, gender, and race) and psychographic (lifestyle) groups.

One example of the use of music in the new soft sell commercials was the "Hilltop Song" ad for Coca-Cola. Airing in 1971, the ad was part of a very successful campaign that lasted into the early 1970s. The first ad featured a group of young adults from many different countries standing on an Italian hillside and lip-synching a newly composed song (by Billy Davis and Roger Cook). Bill Backer, who wrote the lyrics for the song, described the ad as originating during a flight to London that was forced by heavy fog to land in Shannon airport in Ireland. Backer and other disgruntled passengers who had been upset about the delay the night before found themselves feeling jovial the next day, as they laughed and talked over bottles of Coca-Cola in the airport coffee shop. The situation gave him a new idea for the ad:.

> In that moment...[I] began to see a bottle of Coca-Cola as more than a drink...[I] began to see the familiar words, "Let's have a Coke," as...actually a subtle way of saying, "Let's keep each other company for a little while." And [I] knew they were being said all over the world as [I] sat there in Ireland. So that was the basic idea: to see Coke not as it was originally designed to be—a liquid refresher—but as a tiny bit of commonality between all peoples, a universally liked formula that would help to keep them company for a few minutes. (Backer 1993)[5]

Backer collaborated with Davis and Cook on the jingle, which was as long as a pop song and subsequently was marketed as such (example 7.1).

Despite the innovative advertising strategy that led to its creation, the song retained many of the attributes of the older jingle. It incorporated the hook from Coke's previous ad campaign ("It's the real thing") but augmented it with the words "what the world wants today." The name of the product is repeated over and over, usually in counterpoint to the motto. The song's international feel signifies the universality of Coke, even though it is made in America. However, though it retained many attributes of earlier jingles, the song transcended them and took on the characteristics of a pop song due to its length and highly engineered final version recorded by the pop group the New Seekers. The pop version of the song was released shortly after the commercial began to air in the United States in July 1971, the result of more than a hundred thousand fan letters. The demand for the song became so great that many people called radio stations around the country and asked them to play the commercial. Ultimately, Billy Davis asked Bill Backer to rewrite the lyrics without the references to Coke, and the song was rerecorded by The New Seekers and released on the pop charts, where it rose to the top ten in 1972.[6]

The "Hilltop Song" still advertised Coca-Cola, but the message was subtler and the product was lyricized by a song that sounded like a current pop tune instead of a jingle. The subtext of a universal community also supplanted the U.S.P of the Reevesian jingle, indicating that perhaps profits were not the only motive for the soft drink giant. The Coke ad was still a jingle, but it reflects the newer soft sell approach by using a style of music to project an image of the product rather than the product itself.

Eventually the idea of popular songs supplanting jingles took root in television advertising. By the 1980s, advertising agencies recognized that pop tunes were highly desirable for TV commercials, and rather than writing jingles that resembled

Example 7.1. "Hilltop Song" for Coca-Cola (1969). Copyright 1969 by Coca-Cola. Used by permission.

"I'd like to buy the world a Coke"

I'D LIKE TO BUY THE WORLD A COKE

Trade-mark ®

Arranged for Piano by
Debbie McDuffie

Words and Music by
B. BACKER–B. DAVIS
R. COOK–R. GREENAWAY

I'd like to buy the world__ a home and fur-nish it with love__ with ap-ple_ trees_ and hon-ey_ bees_ and snow white tur-tle__ doves__ I'd like to teach the world_ to sing__ in per-fect har-mon-y__ I'd like to buy the world__ a Coke_ and keep it com-pan-y__ I'd It's the re-al__ thing__

Copyright © 1971 · THE COCA-COLA COMPANY

(continued)

Example 7.1. *Continued.*

pop tunes, some advertisers used actual pop tunes.[7] In an article for *Millimeter* magazine, film critic Armond White (1988: 89) recognized that the pop song had supplanted the jingle as the most effective form of musical advertising:

> If jingles are the nursery rhymes of TV advertising, commercials today
> reveal a sophistication of communication skills, a refinement in the way of

subtler, primarily instrumental, musical strategies. It ranges across all genres: rock, country-and-western, blues, soul, New Age, classical, and the *musique concrète* sounds of the *avant-garde*. In agency music departments, producers and jingle writers hear the sound of music as the sound of money: a perfect way of connecting the need to sell with the urge to buy.

Commercials have left "jingles," now a pejorative term, behind, moving on to the pop song, which is advertising plus. It speaks to the spectrum of contemporary life-styles with an emotional resonance.

Jingle composer Steve Karmen (2005) has bemoaned the decline of the jingle and attributed it to two factors, namely, the greed of composers and ASCAP (American Society of Composers, Authors and Publishers) for demanding higher fees, thus pricing themselves out of the market, and the rise of the synthesizer, which, with the touch of a button, put thousands of musicians out of work. Despite White's and Karmen's claims (both of which have merit), the jingle met its demise due more to the evolution of television advertising (which moved from a phase two to a phase three stage) and the growing competency of the audience (who were more receptive to entertaining and clever commercials that reflected their values and tastes) than to the effect of jingles. As television audiences became more sophisticated in the 1980s, so did the music in commercials.

Strategies of Occultation

In a study of print advertising, Winfried Nöth described the dual-level structure of ads: a core pragmatic structure for commodity exchange (i.e., the actual selling of a product) and a textual layer consisting of images, colors, appearance, and so on. Borrowing from semantic frame theory of cognitive psychology, artificial intelligence, and text linguistics, Nöth (1987: 280) refers to these as the "semantic frames" of advertising, which are defined as cognitive units that relate concepts and structures by convention and experience, in the same way that codes work in Eco's theory. Nöth considers these frames as multilayered, with the pragmatic frame as "outer" and the textual frame as "inner," resembling the extradiegetic and intradiegetic televisual spaces, respectively. For television, the pragmatic frame operates in the real world of commerce and accounts for persuasion and selling, the two essential elements of every advertisement. The textual frame is embedded within the pragmatic frame and contains the expressions of these actions within the ad, whether through visual images, sound, dialogue, or music. Although in Nöth's model the texts are closed (with the intent that consumers and producers participate in the act of commodity exchange), the new artistic inner text frame opens the ad to possible additional interpretations. This opening of the text permits the addition of a third cultural or ideological frame that functions much like John Fiske's ideological level in his "codes of television" model, which builds upon shared cultural or ideological beliefs.[8]

Nöth describes the soft sell approach to advertising as advertisers using the textual frame of an ad to cover, or mask, the outer pragmatic frame's appeal to buy a product. The Coke ad is a good example of the practice of masking, as the appeal for commodity exchange is obfuscated by the surface text of the ad—the entertainment value espoused by David Huron (see chapter 3)—and thus has hidden the true intent of the ad. In the masked ad, the pragmatic frame message is often restricted to a mere presentation of the commodity or its brand name without the imperative appeal to purchase the product.[9] Nöth explains that in spite of the closed nature of advertising texts, surface textual messages have tended to use elaborate visual and/or aural components in artistic ways. These surface texts tend to hide or ignore the deeper level of the advertising text in what Patrick Charaudeau (1983) has called "strategies of occultation." Such strategies substitute the deeper level message, "buy X," with a surface message, "enjoy X." Backer's song for Coke takes this masking a step farther: the textual message of the ad does not seem to be "buy Coke" but, rather, "let's share a Coke so that we can become part of a universal community."

Masking can be even more effective on television than in print media because of the added dimensions of sound and music. As pointed out above, the use of a jingle that sounds like (and indeed actually becomes) a pop tune eventually supplants the old-fashioned style U.S.P. jingle. Part of the strategy of occultation in TV commercials is that the pragmatic commodity exchange component of the ad is supplanted by the pleasure of the music. The commercial's primary purpose is no longer to sell, but to entertain. The viewer may find pleasure (*plaisir*) in the musical style that accommodates the viewer's musical taste. As a phase three form of advertising, the focal point of the ad is to match the target audience with the style of music, or in Anahid Kassabian's (2001) terms, to find "affiliating identifications." Following Tedlow's phase three model of advertising, producers frequently try to match targeted audiences with styles of music they like to hear. Music style is thus topical, a unit of social discourse that conveys the affiliating identities of certain groups. The American mass media has made the process of linking musical styles with demographic and psychographic groups relatively simple by tapping into demographics developed by format radio. Format radio provides a ready-made market for affiliating identifications through its own demographic and marketing studies.

American Format Radio and the Categorization of Popular Musical Styles

How advertisers find links between musical styles and targeted demographic groups is similar to how radio stations find these same groups through their choice of programming. Ironically, format radio rose in the 1950s due to the increased competition from television for advertising dollars. Radio was the primary home entertainment medium during the 1930s and 1940s with programming much like that found on television in the 1950s. Along with live music, radio broadcast narrative programs, such as soap operas, mysteries, and children's programming, as well as news, sports, and commentary. As television became more popular in the 1950s, radio found it had to change its broadcasting formula in order to survive. Television became radio with pictures, broadcasting the same formats as radio, only audiences could see the characters as well as hear them. Broadcasting music was an inexpensive way for radio stations to remain on the air, and by the mid-1950s radio stations found it simple to broadcast certain types of music for their particular audiences, in what became known as format radio.

A format has been defined by Eric Rothenbuhler and Tom McCourt (1992: 106) as "a style, genre, or system that defines the musical or informational boundaries of what a [radio] station will present and its overall approach to programming." This somewhat vague definition of the format coincides with Kofi Agawu's (1991: 49) criteria of the "open" musical style topic. Radio formats are open in that they are a complex, or repertoire, of musical components (melody types, instrumentation, harmonic progressions, etc.) along with subject matter that is illustrated by certain song lyrics, audience attitudes, and consensus toward particular styles of music and artists who claim to fall within the category of a genre. Musical style is an important part of what defines a radio format, but it is not the only component. For example, music heard on 1990s contemporary Christian radio stations sounded much like music on easy-listening or lite stations, yet the two formats were distinctly different and drew very different audiences despite the similarity of the music being broadcast. In this case, the difference in format has more to do with its nonmusical components, such as the subject matter of lyrics (words) and audience attitudes and values. While formats may consist of a coalescence of musical traits that create the technical codes of the style (melody, harmony, timbres, forms), they are largely defined by the participants of the culture or what in genre theory is called an audience-response approach to genre.

This audience-response approach lends itself to a fluidity of label, with certain formats continually changing with each passing generation of listeners. For example, music heard on the top 40 or contemporary hit radio (CHR) formats

Adult Contemporary

Album-Oriented Rock (AOR)

Beautiful Music

Big Band

Classical

Comedy*

Contemporary Christian Radio (CCR)

Contemporary Hit Radio (CHR)

Country

Easy Listening Radio (ELR)

Foreign Language

Gold

Gospel

Hispanic

Jazz

Music of Your Life

New Age Contemporary (NAC)

News*

News/Talk*

Nostalgia

Quiet Storm

Religious

Sports*

Talk*

Urban Contemporary

* = nonmusic formats

Figure 7.1. American Radio Formats circa 1988 (Barnes).

of the 1960s became the playlist of the golden oldies formats of the 1990s and 2000s. Formats may also cater to subcategories of styles. For example, the generic style topic of rock was and still is subclassified on radio, with one station playing hard rock (or heavy metal as it became known in the 1990s), others playing rock 'n' roll, and still others playing alternative rock, indie rock, grunge, and so on. Conversely, new formats are created with each new generation: there were no alternative or indie formats in the 1960s, nor was there a New Age format, as there was in the 1990s, just as there are no longer top 40 stations, these having been replaced by a contemporary hits format. Formats are thus flexible and have no definite structures, only generic tendencies based on audience consensus. In this regard, they are similar to my definition of style topics, with many tokens but only idealized types.

Ken Barnes (1988) has provided a snapshot of radio formats in the 1980s, a time in which TV commercials became highly dependent on radio-based musical tastes to identify target groups for their products (see figure 7.1). Barnes identifies some 25 different radio formats (17 delineated by the style of music played; 8, by their nonmusical aspects, such as talk, news, sports, etc.). He describes formats as tools for targeting specific audiences in terms of the demographics of ethnicity, age, and socioeconomic status. This targeting process has resulted in the fragmentation and polarization of the radio-listening public in order to build a market niche for individual radio stations. It also predates the practice of narrowcasting, which found its way into television broadcasting with the rise of cable television in the 1990s.

In addition to the conditions listed above, formats can be considered open because they do not always have the same referential qualities, that is, they are not labeled the same by all members of the participating culture—for example, as just noted, placing rock music into several different subcategories. Conversely, radio's one format for classical music would be considered absurd for musicologists, as it completely negates the multifarious style periods covered in academe. The same might be said for the jazz format, as jazz also has many stylistic manifestations. The universe of formats is thus not fixed, but, rather, is negotiated by musical parameters and audience consensus.

Style, Competency, and Correlation in TV Music

Radio formats provide discursive labels for musical styles in contemporary society as well as identify demographic groups that tend to listen to certain types of musical styles. Barnes's list illustrates that some formats are style driven while others are demographically driven (and some are both). For example, CHR is stylistically diverse: anything that is popular in terms of record sales qualifies for the format. In the 1960s, top 40 radio stations played everything from the Beatles to Frank Sinatra to Sly and the Family Stone. The classical format focuses on Western European classical music, which is popularly viewed within the format as stylistically uniform, even though music scholars have repeatedly shown a diversity of styles within that label—even within a single composer's output. Another example is country-and-western music. It exhibits certain musical traits, such as a blend of acoustic and electronic instruments with a handful of distinctive vocal styles (chest voice, nasal, etc.), and is popularly viewed as a rural format sociographically because it had its origins in rural areas, yet many contemporary listeners and artists are city dwellers and Nashville, the self-proclaimed capital of country music, is a thriving metropolis. Producers of musical television commercials often take advantage of this ambiguity and generality to expand the appeal of their product to television audiences.

Before examining how radio formats have influenced television advertising, it is useful to examine what role musical style plays in radio formats. Despite its prevalence in musical discourse, "style" is a difficult term to pin down, ranging from musical traits to listener's attitudes and proclivities. For the purposes of this chapter, I rely on Leonard Meyer's (1989: 3) definition of style in music, which is "a replication of patterning, whether in human behavior or in the artifacts produced by human behavior, that results from a series of choices within some set of constraints." For music, these artifacts are the paradigms of timbre, texture, volume, harmony, melody, and rhythm, and patterning is how these paradigms are manipulated to create syntax, that is, the same narrative spaces that move music through time.[10] Moreover, the term "style" in music is used hierarchically: it can refer to the work of a single composer, a group of composers, music of a particular geographical area, works composed for some socially defined segment of culture, works composed for some utilitarian purpose, or the music of an entire civilization. For classical music, style is usually delineated by historical periods (the baroque style, the classical style, the Romantic style, etc.) and then delineated further with such subcategories as the music of the Mannheim School, the music of the Second Viennese School, and so on. This hierarchy extends all the way down to the individual composer (e.g., the style of Beethoven). Of paramount importance for style identification and analysis is that some categories be developed and shared with the audience. The basis of much musicology and music theory has been the codification and periodization of musical styles and the identification of generic innovations within individual composers' idiolects.

Meyer's definition implies an audience-response component as well as an ideological repertoire-of-elements component of style. Even more to this aspect of style is Robert Hatten's (1994: 294) definition: "that competency in semiosis presupposed by a work, and necessary for its understanding as a work of music. Competency in interpretation implies an understanding of correlations, and is guided by a hierarchy of principles (ensuring flexibility) and constraints (ensuring coherence)." For a piece of music to demonstrate a style, it must be recognizable to a competent audience, whether in the concert hall or at the TV screen. Gino Stefani (1987a: 7) has defined competence as "the ability to produce sense through music...the ability to realize either individual or social projects by means of music." In Stefani's model, a musical work (or television text) can be viewed as a single work (opus) or as exhibiting a general style according to technical codes or social practice (Fiske's ideologies) or general descriptions.[11] Thus, musical style is more than an aggregation of its syntactical elements; it is also a product of other cultural discourse. In media culture musical styles are associated with demographic groups: for example, popular music, especially rock music, is associated with youth culture; classical music, with older, wealthier audiences; country music, with rural society; and urban contemporary, with urban, often minority populations. Of course, these discourses are highly generalized and stereotyped, as most styles of music enjoy a wide diversity of audiences from both sociographic and psychographic backgrounds. Despite this pluralism, media markets have found it easier to operate on the premise that certain audiences tend to gravitate toward certain types of music.

Both Hatten's and Stefani's definitions of musical style depend on the audience's ability to identify, differentiate, and classify musical artifacts in various ways: physically, musically, and socially. As television advertising reached its phase three level, that of targeting specific audiences, it turned away from using expressive genres embedded within a particular style and toward relying on musical and demographic stereotypes to produce a menu-driven approach to musical styles identified with target groups. Of course, the viewing audience was complicit in this process, as the menu was also based on their own musical preferences. These preferences built the affiliating identifications of certain groups with certain musical styles, created thanks in large part to American format radio.

Strategies of Imbuement: Musical Styles in Two Car Commercials of the 1990s

Format radio provided a convenient way for advertisers to identify and correlate musical styles with targeted audiences. When considering music and TV commercials, there is a useful two-step process of deriving meaning. The first step is that the music used on a commercial would correlate with a preestablished style of music that a competent viewer would identify. This process is the additional correlation listed first by Stefani, in which a musical artifact (with its established structure and syntax) is paired with a musical style category or radio format category. The second step is the structuring correlation process whereby the musical style is paired with the images of the commercial and these images take on the discursive qualities of the musical style. For example, if a car manufacturer wanted to sell to a young (or self-perceived young) audience, that manufacturer might want to use some sort of rock music to correlate the brand of car with the preestablished musical style and its constituent audience. The car would then correlate with being young, cool, with it, and other descriptors associated with youth culture. Rather than cover the product in a strategy of occultation, this process of structuring correlations with musical styles would function more as a strategy of imbuement through which the correlated traits of the musical style of the commercial are newly associated with the product of the commercial, imbuing it with the same traits.

It is precisely this strategy of imbuement that producers of television commercials exploit to match their product with the desired sociographic group. As evident in the radio format system, musical style is a powerful discursive and descriptive tool for the correlation of music and populations within society. Nicholas Cook (1998: 16) has pointed to the use of style on television as an aspect of postmodernism: "Only with postmodernism has the idea of 'composing with styles' or 'composing with genres' emerged, at least as a consciously adopted procedure."

To show how musical style topics interact with other technical codes to produce ideologies, I analyze two television commercials that aired on American television during the early 1990s. Both commercials are for vehicles: one is for Chevrolet trucks, considered as American blue-collar working vehicles (manufactured by General Motors); the second is for an Infiniti, a high-end luxury car (manufactured by a subsidiary of the Japanese car company Nissan). Although selling the same type of product, the commercials use different styles of music with very different musical structures to produce correlations with their products. The ads differ greatly in their audiovisual constructions, with the Chevy truck ad relying on visual montage and a popular song by rocker Bob Seger while the Infiniti commercial uses a mininarrative format (as described in chapter 3) in a comical way, with a protagonist (a woodpecker), an antagonist, (the voice-over narrator), and a narrative enigma (wood paneling on the car's interior). Despite these differences, both ads are tightly constructed with all sensory channels combining to convey the message. Also, musical style is used for its ascriptive properties, not only identifying the product but also connoting the latent demographic of audience intended for each ad.

The Ideology of Work: Chevy Trucks

Unlike the Coca-Cola commercial ad campaign of the early 1970s in which a commercial jingle became a popular song, the ad campaign for Chevrolet trucks in the 1990s used an already popular song as a jingle. When approached by

General Motors to sell them the rights to his 1986 hit "Like a Rock," Seger was initially reluctant, but eventually he did so because he believed he would be helping a then-sagging automobile manufacturing industry in his hometown of Detroit. He also hoped that the ad would put his music before a larger audience, stating that "if an artist can do that, that is the greatest thing."[12]

The Chevy truck campaign was extremely successful, with a broadcast run of more than 10 years beginning in 1992. During that time, the song was played during nearly every Chevy truck commercial (on both TV and radio), many consisting of various mixdowns of the song with montage-like images of strong men using the truck to do their work. One such ad, from the mid-1990s, opens with the darkened images of two men in hard hats hoisting an American flag, which then dissolves into images of two more men throwing construction materials into the back of a truck. The third image shows a portion of the front of the truck (a synecdoche) dissolving into a picture of the side of the truck driving though a field. Additional images consist of construction workers, commercial fishermen, farmers, ranchers, factory workers, all working, lifting, loading, welding, and braving the harsh winter with the help of a Chevy truck bounding through mud and boulders and withstanding various forms of abuse while carrying heavy loads. The commercial seeks a visual correlation of the truck with determined American workers (both rural and urban), as the visual representations of toughness and durability are obvious. The ideology transmitted also is also clear: the American economy is run by rugged, individualistic (and of course predominantly male) blue-collar workers with a strong work ethic. This image carried over to Chevy's print ads, which also featured blue-collar or farm workers. In the photo at the head of this chapter, rural workers are looking at a used Chevy truck that is obviously still in great condition even after heavy use by the previous owner.

While the characters of these ads connote a tough work ethic, the visual techniques used in the TV ads exhibit aspects not commonly associated with toughness. In fact, the visual images rely heavily on some rather unconventional cinematic codes found mostly in art films of the 1920s through the 1970s. First, the use of rapid visual montage effects is usually associated with the highly artistic cinematic technique developed by Russian filmmaker Sergei Eisenstein in the 1920s. Second, most of the visual images are shot in synecdoche, another artistic technique in which only part of an object is photographed. Finally, many of the shots are quite underexposed and dark, revealing an influence of film noir. If anything, these artistic touches of the camera shots might serve to undermine the representation of the tough, American blue-collar worker.

Despite the conflicting representation of the images, the music in the commercial serves to reinforce the representation of toughness. Seger's song serves

217

the primary narrative function and holds the disparate visual images together. The structure of the song and lyrics is one of a narrative or story: the narrator (Seger) sings of his strength ("Like a rock / I was strong as I could be..."). The lyrics, which use the phrase "like a rock" as a tag, are punctuated by Seger's rhetorical delivery that is reminiscent of a gospel minister whose sermon grows with a continuous crescendo to its peak. The song also features an open tonal design: the commercial does not end on a tonic chord, but on a fade-out on the dominant played by electric guitar. Even the fade-out and inconclusiveness of the tonal design signify the longevity of the Chevy truck, as the music appears to keep going, as does the truck.

Two or more topics of popular music can be used to describe the song's style: country-and-western and rock. Although Seger does not consider himself to be a country singer—he describes himself as an American rock artist in the vein of Bruce Springsteen and John Cougar Mellencamp—he could qualify as one due to the timbre of his voice. Indeed, much of the appeal of the song lies in the sound of Seger's husky voice and the repetitive quality of the lyrics.[13] Also, the instruments used in Seger's Silver Bullet Band, electric guitar, acoustic guitar, electric bass, acoustic piano, and drums, create an ensemble that is common for both country and 1980s American rock groups (though acoustic guitar is more prevalent in country groups). The musical parameters of the ad reinforce this notion of style topic. The simple chord progression in the song C–F–Bb–F–C (I–IV–bVII–IV–I) is found in both rock and country styles, though it has been appropriated by country from older rock genres.[14] The diatonic and pentatonic pitches used for the melody also are those used in country music, eschewing the more prevalent blues scale of many rock genres.

The correlation of country music (or country/rock) with the visual images of the blue-collar workers is a powerful force for semiosis in the commercial. Like the images, country/rock signifies the masculine, working-class, blue-collar American worker. This signification transmits the ideology of the ad, much of which is explicit: the preservation of the American work ethic and the American way of life through the economy of the American auto industry. The ideology of patriotism and the other ideologies of capitalism and class are maintained as the status quo. Seger's song has thus become a celebration of the blue-collar American ideology, even though Seger's original intent for the song was quite different.[15]

The use of Seger's "Like a Rock" in the Chevy truck campaign illustrates White's point that pop music supplanted the jingle in the 1990s. While still serving as a jingle with a U.S.P. (Chevy trucks are durable—"like a rock"—even though neither Chevy nor Chevrolet is mentioned in the song), the music also functions to affiliate style topic(s) with a certain demographic group. Seger's song, with its preestablished topic, is associated with the Chevy truck in a structuring correlation in which the qualities of Seger's song (toughness, American patriotism, blue-collar work ethic) imbue the truck with the same attributes. However, though it reflects the durability of the truck, the music relies more on the intended audience of the commercial: those who drive a Chevy truck are likely to be American working-class males. Country music and American rock music both form a cultural bond with this affiliating subculture, as demonstrated anthropologically (see Hebdige 1979) and commercially (Barnes 1988).

Luxury as Ideology: The Infiniti Automobile

About the same time as the Chevy truck campaign, a commercial aired for the Infiniti, an up-scale luxury car catering to upper-middle and upper-class drivers. Unlike the Chevy commercial with its montage effects, the Infiniti commercial follows a tripartite narrative structure that is reflected in all its component parts: visual image, narration, and music. This three-part structure (like that found in the peanut butter commercial discussed in chapter 3) creates a correlation with more highbrow sensibilities.

The ad depicts a large, luxuriously modern house in the country with an Infiniti parked on its cobblestone driveway. The ad opens with a shot of a woodpecker flying toward the Infiniti from a nearby tree. The camera shots alternate between the car and the woodpecker, the latter becoming a sort of narrative protagonist. The shots of the car are presumably the woodpecker's eye view. Moving from long shot to medium shot, ultimately to a close-up of the car's interior (as the woodpecker lands on the car and peers in through the sunroof), they becoming progressively larger and larger giving the effect that the bird (and the viewers) are approaching the car and climbing in. Nested within this visual structure is a tripartite structure of long-shot/close-up/long-shot scheme. Shots at the beginning of the ad are virtually long shots, while shots in the middle of the ad are close-ups of both the car's interior and the bird. The final shot pulls away to a long shot of the car, with the bird flying away above the car. The Infiniti J30 logo at the end of the ad serves as a visual coda and provides the only instance of written text in the commercial.

The tripartite structure of the visual shots synchronizes with the sonic technical codes of the commercial (see figure 7.2). In both the opening and the ending of the commercial, bird sounds are audible while in the middle the bird sounds are muted, thus providing a sort of three-part (A–B–A) sonic design. The ad is narrated by actor Michael Douglas, who in the early 1990s was a major star. Like the visual and sonic codes, Douglas's narration also is organized in a three-part structure, similar to classical rhetorical models. "Ladies and gentlemen, feast your

VISUAL IMAGES

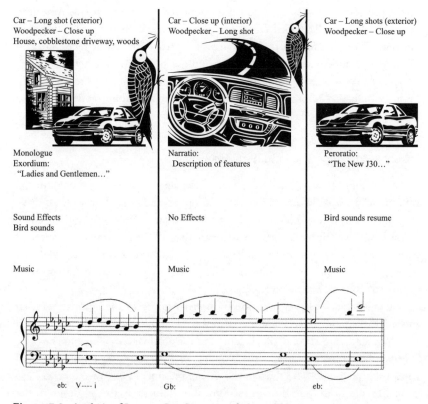

Car – Long shot (exterior)
Woodpecker – Close up
House, cobblestone driveway, woods

Car – Close up (interior)
Woodpecker – Long shot

Car – Long shots (exterior)
Woodpecker – Close up

Monologue
Exordium:
  "Ladies and Gentlemen…"

Narratio:
  Description of features

Peroratio:
  "The New J30…"

Sound Effects
Bird sounds

No Effects

Bird sounds resume

Music

Music

Music

eb: V---- i   Gb: eb:

Figure 7.2. Analysis of Luxury Car Commercial circa 1992.

eyes on the elegant new J30," serves as the introduction or *exordium*. This is followed by the narration or description of the car's features (air bags, leather appointments, wood). Finally, Douglas breaks from the rhetoric and injects himself into the narrative by admonishing the woodpecker, "Hey, pal, don't even think about it!" referring to the woodpecker's view of the "tasty wood interior" of the car. Finally comes the rhetorical *peroratio*: "The new J30 from Infiniti."

Overlaid on the tripartite visual and sonic design, the music of the ad asserts its own three-part structure through gestures and tonal motion from E-flat to G-flat, returning to E-flat for the final A section. The music of the commercial is tonal, using ahemitonic pentatonic pitch material centered on E-flat. The music opens on the pitch B-flat, which serves as dominant of E-flat, the tonic, which is asserted early on. The middle section is marked by bass motion to

G-flat, coinciding with the *narratio* section of Douglas's narration. The final section is marked by the return to E-flat as tonic, coinciding with Douglas's punch line, "Hey pal, don't even think about it!" This little tonal design even concludes on an authentic cadence (V–I) in the final gesture of the piece. The melody also exhibits a three-part form through the deployment of themes. After a three-measure introduction, a principal theme is played by an English horn, with a contrasting theme in the oboe in the middle section. A denouement occurs with a flourish in the clarinets on the original E-flat pentatonic key.

In addition to its three-part design, the Infiniti commercial is structured according to a narrative design. The woodpecker is one of the narrative protagonists, but viewers also are made to be the protagonist as they sense the woodpecker's desire for the car. As mentioned above, the visual shots establish the characters and space of the narrative. The narrative enigma(s) posed include such questions as "what is a woodpecker doing in this ad?" or "how can I afford such a car?" The antagonist is Michael Douglas, the announcer, as he carefully describes the features of the car and ultimately drives the woodpecker away in the denouement ("Hey, pal, don't even think about it!"). Closure is achieved in the rhetorical peroration and the musical cadence, sounding along with the Infiniti logo (with the price—which resolves another enigma—whether or not viewers can afford it!).

The Infiniti ad reveals a highly correlated structure, with the various visual and sonic parameters aligning themselves, joining isomorphically to create an over-arching three-part structure. The commercial is a closed narrative, with a beginning, middle, and end, and the music is also tonally closed as the key of E-flat minor is introduced by its dominant; the tonal center shifts to G-flat; and another tonal shift results in the return to E-flat. The tonally closed design and the narrative correlate. This isomorphism of the musical, rhetorical, and narratological design of the ad unifies it and promotes an internal coherence or introversive or intraopus semiotic.

The internal coherence of the ad is established through the syntagmatic structure of various technical codes. However, it is the paradigmatic or associative aspects of the commercial that ultimately lead to signification. The musical style topics exhibited in the commercial contribute to the extramusical signification. The visual technical codes of the commercial convey a picture of wealth and luxury, particularly one with classical Euro-American connotations. The image of the very large house in the country with a cobblestone driveway conjures up associations of a landed country gentry. The woodpecker lends a comic touch to the visual images but also reinforces a Rousseauian notion of human coexistence with nature (although humans also have dominion/control over nature). In addition to his classical rhetorical model, Douglas's narration contributes to the ambiance of luxury: in pointing out the attributes of the car, he uses such words as "elegant" and "soft, leather appointments" (instead of, say, "seats"), even addressing the audience as "ladies and gentlemen." The focus of the ad is on the car's wood interior, a feature limited to the most expensive automobiles. Overall, the visual and sound codes of the ad transmit the representation of wealth and luxury, which in turn conveys the ideology of materialism and social class (in this case, the upper class).

The musical style employed for this ad serves to locate the music within a cultural context of 1990s America. In fact, like the Chevy truck commercial, the music is an imaginative and creative blend of several styles, perhaps described in turn as easy-listening, smooth jazz, or, more apropos of the 1990s, New Age. New Age music was a popular radio format with middle- and upper-middle-class listeners in the 1990s and thus was appropriate for the target demographic of the Infiniti car. The format incorporated both electronic and classical orchestral instruments as well as modal and consonant harmonies, often in conjunction with sound effects or electronically sampled sounds, especially sounds from nature (e.g., birds, wind, water, etc.). New Age music also often features electronic synthesizers and flutes, piano, acoustic guitar, and a wide variety of non-Western acoustic instruments. Although the music began as an extension of the new age philosophy, it grew to include this soft, ambient music not necessarily related to the philosophy.

Here, the New Age topic is the result of the confluence of the pentatonic melody and diatonic tonal space along with the combination of electronic and acoustic instruments as well as the environmental sounds of birds. Another topic suggested in the commercial is the classical style topic, also transmitted through pitch as well as tonal, timbral, and temporal spaces. Musical gestures and tonal spaces are deployed in the manner of functional tonality of classical music using the tonic-dominant polarity. Timbral space also signifies the classical since it consists of traditional woodwind instruments that are found in such classical ensembles as the symphony orchestra and chamber music ensembles. The temporal space also signifies the classical topic, as the three-part design of the musical score reflects the three part design of many classical pieces. The tonally closed design of the music in this commercial is the same used in many classical ternary forms and even in the classical minor-key sonata form: the tonic minor moves to the relative major and back to the tonic minor. Also, as stated above, the rhetoric of the music reflects that of classical rhetorical models of exposition-development-denouement.

The music of the Infiniti ad is more than just isomorphic with the other technical and representational codes of the commercial. Both the classical and new age topics correlate with advertising demographics identifying certain socioeconomic strata, in this case the upper class for classical music and the nouveau riche (or in 1990s terms, yuppies) for new age music. And, as the music correlates with these groups, it also correlates with the ideologies of these groups. These two demographic groups are the obvious targets, as they would be the most likely groups who could afford the Infiniti. However, another demographic target would be the well-educated or at least those with the cultural capital to appreciate the fine points of the ad. Indeed, if viewers have the appropriate culture capital, they may discern the rhetorical and formal features of the ad's components and also might get the inside musical joke in the ad: the reference to the woodpecker and the "tasty" wood interior of the car is accompanied by woodwinds. Thus, even if they are not an actual part of the targeted demographic, they are nonetheless within it because they get the joke.

Conclusion

The Infiniti and Chevy truck commercials illustrate the stratification of American consumer culture into highbrow and lowbrow by selecting images, sounds, and music that attempt to reinforce existing social distinctions within American society.[16] These class boundaries are maintained through images and music that market research has found appeal to these demographic groups. Musical affinities are mediated through affiliations with recordings and radio formats. The images of the Chevy truck commercial may resonate with American working-class men while also romanticizing or stylizing the work that they (and the truck) do. This stylization is augmented by the use of Seger's song. A naive reading of the truck ad would entail an interpretation that it is a country singer performing a country song. A deeper competency of the music, however, would produce a reading of Seger as an American rock icon of the 1980s with a blue-collar persona. Knowledge of Bob Seger's Detroit roots and the city's tie to the American auto industry also plays a role of significance in deeper meanings of the ad. The Infiniti commercial operates on a similar system of assumptions. A naive reading of this ad connotes an audience of yuppies who listen to new age music in their outer-ring suburban McMansions of the 1990s. However, the design of the ad and the musical techniques reflect a more sophisticated, classical rendering of the product for those with the cultural capital to identify it. The confluence of three-part designs in the ad, while not new or innovative in the ad, leads the sophisticated audience to a deeper reading of the commercial.

The ascriptive powers of music in these ads lead to a reconsideration of Nöth's assertion of the "strategies of occultation" in advertising. By the 1980s (and perhaps much earlier), it is likely that no television viewer would confuse a commercial with a narrative TV show, and viewers were well aware that every commercial contained Nöth's "pragmatic" frame of commodity exchange. So, nothing is really *hidden* in commercials, especially the appeal to purchase the product. Rather, the discourse surrounding the product is elevated to show that the manufacturers of the product are in touch with their potential buyers, that they are trying to connect with the ideal ethos of these demographic groups. Music, as part of the discourse of television commercials, is well positioned to convey this ethos, having been prepped for it through format radio and the recording industry. The Chevy truck commercial appeals to the American workers' sense of patriotism, work ethic, and musical tastes, all embodied in Seger's song as an amalgam of country and American rock. Conversely, the amalgam of new age and classical music, embedded in a humorous setting, make the Infiniti ad appeal to 1990s upper- and upper-middle-class sensibilities. Thus, rather than a strategy of occultation in a closed text, advertisers actually pursue a strategy of imbuement in an open (or at least *more* open) text, in which advertising texts seek to structure a semiotic link between the surface texts of commercials and their products by imbuing the product with certain qualities. Of course, this adheres closely with Tedlow's phase three paradigm of advertising.

The "Like a Rock" ad illustrates a complexity of television commercials that goes beyond a simplistic reading of a single semantic frame. Because television commercials are so brief and ephemeral, they must draw themselves into the viewer's consciousness in as quick and efficient manner as possible. To do this, they often draw upon more than one semantic frame that overlap to produce a single, preferred meaning but ancillary meanings as well. To illustrate, consider four separate frames in a TV commercial, two internal and two external. The internal or textual frames refer to the images and sounds of the ad, including the music accompanying the commercial. The external or pragmatic frames include the product being advertised and the audience.

Beyond music's role as mediator of lyrics and visual images in commercials, musical style is the linchpin of the 1980s and 1990s commercials that link audiences and products by relying on the competency of the viewer to create one of Stefani's signifying correlations. Competency, both musical and televisual, is exactly what occurred in the 1980s and 1990s, as an entire generation, the baby boomers, grew up with television from birth. Perhaps the shift in television commercials also made possible the shift in television programming, into what many call postmodern television, which is the subject of the last chapter of this book.

And now, back to the program.

224

8

"Just the Facts, Ma'am"

Musical Style Change and Markedness in the Police Drama

Cast of *Dragnet*. Officer Frank Smith (Ben Alexander, left) and Sgt. Joe Friday (Jack Webb, right) (Wisconsin Center for Film and Theater Research).

Television Genre: Some Conceptions and Definitions

By the mid-1950s, nearly every American television program fit neatly into one of several genres, most, if not all of them borrowed from radio or cinema. Genre in television has been a subject of scholarly study but is also often brought up in more casual settings among critics and audiences alike. Despite this wide-ranging discourse (or perhaps because of it), defining television genres is not as simple as one might expect. Should genres be based on content alone or other factors? And how does music play a role in defining television genre? Glen Creeber (2001) has listed seven genres for television's golden age (roughly, the late 1940s to the early 1960s): drama, soap opera, comedy, popular entertainment, children's television, news, and documentary. Within each of these general designations he lists sub-genres. Creeber's list relies loosely on content to define each genre, but a closer look at television genre reveals that definitions involve other factors.

Three models have emerged in defining genre in television: an audience-response model, a style model, and a repertoire-of-elements model. John Fiske (1987: 109–110) has defined genre from a sort of audience-response point of view, that is, as a cultural practice that attempts to structure some order into the wide range of texts and meanings that circulate within the culture. In television, this ordering is important in order to triangulate television producers, audiences, and texts within a convenient discourse. The pleasures of genre derive from recognizing structural elements that impart social and ideological concerns while also allowing for innovations that produce new styles of expression. By including both the cultural makeup of the audience and the structure of the television text itself, Fiske touches on two approaches to genre. Stephen Neale (2000) has described the so-called repertoire-of-elements model that depends on the content within the text itself: elements such as character types, setting, iconography, narrative, and style. This conception of television genre is adapted from literature, film, and theater and is well suited to such narrative genres as the western, police drama, science fiction fantasy, and others. In this model, a western is so defined because it has cowboys, horses, an Old West setting, and so on. However, Neale questions this definition's efficacy in terms of nonnarrative TV genres, such as game shows, news programs, and reality series. While acknowledging both Fiske's and Neale's models of genre, Jeremy Butler (1994) has also offered a stylistic model, that is, a model based on the production techniques of sound and/or image. This definition of genre can be applied to film noir, but because many consider film noir to be a filmic style and not a genre, both terms are ambiguous: what is style, and what is genre?[1] Rick Altman (1995) also has described the slippery issue of defining and categorizing genre for Hollywood films by citing two competing theories. One is the ritual approach, through which a number of critics dwell on the mythical qualities of Hollywood genres and on the audience's ritual relationship to genre film. Genre is defined by what audiences want to see and by the Hollywood's desire to both placate the audience and attract the consumers it needs. This approach roughly corresponds to the audience-response model. An alternative to the ritual approach is the ideological approach, which is defined by the identifiable structures through which Hollywood's rhetoric flows. The ideological approach is comparable to Butler's style-and-subject-matter model as well as Neale's repertoire of elements model.[2]

Altman also posits that genre can be considered from a semiotic point of view, notably from both a semantic and syntactic perspective. Like Algirdas Greimas's modalities of "being" and "doing," Altman defines genre by the semantic properties of common traits, attitudes, characters, shots, locations, and sets while the syntactical perspective privileges how these structures are arranged. For example, in a western like *The Rifleman*, the semantic elements of the show are cowboys, an Old West town and ranch, horses, six-guns, and so on. Also worth looking at is the syntax of the genre, with its narrative arc that includes gunfights, chases on horseback, and barroom brawls as well as action scenes specific to the program, such as McCain's struggles to fight off bandits and land cheats while maintaining solidarity with his son and his friends in town—or as John Cawelti (1971: 46) has put it: "the hero protecting the townspeople from the savages, using his own savage skills against the denizens of the wilderness."

Altman's complementary ritual and semiotic approaches to film genre adapt well to television. TV genres may begin as a producer's repertoire-of-elements (the semiotic approach), but because television is continually catering to what is popular, it also has relied on conventional genres that have worked well in the cinema and radio and adapted them for the new medium. Altman's analytic template for genres as semantic and syntactic is useful also in cases where genres are defined by their elements, in others by what happens in the narrative, and still others by the style of the program. Butler summarizes these ideas by describing (if not defining) genre by the three criteria of audience response, style, and subject matter. According to Butler, programs like *Cheers* and *Saturday Night Live* are viewed as comedies because the primary audience response is laughter. Other programs are defined by style; for example, a musical variety show will feature singers and dancers in costumes with well-lit, glittery sets.[3] Still other genres are classified by the subject matter, that is, by the characters and the situations of the narrative, thus incorporating both a semantic and syntactic approach in a broad way. For example, the police drama genre features characters who are police officers, criminals, and victims, and these characters proceed through a narrative formula in which a criminal commits a crime against a victim and the police then investigate the crime and pursue, and finally subdue, the criminal.

Butler's view is that despite a certain stability of elements, TV genres develop through a three-stage evolutionary process. The first is a trial-and-error period during which conventions of the genre are explored. In this period, popular aspects of the genre are retained and unpopular ones discarded. As the genre conventions are codified, the genre enters a classical period, when codes of the genre are solidified and imitated. Finally comes a third period, of self-reflexivity, as the genre turns inward and uses its own conventions for subject matter. Butler (1994: 299–300) claims that this period results in parodies of the genre, genre decay, or genre death. Despite Butler's assertion of genre deaths, many TV genres have been remarkably resilient, resurfacing after several years or even decades of dormancy. The police drama is one such genre that has come in and out of vogue throughout television history.

In addition to resurgence, the late, self-reflexivity stage is characterized by the hybridization of genres. For example, in the 1950s and early 1960s, the TV western was popular and created opportunities for experimentation within the genre, such as the single-parent western listed by Gary Yoggy (1995), of which *The Rifleman* was a part. By the late 1960s, the western seemed to have died out, inasmuch as it had vanished from the airwaves (in prime-time network television at least). However, the genre later resurfaced in the 1970s in programs that exhibited characteristics of the earlier western. For example, *McCloud* (1970–1977) featured a modern-day cowboy sheriff from Taos, New Mexico, playing a crime fighter in New York City. The series shared subject matter of both the western and the police drama and thereby became a sort of hybrid. Another hybrid program from the same time, *Hec Ramsey* (1972–1974), featured a frontier sheriff who solved crimes through investigation rather than violence. It represents the inverse of *McCloud*, as the Old West setting is retained, but the narrative syntax more closely resembles the investigation story lines of the police drama. By the 1980s and 1990s many programs exhibited hybrid characteristics of several genres: some police dramas, such as *Hill Street Blues*, were also soap operas; action shows like *The A-Team* were also detective/PI shows; soap opera–like serials were also comedies, such as *Northern Exposure* (possibly also considered a western due to its Alaska setting); and so on. This hybridity and overlap often lead to new audience-response models for defining a genre or to the creation of new genres.

Musical Style and Television Genre

Throughout the history of television, music has played a role in defining genre, notably as part of the style and techniques or repertoire-of-elements definitions.

As television competency grew among TV audiences, music developed the capacity to signify genres through the correlation of musical *style* with genres and not just specific musical gestures and leitmotifs. This "composing with styles," as Nicholas Cook (1998: 16) has put it, is regarded as a postmodern phenomenon through which style may produce signifiers beyond the individual elements of a musical piece (like motives).[4] This correlation of musical style with television genre is mutable, however, and over the first few decades of television, the correlation changed or evolved within the life spans of genres. Most of these changes have to do with Fiske's notion of the triangulation of audience, producer, and text. Many television producers sought to update certain genres by infusing into some programs music that exhibited newer, more current popular styles. These new musical scores would in turn (producers hoped) attract larger audiences to these shows. The change in music accompanying soap operas is just one example. In the 1950s and 1960s, soap operas were accompanied by studio organists who performed melodramatic music live in the studio. By the 1970s onward, most soap operas featured prerecorded music in a pop style. But perhaps the most apparent change in the correlation of genre and musical style can be found in the police drama, where the correlation of music can be seen as moving in a trajectory from a brassy, military style of music to pop genres, such as jazz and rock.

The term "style" in music as defined in the last chapter is perhaps closer to the term "genre" in film and television, whereas "genre" in music usually refers to specific forms of music or modes of performance, such as the symphony, the lied, chamber music, opera, and so on. (Thus, in music, "genre" may be closer in meaning to "style" as understood by scholars of radio, film, and television!). For the purposes of this study, I again invoke the competency of the television audience and use somewhat grossly partitioned categories of musical style that audiences could easily identify. These styles are those disseminated through highly commodified forms of music, particularly through popular music's correlation with American radio formats. Thus, the styles that are germane to television have rather broad, non-broken-down labels, such as "classical," "rock," "pop," "country," "new age," and others, but like Creeber's theory of genre include nested subcategories (e.g., the category "rock," includes the subcategories of "acid rock," "hard rock," "punk rock," "soft rock," "rock 'n' roll," etc.). The hierarchical nature of these subcategories extends also to the level of an individual composer's own work.

As has been demonstrated throughout this book, television music has drawn from a varied repertoire of musical styles. The radiophonic influences of composers such as Harry Sosnik brought Tin Pan Alley, jazz, and pop styles to television, while the music of B movie composers brought the Hollywood symphonic style to the small screen. While many early television narratives drew upon the cinema, as television evolved through the 1950s, various narrative programs began to experiment with music outside of the Hollywood film music style.[5] One such example is the detective series *Peter Gunn* (1958–1961), which featured an original jazz score by Henry Mancini, perhaps best known for his scores and songs to the films *Breakfast at Tiffany's*, *The Days of Wine and Roses*, and the *Pink Panther* series. *Peter Gunn* episodes were rife with music, sometime as much as 15 minutes in a half-hour show. Some featured songs sung by Lola Albright accompanied on-screen by jazz trumpeter Shorty Rogers and guitarist Laurindo Almeida.[6] The jazz score signified the detective's (Craig Stevens) suave coolness as well as the urban setting of New York City. More importantly, the program demonstrated that musical style could serve as an expressive genre to signify the ambiance of the program.[7] Featuring a musical style like jazz created a new potential for correlating music with certain narrative situations, and composers grew to realize that different musical styles could signify different aspects of American cultural attitudes within a television narrative. Style thus had both an extradiegetic and an intradiegetic signification. Extradiegetically, jazz of the 1950s was popular with the young audiences with which *Peter Gunn* undoubtedly tried to identify. Intradiegetically, jazz signifies the urban setting of the show's narrative and also connotes the suavity of Peter Gunn/Craig Stevens. This correlation, jazz and urbanness, is iconic in the sense that much jazz music is played and heard in large urban areas, but the correlation is cemented by its encoding of the representations of jazz in the urban detective drama in films and television at this time. The correlation becomes a code that TV audiences come to recognize over time.

Similar to signification in jazz, in the 1960s and 1970s rock music came to signify youth culture, but to many it also signified rebellion and political liberalism. As a result, American television was ambivalent about embracing rock (as shown in chapter 6) but at the same time often tried to adapt rock to its own (some would say watered-down) musical vocabulary. As television broadcasting continued through the decades, audience attitudes changed with a new generation of viewers exhibiting new and different sets of musical tastes and competencies. Television had to adapt to these tastes; thus the portrayal of cool, through jazz in the 1950s gave way to rock in the 1970s and 1980s. A particularly interesting example of this transition can be seen in the music to theme songs in police dramas. The remainder of this chapter traces the evolution of the television police drama and how its musical themes evolved from a cinematic model of signifying through the expressive genres of the Hollywood symphonic style to signifying through style *as* expressive genre.

A Brief History of the TV Police Drama

Police dramas have been popular throughout the history of American television, mostly due to the structural elements of the genre but also due to some compelling characters. The plotlines of the genre involve investigation and the search for clues by a (usually charismatic) police detective or uniformed officer, leading toward the apprehension of a criminal suspect. Police dramas have not tended to focus on violence, though at different points in TV history some have featured violence as a marker. American audiences have enjoyed police drama narratives as well as those of its cousin, the detective/PI show. The genre has also involved the portrayal of the police as tough and efficient enforcers of the law. Among the early tough guy cops were Dan Mathews (Broderick Crawford) in *Highway Patrol* and Frank Ballinger (Lee Marvin) in *M Squad* as well as the emotionless but efficient Joe Friday (Jack Webb) on *Dragnet* and Capt. John Braddock (Reed Hadley) on *Racket Squad*. These characteristics of the genre were borrowed from other narrative media, notably the radio drama, mystery novels, and police procedurals on film.

Like most genres on television, the police drama evolved through innovations in plotlines and how the police were portrayed. The 1950s tough cop gave way to the cool cop in such programs as *The Mod Squad* (1968–1973) and *CHiPs* (1977–1983). The tough cop era returned in the 1970s in the form of Lt. Dan "Hondo" Harrelson (Steve Forrest) on *S.W.A.T.* (1975–1976) and Tony Baretta (Robert Blake) on *Baretta* (1975–1978) but then gave way to more "sensitive" cops like Frank Furillo (Daniel J. Travanti) on *Hill Street Blues* (1981–1987), to frustrated, tough cops enmeshed in the complex problems of an ambivalent society like Andy Sipowitz (Dennis Franz) on *NYPD Blue* (1993–2005), to everyday cops dealing with their strengths and weaknesses while also trying to do their jobs in a fatalistically violent society like the cast of *Homicide: Life on the Street* (1993–2000).

The police drama, like all narrative television genres, underwent alternating periods of popularity and unpopularity in the first 50 years of television. The genre was popular in the 1950s, as scripts were easy, if somewhat formulaic, to write and budgets were low. The first TV police drama was Chicago-based *Stand By for Crime* (1948–1949), which aired during the television's breakout year. The show had an interesting twist in that it was interactive with its audience, as during each episode viewers could call into the network and try to solve the murder. Often celebrities appeared and offered their guesses as to the week's culprit (Castleman and Podrazik 1982: 42). Although the show was short-lived, its success led to the development of other investigative police dramas, including *The Plainclothesmen* (1949–1954), which used the subjective first-person camera technique; *Crime Syndicated* (1951–1953), which, like *Dragnet*, documented true crime cases from FBI and police files; the short-lived *Racket Squad* (1950–1951); *Dick Tracy* (1950–1951), which was freshly adapted from the radio show and comic strips; *Dragnet* (1951–1959); and *Highway Patrol* (1955–1959).

In the 1960s, the popularity of cop shows extended to the related detective/PI show in which detectives were freer to bend the rules and which offered a more freewheeling approach to crime investigation. Meanwhile, the police drama also turned toward comedic satires with the airing of such situation comedies as *Car 54, Where Are You?* (1961–1963) and *The Andy Griffith Show* (1960–1968).

In the 1970s, the police drama genre made a comeback in what became its second golden age with the premiere of more than 42 programs during the decade. The trend toward more police dramas actually started in 1968, when four programs debuted almost simultaneously: *Dragnet 1967* brought back Sgt. Joe Friday (this time with sidekick Bill Gannon played by Harry Morgan) and ran for four more years; *Ironside* (1968–1975) featured Raymond Burr of *Perry Mason* fame; *The Mod Squad* (1968–1973) sought to make cops out of young misfits; and perhaps the most long-standing and influential program (at least from a musical perspective), *Hawaii Five-0* (1968–1980). A nearly complete list of TV cops shows during the decade is shown in table 8.1.

Some of the programs during the 1970s pushed the boundaries of the genre by inserting a penchant for violence into the plotline. *S.W.A.T.* in particular was marked for its violent content, which included on-screen shootings of suspects, and others programs followed, such as, *Police Story* (1973–1977), *The Rookies* (1972–1976), and *The Streets of San Francisco* (1972–1977). Soon women also were joining the police force in such programs as *Police Woman* (1974–1978), the glamorous cop fantasy *Charlie's Angels* (1976–1981), and, later, the more realistic and pragmatic *Cagney and Lacey* (1982–1988), thus adding a little pluralism to an otherwise male-dominated genre. NBC gave the genre a particular spin by rotating three or four series under the heading of *The NBC Sunday Mystery Movie* (1971–1977). This umbrella comprised the programs *Columbo*, *MacMillan and Wife*, *McCloud*, and, later, *Hec Ramsey* and other detective series. Several of these programs went on to become independently popular.

In the 1980s the police drama took on two new dimensions as it moved away from investigative plotlines toward, on the one hand, shows marked by the portrayal of violence and, on the other hand, programs focused on the personal lives of the police characters. The programs *T. J. Hooker* (1982–1986), featuring an older William Shatner (aka Capt. Kirk of *Star Trek*), and *Hunter* (1984–1991), featuring retired pro football player Fred Dryer, continued the trend toward violence while programs like *Hill Street Blues* (1981–1987) emphasized the human condition of police officers.

Table 8.1. American TV Police Dramas, 1968–1980

Program	Dates	Theme Music Composer
Dragnet 1967	1967–1970	Walter Schumann
Ironside	1968–1975	Quincy Jones
Mod Squad	1968–1973	Earle Hagen
Adam-12	1968–1975	Frank Comstock
Hawaii Five-0	1968–1980	Morton Stevens
The Bold Ones: The Protectors	1969–1970	Gil Mellé
Dan August	1970–1971	Dan Grusin
NBC Mystery Movie	1971–1977	Henry Mancini
Columbo		David Shire
McCloud		Richard Clements
McMillan and Wife		Jerry Fielding
Nichols	1971–1972	Bernardo Segall
O'Hara, U.S. Treasury	1971–1972	Ray Heindorf
Cade's County	1971–1972	Henry Mancini
The Rookies	1972–1976	Elmer Bernstein
Streets of San Francisco	1972–1977	Pat Williams
Hec Ramsey	1972–1974	Johnny Western, Richard Boone, Sam Rolfe
Police Story	1973–1977	Jerry Goldsmith
Chase	1973–1974	Oliver Nelson
Kojak	1973–1978	Billy Goldenberg (1973–1977) John Cacavas (1977–1978)
Toma	1973–1974	Pete Carpenter and Mike Post
Police Woman	1974–1978	Morton Stevens
Get Christie Love!	1974–1975	Jack Elliott and Allyn Ferguson
Nakia	1974–1975	Leonard Rosenman
Amy Prentiss	1974–1975	John Cacavas
Joe Forrester	1975–1976	Richard Markowitz
Baretta	1975–1978	Dave Grusin and Tom Scott
Starsky and Hutch	1975–1979	Lalo Schifrin
S.W.A.T.	1975–1976	Barry DeVorzon
Bronk	1975–1976	Lalo Schifrin
Charlie's Angels	1976–1982	Jack Elliott and Allyn Ferguson
The Blue Knight	1976–1977	Henry Mancini
CHiPs	1977–1983	John Carl Parker

Also "Police Comedies"

Program	Dates	Theme Music Composer
Barney Miller	1975–1982	Jack Elliott and Allyn Ferguson
Holmes and Yo Yo	1976–1977	Leonard Rosenman
Carter Country	1978–1979	Pete Rugolo
The Misadventures of Sheriff Lobo	1979–1980	Stu Phillips

The success of *Hill Street Blues* led to more police dramas that dealt with the personal lives of police officers as they also apprehended criminals and solved crimes. Notable among these programs are *NYPD Blue* (which fused both violent content and personal treatment of characters) and *Homicide: Life on the Streets*. Other police dramas, such as *Law and Order*, reverted back to Jack Webb's investigative style show with a minimum of violence and a maximum of investigation and dialogue scenes. The show also has its antecedent in the 1960s series *Arrest and Trial* (1963–1964), which featured both police investigation and courtroom scenes.[8]

Music and the TV Police Drama

Despite periods of dormancy, police dramas have not gone into genre decay, as Butler would have it. Rather, the genre has persisted because of innovations in the discursive areas of the genre. Music is one of these discursive elements that has played a large role in the defining the police genre. In terms of musical scoring practices, the police drama was slower than its cousin, the detective/PI show, to move away from the patented Hollywood film scoring techniques, but it has demonstrated stylistic flexibility throughout the past few decades. One reason for the initial reticence to change may lie in the nature of the narrative formula of the genre. As Butler (1997) has pointed out, unlike detectives, the police are viewed as employees of the state who must maintain social order and thus play by the rules. Conversely, TV detectives are free agents who can bend the rules if need be to solve a crime. The constraints of social order appear to have made the police drama genre more conservative than its counterpart, the detective/PI genre. And apparently in the eyes of TV producers, at least in the genre's early years, these unwritten social strictures included adhering to the more conventional musical styles of film for narrative representation.

The musical contrast between police shows and detective shows in the 1950s is striking. As mentioned above, *Peter Gunn* (1958–1961) was known for its jazz score composed by Mancini. The jazz style topic soon correlated to the detective series, as Jon Burlingame (1996: 29–30) has noted that the success of the music to *Peter Gunn* can be attributed to jazz scores in other detective/PI shows, such as *Richard Diamond, Private Detective* (1957–1958) and *Seventy-Seven Sunset Strip* (1958–1964), the latter of which jettisoned a military-type score by Frank DeVol for a jazz score by Pete Rugolo. In contrast to detective shows, early police dramas such as *Dragnet* and *Highway Patrol* employed musical scores that adhered closely to the model of the Hollywood film score and used classic cinematic (or at least radiophonic) orchestras for themes and intradiegetic music.

Among the music topics within Hollywood film style scoring is one that, with its heavy use of brass and percussion instruments, can be described as military.

Concurrent with the success of *Peter Gunn* was at least one police drama, *M Squad* (1957–1960), which made a musical foray into jazz with its theme music composed by Count Basie (example 8.1). The cue music for the series was composed first by veteran film composer Ernst Gold but was then taken up by jazz saxophonist Benny Carter and the up-and-coming composer/arranger/pianist "Johnny" (a.k.a. John) Williams. The musical innovation of *M Squad*'s jazz theme song was not followed immediately by other police dramas, but it did show that other musical styles were possible fits for the genre.

By the 1960s, the police drama took a detour by way of police drama parodies, most notably, *Car 54, Where Are You?*, with a jingle-like theme composed by John Strauss, and *The Andy Griffith Show*, with its famous theme song, "The Fishin' Hole," composed by Earle Hagen. In addition to the theme, Hagen's music on *The Andy Griffith Show* included regularly recurring motives spoofing the *Highway Patrol* and *Dragnet* series (complete with motifs played by a trombone ensemble), used especially to accompany the bumbling antics of Deputy Barney Fife (Don Knotts). These were followed by satires of the police drama, including *Carter Country* (1977–1979), with a theme by Pete Rugolo, and *Barney Miller* (1975–1982), with an urban-jazz/funk theme by Jack Elliott and Allyn Ferguson.

The 1970s are seen as the second golden age of the police drama, with dozens of like shows premiering during the decade. The significance of these programs is the changing social view of the police, as reflected in the music. Beginning with cop shows like *Hawaii Five-0* and *The Mod Squad*, theme music contained an influence of rock music. *Hawaii Five-0* can be seen as a progenitor to many pop/rock style (or at least television's version of rock) musical themes in police dramas up to *Miami Vice* (1984–1989) and beyond.

The 1980s trend toward rock was revised somewhat in the 1990s. Programs like *NYPD Blue*, *Law and Order*, and *Homicide* used musical themes inspired

Example 8.1. Excerpt from Theme to *M Squad* (Music by Count Basie).

from contemporary pop but toned down from the raucous rock themes of the 1980s. The decade also witnessed the innovation of the police drama musical with the short-lived *Cop Rock* (1990).

The Innovation/Assimilation Model

The slow foray of police drama music into jazz in the 1950s and rock in the 1970s and 1980s reflects television's conservatism, on the one hand, but also its attraction to what's popular, on the other hand. As a medium driven by corporate sponsorship, American television has been very reticent to change formulas or to experiment with narratives that diverge too far from established norms. Despite this reticence, change does occur in television genres when a particular program that varies from the standard norm becomes popular, attracts many viewers, and thus also attracts many sponsors. The evolution of the police drama is an example of what Cawelti (1971) has called the "invention/convention" model of genre. In this ritual approach model, ratings success, and sometimes even critical approval of a newly created and innovative program (the invention aspect) will bring about an imitation of that success through the production of takeoffs with similar traits. As many programs begin imitating the innovative one, the invention aspect of the genre becomes conventional. The history of television is rife with examples of this process: the persistence of such genres as the situation comedy, the police and detective drama, and the soap opera (even subsequent programs that are not particularly innovative) are testaments to this process. Music in these genres follows a similar pattern to the program genres themselves, as evidenced by the police dramas evolution from the Hollywood film style of early TV to a pop/rock style prevalent in television in the 1980s and 1990s.

The invention/convention model can be viewed aesthetically as well as commercially. Innovations to television genres leave artistic imprints on a show, whether through the diegesis of the program, such as the narrative structure, characters, and settings, or through stylistic or discursive aspects of the program, such as camera shots, lighting, or music, or through any combination of parameters. The opening visual montage of *Hawaii Five-0* (described below) is one such example of aesthetic innovation to the police drama. Ultimately, the artistic success of genre innovations is linked to the commercial success of a program. Programs that display successful innovations tend to be more popular and have higher Nielsen ratings. Other programs are soon developed to copy this success (while perhaps making their own imprints) in order to achieve similarly high ratings and commercial success. Soon the innovative aspects of a program become conventional.

Rather than using Cawelti's term "invention/convention," it seems that a more accurate description of television genre is "innovation/assimilation," where an innovative feature (such as using music with a new/different style topic) results in an imitation by other programs, thus assimilating that innovation into conventional codes. Although this process is viewed both economically and aesthetically, it is important to point out that it occurs in other art forms as well as on television. Economic and artistic success breeds imitation in many areas, as pointed out by Harold Bloom's (1997) "anxiety of influence" theory for poetry. Joseph Straus (1990) has described a similar process for classical music, wherein composers, like poets, feel the need to be creatively innovative in order to supersede the music and poetry of earlier composers, thus creating space for themselves in the creative pantheon. Successive composers assimilate such innovations until further innovations are developed by artists responding to this anxiety of influence.[9]

Markedness

The innovation/assimilation model can be illustrated musically by tracing the musical styles used in various police dramas throughout the history of the genre. Music style analysis of themes in police dramas shows a gradual shift in the types of music accompanying programs, with most programs having musical themes that conform to other programs within a genre. In this process, a program that innovates through a shift in the musical style is, if successful, imitated by other like programs until the innovation is assimilated into the genre. Jazz and rock musical styles were innovations when introduced to a dramatic series and had to be assimilated through repetition for eventual acceptance by the audience. At first, the innovative style is marked, that is, without counterpart, and either spawns imitations until the style is no longer marked or dies out for lack of imitation/assimilation.[10] One example of the latter scenario is the program *M Squad*, which used jazz tracks instead of the traditional, Hollywood-style military music tracks used in most narrative police dramas of the era. Basie's jazz theme music to the show can be seen as marked vis-à-vis other police drama themes of the time. In the simplest form of markedness, one term in a binary opposition is marked, the other unmarked, with the terms of such an opposition having an unequal value or asymmetry in which the marked term is the more restrictive and the unmarked the more inclusive or generic (e.g., in this case one jazz theme versus many military themes). Marked TV themes are those perceived to be stylistically unique, such as the use of jazz in *M Squad*. As understood in linguistics, a marked term asserts the presence of a particular feature, and an unmarked term negates that assertion. The marked term usually covers a smaller semantic space than the unmarked and thus is more specific, conveying a narrower range of expressive content. Markedness can also be viewed as a comparatively significant event within a semantic space filled with insignificant events. It can be explained as the innovation aspect of the innovation/assimilation model that, in terms of TV music, may or may not produce a change in the musical style of a particular genre. In this sense, innovation shares a commonality with Butler's trial-and-error period of television genre. For *M Squad*, the jazz style of music used on the show is marked versus the unmarked Hollywood film music style of that time.[11] Ultimately, the jazz style of *M Squad* did not continue, or "take," within the police drama of the 1950s, and thus the assimilation aspect did not take place.

As a popular medium, television is largely unmarked, adhering closely to the conventional codes of genre in both the repertoire-of-elements and ritual models. Television producers, owners, and sponsors find it necessary to maintain a symbiotic relationship with audiences and thus strive to keep television unmarked in order to keep viewers socially comfortable and watching. At the same time, every program must have some marked aspect in order to make it distinctive.[12] These markers are usually most apparent in the diegetic aspects of the program, but they can come from any of the three spaces of television. Extradiegetic markers, or markers extrinsic to the narrative of a particular show, entail such aspects as time slot, production studio, director, and so on. For example, during most of its run *NYPD Blue* was broadcast over the ABC network on Tuesdays at 10 P.M. (Eastern Time). The show was thus marked as the "Tuesday 10:00 P.M. (prime-time) show on ABC," distinct from other cop shows broadcast at other times.[13] Other extradiegetic markers include the production studio or production crew of a particular show. Programs produced in the 1950s and 1960s by ZIV studios, for example, were marked in that they were not affiliated with one of the three major networks. Television programs are also marked through the intradiegetic markers of celebrity, camera shots, lighting, setting, and music. For instance, *NYPD Blue* was visually marked by jump cuts and jerky camera movements that appeared to be due to the use of handheld cameras. Most every program produced and directed by Stephen Bochco in the 1980s and 1990s featured a repertory company of actors and multiple narrative plots as well as music by Mike Post. Finally, markers occur within the diegetic realm through characters, setting, plot type, and so on. *The Rifleman*, for example, showed that the western was unmarked as a genre in late 1950s American television, but the show itself had marked aspects, including Chuck Connors as the star (discourse), the character Lucas McCain as a widower father, and the customized rifle fired in every episode.[14] *Star Trek* (1966–1969), meanwhile, showed that the sci-fi fantasy was an unmarked genre in the late 1960s (following *The Twilight Zone*, *The Outer Limits* [1963–1965], *Lost in Space* [1965–1968], *The Time Tunnel* [1966–1967], *Voyage to the Bottom of the Sea* [1964–1968], and others), but the show itself was marked with William Shatner and Leonard

Nimoy as actors (discourse) and the fact that Nimoy portrayed a nonthreatening alien allied with the good guys (story). For many years the plots of police dramas were investigative—cops discovered a crime and then investigated the crime by the book until a suspect was caught. As the genre matured, new marked plots developed, such as the depiction of violence (cops not only investigated, but they also participated in gun battles and car chases), a trend that was assimilated in the 1970s. Later programs depicted personal aspects of cops' lives, creating a marked hybrid genre of cop show/soap opera.

In short, Cawelti suggests that in order for television programs to be successful, they must balance marked features with unmarked ones. The trick is for the program to provide enough characteristics of the genre to attract viewers while also providing some innovation, or markedness, that makes the program stand out in the viewer's mind. Tendencies toward unmarkedness in the police drama would include plot (police must solve crimes, violently or not), setting (usually urban, usually New York, Chicago, or Los Angeles), and characters (must be cops—enforcers of the law—and likeable or at least sympathetic to viewers).

Style Growth/Style Change

The second scenario for a marked aspect of a program would be for the innovative marker to be imitated and thus assimilated into a TV genre. Theme music to a program in a genre can imitate its predecessor, as the theme to *Highway Patrol* imitated the theme to *Dragnet*. However, later shows often seek to have their themes "marked" by changing the style of the theme music. Such a scenario is similar to Robert Hatten's (1994: 33) term "style growth," which I borrow here to show the evolution of musical style in police drama theme music. Composers of music for new shows often draw upon successful musical formulae of the past while also infusing new elements into the theme music. As has been noted, the military march style was popular in early police drama themes, but as the popularity of rock music increased, composers began to draw from both styles. Eventually, rock and pop styles replaced the old military musical style, in a process that I (again borrowing from Hatten) refer to as style change. The remainder of this chapter focuses on how style growth and style change occurred in the police drama from 1952 to 2002.

TV Theme Music as Marker in the American Police Drama

TV theme music can be considered as part of both the extradiegetic and intradiegetic aspects of a program in that it transitions the audience from the flow of the televisual into the narrative realm of the program (the extradiegetic aspect) while also conveying traits of the program about to be watched (the intradiegetic). TV themes are marked in one sense, that each is unique to its particular program. In this regard, TV theme songs serve as labels (or leitmotifs) for specific programs. However, the style of music used for a particular TV show can reveal much about how the show is to be perceived by an audience as well as relay information about the genre in which a show belongs.

Because musical style has the ability to signify certain cultural phenomena, such as place (urban versus rural) or demographic/sociographic groups (African Americans, Latinos, the wealthy, etc.), it is a powerful tool to attract viewers extradiegetically as well as to signify intradiegetically. Over a 50-year period, the musical style of the police drama gradually changed from a military march style to rock music and then to a new age or smooth jazz style. The following analysis of the theme music to several police dramas from the first 50 years of American TV offers several views of the innovation/assimilation process at work, reflecting its twofold purpose of attracting new (often younger) audiences while also exhibiting a visual and musical reconception of the TV cop.

Dragnet

One of the pioneering programs of the police drama genre on television was *Dragnet*. This program made its way to American television in 1951 by way of the radio drama of the 1940s. The musical theme to the program, especially the opening four-note motif, became famous as exemplifying the cop show genre in American television (see example 8.2). The motif serves as a dramatic introduction to both the theme music and the program itself. In fact, the opening motive has been highly influential in identifying the program, even many years after its demise, and has been thoroughly assimilated into the American psyche. In semiotic terms, it can be said that the motif serves as a sort of leitmotif for the program. In layman's terms, this is one of television's greatest hits.[15] The ascending minor key melody in the first four notes of the motif signals that the program is a drama. This four-note motif is repeated with a final note sounding a tritone away from the tonic pitch, the discordant interval signifying the

Example 8.2. *Dragnet* Four-Note Motif (Music by William Schumann and Miklós Rózsa).

dissonance of crime within society. The dotted rhythm of the motif does not signify the action and heroism found within a similar rhythm of the *Rifleman* theme but rather is more likely an iconic representation of the fateful knock on the door by the police or the pounding of a judge's gavel.

In addition to the motif, the closing credits of the program are accompanied by a full-blown theme that is characterized as a military march (see example 8.3). The compound duple meter with the preponderance of brass instruments recalls the conventional 6/8 march performed by military bands. Due to its association with military band music, the 6/8 march has the expressive function of signifying authority, especially military authority. The narrow compass of the melody could signify the straight-and-narrow path of law and order, and the repetitious nature of the melody can be thought to signify the methodical persistence of the police in tracking down suspects. As shown in example 8.3, the end of the theme shifts from its ambiguous minor key basis (ambiguous due to the persistent parallel fifths in the trombones) to end in B-flat major. The piece thus represents a sort of miniature expressive genre in Hatten's Beethovenian sense, signifying a movement from one emotional state to another, in this case from serious investigation to triumphal resolution. In the post–World War II, Cold War mindset of the 1950s, the expressive qualities of a military style topic transferred easily to the authority of the police. The terse march music reinforces the narrative aspects of the program, which include a pseudodocumentary form of narration (Jack Webb's voice-over) and depictions of the lead characters (Webb and Ben Alexander) as authority figures who are very good at their jobs.

Example 8.3. *Dragnet* March (Music by William Schumann and Miklós Rózsa).

The program emphasizes careful police work and the characters' professional (not personal) lives. Moreover, the crime is always solved at the end of each episode, followed by an epilogue describing the outcomes of the resulting criminal trials.

Other police dramas in the 1950s and 1960s followed *Dragnet*'s lead. One such program was *Highway Patrol* (1955–1959), which featured a dour Broderick Crawford as Lt. Dan Mathews. The theme music was believed to have been composed by David Rose working under the pseudonym Ray Llewellyn, a name reportedly used by several ZIV-TV composers who worked under buyout contracts with the studio.[16] Rose was a veteran film composer best known for composing scores for Bob Hope movies. He broke into television in 1951 as composer and conductor on *The Red Skelton Show*, using the theme "Holiday for Strings," which he had composed for the film *The Unfinished Dance* (1947). For *Highway Patrol*, Rose copied the marked qualities of the theme music to *Dragnet*, that is, the military style topic performed in another 6/8 march, and assimilated it, virtually to the point where it was unmarked by the 1960s.

Adam-12

Following the long-running success of *Dragnet*, Jack Webb went on to produce and direct *Adam-12* (1968–1975) and *Dragnet 1967* (1967–1970). Like *Dragnet*, *Adam-12* is a realistic police drama following the lives of two officers of the Los Angeles Police Department (LAPD), veteran Pete Malloy (Martin Milner) and his rookie partner, Jim Reed (Kent McCord). Done in a sparse, almost docudrama style, each episode covered a variety of incidents, from the tragic to the trivial, that the officers encountered while on patrol on the streets of Los Angeles. The program featured a little bit more of the personal side of the two characters than in previous police shows, with Milner portraying the veteran cop (whose former partner was killed) and McCord portraying the rookie cop who matures as the show progresses.

The theme to *Adam-12* was composed by Frank Comstock, a successful film composer, conductor, arranger, and accompanist (example 8.4). Comstock arranged music for several bands, including Les Brown's Band of Renown (with whom he worked for 17 years), and was also a freelance arranger/composer for Doris Day, for the *Bob Hope* and *Steve Allen* shows (both radio and television), and for films. His other television credits include *Rocky and His Friends*, the wacky Jay Ward and Bill Scott animated cartoon show, and music for the comedies *Gilligan's Island* and *F Troop*, among others. For *Adam-12*, Comstock imitated Schumann's military-style topic from the *Dragnet* theme but updated it somewhat by creating a more angular melody and dissonant harmonies.

Example 8.4. Excerpt from Theme to *Adam-12* (Music by Frank Comstock).

The *Dragnet/Highway Patrol* pairing illustrates the innovation/assimilation paradigm in television. The first program is marked by the use of an innovative musical style topic, and with the imitation of that topic by other programs (like *Highway Patrol*) the style becomes unmarked for the genre. The *Adam-12* theme illustrates style growth, as the older military march topic is retained but adapted and crafted into a more modernistic, contemporary style. The meter has shifted from the swingy compound duple (6/8) to the more angular simple quadruple (4/4), the harmonies are more dissonant, and the melody features wide dissonant leaps sustained over long periods of time to accentuate the dissonance. The all-brass and percussion ensemble of *Dragnet* is augmented by woodwinds, particularly a piccolo that plays the extremely high dissonances. Although more modernistic in its pitch elements, the snare drums and timpani retains the notion of a military style topic with the persistent drum cadence under the melody and harmonies of the theme. A bass guitar and electronic guitar furnish a rhythmic backdrop to the theme, foreshadowing the use of rock/pop instruments in other programs to follow.[17]

Hawaii Five-O

Comstock's theme music to *Adam-12* demonstrates how the military march of the police genre evolved in the late 1960s through style growth. Not all programs, however, demonstrate this type of development. The use of jazz in *M Squad* has already been noted. Although it proved to be an innovation, police dramas of the time did not follow the program's lead, adhering instead to the military march topic of shows like *Dragnet*. Thus *M Squad*'s innovative musical score was not assimilated by other programs—at least not immediately. It did resurface, however, in 1968, with the premiere of *Hawaii Five-0*. This police-on-the-beach program featured a theme that was essentially a hybrid style incorporating big band jazz and rock elements thus becoming one of the first police dramas to use elements of rock music. The longest running police drama (1968–1980) until *NYPD Blue* (also 12 seasons [1993–2005]), *Hawaii Five-0* evolved from an unmarked police procedural (albeit with a diegetic marker in its Hawaiian location) to a show in which the characters became increasingly involved with mastermind criminals and international political intrigue.

The theme to *Hawaii Five-0* was composed by Morton Stevens, a Juilliard graduate who began his career as musical director for Sammy Davis Jr. By the time he composed *Hawaii Five-0*, Stevens was music director for CBS as well as a veteran TV composer, having supplied music for the shows *Thriller*, *The Man from U.N.C.L.E.*, *Gunsmoke*, and many others, primarily for Revue and MGM studios.

Stevens's theme can be considered as an important turning point for music in the police drama. The theme music for the opening credits to the program featured four trumpets, four trombones, four French horns, six woodwinds, six cellos, and four percussion players, an instrumentation not unlike that for the march topics of other police dramas.[18] However, the rock style of the music was markedly different. Although Stevens used conventional orchestral instruments, he added heavy percussion with a rock-like feel that distinguished the theme from other police shows at the time. The heavy percussion at the very beginning is also made to sound Hawaiian or Polynesian, depicting the location of the series, but the remainder of the percussion during the theme (along with the heavy bass) is pure rock. Stevens's use of brass instruments retains a trace of the expressive genre of the military march found in *Dragnet* and *Adam-12*, but it also gives the theme a big band jazz feel. As a result, the *Hawaii Five-0* theme is a hybrid style of big band jazz and what can be called

Example 8.5. Excerpt from Theme to *Hawaii Five-0* (Music by Morton Stevens).

TV rock, which at least partly supplanted the military march topic as a portrayer of the police (example 8.5).[19]

The active percussion parts (not shown in the example) and the minor key also illustrate that rock (whether authentic or faux) carries expressive genres signifying both the drama and the action-packed nature of the drama. The use of the rock style topic, along with Jack Lord's famous line, "Book 'em Dan-o," became marked aspects of the series. The retention of brass instruments signifies the police as authority figures, but the driving rock beat of the augmented percussion section apparently signifies more on-screen action and violence than the authority of the police.

The weekly installment of the program opened with the theme music accompanying another marker, a rapid cinema-style montage compiled by editor Reza Badiyi. The montage of scenes from Hawaii with the powerful music remains a tour de force of American television. Stevens's theme was so popular, in fact, that it was recorded by the instrumental rock group the Ventures, first making its way into the top-10 hit list and, in 1969, becoming a gold record.

Light Rock Themes in the 1970s

Stevens's theme to *Hawaii Five-0* represents a musical innovation in the police drama in the 1960s and, following the success of the program, became a convention during the 1970s, an era known as the second golden age of the police drama. However, Stevens was not the lone composer of jazz/rock scores at this time. Earle Hagen's theme to *The Mod Squad* (1968–1973) and Quincy Jones's theme to *Ironside* (1967–1975), both performed in several different arrangements over the seasons, featured similar jazz/rock influences and came out at the same time as *Hawaii Five-0*. These successful programs led to dozens of jazz/rock scores in the 1970s. Just as in the 1950s Americans looked to the police drama for reassurance during the Cold War, so in the 1970s Americans may have looked again to the genre to recuperate from the political devastation of the Vietnam War and the Watergate scandal.

One good example of the growth of the jazz/rock style in cop show theme music can be found in the program *CHiPs* (1977–1983). *CHiPs*, an acronym for California Highway Patrol (not actually used in California before the show aired), followed the daily beat of two state motorcycle cops as they patrolled the freeway system in and around Los Angeles. Officer Jon Baker (Larry Wilcox) was the straight, serious officer while Frank "Ponch" Poncherello (Erik Estrada) was the more freewheeling member of the duo. Each episode presented a compilation of incidents, ranging from the humorous (e.g., stranded motorists) to the criminal (hijackings) and the tragic (fiery, multicar pileups involving multiple deaths). Aspects of Ponch and Jon's daily work were highlighted, and unlike *Dragnet*, their social lives (both officers were single) also were depicted, often providing for the show's lighter moments.

The theme to *CHiPs* was composed by John Carl Parker, a veteran TV composer who got his start in 1955 by contributing music to episodes of *Gunsmoke*. Parker went on to provide music for several television programs, in particular, the distinctive theme music for the detective series *Cannon* (1971–1976).[20] Parker's theme to *CHiPs* is another amalgam of military march and light rock style topics, and like the *Hawaii Five-0* theme, it utilizes conventional orchestral instruments. This type of scoring portrayed the police characters as men of power and authority but also socially cool (especially to enhance Estrada's off-screen persona). The high, blaring trumpet in the middle of the theme also imitates a Latino, mariachi style of playing, thus signifying Poncherello's Latino persona, as well as the multicultural scene of L.A. in the series.

By the 1970s, not only had the pop style caught on in police dramas, but some theme songs became hits on the *Billboard* charts. Barry DeVorzon's theme to *S.W.A.T.* (1975–1976) was arranged in a disco version by the group Rhythm Heritage and became the first single from a prime-time series to hit number one on the *Billboard* pop chart since "The Ballad of Davy Crockett" 20 years earlier (Burlingame 1996: 58). The disco style topic was adopted by at least one other police show, *Charlie's Angels* (1976–1981), with a theme by Jack Elliott and Allyn Ferguson.

Hill Street Blues

A new, marked type of police drama emerged in the 1980s with the program *Hill Street Blues* (1981–1987). *Hill Street Blues* was one of the first shows in which the boundaries of genre began to blur through the portrayal of characters not only as members of the police force but also as actual human beings both in and out of the squad room and police car. As members of the squad pursued myriad criminals, other aspects of their lives crept into the story line, such as romantic involvements, divorce, alcoholism, personality disorders, drug addiction, and financial problems. In short, the program was a virtual hybrid of police drama and soap opera.

The theme music, composed by Mike Post, signifies within this hybridization conveying the topics of soft rock or easy listening, as it was called in the 1980s (example 8.6). Post's use of rock and other popular style topics was intentional from his first project, the theme to the detective series *The Rockford Files* (1974–1980). Post differs from his predecessors in that he began his career as a rock musician and was not a formally educated film scorer. He has a remarkable ability to manipulate musical style topics and expressive genres according to a program's theme, thus demonstrating an ability to fuse style topics and social codes. As a window into his compositional process and aesthetic, Post has described his conception of his music to *Rockford Files*:

> The whole story of that is [James] Garner. . . . He's Oklahoman—a little southern, but not completely—so a harmonica makes sense. I had just gotten a mini-Moog [synthesizer] with that sassy sort of weep, "nya-nya" to it. And I'm very guitar-oriented, and nobody had done it on TV.
>
> *Rockford Files* isn't real rock 'n' roll, but it's close. We got calls from the dubbing stage [saying] "What is this?" What it was, was our turn: guys who were raised on Chuck Berry, Bo Diddley, and the Rolling Stones. . . . It's going to be thundering guitars now, guys. That's all there is. It isn't five saxophones anymore: it's thundering guitars. (Quoted in Burlingame 1996: 61–62)

In a sense, Post personifies the innovation/assimilation model for television music in much the same way that Beethoven personified it for classical music. Post's move to rock music in television has revolutionized the medium. Since *Rockford Files*, Post has experimented with other style topics, notably soft jazz, as heard in the *Hill Street Blues* theme. His other themes are similar: *The A Team* (1983–1986) is similar to *CHiPs* as an amalgam of military and pop styles, *Magnum, P.I.* (1980–1988) is more rock-oriented, as is the theme to another police drama, *Hunter* (1984–1991). Post's efforts to infuse rock music in television were helped by the rise of the music video and MTV in the 1980s and

Example 8.6. Opening to *Hill Street Blues* Theme (Music by Mike Post).

1990s, but his influence as an innovator of television theme music in this period cannot be overstated.

Although Post composed the breakthrough rock score for *Rockford Files*, his theme music to the police drama remained restrained and conservative. The *Hill Street Blues* theme, with its soft jazz/rock topic, signifies a soap opera more than a police show. Heard against the visual images of the opening titles, the theme has an ironic effect: the rushing and skidding of police cars down slippery city streets is accompanied by Post's somber easy-listening theme music. In Cook's (1998) terms, the music and visuals of the scene are not "conformant," but the opening nonetheless signifies the sense of melancholy, futility, fatalism, and human drama in the show.

Miami Vice

While Post paved the way for greater stylistic diversity on television (including some use of rock), authentic rock music came to the television with the program *Miami Vice* (1984–1989). By 1984, music videos had become influential purveyors of popular music, and the editing techniques of quick cuts, montage, and surrealistic images became compelling for television as well. NBC president Brandon Tartikoff decided to try these techniques in a television series. Michael Mann, the appointed executive producer of the show, chose Jan Hammer, a Czech-born keyboardist who played with the popular jazz-fusion group the Mahavishnu Orchestra to compose music for the series.

Hammer's theme is truly progressive rock of the 1980s, utilizing synthesizer, distorted guitar, and Latin-style percussion. The score to *Miami Vice* can be seen as a continuation of the expressive topics of Morton Stevens's *Hawaii Five-0* and Post's *Rockford Files* themes. The *Miami Vice* theme, perhaps not coincidentally accompanied by a visual montage similar to that of *Hawaii Five-0*, signifies action and excitement. However, the theme is not a jazz-pop-rock amalgam as is Stevens's theme, but real 1980s techno-rock. This topic signifies many social codes of interpretation, both from audience-response signifiers of youth and masculinity (i.e., the desired audience demographics) as well as narrative signifiers of counterculture aspects, like drugs, armed conflict, and antisocial behavior. These signifieds can be found within the intradiegesis of the narrative and its characters. As Fiske (1987: 133) has pointed out, "Crockett and Tubbs... move literally between the worlds of the vice squad and the drug runners, and, in embodying certain values of both, they act mythically as mediators between both sides of the opposition. Their embodiment of the values and lifestyle of both demonstrates an imaginative way of coping with the conflict, which is a crucial mythic function, for the conflict itself can never by resolved." Also, as noted by David McQueen (1998: 85), "Crockett drives a Ferrari, they wear designer clothes, they become involved with women associated with the gangs they are investigating, they act the parts and seemed to flirt with the roles of cocaine dealers or users...and all this set against a backdrop of images and music that seems at once to celebrate and condemn Miami's vice." Ideologically, the rock style topic is, at best, ambivalent to the role of the police, and, at worse, it mitigates against the police by venerating the countercultural aspects of the program.

Beyond Rock in the 1990s

The assimilation of both the hard rock and soft rock style topics can be found in another Post theme score, to *NYPD Blue* (1993–2005). Like *Hill Street*, this controversial and often graphic program depicts police both on and off the job, and thus continues the cop show/soap opera hybrid (not coincidentally, Stephen Bochco was the producer of both programs). The theme music, with its interesting blend of style topics, reflects both of these areas (see example 8.7).

The hard-driving percussion typifies a hard rock style topic, signifying the action/violence that the viewer will see in the program. However, in the electronic keyboard part, a long quasi-melody meanders in no particular direction. This line is more like the easy-listening or soft jazz style of Post's *Hill Street* theme. The *NYPD Blue* theme is thus marked as a double assimilation of both the hard rock topic of *Miami Vice* and the easy listening topic of *Hill Street Blues*. However, it is marked also by another topic: the popular music categories of the 1990s called New Age. The use of Asian-sounding drums at the beginning of the theme, giving it a one world music quality, links this topic with one of the features of New Age music of the 1990s. This one world music topic signifies the multicultural aspects of the program (reinforced by African American and Hispanic characters on the show) and (perhaps more importantly) seeks to ameliorate the prevailing notion in America that cops are primarily white and racist, as the LAPD was accused of being at the time (the show was contemporaneous with the Rodney King beating by Los Angeles police officers, and with the O.J. Simpson trial, in which some tried to project Simpson's race onto the case). The theme can be seen as a conscious attempt by Hollywood producers to portray the police in a positive light.

Finally, one other cop show of the 1990s with a marked theme is *Homicide: Life on the Streets* (1993–1999), produced by Barry Levinson. This critically acclaimed program portrays police (again) both on and off the job, but characters are no longer authority figures; rather, they are portrayed as fatalistic professionals who go about the job of solving murder upon murder on the streets of

Example 8.7. Excerpt from Theme to *NYPD Blue*
(Music by Mike Post).

Baltimore.[21] The theme is a musical collage replete with electronic and electronically manipulated environmental sounds. The score features a synthesizer playing slowly moving sustained notes along with panflute, forced air sounds, electronic telephone ringing, and heavy percussion in a ponderous, repetitious pattern. The theme music signifies the dramatic if not chaotic and entropic nature of "life on the streets." The theme is marked by its musical modernist style topic, and it remains to be seen whether or not it will be assimilated in subsequent police dramas.

Police Show Themes: An Ideological Reading

Musical style has the ability to signify extramusically by its associations with performers and audiences who are attracted to a certain style and also by attitudes, critical writings, and impressions formed by the supporting culture. In this sense, music style in TV themes seems to fit in with the audience-response approach to genre. In Fiske's terms, ideologies would form around different musical styles while, in Eco's terms, codes would form based on habit and belief. These codes lead to correlations of music and extramusical traits that help define the police drama, and they also steer the viewer toward preferred or intended meanings within the genre.

TV themes also participate in the repertoire-of-elements model for genre by signifying intradiegetic aspects of the programs. The theme to *Dragnet* conveys a military style topic that reflects the image of the police in the 1950s as authority figures serving and protecting the larger society. Such an image was comforting to American middle-class TV audiences concerned about the Cold War, the supposed infiltration of communism, and other social disruptions of the day. *Dragnet's* Sgt. Joe Friday is portrayed as a no-nonsense police investigator who remains cool and seeks "just the facts" when interviewing someone. His personal life was irrelevant to the series. Broderick Crawford was portrayed similarly in *Highway Patrol*, though narrative resolutions on this series tended to be more punitive and violent than on *Dragnet*. Violent scenes in which the bad guys were killed by the police may have been cathartic to some middle-class, law-and-order viewers in the 1950s. It was the police procedural, though, and not police violence, that endured throughout the history of the genre. The ethos of authority was carried into the 1960s and 1970s with such programs as *Adam-12* and *Dragnet 1967* (1967–1970) (both produced by Jack Webb). The desire to bolster police authority, to show police in a positive light, was undoubtedly a result of the Vietnam War and the social unrest of the 1960s and early 1970s.

The infusion of popular styles of jazz in the 1950s and rock in the 1960s and 1970s represents an attempt to portray police in a more personal, personable light. That the jazz score of *M Squad* reached a dead end may be due in part to the fact that jazz was perceived by many as cerebral, a style with little emotive, expressive capacity. Jazz does signify sophisticated, big-city settings due to its roots as an urban art form (see the discussion of the "Steel" episode of *The Twilight Zone* in chapter 2). But though jazz was popular among young intellectuals in the 1950s, it could be that it did not have the extramusical expressive power of the post-Romantic Hollywood film style. In other words, the jazz of Count Basie and Benny Carter may simply have been too exotic or too foreign-sounding for most television viewers at the time.

251

The growth of musical style in the police drama can be traced more directly in the fusion of the military topic with the pop/rock style. The program *CHiPs* represents an attempt to portray police as benevolent authority figures in touch with the needs of common people, and its theme contains music that reflects a bent toward the popular. The jazz-rock topic of *Hawaii Five-0* with its accompanying montage intended to portray action and excitement exploited not only a new style, but also an expressive genre of seriousness and action. Likewise, *Adam-12*'s theme is meant to refer back to the military style topic while also portraying a sense of contemporary action. *Miami Vice* continues the trend by featuring a musical theme (and music on the series) that was truly pop rock music of the time.

Mike Post's themes to the police shows *Hill Street Blues* and *NYPD Blue* signify in a different way, perhaps more in keeping with television's desire not to be on the cutting edge. The soft rock or light jazz topic of *Hill Street* signifies intimacy (the piano chords at the opening), gentility, even humor. As Burlingame (1996: 63) has noted, "Post created a gentle counterpoint to the main title visuals of police cars careening around corners and down mean city streets." This counterpoint also provides a narrative distance and objectivity to the opening—one that seems melancholy, almost tragic (the theme is often replayed during tragic scenes). The theme reflects the portrayal of police officers as individuals who perform their jobs but who also experience the same joys and sorrows of other people. Although they are still authority figures, the police on *Hill Street* are nonetheless real people. Finally, the *Hill Street* theme music signifies within the repertoire of the soap opera, thus highlighting the genre hybridity of the program.

The other Post theme considered here, the one for *NYPD Blue*, is an interesting amalgam of rock, new age, and one world music. The drums are ethnic-sounding tom-toms and are accompanied by electronic keyboard that produces a static melody, thus signifying a new age topic. All these styles blended together in popular music of the 1990s. The drums signify the diverse ethnicity of residents of the big city as well as officers within the New York Police Department (complete at times with an African American chief of police and a Hispanic detective). The drums can also be seen as iconic to the noise of the city (it accompanies a montage of an elevated train) while also signifying action and violence. Like *Hill Street*, the police in *NYPD Blue* are portrayed as characters that perform their duties but have real life problems as individuals. In this sense, the program is a 1990s' version of *Hill Street*.

Quite a different view of the police is seen in *Homicide*. The theme is an aleatoric sounding mass that resembles more progressive new age music but is reminiscent of a more highbrow style, notably the *musique concrète* by twentieth-century art music composers like Karlheinz Stockhausen, Edgar Varèse, and John Cage.

The interweaving of electronic musical sounds with electronically manipulated environmental sounds, like voices on police band radios and telephones ringing, produces an almost hallucinatory effect to the opening. Police on the program are portrayed in many ways: some are dedicated, efficient, and almost addicted to their jobs; others are overcome with problems; some are crooked; some are alcoholics; one is gay, and so on. While the program has its comic moments, it also lends an air of fatalism in which police struggle against criminals but also against themselves. The theme music signifies this almost chaotic fatalism. However, the theme may present more of a commentary on the program itself as a perceived high art form than a true societal reflection of policework.

Conclusion

This snapshot historical survey of style in police drama themes serves to illustrate the process of style change in television music over a 50-year period. Though participating in a repertoire-of-elements approach to genre, the musical styles of theme music in some TV genres also function as part of the audience-response model in which music maintains its signifying power with an audience. In the police drama, theme music shifted gradually from a military style topic in the 1960s to pop styles like rock and disco in the 1970s to smooth, easy-listening and new age topics in the 1990s. Yet this shift in topics was not always cut-and-dried but, rather, moved smoothly through a series of hybrids or amalgams of musical styles. Many shows of the 1960s retained a musical sense of the military through the use of brass instruments and heavy percussion, but these same themes also contain a contemporary rock beat. The retention of such features can be viewed as an attempt to keep the musical signifiers of action, violence, and/or authority. Where the musical shift was not smooth, as in the case of *M Squad*, the new style was less likely to assimilate. Figure 8.1 illustrates the process of style change for cop shows from 1952 to 2002 along with extrinsic influences on it, from both the musical world and other genres. These features are assimilated into a show's own fingerprint.

The theme music for police dramas in the early 1950s adopted the military march style topic, and the assimilation of this style became unmarked for police shows (*Highway Patrol*). Style growth in the 1960s is illustrated by the military march being updated with some big band and jazz influences, as in *Adam-12*. With *Hawaii Five-0*, Morton Steven's score retains the predominantly brass instrumentation of the march topic but is infused with the innovative, driving rhythms of rock music. *Ironside* (1967–1975) and *Mod Squad* (1968–1973) followed suit. Many themes of the 1970s retain this use of brass while adopting pop music topics, thus making these themes unmarked. Jan Hammer's score to *Miami*

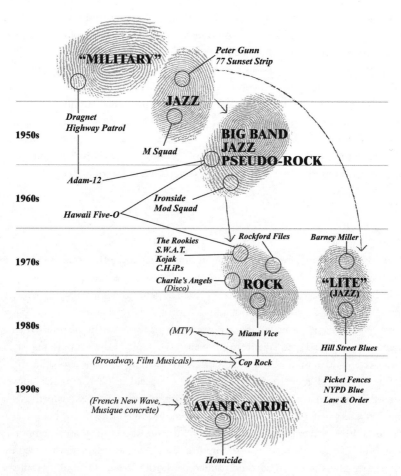

Figure 8.1. Musical Styles of Police Drama Themes, 1952–2002.

Vice, perhaps the first true rock TV score, resulted from the influence of Mike Post's detective dramas scores, especially *The Rockford Files*. Lite themes also made their appearance in the 1970s, with such programs as the situation comedy/police show *Barney Miller* (1975–1982) helping to pave the way for the lite theme to *Hill Street Blues*. By the 1990s, themes used style to reflect the times. The score to *NYPD Blue* retains some of the rock characteristics of *Miami Vice* but is imbued with new age and non-Western elements, both popular in the 1990s. *Law and Order* reverts back to a cool jazz or urban contemporary topic while the theme to *Homicide*, like many other aspects of the program, is definitely marked by the elemental sounds of *musique concrète*.

In this sense, the shift in musical styles in police themes is a process of style growth and style change, which can be seen as extensions of Hatten's (1994: 33) cyclical process used to illustrate the music of Beethoven. In adapting Hatten's model to television music, I use the more generic (and perhaps cruder) categories for contemporary styles found in film and format radio. In television programs of the 1950s, such as *Dragnet*, the musical styles heard on television ranged from the Hollywood symphonic style (with its many expressive genres) to jazz to light music to Tin Pan Alley, to some contemporary classical music, folk, and country music. By the 1960s, rock 'n' roll had made inroads to some narrative television genres. Certain styles and expressive genres of music become correlated with certain genres of television programs, and viewer's competencies with these correlations produce meaning. In early television programs, the military march topic correlated with the police drama, light music with the filmed situation

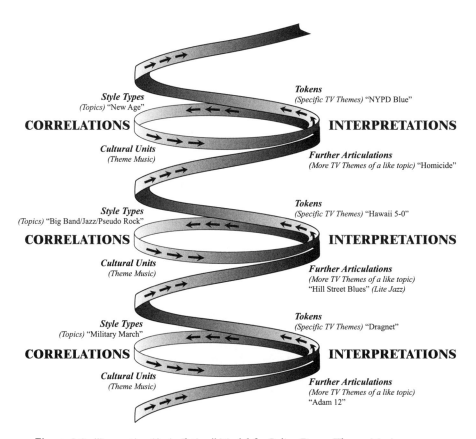

Figure 8.2. "Innovation/Assimilation" Model for Police Drama Theme Music.

comedy, and dramatic Romantic music with the soap opera. These style topics were inherited from radio dramas and film as well as musical theater and were assimilated into television.

This process can be summarized as follows: One, music is marked in some way—though not always through the style topic. It remains a token of a style type, for example, rock, jazz, classical, and so on. Two, a show comes along that is marked through music (such as *M Squad* or *Hawaii Five-0* or *Homicide*) and, if it is successful, is imitated and thereby becomes unmarked. Three, while the entire process of style growth in theme music is more menu-driven than binary, when it is viewed as a binary opposition, the process creates a stylistic spiral. This spiral can be expressed as Hatten's growth model, or series of growth models, connected with the unmarked or breakout style. For police drama themes, this model is shown as figure 8.2.

In this model, the assimilated themes remain within the correlation of the marked style while the new, unmarked styles break out of the correlation cycle to restart the process anew. So, for police drama, *Adam-12* lies within the correlation of the military march style (though it has grown) while *Hawaii Five-0* breaks out of the style by injecting the new stylistic characteristics of jazz and rock. However, despite these characteristics, some aspects of the *Hawaii Five-0* theme retain the military march topic, such as the loud, brass instrumentation.

At this writing, it is unclear how the genre will play itself out and which styles will become unmarked. New programs, such as the *CSI* series on CBS and the *Law and Order* spin-offs on NBC, differ, with the *CSI* programs utilizing old pop tunes ("We Won't Get Fooled Again" by The Who) and the *Law and Order* spin-offs reorchestrating Post's original jazzy *Law and Order* theme. Also up to this writing, no program has yet to copy the avant-garde theme of *Homicide*.

Stay tuned for more.

9

"The Truth Is Out There"

Music in Modern/Postmodern Television

Gillian Anderson and David Duchovny in *The X-Files—The Movie* (Photo by FOX/ Liaison; Getty Images).

TV in the 1980s and 1990s

Many consider the 1980s as a turning point, the period when television came into its own, decoupling the influences of radio and the cinema and developing into a unique medium with its own visual and sonic production values. Jimmy Reeves, Mark Rodgers, and Michael Epstein (1996: 24) have described 1980s television as representing "the most extreme shift the American mass communication complex has experienced since the 1950s (when broadcast television displaced the movies as the culture's central narrative medium)." They attribute this shift to economic, technological, political, and societal developments that included: (1) the drift from a manufacturing "Fordist" economy to a niche-market, post-Fordist service economy, (2) the diminished role of broadcasting after the diffusion of new communication technologies (i.e., personal computers), (3) the displacement of the Cold War, (4) the triumph of Reagan's politics of division (signaling the end of the New Deal), (5) the postmodern turn in everything from architecture to advertising, and (6) the fragmentation of American society into special interest groups and various types of racial, ethnic, and sexual subgroups. A new type of television emerged during this TV II generation (as opposed to TV I, that is, the era of the big three television networks—and the subject matter of much of this book). TV II is marked, in part, by narrowcasting, through which networks develop programming directed to a specific audience demographic. One result of narrowcasting is the genre of cult television, beginning with MTV, specialty cable channels (Comedy Channel, the History Channel, BET, MTV, the Food Network, etc.), and programs that tend to draw avid viewers, such as *The X-Files* and *Twin Peaks*. This process of fragmentation in television is similar to that of radio in the 1950s (described in Barnes 1988), when networks abandoned the variety programming format and developed format music radio stations. This narrowcasting filtered into television commercials especially (as discussed in chapter 7).

John Thornton Caldwell (1995: 5) has identified a new style of television that developed in the 1980s, one featuring a new mode of visuality, or "televisuality," through which "style itself became the subject, the signified...of television." This change resulted in a bifurcated mode of visual presentation wherein some programs emulated film in cinematic quality, complete with enriched color and sound (stereo television made its impact in the 1990s), while other programs developed a videographic look featuring split screens, textual crawls, computer graphics, and other explicitly video visuals. This bifurcated mode of visual presentation followed genre lines: narrative television tended toward the cinematic (*Miami Vice, Moonlighting, Max Headroom, thirtysomething*) while news and documentaries (later reality TV) gravitated toward the new videographic mode (*Entertainment Tonight, A Current Affair, America's Most Wanted*, and *CNN News*).

Caldwell's bifurcation of televisual presentation is actually the intensified continuation of a duality that existed from the very earliest days of television. As has been mentioned, television has always contained two modes of visual presentation, beginning with the live videographic look (presented through videotape and/or kinescope) followed by the cinematic look of narrative TV in the early 1950s, especially with the Desilu studio sitcoms and the Four Star and Warner Bros. westerns. Narrative TV films contrasted with the videotaped look of live daytime soap operas, game shows, and news programs, but the look was always somewhat mitigated by the black-and-white picture of both visual formats. As color TV became the norm in the 1960s, the looks remained distinctive, with improvements to both film and videotape. By the 1980s, the rise of computer-generated graphics further enhanced both the cinematic and video appearances, improving video color techniques as well as stereo sound, all of which contributed to making each of these visual modes more distinctive and appealing in their own ways.

Along with the technological forces that improved the appearance and sound of television, televisuality of the 1980s was influenced also by economic and aesthetic factors. Cable TV began to proliferate early on in the decade, and the migration of audiences from the traditional networks to cable threw the big three networks into turmoil. The loss of audiences due to cable, music videos, and other new media forced TV producers to look for something to revitalize their programming. They tried new marketing strategies to identify target demographic groups for particular shows, the practice of narrowcasting discussed above. This strategy in turn led to the development of cult TV shows whose fans not only watched the shows religiously but also taped them on their VCRs, bought ancillary merchandise associated with the program, and created Web sites on the Internet, which also was growing in popularity during this time (see Reeves, Rodgers, and Epstein 1996).

The shift in the perceptual and conceptual broadcasting practices of television in the 1980s coincided with a new generation of television viewers who were competent and comfortable with the broadcasting and narrative codes of television. By the 1980s, television was no longer a novel new medium; the baby boom generation had grown up with television as a new medium, and the next generation, the Gen X-ers, were fully competent and comfortable with it. As broadcasting practices were well established, television producers sought to stretch the boundaries of programming in order to create new, innovative programs. At the same time, producers sought to expand the revenue-creating aspects of television by finding more airtime in which to broadcast commercials. In service of both of these principles, television makers sought to reduce portions of programming that exhibited the practices of overcoding (discussed in chapter 2) in order to streamline programs that were already intelligible to the competent viewer. Such overcoded redundancies included the openings and conclusions to programs, which were now considered redundant and excessively telegraphed to the audience. Many extradiegetic transitional practices, such as theme music and lengthy opening and closing visuals, were felt to be no longer necessary for a competent viewing audience, and they also cut into time that could be spent airing revenue-enhancing commercials.

Pursuing the audience's desire for new and innovative material, the networks developed programs that transformed the nature of television genre. *Hill Street Blues* (1981–1987) and *St. Elsewhere* (1982–1988) were essentially genre hybrids that combined characteristics of the police and hospital drama, respectively, with traits of the serial soap opera and the situation comedy. *thirtysomething* (1987–1991) and *Tour of Duty* (1987–1990) imitated the niche-market strategies of cable TV by essentially targeting specific audiences and narrowcasting to them. Still other programs sought to draw larger audiences. Programs like *Pee Wee's Playhouse* (1986–1991) and *The Simpsons* (1989–) turned the Saturday morning children's show and the animated cartoon into satiric and often bizarre postmodern texts that pitched irony and satire to children and adults alike.

The use of music in new programs for the TV II generation underwent similar transformations to keep up production values. New innovative musical scores were composed to fit the hybridization of these new shows, such as Mike Post's easy-listening score for the cop drama *Hill Street Blues*. Music was also a participant in the self-parodying postmodernism of many programs, such as *The Simpsons*, that often featured preexisting music to satirize a narrative situation. Other programs featured music with a diversity of musical styles, some of which did not seem to fit the narrative of the program, at least not in the traditional sense. *Miami Vice* is one such program; current pop hits often accompanied search or traveling scenes, with little narrative tie-in with the visual images.

Yet, for all the postmodernist traits listed above, TV music actually continued in the modernist innovation/assimilation model, always striving, on the one hand, to be original with its innovations attaining high Nielsen ratings, and on the other hand, to be able to fit in with the audience's more conventionally conceived notions of musical style and genre. In fact, TV music of the 1980s and 1990s seems to illustrate both modernist and postmodernist traits. While television in these decades does demonstrate some new and unique production values, especially with regard to music, in other ways it can be seen as a continuation of television production values from the very beginnings of broadcast television, albeit with better technological tools and a greater palette of musical styles. In this chapter, I investigate both the modernist and postmodernist traits of TV music in these decades and show how television music is a product of both camps.

TV Music as Modernist Avant-Garde: "Relativization" of Music on TV

The effort to make TV programs unique and successful led to some innovative technological and artistic practices in the last two decades of the twentieth century. The use of music in television was one of these innovations, and in some TV shows music functioned in different ways than the traditional denotative and connotative models of early narrative television. In fact, musical practice on several shows resembles processes for cinematic speech that Michel Chion (1994) has called "relativization." In the context of speech on film, Chion defines relativization as a modernist, avant-garde practice wherein attempts are made to decenter speech as the primary element of filmic discourse, thus expanding its artistic expressivity. Chion (1994: 171) delineates three types of speech for film sound: textual speech, theatrical speech, and emanation speech.[1] Chion delimits these three types of cinematic speech as a way to describe the ways filmmakers sought to "relativize" speech since the beginnings of sound film. Relativizing speech means the attempts to inscribe speech in a visual, rhythmic, gestural, and sensory totality where it would not have to be the central and determining element of conveying narrative in a film (Chion 1994: 178). According to Chion, once speech was established as a primary mode of furthering the narrative of film, filmmakers sought to decenter speech as the primary element of filmic discourse as a means of expanding the artistic expressivity of film.

Chion lists seven techniques used by filmmakers (mostly art film makers as opposed to popular film makers) as means to relativize speech in film (figure 9.1). While Chion provides specific examples of all these techniques in avant-garde films, these same techniques can be observed (though adapted) for television music, even in its first decade, and as they proliferated in the 1980s and 1990s.

Although Chion's observations on relativization pertain to the sensory channel of verbal speech, television music also underwent a sort of relativization in the 1980s and 1990s. Chion's categories of theatrical speech resonate with the semiotic spaces of music described elsewhere in this volume: substituting "music" for "speech," "theatrical" music becomes intradiegetic; "textual" music becomes extradiegetic; and "emanation" music becomes "diegetic" or "source" music. One primary difference between relativizing music versus relativizing speech is that, unlike speech, music is usually *not* at the center of narrative discourse in television drama, and a postmodern turn would invert this relationship, where music could potentially be centered in a relativized text. A program containing relativized music might have music suddenly center itself in the narrative, appropriating such genres as the musical variety show or the music video (for example, with *Miami Vice* and *The Monkees*, though in different ways). While music may still not be the *center* of discourse (speech is still the center in TV, as it is in

1. *Rarefaction*, where the presence of speech is limited or rarefied.

2. *Proliferation*, where the soundtrack is bombarded with characters speaking simultaneously, canceling each other out.

3. *Narrative commentary over dialogue*, textual speech overlaying theatrical speech.

4. *Multilingualism*, use of foreign languages where language is not understood by most viewers.

5. *Submerged speech*, similar to proliferation only the soundtrack is submerged in a mass of speech, bits of which become intelligible.

6. *Loss of intelligibilty*, or the viewer's inability to track the flux and reflux of speech in a soundtrack, where intelligibility of speech fades in and out.

7. *Decentering*, situation where speech is undermined by other aspects of the film's mise-en-scène, where visual images or other sensory channels undermine the intelligibility of speech.

Figure 9.1. Chion's (1994) Techniques for "Relativized Speech" in Avant-Garde Film.

film), the critical viewer will note the change or shift of function in the postmodern TV text. An application of Chion's theory of relativized speech for TV music is found in figure 9.2.

Many television programs of the 1980s and 1990s sought to be distinct by employing one or more of these avant-garde procedures in their musical scores. What follows are analyses and commentaries of some of these programs and

1. *Rarefaction*, where the presence of *music* is limited or rarefied. Another form of rarefaction is where a sense of musical motion is attenuated.

2. *Proliferation*, where the soundtrack is bombarded with music, perhaps overpowering dialogue or other sounds on the screen.

3. *Narrative commentary over dialogue*, or, music overlaying theatrical speech. For music, this would entail an intrusion of music into the narrative, especially during dialogue. This music could be either diegetic or intradiegetic.

4. *Multilingualism*, the use of diverse style topics in one television text, or the use of non-Western or foreign (to a specific culture) music, or perhaps where the musical style is not understood by many viewers.

5. *Submerged music*, a situation similar to proliferation, only the soundtrack is submerged in a mass of sound and becomes unintelligible.

6. *Loss of intelligibility*, or the viewer's inability to track the flux and reflux of music in a soundtrack, where intelligibility of music fades in and out.

7. *Re-centering*, where music becomes a central feature of the narrative television text. This situation could occur diegetically or intradiegetically, where music plays a more prominent role in the narrative discourse than in traditional narrative television.

Figure 9.2. Techniques for "Relativized Music" for Television (after Chion 1994).

how Chion's notion of relativized speech is adapted for music in these TV shows.

Rarefaction

One trait of programs in the 1990s was to use music sparingly. In the 1990s, the NBC and ABC networks, in particular produced some of their situation comedies with either no opening theme song or greatly attenuated music. Opening credits for these shows remained but were superimposed on the screen during the narrative action. The rationale for the brevity of these programs' openings was to get the viewer into the show more quickly and to make more time available to air commercials.[2] TV networks probably made such theme music decisions from the perspective of a Fredric Jameson–style postmodernism of consumption, and one effect on the TV text itself can be found in Chion's avant-garde notion of rarefied speech. Two notable programs that featured attenuated or rarefied music tracks were the popular situation comedies *Frasier* (1993–2004) and *Seinfeld* (1990–1998). Both opened with a teaser that got the story line going and was followed by an extended commercial break. Neither program featured an opening theme song but, rather, a short musical tag at the beginning or in some cases no music at all.

Frasier was a popular spin-off of the sitcom *Cheers* (1982–1993) featuring as the central character Frasier Crane (Kelsey Grammer), a psychiatrist who has just moved to Seattle after his divorce in Boston.[3] Like earlier sitcoms, the program's narratives revolve around Frasier's life at home, an elegant Seattle apartment he shares with his father (John Mahoney) and English physical therapist/housekeeper, Daphne Moon (Jane Leeves), and at work, a local radio station where, as a therapist, he counsels callers to his talk show, assisted by his technical assistant, Roz Doyle (Peri Gilpin), and interacting with the station's other hosts. Frasier's home life often focuses on his close relationship with his brother, Niles (David Hyde Pierce), especially during his divorce from his wife, Maris (who is never shown on-screen), and his infatuation with and eventual marriage to Daphne.

Each episode opened with a visual image of a black-and-white line drawing of the Seattle skyline, complete with the Space Needle, with slight variations to the drawing occurring with each episode (such as a red light blinking from the top of the Space Needle or an ascending light going up the Needle like an elevator, a schematic moon rising over the skyline, or fireworks appearing in the background). A musical leitmotif sounds during this very brief introduction, played by a jazz combo consisting of vibraphone, piano, bass, and drums. Beyond this motif, there is very little music on the program, even in transition sections. Most scenes are introduced silently with an extradiegetic intertitle (a device used in silent film but here an innovative device seldom used in television narratives), even after commercial breaks. Breaking this musical rarefaction is a theme song that is performed at the end of the program. It features Grammer, accompanied by a jazz combo, singing "Tossed Salads and Scrambled Eggs," a jazzy-blues number he composed for the program. The jazz style topic reinforces the urban and urbane style of the program, with Frasier and Niles as upper-class sophisticates, and contributes to the closure of each episode.[4]

Another example of musical rarefaction is the program *Seinfeld* (1990–1998), which enjoyed an eight-season run on NBC. Many critics hail this situation comedy "about nothing" as the greatest television show ever. As one critic (Wyman: 2002) has put it:.

> It's possible that the people in previous eras looked at Michelangelo's frescoes in the Sistine Chapel, or gazed on a Bernini statue, and simply took it for granted.
>
> Perhaps today we take things for granted as well? What if the true cultural brilliance of our time existed right under our noses?
>
> It might be something that was well liked and even respected, but might not be recognized for its mastery. It might be something that we'd not even suspect of such artistry, precision and meticulous attention to detail. It might be a TV show. It might even be a sitcom.
>
> It might be . . . *Seinfeld*.

Seinfeld's music is limited to transitions between scenes, consisting of bass guitar riffs, actually played by synthesizers sampled to be made to sound like an electric fretless slap bass.[5] The timbre and wide leaps of the transition music could certainly fall into a topic of comedic. During early years of the series' run, programs open with Jerry Seinfeld performing a comedy monologue in a nightclub setting; later, they open with a brief vignette accompanied by a slap bass accompaniment. These short riffs, played in an improvised funk style, were composed by Jonathan Wolff and vary throughout each episode. Like *Frasier*, the program ended (during some seasons) with a more extended closing theme featuring the synthesized slap bass with an additional synthesized midrange brass sound. Perhaps Wyman's criticism of the piece states its aesthetic most accurately: the program's plainess, its "patina of sparseness," is its strength. And the sparseness, or rarefaction, of music with its minimal character involvement made it the most recognizable music on television at the time.

Proliferation

Proliferation of music in 1980s and 1990s television is most apparent in music videos. Since the debut of MTV in 1981, music videos have branched out from mainstream popular music to include many genres, most notably country music broadcast on the cable channel Country Music Television (CMT) and rap/hip hop (on BET and "Yo! MTV Raps"). As was noted in chapter 8, some police dramas from the 1980s and 1990s contributed tracks in which music proliferated throughout the story line, for example, *Miami Vice*, particularly during chase scenes, when pop tunes from the era played almost in their entirety over the narrative. In the 1990s, the critically acclaimed series *Homicide: Life on the Street* occasionally featured teasers and extended scenes with pop tunes playing.

One police drama, *Cop Rock* (1990), appropriated the genre of the film musical, resulting in an extreme saturation of music in every episode. *Cop Rock* is a genre hybrid par excellence: an attempt to combine the police drama with the film musical. The experimental police drama was produced by writer-producer Steven Bochco, the writer–producer of *Hill Street Blues*, who achieved a sort of auteur status for his creation of that program. The series was set in the toughest neighborhoods of Los Angeles and featured veteran actor Ronny Cox as Police Chief Roger Kendrick, a quasi-cowboy with a brash attitude. Larry Joshua played Captain John Hollander, the honest commander who tries to keep his precinct together. David Gianopoulos and Anne Bobby played street cops who were romantically attracted to each other; James McDaniel played officer Franklin Rose, and Barbara Bosson (who was married to Bochco at the time) played the corrupt, publicity-greedy mayor, Louise Plank.

Composers for *Cop Rock* included Greg Edmonson, Alan Elliott, and such luminaries as Randy Newman (who composed and performed the theme music, "Under the Gun," on camera during the opening of the program) and Mike Post. In typical Broadway and film musical fashion, every few minutes the narrative action stopped for a full-blown musical number, ranging from rock ballad love songs to gospel/soul pieces, to 1990s rap. In the pilot episode, gang members threaten to attack the cops who arrested them, rapping "On these streets, we got the power!" The mayor and her staff sing about the glories of bribery while a judge and a jury convict a criminal gospel-style with the refrain "he's guilty." And of course, there is the poor upscale yuppie whose BMW was taken away after he was arrested for buying cocaine. He sings a bluesy ballad, "I want My Beemer Back!" to lament his loss. The program even featured the dispatching sergeant singing to the squad, "Let's be careful out there!" a signature motto of the dispatch sergeant in Bochco's predecessor show, *Hill Street Blues*.[6]

Cop Rock may be considered avant-garde due to this extreme hybridization of such disparate genres. However, the Broadway musical style of presentation for the show proved to be too much for audiences and critics alike, and the show was canceled after only 10 episodes. Although the experiment was seen as a failure (critics expected more from Bochco, whereas audiences were not ready for a police drama *cum* Broadway-style musical), the model of musical prolifera-tion translated to other programs of the decade. An episode of the medical drama *Chicago Hope* (1994–2000) featured the regular cast breaking out in song on several episodes. In November 2001, executive producer Josh Whedon com-posed a musical episode for his series *Buffy the Vampire Slayer* (1997–2003). Entitled "Once More, with Feeling," the episode blended a number of musical genres performed by the regular cast, and critics cheered the effort (Spadoni 2004). Also, some episodes of *The Simpsons* featured full-blown musicals (and musical parodies).[7]

"Multilingualism"

Chion's notion of relativization for speech in the cinema also includes "multi-lingualism," or the use of multiple languages in a film, some (or all) of which are not intelligible to the audience. The employment of these diverse languages reflects a postmodern tendency toward diversity and eclecticism while at the same time creating a modernist uniqueness within the text itself. I would trans-late multilingualism for television music as the use of an eclectic and diverse mixture of musical styles, some of which may not necessarily reflect the narra-tive in a classic semiotic sense.

The popular TV series *Northern Exposure* (1990–1995) is a good example of the use of multiple musical styles in a single series. The program was written and produced by Joshua Brand and John Falsey, who earlier co-scripted the popular hospital program *St. Elsewhere* (1982–1988), which also became a sur-prise hit. *Northern Exposure* broke new ground on television for many reasons. Although it is often labeled as a "dramedy" (a drama + comedy), which reflects yet another tendency of 1980s television for genre hybridity, aspects of the program's narrative suggest a mixture of the western, screwball/romantic/situ-ation comedy and serial drama genres. The narrative revolves around Dr. Joel Fleischman (Rob Morrow), a Jewish doctor from New York, who accepts an offer to serve the denizens of Cicely, Alaska, for two years in order to pay off his medical school debts. The series progresses through Fleischman's initial abhorrence and hostility to the backwater town and toward his gradual soften-ing and acceptance of the town and its people. A second important aspect of the narrative is Fleischman's sexual love/hate turmoil with Maggie O'Connell

(Janine Turner), a local bush pilot and Joel's landlady, with whom he becomes engaged in a tangled romance reminiscent of 1930s and 1940s screwball comedies. Intermingled in this narrative is a wide array of characters of various cultural and ethnic backgrounds, including former astronaut and wealthy entrepreneur Maurice Minnifield (Barry Corbin), septuagenarian and general store owner Ruth-Anne Miller (Peg Phillips), Native Americans Ed Chigliak (Darren E. Burrows) and Marilyn Whirlwind (Elaine Miles), Holling Vincoeur (John Chillum), who owns and manages Cicely's bar, the Brick, along with his live-in girlfriend, Shelly Tambo (Cynthia Geary), an ex-beauty queen some 40 years Holling's junior.

Northern Exposure was innovative from several perspectives, including the portrayal of intermittent characters that appeared on the series. Chris Steven's (John Corbett) African American half-brother Bernard (Richard Cummings Jr.), and Marilyn's healer cousin Leonard Quinhagak, played by noted film actor Graham Greene, deepen and enhance the show's representation of multiculturalism. Gender and sexuality are explored through Ron (Doug Ballard) and Erick (Don R. McManus), proprietors of the local inn, whose gay wedding was a prime-time television first. Ron and Erick's arrival also helped to provide a larger context within which to recollect the town's founding by a lesbian couple, Roslyn and Cicely, later featured in a flashback episode. Eccentric bush couple Adam (Adam Arkin) and Eve (Valerie Mahaffey) shadow the ongoing battle of the sexes rendered by Joel and Maggie and, with their exaggerated, back-to-nature facade and conspicuously consumptive habits, reach out beyond the narrative to poke fun at the program's yuppie audience.

The music featured on the program reflects the multicultural theme of the show. Of musical interest to the program is the character of Chris Stevens, an ex-con and DJ for Cicely's one radio station, KBHR, known as Kaybear radio. Stevens's "Chris in the Morning Show" features a soundtrack peppered with eclectic musical selections, philosophical musings, and Greek chorus–like commentary. At points during episodes, acousmatic music, eventually found to be emanating from radios playing throughout town, saturates the narrative.[8] In fact, through its six seasons on the air, music in the series ranges widely, from classical pieces (opera arias from Mozart's *Magic Flute* and *Don Giovanni*, Mascagni's *Cavalleria Rusticana*, and other pieces, such as Chopin nocturnes, the *Light Cavalry Overture* by Suppé, and pieces by Beethoven, Bach, Haydn, Kromer, and others) to big band jazz (Benny Goodman, Glen Miller, Louis Armstrong), contemporary jazz (Bela Fleck, Bobby McFerrin), Broadway musicals (*The King and I, Pacific Overtures*), and a healthy dose of country music (Travis Tritt, Kitty Wells, Ricky Skaggs, the Dixie Chicks) and rock (Chuck Berry, Booker T and the MGs, many others).

One example of the use of the wide variety of musical styles is found in the fourth episode of the first season, entitled "Dreams, Schemes, and Putting Greens." The story line for the episode is constructed in the program's typical threefold narrative structure with each narrative thread woven into the single episode. The first story line involves Maurice, who is entertaining two Japanese businessmen who he hopes will establish a recreational resort and golf course in town (the competition is a location in Hawaii, so Maurice opens the program extolling the virtues of Alaska!). The second thread is Fleischman's desire to cooperate with Maurice on the sale in order to become the resort's medical doctor and thus receive free golfing greens fees and to reduce his sentence in Alaska. The third thread is the discovery that Shelly is pregnant and Holling's subsequent proposal of marriage. The wedding begins in the town chapel, but Holling pulls out for fear that he (ironically), as a 62-year old, will outlive his 18-year old bride.

The music for the episode, like many of the episodes in the series, is an eclectic mixture of artists and styles from a wide period of time. To reflect the oriental nature of Maurice's business dealings, excerpts from Gilbert and Sullivan's *Mikado* are played intradiegetically (and with an ironic stereotype). Fleischman's construction of a temporary Astroturf golf course is accompanied (intradiegetically) by "Sukiyaki" by techno artist Ryuichi Sakamoto, reflecting another stereotypical portrayal of the Japanese businessmen. Scenes in the Brick are accompanied by diegetic but acousmatic songs, "Diet of Strange Places" by kd lang and "Honky Tonk Angels" by Kitty Wells played on the ubiquitous radio soundtrack. The almost-wedding scene (between Shelley and Holling) features Maurice singing "Hello Young Lovers" from the *King and I* diegetically in the Cicely chapel.

The mixture of musical styles on the show reflects the eclectic nature of Chris the DJ's musical tastes diegetically and undoubtedly also the vicarious musical tastes of Brand and Falsey. But the mixture of music also reflects an ideology of the postmodern, where all pretense of a distinction between high and low art is eradicated. In Brand and Falsey's setting of Cicely, Bach, Haydn, and Mozart are on an equal, not higher, footing with Kitty Wells, Lionel Hampton, Procol Harum, and the Broadway cast of *My Fair Lady*. The eclecticism of multiple musical styles serves not only to entertain a pluralistic audience in a wide variety of musical styles but also to connote the consciously multicultural and postmodern theme of the program. According to Christine Scodari,

> the "fish out of water" narrative exemplified by Joel's gradual softening
> toward Cicely, Cicelians, and small-town life is replicated again and
> again in episodes about visitors who give of themselves in some fashion

while becoming enriched by their interactions with worldly wise, innately intelligent, and accepting locals. Humanity's place within the larger natural environment is another significant thematic thread running through the program's extended text. Behavior and temperament are often seen to be influenced by phenomena such as seasonal winds, Northern Lights, midnight sun, and ice breaking in springtime. The lesson is clear: nature tames human beings—not the other way around. An even more prevalent theme is that the educated New York elitist Joel Fleischman is, ironically, the buffoon in the series, as his attempts to escape or at least "civilize" the Alaskans is continually frustrated. Rather, it is the simple, multicultural locals who are the wise ones in the series, and those who contribute to the well-being of the community.

While illustrating Chion's modernist avant-garde notion of multiplicity of musical languages (styles), the program also is a musical bricolage of eclecticism that aligns with postmodern thought. The program thus reveals both postmodern and modernist, or at least "anti-postmodern," traits simultaneously.

Submersion/Loss of Intelligibility

Many would argue that television (and film) music is already submerged within the narrative, as it has often been described as "unheard." Recalling Roger Bowman's and Claudia Gorbman's lists of musical functions on television (see chapter 4), they and others remind the reader that music should not interfere with dialogue on television. Playing with this code of underscoring, some TV composers sought to combine music and sound effects into a single sound effects track in some TV shows, and these efforts were assisted by developments in the technology of sound production in the 1980s and 1990s. One notable program that combined sound and music was the sci-fi drama *The X-Files* (1993–2002), with music *and* sound by Mark Snow.

Like most programs considered postmodern, *The X-Files* is an amalgamation or genre hybrid, in this case, a hybrid of the police procedural and the sci-fi drama, with FBI agents Fox Mulder (Michael Dukovny) and Dana Scully (Gillian Anderson) investigating cases of paranormal activity, such as UFOs, alien abductions, psychic phenomena, and even vampires. An overriding narrative for each episode is Mulder's attempts to expose the truth about these phenomena and uncover the grand conspiracy of cover-ups of these phenomena by the U.S. government—including his own FBI colleagues. Scully is the skeptical medical doctor who accompanies Mulder and eventually (after five seasons) is won over to Mulder's thinking. Each episode deals with Mulder's frustrations with his attempts to get at the truth, combating Scully's skepticism, and maintaining his job despite antagonistic superiors.

The music to the series was composed by Mark Snow. Snow studied music at New York's Art and Music High School and went on to Juilliard, where he concentrated on composing and studied with oboist Melvin Kaplan, jazz arranger Hall Overton, 12-tone composer George Tremblay, and composer Earle H. Hagen, from whom Snow learned the basics of writing a TV theme (see Aswad 2008). (As has been noted, Hagen composed music for *The Andy Griffith Show*, *I Spy*, and *The Mod Squad*, among others). After graduating in 1968, Snow formed the New York Rock 'n' Roll Ensemble with Michael Kamen, a classmate at Juilliard. The band recorded and toured actively between 1968 and 1972. Snow's interest then turned to composing film and television scores. He relocated to Los Angeles in 1974, and his first TV contract began soon thereafter with the series *The Rookies* (1972–1976) and continued with *Starsky and Hutch* (1975–1979), *Crazy Like a Fox* (1984–1986), and several TV movies and miniseries. He is best known for his work on *The X-Files* and *Millennium*.

Snow's theme to the *X-Files* is harmonically static and played on a synthesizer that never moves away from the A-minor harmony of its home key (example 9.1). In this regard, the theme has its own sort of "rarefaction," here referring to the lack of harmonic motion that leaves the listener with an unsettled, ambiguous feeling. The lack of harmonic motion may be compared to other sci-fi themes, particularly classics like *The Twilight Zone* (see chapter 2), *Night Gallery* (1970–1973; music by Paul Glass), *The Outer Limits* (1963–1965; music by Dominic Frontiere), *One Step Beyond* (1959–1961; music by Harry Lubin), and others.[9] Snow's theme retains an ambiguous quality, reflecting the vague, frustrating aspects of Mulder's search for the truth.

In writing about the music to *The X-Files*, Lawrence Kramer (2002: 189) viewed the theme as portraying Mulder's frustration with the impediments to

Example 9.1. Theme to *The X-Files* (Music by Mark Snow).

his progress on finding the "truth that is out there": "The net effect is complex: at once an impression of the obsessional element in Mulder's relentless goal-directed quest and, with the constant harping by the melody on the fifth degree and the bass on the dissonant sting, the impression of an expectancy never satisfied and never meant to be, of the obsession as self-sustaining, unfolding not in an effort to find the truth but to defer finding it, to make sure that the truth is indeed still 'out there.'"

Snow's intradiegetic musical cues are also unusual and avant-garde in Chion's sense, in some cases feeling submerged with a loss of intelligibility. First, in many episodes the static quality of Snow's theme is translated in the intradiegetic music. Many cues are limited to long, sustained chords on Snow's synthesizer, with the electronic sounds providing an otherworldly and futuristic sense. Scenes of foreboding are accompanied by sustained sounds in the very low register of the synthesizer. The synthesizer also has the capability of providing sound effects as well as music, and Snow uses the instrument and other audio engineering techniques to achieve these effects. In this regard, the musical score for *The X-Files* can be seen as influenced by Vangelis's electronic score for the film *Blade Runner* (1982), in which musical sounds are mixed in with electronic sound effects.

The mixture of music and sound effects is found in many of the episodes, but I will take one from the first season, entitled "Fallen Angel," as an example. In the plot to that episode, the U.S. military has cordoned off an area in rural Wisconsin in which a UFO has crashed. As Mulder sneaks into the area to investigate, the viewer sees the area through a fish-eye camera lens. A laser fence erected around the restricted area emits a pair of red laser beams. A slow static musical cue sounds in D minor, with a high-pitched F-sharp (apparently emanating diegetically from the fence) submerged within the score. The dissonance between the D minor tonality of the cue and the F-sharp (which conflicts with D minor's F-natural) creates a feeling of dissonance and suspense. The viewer is left to wonder: is the sound of the electric fence part of the music track or part of the sound track? The musical cue is so submerged and intermixed with the sound effects that both blend into an ethereal soundscape. The scene ends with a nearly invisible, blurry shape (undoubtedly the alien presence) bursting through the fence, whereupon the viewer realizes that the fish-eye lens is from the alien's point of view as the blur crosses the road into the forest. As it crosses, the D minor chord of the music track and the fence's F-sharp sound undergo a slow glissando up to a screeching high register.

The narrative of *The X-Files* is a constant puzzle about whether or not alien life really exists and whether or not the U.S. government knows about it and is covering it up or whether the alien sightings are in fact trappings of a top-secret

U.S. government cover-up. The viewer must process a large amount of narrative material about this puzzle, through which the program takes a postmodern view of the relativity of truth and representation, as some UFO sightings are shown to be hoaxes, whereas others remain a mystery. Some UFO sightings seem to be of high-tech government aircraft while others seem to be of actual aliens, which the government tries to cover up.

In *The X-Files*, television has moved from an arbiter of cultural truth and mores to an ambiguous skeptic. Douglas Kellner (1999: 8) has written that "television has instilled an attitude of trust toward existing institutions and authorities and fear of those forces outside of the dominant order who would threaten it. *The X-Files* reversed this way of seeing by instilling distrust toward established authority, representing institutions of government and the established order as highly flawed, even complicit in the worst crimes and evil imaginable. *The X-Files* draws on and intensifies popular paranoia that government is bad, that the CIA, FBI, and military and other institutions of government are filled with individuals who carry out villainous actions and constitute a threat to traditional humanist moral values and human life itself." Both the static nature of the musical theme and its submerged musical cues contribute to the moral and emotional ambiguity of the series. This recalls the role of the opening credits to *The Rifleman* (see chapter 1), in which the narrative enigma of Chuck Connors is reflected in the way he fires his rifle and glares into the camera. The heroic sounds of the horns of the theme lead the viewer to believe that Connors a hero, thus reinforcing the social codes of individualism, patriarchy, and violence as a source of law and order in the American west. In the harmonically static theme of *The X-Files*, however, there is no solution to the narrative enigma. The music has no beginning, middle, or end but rather is a static harmonic structure with a circular, oscillating melody. Kramer (2002: 189) has described the shrill sound of the melody as "one who is whistling out of the fear of the dark in woods." Through neither the theme nor its submerged score is the audience reassured of the truth.

Television as a Modern/Postmodern Medium

The notion of avant-garde is usually defined as the modernist high-art trait of wanting a work of art to be absolutely original and unique, to the point of withdrawing to a position of detachment from all aesthetic and political realms. Connor (1989: 237–239) summarizes Theodor Adorno's concept of the avant-garde as a negative dialectic of an art whose political force consists of its obstinate denial of the alienating influences of mass culture and bourgeoisie rationalization by insisting on its own untranslatable, abstract specificity of form. Similarly, Connor describes Clement Greenberg's concept of the avant-garde as those works that leap into abstraction in order to maintain a world of absolute, self-legitimizing value. So, to regard the television programs listed above as avant-garde texts may seem ironic in the extreme. Television is anything but abstract, and certainly it is not designed to alienate mass culture. So, if television cannot be avant-garde, can it be postmodern? Given Chion's assertions that techniques of sound in art cinema follow a modernist avant-garde path, and my own assertion that television music resembles much of Chion's principles, many of the techniques of 1980s and 1990s television music may also be considered postmodern. Authors writing about television in this period indicate that something different was happening at this time, and they usually refer to this "something different" in the context of postmodernism. For example, Caldwell's (1995) theory of televisuality was prompted by developments in television in the 1980s, many of which tended to emphasize traits associated with postmodernist thinking. First, according to Caldwell, televisuality emphasizes a stylized performance often at the expense of content, an exhibitionism that utilizes many different looks, from opulent cinematic spectacles to graphic-crunching split-screen effects. Even though the cinematic versus videographic bifurcation is in place, television production tends to negate any accounting for a highbrow versus lowbrow form of television—TV broadcasts all forms indiscriminately. Caldwell also asserts that the new emphasis on televisuality created a "structural inversion" in television programs in which the roles of narrative and discourse, form and content, subject and style, and other aspects are inverted. Television luxuriated in its new visual forms and emphasized these over narrative function. The mode of exhibition becomes all-important, often at the expense of content. Essentially, televisuality is an industrial product, manufactured and ruled by the technologies, economies, and mechanisms of production.

Many of Caldwell's assertions resonate with theories of postmodernism posited by media theorists throughout the 1990s. Although postmodernism is a concept that defies definition, many writers have been able to circumscribe a list of traits and characteristics even though these same writers may disagree on an overarching conception. These divergences of conception range from definitions of postmodernism as a distinctive style, a movement that emerged in the 1960s, 1970s, or 1980s depending on the medium or genre in question, a condition or milieu that typifies a set of socioeconomic factors, a specific mode of philosophical discourse, a particular type of politics, and an emergent form of cultural analysis shaped by all of the above (Collins 1992: 327).

Jim Collins has speculated that one way of defining postmodernism is by comparing it against modernism, a term that also has varied definitions.

Modernism is usually defined in two ways: one, as a heroic period of revolutionary experimentation that sought to transform entire cultures; and, two, as a period of profound elitism and avant-garde (Collins 1992: 328). As I have adapted Chion's avant-garde principles of filmic speech for television music, I have (at least tacitly) assumed that television music has functioned within a modernist paradigm. Postmodernism, then, is the movement that leads away from modernism, either as a backlash from this experimentation or as a move away from elitism back to day-to-day life.

Collins and others argue that television really did not have a modernist tradition from which to develop but, rather, was/is essentially a postmodern medium from its inception. One basis for this assertion is that television has always been a *popular* mass medium as opposed to an *elitist* medium, such as art films, theater, or opera. Moreover, television has demonstrated, and continues to demonstrate, certain traits (or themes) that resonate with much thought about postmodernism. Collins and others have identified several themes for postmodernism in television narratives, including: (1) a continual proliferation of signs, (2) the pervasiveness of rearticulation and appropriation of previously articulated signs or the foregrounding of intertextual references, (3) subjectivity, bricolage, and eclecticism, and (4) commodification, politics, and value.

As for the proliferation of signs, since its earliest years television has been on a continual broadcast schedule in which the televisual flow has been the order of the day, at least for most of the day and evening. With the rise of cable, more networks and stations proliferated, all broadcasting 24 hours a day in a saturated, seemingly never-ending televisual flow. Indeed, much of this book has focused on how music has helped to mediate the televisual flow into the three semiotic spaces of television. So, television has always produced a continual proliferation of signs, whether visual, auditory, or musical.

The foregrounding of intertextual references also has been an ongoing feature of television. As has been shown, television began by appropriating the sound, celebrities, and production values of radio and later of the cinema. Early TV programs that spanned many genres were transplants from radio, such as *The Lone Ranger* (western), *The Burns and Allen Show* (comedy), *Dick Tracy* (police drama), and others. This appropriation turned to parody and irony in some narrative television programs, for example, *The Munsters* (1964–1966), which parodied classic horror movies, and its contemporary and more sophisticated counterpart, *The Addams Family* (1964–1966), which provided a televisual realization of the comics of Charles Addams featured in the *New Yorker*. By the 1980s the self-reflexive intertextuality of television became more subtle. Programs not only parodied other genres; they often also made satirical references to their own production companies. Take the medical drama *St. Elsewhere*,

274

for example. The show dealt with serious issues of life and death, but every episode also included a substantial amount of comedy and parody. In one episode, an amnesia patient comes to believe that he is Mary Richards from *The Mary Tyler Moore Show* (1970–1977), MTM Enterprises' first television production and also the production company of *St. Elsewhere*. Throughout the episode the patient makes oblique references to MTM's entire program history. In the series finale, a scene from the last installment of *The Mary Tyler Moore Show* is restaged, and the cat that for 18 years appeared on the production logo at the end of every MTM show dies as the final credits roll. Such reflexivity reached its peak in the 1990s in the animated series *The Simpsons*, with nearly every episode referencing and parodying some aspect of American life, everything from fast food to Broadway musicals and, most often, the media, including television news (Kent Brockman, the aging, mediocre, local newscaster) and kid shows (Krusty the Klown, the jaded, middle-aged, chain-smoking local TV kiddie show host). The program is rife with what Collins (1992: 335) has referred to as hyperconsciousness or a hyperawareness of the text and its critical status, function, history, and conditions of its circulation and reception.

According to Collins, audiences decode television representations as social constructions rather than as value-neutral reflections of the real world. As social constructions, they are subject to varying interpretations by a multicultural and diverse audience. The idea of multiple interpretations is also one of Fiske's main points, that conventional television attempts (mostly unsuccessfully) to assemble preferred meanings to a homogeneous audience. Television texts in the postmodern era are produced to be consumed as forms of bricolage or texts that are conscious of the multiple ways in which they might be understood. Fiske (1987: 345) illustrates this issue in discussing the program *Twin Peaks* (1990–1991), describing it as "aggressively eclectic, utilizing a number of visual, narrative, and thematic conventions from Gothic horror, science fiction, and the police procedural as well as the soap opera." The mélange of genres within a program attracts a diverse audience interested in a particular genre, though not everyone is interested in the *same* genre.

Postmodern texts also tend to be consumerist oriented. Fredric Jameson (1991) has argued that postmodernism is best understood as the end result of capitalism's relentless commodification of all phases of everyday existence. The eclecticism of popular culture is a mere cannibalization of the past and a sheer heterogeneity without decidable effects. In writing about MTM television shows, Jane Feuer has described what she calls the relationship between "textual production and commodity production." She defines quality programs (in this case, shows produced by MTM Enterprises) as "those that maintain a fairly consistent demographic profile and display an authorial style evinced at the textual level by two key characteristics: self-reflexivity and liberal humanism" (quoted in Williams 1994: 142). As Betsy Williams (1994) has posited, the networks allowed *Hill Street Blues*, *The Bob Newhart Show*, and *Northern Exposure* to have long runs even though, despite their high production values, they never drew top ratings. These programs had especially avid viewing audiences (maturing baby boomers) who represented a consistent *consumer* demographic. This consumer demographic translates as postmodern, and is evident in the interruption of programming for commercials, which actually become little programs in themselves (see Himmelstein 1984). Such TV consumerism led to the development of the info-mercial, shopping channels, and product lines of consumer goods taken from TV, such as toys based on Saturday morning cartoons or cosmetics from soap operas.

Finally, a large issue of postmodernism is that of "antifoundationalism," most often associated with the philosophers Jean-François Lyotard and Richard Rorty, among others. This view rejects the concept of "master narratives" or any set of all-embracing laws governing human behavior, science of history, or the ways and means of capital. The postmodern condition is that of the Promethian outsider or cultural guerilla. Many have taken the "antifoundational foundation" of Lyotard's thinking to generalize on postmodern texts as "decentering the central." Another central tenet of this mode of thinking is to place modernism's tendency to value the unique and search for the universal in sharp relief to post-modernism's tendency to embrace the popular, the everyday, and the eclectic and diverse.

In contrast to Collins's postmodernist assertions, Kellner implies that perhaps television has had a modernistic period or at least a tradition to which postmod-ern thought can react. During the 1980s and 1990s, according to Kellner, tele-vision turned toward a cultural populism that valorized audiences over texts, and its production apparatus began to foreground the pleasures of television and popular culture over their ideological functions and effects, thereby refocusing television criticism on the surface of its images and spectacle rather than on deeper embedded meanings and complex effects. Indeed, much of what has been covered in this book can be seen as a modernist aesthetic for music in television narratives in that these narratives have a traditional pattern of develop-ment. But perhaps television is postmodern because it produces popular images that are fun to watch regardless of what cultural meanings are produced.

Despite the debate on the modernist/postmodernist aspects of television, *something* was different about television in the 1980s and 1990s. As Caldwell has pointed out, where content of TV narratives was important in a modernist tele-vision narrative, by the 1980s that narrative has been decentered by an emphasis on visual style. As this style becomes popular on TV (i.e., consumed by the populace), the style is appropriated and imitated and even parodied. All of these are postmodernist traits, but they are also the traits of the innovation/assimilation model posited in this book, a model that is at the very core of modernism.

Postmodernism, Music, and the Auteur

Traditional musicology has always valued the traits of modernism in art music, especially unity, organicism, coherence, and textuality in classical art music. Above all, musicology is primarily about the auteur, that is, the life and works of a particular composer. Despite continuing modernist biases, several musicologist and music theorists have sought to engage postmodern thinking through their analyses of new works. Lawrence Kramer (1995) has proposed a musicology in which the traditional boundaries between the musical and the extramusical are dissolved. He also interrogates the notion of unity versus diversity, immediacy versus transcendence, and the performative versus the constative. As to decentering, several musicologists have engaged other milieus of analysis that traditionally have been included in the postmodern canon, for example, Susan McClary (1991) and feminism; Eero Tarasti (1994), Raymond Monelle (2000), Jean-Jacques Nattiez (1990) and semiotics; Walter Everett (1999, 2001) and John Covach (1997) and analysis of pop music. Rather than explore the multiplicity of musical postmodernism, Jonathan Kramer (2002: 16–17) lists traits of postmodern music based on the tenets of unity, intertextuality, and eclecticism. These traits are presented in figure 9.3.[10]

By its very nature, television, and by extension television music, participate in the postmodern agenda. Television is certainly a fragmented medium, broadcasting a constant flow of diverse texts. Television embraces both high and popular culture and is used indiscriminately in television to promote whatever an audience will watch and whatever an audience will buy. Binary oppositions on television give way to a menu-driven selection of genres, programming, and musical styles. And as a technological marvel of the middle part of the twentieth century, television does indeed consider "technology not only as a way to preserve and transmit music but also as deeply implicated in the production and essence of music" (Kramer 2002: 16).

With all of its postmodern traits, music on television especially resonates with Kramer's first point. As implied throughout much of this book, the practice of composing television music represents not so much a break with the past as a continuation and adaptation of music broadcasting in predecessor media, such as film and radio. While the music of some television shows exhibit postmodern traits, other music, especially on programs that are considered

Postmodern music:

1. is not simply a repudiation of modernism or its continuation but also has aspects of both a break and an extension;

2. is, on some level and in some way, ironic;

3. does not respect boundaries between sonorities and procedures of the past and of the present;

4. challenges barriers between highbrow and lowbrow styles;

5. shows disdain for the often unquestioned value of structural unity;

6. questions the mutual exclusivity of elitist and popular values;

7. avoids totalizing forms (e.g., does not want entire pieces to be tonal or serial or cast in a prescribed formal mold);

8. includes quotations of or references to music of many traditions and cultures;

9. considers technology not only as a way to preserve and transmit music but also as deeply implicated in the production and essence of music;

10. embraces contradictions;

11. distrusts binary oppositions;

12. includes fragmentations and discontinuities;

13. encompasses pluralism and eclecticism;

14. presents multiple meanings and multiple temporalities;

15. locates meaning and even structure in listeners more than in scores, performances, or composers.

Figure 9.3. Traits of Musical Postmodernism (Kramer 2002: 16–17).

postmodern, follow a traditional arc of composition in broadcasting media. Ironically, many television programs of the 1980s and 1990s that are considered to be postmodern are validated by their modernist attributes, which includes music. One of these traits is auteur theory, which posits that great films are created by singularly genius artists (usually directors) who have a vision for their films. For example, *Miami Vice*, *Homicide*, and *Twin Peaks* were directed by Michael Mann, Barry Levinson, and David Lynch, respectively, all of whom are also notable film directors or producers. These producer/directors give their programs a very cinematic quality (per Caldwell's terminology), but they also have created a critical literature similar to auteurist cinema in which their artistic traits are highlighted.

The same auteurist traits have followed musical scholarship of film and TV. Although the topic of film music might be considered a potential area of postmodern academic scrutiny (since the music is arguably not *art* or *concert* music), recent work on film music and even television music reflects this traditional auteurist focus: Claudia Gorbman (1987) has focused largely on composer Max Steiner while Kathryn Kalinak (1992) has covered Erich Korngold. Roy Prendergast (1990) is indebted to David Raksin, and when writing on television music he uses Jerrold Immel's score to *Dallas* as an example. For television, Jon Burlingame's *TV's Biggest Hits* (1996) follows the traditional path of recounting television composer biographies and interviews by compiling a comprehensive list of composers through the first 50 years of television. This book also taps into this modernist agenda, given its brief biographical and analytical accounts of composers Harry Sosnik, Gerald Fried, and Hershel Burke Gilbert.

This blend of the modern with the postmodern reflects Kramer's assertion that the postmodern relies on the modern for its own existence. Both postmodern and modernist interpretations of these programs can and usually do exist in the same textual universe. In spite of television's postmodernist stance (it is a medium for the mass culture, it operates in a universe of commodification, it contains bricolage through its continual extradiegetic flow, etc.), by the 1980s and 1990s TV programs were operating within the same modernist innovation/assimilation paradigm as always. Writers, producers, and directors were trying to make some television programs different, even unique. *Miami Vice*, for example, carved out its uniqueness as a modernist text by taking the police drama and giving it the look and sound of a music video with a postmodern turn. Other programs, like *The X Files* and *Twin Peaks*, have been singled out for both their modernist and postmodernist tendencies, depending on the critic. As Kellner (1999: 4) has written of *The X-Files*, "Most interpretations … perceive it as one-sidedly modern or postmodern, failing to see how it negotiates the boundaries between them, participating in both sides of the Great Divide." Such a program is viewed as "blurring the boundaries" between the two camps while also being seen as "post-postmodern" or anti-postmodern. And musically, despite their postmodern intentions, composers Jan Hammer of *Miami Vice*, Mark Snow of *The X-Files*, and Angelo Badalamenti of *Twin Peaks* become the next auteurs of television music.

This leads to the question: can a postmodern work also be avant-garde? Connor seeks to answer the question by pointing out that postmodern theory reacts to modernism in two distinct ways. The first is by glorifying the banal, where the pose of aristocratic aloofness from the mass culture is put aside and kitsch and popular culture, such as works by Andy Warhol and Kurt Vonnegut, are embraced. However, a second mode in postmodern theory seeks to recapture and purify avant-garde strategies and ideas. In this mode, "a purified or invigorated avant-garde practice is to be found in an art that breaks out of its mutely self-mirroring trance [of modernism] to reflect upon institutional contexts and functions" (Connor 238–239). Here, the works of John Cage, Laurie Anderson, Robert Smithson, Joseph Kossuth, and others require viewers not merely to adore an object but to actively reflect on its nature as a work of art. In this process, postmodernism recovers much of the energy of the beginning of modernism, but the artifact remains a postmodern work.

In his discussion of music videos, Andrew Goodwin (1992: 17) writes that "the postmodern analysis of the convergence of *avant-garde* modernist and popular/realist texts...is insufficiently grounded in an understanding of pop music debates." Indeed, the scope of his book is a refutation of the many analyses of music videos (mostly from film scholars) that view the genre as postmodern. The same dilemma exists for narrative television music. Although Goodwin acknowledges that TV shows like *Miami Vice* and *Moonlighting* may be viewed through a postmodern lens, these programs operated through the same network system employing the innovation/assimilation model of their predecessors. While some television programs of the 1980s and 1990s sought to break out of their generic molds in certain ways to become unique and, in some cases, postmodern, this process was still an application (albeit an interesting one) of the innovation/assimilation model, and also smacks of the modernist avant-garde.

Postmodern TV as Avant-Garde: The Case of Twin Peaks

Aside from *The X-Files*, the program that has been equated with postmodernist thought of the 1990s is *Twin Peaks* (1990–1991). Though many consider the program to be postmodern (see Collins 1992), the intent of *Twin Peaks* was arguably to be a rare example of television art in the more elite, modernist sense. The program was originally scheduled to appear as a limited-run, midseason replacement series on ABC in the spring of 1990. The program was publicized extensively (as an "event" in the Jameson postmodern sense) and attracted considerable critical attention even before its premiere. The critical acclaim and publicity were intended to draw a more select, upscale audience demographic to the program. The appeal to the elite is modernist, but the notion of narrowcasting is postmodern.

Jeffrey Sconce has written that the artistic status of *Twin Peaks* stemmed from the unique pedigrees of the series' co-creators, writer/producer Mark Frost and writer/director David Lynch. Frost became famous as the writer and story editor for *Hill Street Blues*, where he mastered the techniques of orchestrating a large ensemble drama in a series format. Lynch is an eccentric cult figure in the cinema, directing such films as *Eraserhead* (1978), the Academy Award–winning *Elephant Man* (1980), the sci-fi epic *Dune* (1984), and his tour de force for the avant-garde, *Blue Velvet* (1986). As a prominent American auteur, Lynch contributed his cinematic techniques to the small screen of *Twin Peaks*, including his oblique narrative strategies, macabre mise-en-scène, and obsessive thematic concerns.

Twin Peaks is an interesting combination of the strengths of both Frost and Lynch. The program features an ensemble cast, similar to that in Frost's *Hill Street Blues*, that inhabits Twin Peaks, a small town in Washington state that becomes more and more sinister as the serial narrative progresses. In a sense, Twin Peaks becomes much like the small town setting of the earlier *Blue Velvet*. The story line of the show is that of a murder mystery, as the series centers on FBI agent Dale Cooper's investigation of a murder in the town. The victim is teen prom queen Laura Palmer, whose body is discovered floating in a lake. As Cooper tracks Laura's killer, he uncovers many and varied secrets of the townspeople, and the mystery surrounding the murder leads him to think that the town is inhabited by an evil presence. Eventually Cooper begins to track Killer Bob, a demonic and apparently supernatural entity inhabiting the deep woods.

Many consider *Twin Peaks* a pivotal postmodern television program. Sconce (2007) has described the show as "an avowedly 'artistic' text" that was "in many ways more about style, tone, and detail than narrative. Many viewers were attracted to the series' calculated sense of strangeness, a quality that led *Time* magazine to dub Lynch as 'the czar of bizarre.' As in Lynch's other work, *Twin Peaks* deftly balanced parody, pathos, and disturbing expressionism, often mocking the conventions of television melodrama while at the same time defamiliarizing and intensifying them." Here, Sconce resorts to a very modernist auteur theory to analyze the program.

Jim Collins has written about the program as a prime example of a modernist/postmodernist struggle within a television text. He (1992: 345) asked: "What does it mean to be culturally literate about *Twin Peaks*? Should one regard it as an unprecedented *auteurist/avant-gardist* incursion into the vast wasteland of mere TV? Or should one adopt a sense of knowing detachment that asserts, 'I know it's just all TV trash, but I enjoy it ironically'?" He explains that the series may be considered postmodern first because of its creation by Lynch, who is considered a postmodern filmmaker; second because it employs a number of postmodern stylistic conventions; and third because it generated so many commodity intertexts. In addition, Collins labels the program postmodern in terms of how it circulated through American audiences in the 1990s, when cable TV and the VCR were leading to the decline of network revenues such that networks began experimenting with new types of programming. *Twin Peaks* was critically acclaimed by reviewers and thereby appealed to a connoisseur type of viewer (yuppies, perhaps?) who consumed other like forms of entertainment.

The development of *Twin Peaks* thus represents a new way in which the television industry envisioned the public. The program adapts conventions of several genres—the murder mystery, the police drama, the soap opera, the western, the situation comedy, the Gothic horror genre—and presents them in a series of interlocking and discrete segments that potentially appeals to a wide, yet heterogeneous audience demographic. The program thus meets at least one criterion for postmodernism, the trait of eclecticism.

In addition to the critical reception of the program, the semantic/semiotic dimensions of the program align themselves with postmodernist thinking. First, the series often foregrounds style over substance. The story line moves at a snail's pace, and as the series progressed, the proliferation of sinister enigmas led the viewer deeper into ambiguity and continually frustrated any hope of definitive closure. On a *Twin Peaks* page on the Museum of Broadcast Communications Web site Sconce describes the protracted emplotment of the first season:

> The entire first hour of the premiere episode, for example, covered only a single plot point, showing the protracted emotional responses of Laura's family and friends as they learned of her death. This slow yet highly overwrought emplotment was apparently considered so disruptive by ABC that the network briefly discussed airing this first hour without commercial interruption (although this too could have been a strategy designed to promote the program as "art"). Throughout the run of the series, the story line accommodated many such directorial set-pieces, stylistic *tours-de-force* that allowed the "Lynchian" sensibility to make its artistic presence felt most acutely. The brooding synthesizer score and dreamy jazz interludes provided by composer Angelo Badalamenti, who had worked previously with Lynch, also greatly enhanced the series' eerie, bizarre, and melancholy atmosphere.
>
> As the series progressed, its proliferation of sinister enigmas led the viewer deeper into ambiguity and continually frustrated any hope of definitive closure. Appropriately, the first season ended with a cliffhanger that left many of the major characters imperiled, and yet still provided no clear solution to Laura Palmer's murder. Perhaps because of the series' obstinate refusal to move toward a traditional resolution, coupled with its escalating sense of the bizarre, once-high ratings dropped over the course of the series' run.

Second, the series is a genre hybrid par excellence, as the narrative itself shifts to conventions found in various genres, often many times within a single episode. Agent Cooper's presence signifies a police drama, and the overarching plot follows the police procedural of a murder. However, the actions of other characters evoke plotlines of soap opera, the western, Gothic horror, and so on. Overlaid upon these shifting genres is the sense of the hyperconscious ironic, as Cooper's lines are often spoken as if coming out of a detective dime novel. (Example: Waitress: "How do you like your coffee?" Cooper: "As black as a moonless night at midnight.") Cooper's obsessions with coffee, cherry pie, and Zen Buddhism lend a literary air to the program, as does borrowing from the theater of the absurd. Furthermore, the hyperconsciousness of the program is evident in the soap opera "An Invitation to Love," which is shown running on TV sets in the mise-en-scène, its events shadowing the *Twin Peaks* story line.

Despite the argument for postmodernism, the program actually contains several traits of modernist thinking and the avant-garde. Lynch is indeed postmodern, but he is also an avant-gardist director. The program sought to be unique and thus attract an audience, a modernist trait. *Twin Peaks*, then, is not a matter of either/or but both because a postmodern cultural literacy recognizes exactly this kind of variability. As Lawrence Kramer (1995: 5–13) has intimated, postmodernism includes modernism for its own identity and purpose.

Music and *Twin Peaks*

The music to *Twin Peaks* was composed by Angelo Badalamenti, a native of Brooklyn and graduate of the Eastman and Manhattan schools of music. After scoring some minor films, his big break reportedly occurred when he was brought in as a singing coach for Isabella Rossellini, who was to sing the title song, "Song to the Siren," in the film *Blue Velvet*. Lynch was unable to secure the rights to use the song, though, so he asked Badalamenti to collaborate with him, and together they wrote "Mysteries of Love," combining Lynch's lyrics and Badalamenti's music. Lynch then asked Badalamenti to appear in the film as the piano player in the club where Rossellini's character performs. This film would be the first of many collaborations, with Badalamenti providing scores to Lynch's films *Wild at Heart, Twin Peaks: Fire Walk with Me, Lost Highway*, and *Mulholland Drive* as well as the TV series.

Badalamenti's music for the series, like much TV show music, falls into the category K. J. Donelly (2005) has termed "music blocks," that is, a few cues composed and recorded and then reused over and over again to establish leitmotifs for certain aspects of the series and a few musical cues that recur over the life of the series—similar to Hershel Burke Gilbert's music for *The Rifleman* more than 30 years before. Despite the relatively few cues of the show, Badalamenti's music shadows the program's postmodernist traits of eclecticism and ironic parody while adding a dimension of the avant-garde in Chion's sense. The music adheres to Chion's "multilingualism" or eclecticism through the use of differing styles, but unlike the mixture of originally composed music and stock pop music in *Northern Exposure*, all of the music for *Twin Peaks* was originally composed and performed on Badalamenti's synthesizer. On occasion, the music tends to decenter the narrative and call attention to itself, often ironically. The music also exemplifies Chion's avant-garde traits of submersion and loss of intelligibility.

Like the hybridity of the program itself, the musical cues for *Twin Peaks* are a bricolage of musical style topics, tapping into a diversity of styles ranging from soap opera–sounding ballads of the theme to progressive bebop, jazz, country music, new age music (in the 1990s sense), fifties rock, and even modernist avant-garde art music. Most cues also contain elements of minimalism, with repetitious chord progressions, slow, meandering melodic gestures, and nonconclusive cadences, almost as if the cues were looped to be repeated endlessly, similar to Snow's music to *The X-Files*. One fully composed song in the series, "The Nightingale," features the vocals of Julee Cruise and contains the stock chord progression of many rock ballads of the 1950s and 1960s.[11] The cue, "Night Life in Twin Peaks," compares with many modernist art pieces considered to be avant-garde. Cues such as "Audrey's Dance" and "Dance of the Dream Man" are in a progressive jazz style.[12] The employment of these diverse musical styles reflects the genre hybridization of the show, often mirroring previous genres in an ironic way.

The *Twin Peaks* theme is itself a subtle blend of musical styles that connotes several television genres (example 9.2). The images of the opening sequence are a peculiar visual blend of the outskirts of the town of Twin Peaks, with a beautiful waterfall in juxtaposition to a ramshackle factory building in which can be seen machines sharpening saw blades. As the sparks fly from the machines in a precise manner, Badalamenti's slow, melancholy theme plays. The slow, free tempo of the theme counterbalances rhythmic precision of the machines.

The theme contains at least two style topics. The first is the sampled electric bass (similar to the *Seinfeld* slap bass sound) engineered for a cutting-edge sound, much like that heard in country-and-western music of the 1950s–1970s. The bass signifies the rural, Pacific Northwest setting of the narrative. The static

Example 9.2. Opening of Theme to *Twin Peaks* (Music by Angelo Badalamenti).

melody in the upper part, however, signifies a quite different topic—more of a Romantic love theme found on many TV soap operas of the 1960s and 1970s. This topic correlates with soap opera music of that time and affiliates itself with the genre as a never-ending serial drama. The slow, repetitious quality of the theme opens a fantasy, a dream-like, melancholy narrative world, which (incidentally) does nothing to suggest that the program is a police drama.

The disconcerting atmospherics of Badalamenti's music create an effect similar to that in Snow's synthesized score to *The X-Files*. The minimal amount of musical material along with the engineered-in soft dynamics create more of an effect than a sound track. For example, many of the cues taken in the program, especially for scenes that recall the tragic death of Laura Palmer or the various discoveries of evil, are accompanied by the two chords that introduce "Laura Palmer's Theme": an F minor chord in second inversion resolving to a C minor chord in root position (see example 9.3). The low, soft voicing of this simple sonority signifies a tragic topic.

Yet not all of the music in the series is submerged in such a way. In the fourth episode of the first season, a scene in the Double R Diner opens with a country-and-western song acousmatically presented but apparently sounding from the jukebox. In that same episode, Donna Hayward (Lara Flynn Boyle) and others are sitting in the diner, where they notice Audrey Horne (Sherilyn Fenn) sitting on a stool at the bar. Audrey walks over to the jukebox and inserts some coins, and an avant-garde sounding jazz piece begins to play. The music (Badalamenti's cue, "Audrey's Dance") is very dissonant, featuring layers of instruments: a drum set with brushes, a "walking" bass, clarinets playing an improvised-sounding melody, and electronic instruments playing dissonant intervals and high-pitched tone clusters. As Audrey and Donna discuss coffee and agent Cooper, Audrey remarks that the music is "dreamy" and gets up and dances in the middle of the diner, much to the embarrassment of the few patrons therein. The sinister sound of the music foreshadows Killer Bob, the force of evil revealed later in the series. The cue "Audrey's Dance" decenters the narrative temporarily while at the same time reinforcing it and foreshadowing the outcome.

Kathryn Kalinak (1995) has written on the show's musical score, which she suggests subverts the standard conventions of music and television narrative in various ways. Badalamenti's music aids the disruption and disorientation of the narrative that Lynch and Frost also employ in the visuals, dialogue, and sound. In particular, Kalinak notices how often the viewer is fooled by seemingly nondiegetic music that turns out to be diegetic through the visualization of phonographs, car radios, and the jukebox at the Double R Diner. Another postmodern trait of music is the imprecise nature of the representation of musical performance on the show, where characters obviously lip-synch prerecorded songs diegetically. Here, the musical performances foreground visual style over narrative substance, as viewers are captivated by the artistic imprecision of the music rendered. Yet another trait is the over-the-top nature of many of the music cues. Cues are often played so loudly and so persistently that viewers get the irony of the scene. Laura's theme, for example, saturates the music track and soon evinces a parody of soap opera–like tragedy. Rather than feeling the tragedy of the murder, the viewer realizes the foregrounding of the expressive aspects of the soap opera genre through the exaggerated repetition of the music.

A final significant point that Kalinak brings up with regard to the music of *Twin Peaks* is that musical themes tend to migrate between characters and situations in the show. In the modernist cinema and on television programs (as noted throughout this book), music serves to identify characters and situations, what Roland Barthes has termed "ancrage": anchoring the image in meaning, authorizing, indeed helping to create, a dominant reading of the visual image which is confluent with narrative objectives (quoted in Kalinak 1995: 89). How ancrage works is shown in the *Star Trek* leitmotifs and the *Rifleman* score, where the themes serve to signify a particular character or situation. However, in *Twin Peaks* there is no such allegiance of leitmotif to character. For example, "Audrey's Dance" migrates from the Double R Diner's jukebox and its connotation of Audrey as a promiscuous and rebellious character to later becoming associated with Mike and Bobby and still later with agent Cooper, signifying him as a cool detective in a film noir sense. While Kalinak regards the migration of leitmotifs as contributing to the disorienting and disrupting effects of the program, the practice can also be viewed as the quintessential element of style over substance in postmodernism.[13] The few leitmotifs composed by Badalamenti are highly stylized topics—indeed "over the top" as Kalinak states—and signify not through specific denotation of character, but through denotation of the topics themselves. The opening chord progression of Laura's theme is firmly situated in the style topic of the tragic and denotes not only Laura's untimely death, but also the collective grief of the denizens of Twin Peaks. It continues on through the episodes to become the more generic and tragic prevalence of evil in the town, as exemplified by Bob (example 9.3)

As the tragic chord progression morphs into the soap opera–like melody associated with "Laura's Palmer's Theme," it is obvious that this is a lush, exaggerated topic of emotion, and at the same time, it parodies the emotional excess of soap opera music (example 9.4). The theme migrates from fond memories of Laura to a love theme for Donna and James and later for James and Madeleine. It also accompanies Bobby's breakdown in a family counseling session with Dr. Jacoby and Audrey's attempted seduction of agent Cooper.

Through the migration of the leitmotifs, Badalamenti and Lynch decouple the denotative aspects of the leitmotifs from single characters on the show. The

Example 9.3. Part 1 of "Laura Palmer's Theme,"
Twin Peaks (Music by Angelo Badalamenti).

Example 9.4. Part 2 of "Laura Palmer's Theme,"
Twin Peaks (Music by Angelo Badalamenti).

themes become connotative signifiers expressing pure emotional states: tragedy ("Laura Palmer's Theme," pt. 1), love ("Laura Palmer's Theme," pt. 2), coolness or the sinister ("Audrey's Dance"). These musical blocks become pure connotators and thus seemingly lose their ascriptive value. However, as the leitmotifs are emptied of denotative signification, they signify on another level of the text as metasignifiers, or musical cues that migrate from signifier to signifier. Thus, musical leitmotifs no longer signify through characters or narrative but through the *conventions* of television narrative itself.

Conclusion

Despite the descriptions of television as postmodernism, it is apparent that TV music of the 1980s and 1990s still followed the innovation/assimilation model described earlier in this book. Television is, was, and has always been a postmodern medium in that it broadcasts mass-produced, commodified images and sounds. It is also an eclectic medium, broadcasting many different types of programs in various ways. At the same time, producers, writers, directors, composers all strive to make their individual television programs a commercial success. Traditionally, this has meant that programs must adhere to long-standing narrative conventions while also exhibiting some unique features that will reach a potential new audience. Each program seeks to exploit this unique feature extradiegetically, intradiegetically, or diegetically while at the same time conforming to recognized constraints of the genre. In the 1980s and 1990s, the television programs *Miami Vice*, *Frasier*, *Northern Exposure*, *The X-Files*, and *Twin Peaks* challenged the conventions of genres and opened up new realms of television with new visual, sonic, and narrative innovations. These traits are often described as postmodern, but they are also uniquely avant-garde and thus modernist. Both "modern" and "postmodern" are viewed here in the sense described by Jonathan Kramer, that they are dependent upon each other for their existence and continued articulation. So to be a "post-" of modernity is not to come after, but to be a borrower. Such borrowing is common in the history of the theater and the cinema, as it has always been to television. Perhaps one of the most notable traits of postmodernism in television is the borrowing of the traits of modernism, and of the avant-garde, as demonstrated by the music discussed in this chapter.

Thus, television music since 1980 can be considered as two sides of the same coin: as modernist texts with postmodern twists. Music in these programs is modernist in its striving to be original, to build on what has come before it but in a new, fresh and different way. At the same time, television is, as it has always been, postmodern in its borrowings from every other media possible and in its reflexivity, whether in television shows about television or in parodies of itself. Music has participated in both of these aesthetic arenas as part of new, modernist artistic endeavors, such as the use of jazz for *M Squad* or tonal coherence for episodes of *The Rifleman* or the delineation of televisual form for the *Philco Television Playhouse*. But music has also played the postmodernist joker in its borrowing of cinematic leitmotifs, as in *Star Trek*, or the self-parodying of musical style, as in *Twin Peaks*. As with all art forms, postmodern and modernist traits are found on television.

Despite the ongoing battle of modernist versus postmodernist aesthetic, television continues broadcasting because it resonates with its audience. And sponsors continue to tap into this resonance and, along with the networks, to commodify television. Television is the relationship of a particular text of images and sounds to another more general and diffuse text known as the audience. It is what producers (and composers) and audiences agree it is. And music on television will enhance/complement/signify/represent whatever we collectively believe it enhances, complements, signifies, or represents. This is the essence of televisual verisimilitude.

We now conclude this broadcasting day...

("The Star-Spangled Banner" plays...)

Appendix A

Morris's Definitions of the Three Dimensions of the Sign

Syntactics: The branch of semiotic that studies the ways in which signs of various classes are combined to form compound signs. It abstracts from the signification of the signs it studies and from their uses and effects; hence, it is distinguished from semantics and pragmatics.

Semantics: The branch of semiotic that studies the signification of signs. It is distinguished from syntactics and pragmatics.

Pragmatics: The branch of semiotic that studies the origin, the uses, and the effects of signs. It is distinguished from semantics and syntactics.

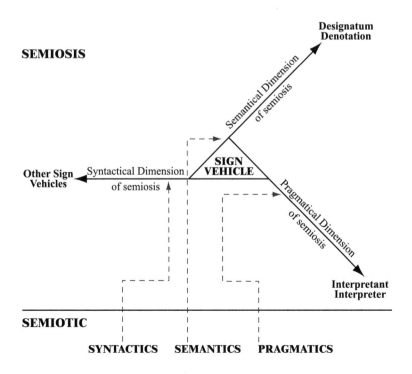

Appendix B

Propp's Functions of the *Dramatis Personae* in Russian Folktales

    I. One of the members of a family leaves home.

    II. An interdiction is addressed to the hero.

    III. The interdiction is violated.

    IV. The villain makes an attempt at reconnaissance.

    V. The villain receives information about his victim.

    VI. The villain attempts to deceive his victim in order to take possession of him or of his belongings.

    VII. The victim submits to deception and thereby unwittingly helps his enemy.

    VIII. The villain causes harm or injury to a member of a family.

    a. One member of a family either lacks something or desires to have something.

    IX. Misfortune or lack is made known; the hero is approached with a request or command; he is allowed to go or he is dispatched.

    X. The seeker agrees to or decides upon counteraction.

    XI. The hero leaves home.

    XII. The hero is tested, interrogated, attacked, etc. which prepares the way for his receiving either a magical agent or helper.

    XIII. The hero reacts to the actions of the future donor.

    XIV. The hero acquires the use of a magical agent.

    XV. The hero is transferred, delivered, or led to the whereabouts of an object of search.

    XVI. The hero and the villain join in direct combat.

    XVII. The hero is branded.

    XVIII. The villain is defeated.

    XIX. The initial misfortune or lack is liquidated.

    XX. The hero returns.

    XXI. The hero is pursued.

    XXII. Rescue of the hero from pursuit.

    XXIII. The hero, unrecognized, arrives home or in another country.

    XXIV. A false hero presents unfounded claims.

    XXV. A difficult task is proposed to the hero.

    XXVI. The task is resolved.

    XXVII. The hero is recognized.

    XXVIII. The false hero or villain is exposed.

    XXIX. The hero is given a new appearance.

    XXX. The villain is punished.

    XXXI. The hero is married and ascends the throne.

Notes

Introduction

With apologies to Fred Steiner and his now-famous article "What Were Musicians Saying about Movie Music during the First Decade of Sound?" in McCarty 1989.

1. These three programs were based on the films *Casablanca* (1942), *Kings Row* (1942), and *Cheyenne* (1947); each program was 45 minutes long, with the last quarter-hour devoted to promoting the studio and its upcoming movie releases. After the initial (1955–1956) season, only *Cheyenne* remained, later becoming a major hit and a watershed mark in network television's move to studio-produced, hour-long telefilm series, especially westerns.

2. The notion of "continuous performance" can be traced back to 1885, when Benjamin Keith decided to feature live acts in his Boston theater (and his later Manhattan theater) each day from 11:00 a.m. to 11:00 p.m. Within a decade, these live acts were supplemented with Thomas Edison films (Hawes 1986: 4).

3. History of Television Technology Web site, http://en.citizendium.org/wiki/History_of_television (accessed Sept. 18, 2008).

4. Toscanini, of course, was the long-standing conductor of the NBC Orchestra for both radio and television from 1937 to 1954. That a TV station employed a full-size symphony orchestra seems unbelievable in the twenty-first century!

5. Kempinski was best known for having composed stock music for several B film musicals in the 1930s and 1940s. Mamorsky's claim to fame was as composer of the film *With These Hands*, produced in 1950 by the International Ladies Garment Workers Union. Belviso was music director at Paramount Theaters in New York.

6. Jon Burlingame (1996) believes that Milhaud's two scores for the program were his only scores for American television. The two episodes were "Peron and Evita," in 1958, and the World War II film "Burma Road and the Hump," in 1959. John Briggs (1959) reports that French composer Georges Auric made his television-composing debut with the "Battle of Stalingrad" episode.

Chapter 1

1. There is much controversy over who invented television. Farnsworth received a patent for the cathode ray tube in 1927 (at age 21; he reportedly had the initial idea at age 14), whereas Zworykin claimed to have invented the iconoscope in 1923. Zworykin's patent was not approved until 1930, and he is reported to have revised his invention after visiting Farnsworth's lab.

2. Some very early nationally broadcast music programs included *King's Record Shop* (1945–1946), *Broadway Previews* (1946–1947), *Musical Merry-Go-Round* (1947–1948), *Showcase* (1947–1948), *Chevrolet on Broadway* (1948–1949), and *Toast of the Town* (1948–1972), which later became *The Ed Sullivan Show*. See Castleman and Podrazik 1982 for a complete listing.

3. The term "flow" was coined by Raymond Williams ([1974] 1992) and is discussed in more detail in chapter 2.

4. For specific information on a variety of communication models, see McQuail and Windahl 1993.

5. Fiske's codes of television model constitutes a practical application of the semiotic model of Peirce and Morris in that the codes reflect the tripartite aspect of the sign. "Reality" correlates to the Peircian sign-vehicle (or representamen); representation, to the object; and ideology, to the interpretant, where the receptor of the sign is free to make unlimited associations and further correlations of the original sign-vehicle. Fiske's model is an amplification also of Morris's (1946) "dimensions of the sign" theory, which in turn amplifies the tripartite Peircian conception of the sign wherein reality is actually syntactics, or an amplification of the "sign-vehicle" or "representamen," the representation level is semantic "object," and the "ideology" level is pragmatic. Fiske's reality level is Morris's syntactics, an area that deals with the examination of the physical elements of the sign-vehicle itself. "Representation" is Morris's "semantics" dimension, which deals with the meaning generated by the sign, and "ideology" is Morris's "pragmatics," or interpretation of the object (or sign vehicle, or both). These dimensions become courses of study in themselves, as syntactics for language translates into the study of grammar, semantics into hermeneutics, and pragmatics into several humanistic fields of study, such as philosophy, sociology, and so on.

6. Metz's sensory channels idea is a borrowing from Claude Lévi-Strauss's "sensory codes" that he uses for analysis of ritual in societies. Lévi-Strauss has used the term for the enlistment of each of the senses to develop a vocabulary and grammar founded on it to produce messages in various cultures. For example, the burning of different types of incense at different points in a ritual performance communicates different meanings, gestures and facial expressions are assigned meanings with reference to emotions and ideas to be communicated, soft and loud sounds have conventional meaning, and so on. The master of ceremonies, priest, conductor, producer, or director creates art from the ensemble of media and codes, just as a conductor in the single genre of classical music blends and opposes the sounds of the different instruments to produce an often unrepeatable effect (see Turner 1986: 23). Applied to television, TV often serves as an electronic

master of ceremonies or conductor, coordinating all sensory codes into a single preferred meaning.

7. A persistent criticism of Metz's categories is that image provides too much information to be listed as a single category. This brief example illustrates this, as we note Connors's costume, the setting, and Connors's actions, all of which convey much different information. Fiske seems to understand this limitation by listing costume, makeup, setting, etc., in his codes of television model. Images show both objects and actions, or what Algirdas Greimas (1987) calls the "modalities" of "being" and "doing," both of which are essential to conveying narrative. Film and television images are powerful and rife with interpretations for meaning, and the images' complexities are undoubtedly why many media theorists concentrate so heavily on them in their own analyses.

8. It is not a universally agreed upon notion that music is a semiotic system. Many theorists, including Eco, claim that music is an incomplete semiotic system with an expression plane but no content plane. Others have questioned music's ability to convey any sort of meaning outside of itself, that is, it has no potential for *extramusical* meaning. However, it is the central thesis of this book that music, especially music combined with images and sounds, does indeed act as a complete semiotic system, and sources are quoted throughout the book that also take this view.

9. See Hatten 1994 for an extended discussion of types and tokens in musical meaning.

10. For the nonmusic theorist reader, Schenkerian analysis is a method developed by Austrian musician Heinrich Schenker (1868–1935) as a means of finding a common fundamental structure for all tonal music. The graph in example 1.2 illustrates the Schenkerian fundamental structure, composed of the bass arpeggiation of the tonic and dominant chords (I–V–I) along with the descending fundamental line from scale degrees 3–2–1 in the top voice. Of course, the complication here is that the *Rifleman* theme actually ascends at the end rather than descends, as Schenker's model would have it. Schenkerian analysts would read this ascending figure as a foreground manifestation of an implied fundamental descent. See Schenker [1935] 1979.

11. An "energetic" interpretant is described by Peirce (1931–1958, 2:230) as one that prompts a physical response, in this case flinching from the noise of the rifle. Other energetic interpretants to music may be the desire for bodily movement (dancing, head bopping, clapping hands, and so on).

12. For a detailed account on the use of the horn for musical expression throughout music history, see the description in Tagg 2000.

13. In finding historical precedents for musical styles and genres, I am following the example of Philip Tagg (though not as extensively). See Tagg 2000 and 1982.

14. Gilbert did indeed have a fertile period of composing music for film before the *Rifleman* series; he was nominated for two Academy Awards for scoring, in 1952 and 1954, for the films *The Thief* and *Carmen Jones*, and he was also nominated for best song composed for the film *The Moon Is Blue* (1953).

15. For the reader not familiar with these labels for chords and scale degrees, tonic refers to the keynote pitch or the chord based on the keynote pitch (e.g., the pitch D in

D major is tonic); subdominant refers to the pitch or chord based on the fourth scale degree (in D major subdominant would be the pitch/chord G); and dominant is the pitch/chord based on the fifth scale degree (in D dominant would be A). In tonal music the arrival on the dominant almost always signals the return of tonic.

16. For an in-depth study of signification in Copland's music, see Lerner 2001.

17. These draw from Peirce's conception of iconic and symbolic signs, which lie in the representation part of the three-part sign. The third is indexical, and many music signs also may be viewed as indexical because they often point to extramusical meaning.

18. See Peter Kivy's *Sound and Sentiment* (1984) for an in-depth discussion of music's mimetic qualities.

19. A third mode of signification for music has been cited by Peirce as the ability for music to prompt bodily movement, motion, or dancing. Peirce calls this the "energetic interpretant" (as distinguished from "emotional" and "logical" interpretants), and while it is a significant feature of music, is not so important for music in television. I discuss the property briefly in chapter 6. For Peirce's quote on interpretants, see Martinez 1997: 75–76.

20. The term "Hollywood symphonic style" is used by Neil Lerner (2001) to describe the film music tradition of Hollywood in the mid-twentieth century. I shall use this term to describe much television music of the 1940s–1980s as deriving from this tradition.

21. A couple of westerns did actually use jazz style music; *Shotgun Slade* (1959–1961) starring Scott Brady, and *The Deputy* (1959) starring Henry Fonda (in a rare and unsuccessful TV role), both of which used a solo electric guitar, the timbre of which imparted a sort of jazz style. Music for *The Deputy* was composed and played by Jack Marshall.

22. The new meaning that is developed as the result of the structuring correlation is referred to as a trope.

23. There are exceptions in film. *High Noon* (1952) provides an opening that shows the outlaws assembling together to fulfill their plot to kill the Sheriff (Gary Cooper), who is not shown until the opening credits end.

24. Lawrence Kramer (2002) also discusses the concept of the "musical remainder," that while music contributes to the semantic meaning of a multimedia text, a nonsemantic remainder also is present (the musical artwork itself) and often is ignored by the spectator/listener.

Chapter 2

1. Seymour Chatman (1978: 19) has defined a story (*histoire*) as "the content or chain of events (actions, happenings) plus what may be called the existents (characters, items of setting)" and a discourse (*discours*) as "the expression, the means by which the context is communicated. In simple terms, the story is the 'what' in a narrative that is depicted, discourse is the 'how'."

2. Music can be part of the story, of course, in musicals and musical variety shows. Music as story is explored in chapter 6.

3. Levinson's article "Film Music and Narrative Agency" deals with film, not television; thus, I am paraphrasing his terms "film story" and "world of a film."

4. For this study, I use the narrative agency theory of Gérard Genette (1980: 213), who describes agency as "the mode of action . . . of the verb considered for its relation to the subject—the subject here being not only the person who carries out or submits to the action, but also the person . . . who reports it, and, if need be, all those people who participate, even though passively, in this narrating activity. We know that linguistics has taken its time in addressing the task of accounting for what Benveniste has called *subjectivity in language*, that is, in passing from analysis of statements to analysis of relations between these statements and their generating instance—what today we call enunciating. It seems that poetics is experiencing a comparable difficulty in approaching the generating instance of narrative discourse, an instance for which we have reserved the parallel term *narrating*."

5. These two modalities of narration were posited as far back as Aristotle. See Bordwell 1985 for a full discussion on telling and showing narration.

6. Chatman (1990: 113) has made the case for a similar mimetic narrator in fiction films, writing that "film has nothing like a narrative voice, no tell-er. Even the cinematic voice-over is usually at the service of a large narrative agent, the cinematic show-er. But that show-er can reasonably be called a presenter."

7. David Bordwell disagrees with Chatman's model and places the onus for meaning in film narrative on the audience, who supposedly cobble together narrative meaning from a set of narrative cues in a film. According to Bordwell (1985: 62), "Literary theories of the implied author, such as Seymour Chatman's, take the process of narration to be grounded in the classic communication diagram: a message is passed from sender to receiver. . . . I suggest, however, that narration is better understood as 'the organization of a set of cues for the construction of a story.' This presupposes a perceiver, but not any sender, of a message." Bordwell's audience response model is similar to discussion of the semiotic theory of television, though I would suggest here that meaning is negotiated between a presenter, who displays the representational codes of television (through images, sounds, music), and the viewer, who interprets those codes. The position taken here is more in line with the view of Jerrold Levinson (1996: 252), that narration in film is through the presenter, who is a perceptual enabler, who provides perceptual access to the fictional world, which the audience in turn perceives as what the narrator perceives in a story, even imaginarily, in the manner and order in which the audience receives it.

8. However, such master log schedules are a staple at network and local television stations, where newsbreaks, commercials, weather reports, etc., are placed on a master schedule for broadcasting.

9. Antin then postulates that television time is reducible to the 10-second spot, upon which all television is assembled, like building blocks. Advocating Antin's view, Robert Fink (2005: 132) states that these temporal units pile up into complex additive blocks, acting as small gears driving the larger ones. Since all television texts have the same syntax (programs, commercials, etc.), all TV builds from the smallest temporal building block. However, neither Antin nor Fink defines the properties of this minimal unit.

10. In all fairness, Fink's task in his book is to demonstrate the similarity between minimal music and the televisual practice of flow, not to provide a detailed discussion of television broadcasting practice.

11. The metaphor of space in Fauconnier and Turner's blended space networks is discussed in chapter 1. Music has also invoked the metaphor of space, from Heinrich Schenker's (1935) "Tonraum" (tonal space) to spatial applications by David Lewin (1987), Fred Lerdahl (2001), and others.

12. Prendergast (1992: 281) opines that bumpers are functionally worthless on television, and he somewhat cynically describes them as a means of hoodwinking the audience into believing that the program is about to resume after a commercial break, thus drawing people who may have been out of the room back to the set—to watch more commercials. While his opinions are probably held by many TV viewers, another way of considering this device is that they carry a proairetic function, that is, they tantalize the viewer to stay engaged in the program.

13. Immel began his career as a copyist at Four Star Studios and as a supervising copyist/librarian at CBS. He worked on some scores for the western series *Gunsmoke* and composed an elegant theme for the television special *How the West Was Won*.

14. See Prendergast 1992: 285 for Immel's facsimile score of the bumper.

15. Identificative mode is one of Morris's "modes of signification" that differentiate signs in terms of the most general kinds of significata. He distinguishes five modes of signifying, three of them "pragmasemantic": designative (statements), appraisive (valuations), and prescriptive (imperatives), and two of them less important modes: identificative (locators in time and space) and formative (contextual functions, such as conjunctions and quantifiers, as well as punctuation marks).

16. See Prendergast's discussion of the piece in Prendergast 1992: 279.

17. The DX7 was thought to be one of the most influential digital synthesizers ever produced. It was the first commercially successful synthesizer due to its range of digital sounds. When the DX7 was originally introduced in 1983, it was so popular with musicians that Yamaha quickly found out that they simply could not produce enough of them. Some 160,000 of these synthesizers were manufactured between 1983 and 1987. The DX7 was used by many popular music artists at the time, notably, Sting, Herbie Hancock, Phil Collins, Madonna, Jan Hammer (for *Miami Vice*), and Mike Post (for many TV shows). See Cox and Warner 2004.

18. Prendergast complains that act-ins and act-outs are so constraining that the composer really has no musical time for any sort of expression. As I have intimated, Immel's use of instruments and harmonies seems to convey suspense quite well, with a maximum amount of musical signification within a minimum amount of musical time.

19. See Gorbman 1987; Kalinak 1992; and Prendergast 1992, among others, who label it as "source music."

20. See Wilk 1976: 125–138 on some of the legal battles that Philco had to overcome.

21. According to Harman (1951), more and more dramatic music on television had by that time moved from live performance to recordings. A music supervisor would simply play LP records as part of the production process. The records would be part of the

studio's music library but might also come from the emerging program services who furnished library music.

22. Sosnik's biographical information is taken from the Sosnik collection at the Wisconsin Center for Film and Theater Research (unpublished).

23. Sosnik's theatrical terminology in the labeling of cues is telling in that producers of early television viewed their work as theatrical rather than as a mass electronic medium.

24. The G#7 is an enharmonic respelling of a German augmented 6th chord that resolves to the I 6/4 chord but omits the dominant at the final cadence. It is comical in that it can be seen as an ellipsis that omits the dominant.

25. Sosnik's terminology on these musical cues reflects an influence of incidental music for the theater rather than broadcasting. Some of his terms for transition music for musical variety shows are similar, where he calls transition cues "play ons" and "play offs" rather than act-ins and act-outs.

26. I viewed this program on the original kinescope at the Wisconsin Center for Film and Theater Research.

27. Complete musical structures are those that illustrate musical closure, as shown in such methodologies as Schenker's theory of the *Ursatz* or Hugo Riemann's harmonic/tonal cycles, or in more rudimentary demonstrations of musical closure, in which musical structures, like phrases, demonstrate closure through authentic (V–I) cadences.

28. For example, a minuet cue might be more appropriate for the late-eighteenth-century setting of the play rather than the more nineteenth-century waltz cue. In this context, however, a minuet may sound excessively antique, so the waltz is probably a good choice.

29. Overcoding proceeds in two directions: first it can assign additional meanings to objects or, second, it will analyze objects into more analytical entities. Eco uses the example of how paralinguistics pronounces a word in several different ways or stresses different syllables. Also, overly flowery courtesy formulas, such as "s'il vous plait" or "I beg your pardon," are traditional overcodings. These are overly polite and verbose ways to convey "please" and "excuse me," respectively. Richard Middleton (1990: 173) describes over-coding in terms of popular music where every detail of the music is covered by a network of explicit codes and subcodes.

30. For more information about the series, see Zicree 1982.

31. More on jazz in 1960s TV in chapter 8.

Chapter 3

1. Most, but not all, sources cite the Bulova watch commercial as the first TV advertisement. According to the Web site answerbag.com, the Bulova ad was preceded by one for I. J. Fox Furriers in Boston in 1930. Given that in 1930 the Federal Communications Commission did not yet license commercials, however, the Bulova ad is technically the first to be aired on the new medium.

2. One example I viewed was a demonstration of the new Philco record player that was developed for the new 33 1/3 rpm records in 1948. The commercial was narrated by band leader Paul Whiteman, was over five minutes in length, and was inserted as an intermission to a *Philco Television Playhouse* teleplay.

3. This trend is explored in detail in chapter 7.

4. Background music is what Claudia Gorbman (1987) refers to as the "unheard" underscored music of narrative films.

5. "Supradiegetic" is Rick Altman's (1987a: 69–70) term for transcendent fantasy music in film musicals, wherein actors suspend the narrative in order to sing. The singers on-screen appear to be singing but in fact the music on the track was recorded prior to the filming and the actors lip-synch on film. In addition to its fanciful nature, supradiegetic music differs from diegetic music in that the music seems to emanate from the screen, but the orchestral accompaniment (usually) does not appear on screen.

6. The seminal radio bite—"Have You Tried Wheaties?"—was first released on Christmas Eve in 1929. It featured four male singers (eventually christened the Wheaties Quartet) singing the following lines:

Have you tried Wheaties?
They're whole wheat with all of the bran.
Won't you try Wheaties?
For wheat is the best food of man.

7. Huron (1989) described the musical structure of the Pepsodent jingle, citing the two-part structure of the theme in which the first part contains the blue note (the lowered 7th scale degree as in jazz and blues music) on "you'll wonder where the yellow went," followed by the diatonic dominant 7th chord resolving to tonic on "when you brush your teeth with Pepsodent." These brief musical gestures represent two style topics: the blues (at having "yellow" teeth) and a happy, up-beat diatonic (nonblues) gesture of resolution.

8. Reeves spelled out the concept of the U.S.P. in his first book, *The Reality of Advertising* (1961). As the name implies, the U.S.P. enumerates all the unique characteristics of a product, even if all that is unique is that it is easier to use or simply new.

9. Reeves also insisted the product being sold actually be superior and argued that no amount of advertising could move inferior goods. He also disagreed that advertising created demand where it did not exist. Moreover, he did not shy away from questionable ethics, including using doctors to sell cigarettes. Despite some decline in receptivity to Reeves's style of ads, many companies still use his techniques when producing television commercials, and his methods and ideas are still taught in many marketing schools.

10. This is, of course, the same Harry Sosnik mentioned in chapter 2: during his career he also worked as a jingle writer for the Ted Bates Advertising Agency in New York.

11. Quote is from an unpublished interoffice memo.

12. When *The Flintstones* premiered in 1960, ABC promoted the animated Stone Age family show as an adult cartoon, so the network contracted with adult-oriented sponsors

Miles Laboratories (makers of One-A-Day vitamins and Alka-Seltzer) and the R. J. Reynolds Tobacco Company (makers of Winston cigarettes). The series began as an animated version of *The Honeymooners* (1955–1956) but eventually found an audience with children.

13. A ban on cigarette advertising on television and radio was proposed in Congress in 1969 and became law in 1971, thus ending the tobacco companies' involvement with the electronic media (Barnouw 1978: 435). Cigarette advertising was not banned in print media, where it remains to this day.

14. Permission to use Sosnik's material has been granted through the Wisconsin Center for Film and Theater Research.

15. I have seen ads that use this light jazz topic to sell products ranging from cigarettes to beer to soft drinks. One other interesting use of this topic was the early 1960s ad campaign for Pepsi that featured the jingle "Be Sociable, Have a Pepsi" and showed adults drinking Pepsi while dancing to an on-screen jazz combo.

16. Despite the craftsmanship of the commercial, I can find no evidence that Sosnik's jingle ever aired. Rather, the ad campaign at the time for this brand of cigarette featured a rhythmic monotone patter on the "not too strong, not too light" U.S.P. by an unknown (to me) composer.

17. Merrick was also involved with such programs as *The Bob Cummings Show, The Burns and Allen Show, Blondie,* and others, but his primary tenure on television was as Jack Benny's music director, a position he held for fifteen years. Merrick also composed the fight song for Washington State University, his alma mater. See the "Guide to the Mahlon Merrick Papers 1953–1967," http://nwda-db.wsulibs.wsu.edu/findaid/ark:/80444/xv35570 (accessed July 15, 2008).

18. The *Cavalcade of Sports* was indeed one of the very earliest and longest running American television programs, debuting in 1944. It began as a radio show in 1942 as an outgrowth of Gillette broadcasts of the annual World Series. The program moved to television in 1944 and was renamed *The Gillette Cavalcade of Sports* in 1948. The show was noted for broadcasting a wide variety of sporting events but was best known for its Friday night boxing matches. See Castleman and Podrazik 1982.

19. The song was originally composed for the musical *Sweet Charity* and has been covered many times, perhaps most famously by Peggy Lee in 1966 and Shirley Bassey in 1967. Adams was no stranger to television. She began her career by winning the 1950 Miss U.S. Television pageant on the DuMont Television Network. Soon afterward, she appeared on the Ernie Kovacs Show and ended up marrying Kovacs in 1954. An accomplished singer (a Juilliard graduate), she won a Tony Award for her role in *L'il Abner* on Broadway in 1957 and appeared in more than a dozen films.

20. The semiotic square is an adaptation of the 'logical square' of scholastic philosophy and is used as a means of analyzing paired concepts more fully (Greimas 1987: xiv, 49). The semiotic square is intended to map the logical conjunctions and disjunctions relating key semantic features in a text. Fredric Jameson has noted that "the entire mechanism . . . is capable of generating at least ten conceivable positions out of a rudimentary binary opposition" (see Greimas 1987: xiv). These positions suggest possibilities for

signification in a semiotic system richer than the either/or of binary logic, but they are still subject to semiotic constraints—deep structures providing basic axes of signification. The terms on the upper corners of the Greimasian square represent an opposition between S1 and S2 (e.g., white and black), while the lower corners represent positions that are not accounted for in simple binary opposition: Not S2 and Not S1 (e.g., not white and not black). Not S1 consists of more than simply S2 (e.g., that which is not white is not necessarily black). The horizontal relationships represent an opposition between each of the left-hand terms (S1 and Not S2) and its paired right-hand term (Not S1 and S2). The terms at the top (S1 and S2) represent presences while their companion terms (Not S1 and Not S2) represent absences. The vertical relationships of implication offer us an alternative conceptual synthesis of S1 with Not S2 and of S2 with Not S1 (e.g., of white with not black or of black with not white). Greimas refers to the relationships between the four positions as contrariety or opposition (S1/S2), complementarity or implication (S1/Not S2 and S2/Not S1), and contradiction (S1/Not S1 and S2/Not S2).

21. In logic, contrariety is the relationship between contraries, that is, things that are opposite in nature but so related to each other that both may not be true even though both may be false, whereas contradiction is a relationship or proposition that denies another or itself and is logically incongruous. In a contrary proposition, both may not be true though both may be false, as with the propositions "all judges are male" and "no judges are male"; in contrast, contradictions are propositions so related to a second that it is impossible for both to be true or both to be false and thus cancel each other out, such as in the statement "he is brave and he is not brave."

22. Altman (1987a: 62–74) calls this relationship "audio dissolve" (see chapter 6).

23. Patter ads are perhaps a possibility for dialogue mediating lyrics and image, wherein a rhymed verse would be chanted in rhythm but without musical pitch. One example of a patter ad is the famous Pepsodent commercial, in which patter was sung interspersed with the tag of the jingle.

24. Robert Hatten (1994: 291) has defined markedness as the "asymmetrical valuation of an opposition (in musical structure, language, culture) given to difference." More on markedness in chapter 8.

Chapter 4

1. Coyne Sanders and Tom Gilbert (1993: 36) have described as a "myth" the idea that the Arnazes dipped into their own pockets to finance the pilot. According to producer Jess Oppenheimer, the pilot was always underwritten by CBS.

2. *I Love Lucy* was not the first TV program on film, but at the time it was the most popular by far. The three-camera technique of filming on 16mm film was first used by the NBC network on the 1947–1948 program *Public Prosecutor*, the 1949 anthology series *Silver Theater*, and Frank Edwards's game show, *Truth or Consequences*. CBS adopted a more sophisticated format, using 35mm film stock and an enhanced communication system

between the control room and studio floor, which became known as the Fairbanks-Simon technique, first used on the *Amos 'n' Andy* series in 1950 (see Sanders and Gilbert 1993: 38–39).

3. The score is part of the CBS Television Collection housed at the Music Library Special Collections Department at UCLA.

4. Chion was correct up to the time his book was published; in the early 2000s, however, films like *The Matrix* began to experiment with different visual effects, such as stop action and slow motion.

5. Chion's analogy breaks down somewhat when one considers that early TV cameras were actually massive, bulky apparatuses that had to have wheels to move.

6. I use the term "Hollywood film style" to describe the post-Romantic style of music found in many classical Hollywood films, that is, music from the mid-1930s through the 1950s and beyond. This style, described by Claudia Gorbman (1987), Kathryn Kalinak (1992), Roy Prendergast (1992), and especially Caryl Flinn's *Strains of Utopia* (1992), was typified by such film composers as Max Steiner, Erich Korngold, Alfred Newman, Franz Waxman, and others. Flinn (1992: 13) asserted that most film scores "were composed in a manner deeply influenced by late romantic composers like Richard Wagner and Richard Strauss." Prendergast (1992: 98–179) points out, however, that in the 1950s, film music, like that of television, became more pluralistic with regard to style and genre, using jazz and rock styles as well as 12-tone and electronic scores. So, TV and film music both took advantage of the rich variety of musical styles available to composers during that decade and beyond.

7. One episode in particular, "The War of the Robots" (broadcast during the first season on February 9, 1966), uses Bernard Herrmann's music from the film *The Day the Earth Stood Still*, complete with the electronic Theremin.

8. The concept of leitmotif was developed and popularized by German composer Richard Wagner in his musical dramas of the nineteenth century, but the notion of repeating motifs to signify characters or ideas predated Wagner in works by Hector Berlioz and Franz Liszt, among others. However, Wagner is viewed as the innovator of the leitmotif, due to the ubiquitous use of them in his musical dramas and his extensive writings on the subject. Wagner asserted that leitmotifs could have dramatic value throughout an entire opera when introduced first as a union of text and music (see Wagner 1900: 237–376). In practice, musical gestures would accompany the sung dialogue of a character to introduce the motif. With the establishment of this "memory motif," the motif could recur later in the opera without reinforcement of language to spur the memory of the audience. Gorbman (1987) uses the "curse" motif from Wagner's opera *Das Rheingold* as an example. The motif is introduced by the sung line "Wie durch Fluch er mir geriet, verflucht sei dieser Ring!" ["As by a curse it came into my power, cursed be this ring!"] As the motif recurs throughout the opera (such as the slaying of Fasolt by Faffner), the audience is able to recognize the curse in the course of narrative events. Cinematic and televisual leitmotifs do not live up to Wagner's practice of musically developing motifs throughout his music dramas and, for the most part, only represent signposts of signification through simple repetition in a film or TV show.

9. Musical leitmotifs in film and television can be seen as small units of denotation or musical meaning, though perhaps not the smallest possible unit. (Stinger chords that carry the dynamic or iconic interpretant may be a smaller meaningful musical unit, for example). Indeed, one of the issues of musical (and for that matter linguistic) meaning is defining and identifying the smallest unit of meaning and how these units are strung together to create larger ones. Such studies of metalanguage (the language of the theory of language) have been ongoing for a very long time, but here I deal with one dimension. Linguist Ferdinand de Saussure (1959) identified two dimensions of language, the paradigmatic and the syntagmatic. The paradigmatic consists of linguistic units forming categories wherein units could be substituted for other units within that category. In language, for example, any noun can be substituted for another noun, any verb for another verb, and so on (though many substitutions would result in nonsensical or absurd sentences). For example, one could change the sentence "the cat walked across the street" with "the giraffe walked across the street," and the meaning would change but would be intelligible nonetheless due to the substitution of like paradigms. Other substitutions could further transform the sentence ("the giraffe *ran* across the street," "the giraffe *looked* across the street," "the giraffe looked *for* the street," etc.). Paradigms, then, are discrete linguistic categories that convey meaning. In some theories of language, the word is viewed as the smallest unit of meaning. In Saussure's view, every word is a sound-image that combines signifier with signified. However, there are smaller units of meaning than the word. Prefixes and suffixes to words also impart meaning. "Pre-" and "post-" refer to time (before and after), whereas such endings as "-itis" or "-ism" refer to illnesses or belief systems, respectively.

Given the paradigmatic, or "vertical" conception of language, words are combined "horizontally" (or "syntagmatically") to create larger linguistic units, for example, phrases, sentences, paragraphs, and so on. The linking of syntagms gives rise to syntax (or syntagma), that is, the sequential ordering of paradigms in a string. In English, conventional syntax calls for a noun phrase followed by a verb phrase in a sentence. "The cat walked across the street" is intelligible because of commonly accepted English syntax, whereas "across the street the cat walked" is still intelligible, though the phrasing is less commonly accepted (except perhaps in poetry). "Across the walked street cat the" becomes unintelligible due to unfamiliar syntax or syntagma. Music also possesses paradigms and syntagms, and television music uses both these dimensions to help convey meaning in a narrative. Leitmotifs are musical paradigms that are used to great theatrical effect on television.

10. Light music is a somewhat generic style topic that is attributed to many American and English composers and arrangers of the early twentieth century, the most famous perhaps being Leroy Anderson, Morton Gould, Percy Faith, and Mantovani. Either these composers/arrangers had their own orchestras and choirs or their works were played by ensembles like the Boston Pops Orchestra. Repertoire consisted of lush arrangements of Tin Pan Alley standards or original compositions, such as those by Leroy Anderson, Eric Coates, Frederic Curzon, and others. The most coherent grouping of this type of music I have found can be found on the Robert Farnon Society Web site at http://www.rfsoc.org.uk/.

11. I am describing the early incarnation of the theme, as in the show's later years; the theme was rearranged into a swing jazz number to reflect (somewhat naively) the Beaver character as a teenager.

12. I am referring here to comedy shows like *Saturday Night Live* and *Mad TV*, which have lampooned sit-coms, such as *Leave It to Beaver* and others.

13. I am paraphrasing and glossing Hatten rather freely here. Hatten's definition is actually as follows: "Category of musical works based on their implementation of a change-of-state schema (tragic-to-triumphant, tragic-to transcendent) or their organization of expressive states in terms of an overarching topical field (pastoral, tragic)" (Hatten 1994: 290). The point here is that expressive genres define works by the extramusical traits they express rather than by their musical structure (sonata, rondo, etc.) or by their genre or performance practice (string quartet, symphony, etc.).

14. "Many of the current differences in the attempt to differentiate 'statements,' 'valuations,' and 'imperatives' comes from the different bases upon which the various classification are made. The classification of the major modes of signifying is not itself an exhaustive classification of signs, but only a fragment of such classification.... There is a common tendency to say that such a term as 'war' is 'referential' if it produces no emotion in its interpreter and 'emotive' if it does produce an emotion" (Morris 1946: 63).

15. More recently, Kivy (1989) wrote extensively about emotions and music, stating that music is more a representation of emotion than emotive itself.

16. Agawu describes style topics for eighteenth-century classical music. He (1991: 49) has defined the style topic as follows: "Topics are musical signs. They consist of a signifier (a certain disposition of musical dimensions) and a signified (a conventional stylistic unit, often but not always referential in quality). Signifiers are identified as a relational unit within the dimensions of melody, harmony, meter, rhythm, and so on, while the signified is designated by conventional labels." Agawu defined topics as musical signs that link musical syntax (disposition of notes, rhythms, etc., as a signifier) to a signified of a stylistic label, thereby creating a sign of musical discourse that provides a framework for describing various kinds and levels of associative signification in music. Monelle (2000) described topics in relation to the musical object (as opposed to sign-vehicle and interpretant), describing topics in Peircian terms of the symbolic, iconic, or indexical features. According to Monelle (2000: 17), the topic "is essentially a symbol, its iconic or indexical features governed by a convention and thus by rule. However, topics may be glimpsed through a feature that seems universal to them: a focus on the indexicality of the content, rather than the content itself." Here Monelle stresses two important aspects of topic: (1) that it may contain a musical figure that signifies through its indexicality to a nonmusical idea and (2) that this indexicality must be recognized by the culture in which it is produced. The topic is a musical abstraction of something it may or may not have once represented, through iconicism or indexicality. Tarasti considers topics as exteroceptive (extramusical) icons (again, a category of the object part of the sign) because they function musically as part of human sociocultural praxis, that is, through the individual habits and beliefs within a culture. As the same topic is repeated in a composition, the extramusical nature of the topic dissolves into an intramusical iconicity dealing with the structure and semantics of

the work itself. Tarasti has attributed the success of many compositions to the composer's ability to ensure that the extramusical and intramusical networks support each other.

17. In Morris's terms, topics are like "lansign-systems" or sets of plurisituational signs with interpersonal significata common to members of an interpreter-family (Morris 1946: 350).

18. See Kalinak 1992 and Gorbman 1987 for the use and functions of music in the silent film era.

19. Rapée's list is much longer, and I use only a few of his many examples to make my point.

20. This information is on the Internet Movie Database (imdb.com).

21. These cues are actually called "standard orbit" and "captain's log," according to Bond (1999: 41–55).

22. Gorbman (1987) illustrates this phenomenon with a theme that represents "attacking Indians" in John Ford's film *Stagecoach*. According to Gorbman (1987: 28), the motif denotes Indians through its cultural-musical properties, including "rhythmic repetition in groups of four with accented initial beat, and predominance of open intervals of perfect fourths and fifths—already signify[ing] 'Indian' in the language of the American music industry."

23. For the music of Beethoven, Hatten has identified these schemas as "comic to tragic," "tragic to triumphant to transcendent," and so forth. In the context of twentieth-century television music, I describe these expressive genres more as menu-driven than as binary oppositions, as Hatten would have it. Thus, for TV music, expressive genres would include a list containing the topics of "comic," "tragic," "romantic," danger/suspense," "mystery/enigma," "fantasy," "heroic," and others. These are derived from Rapée (1924)'s list of "moods" for silent film music, with many topics to select from.

Chapter 5

1. Chatman lists events and characters as two of the three signifieds of narrative, the third being detail of setting.

2. Similar to Chatman's oppositions, Algirdas Greimas (1987) refers to a "generative course" of narrative that reflects the semiotic modalities of "being" and "doing." These two modalities, more generically referred to as "referencing" and "action," are the two ways of viewing the narrative world.

3. Leitmotifs can also signify time and place in a film or television score, as demonstrated by Ernö Rapée's silent film music catalog. Royal Brown (1994: 52) has described how Max Steiner quotes "Dixie" and another motive on banjo in the film *Gone with the Wind* to evoke what Roland Barthes would call "old-southicity," that is, denoting the South during the American Civil War. Various other ethnic-"icities" are part of the semantic field of television audiences, as evidenced by the open fourths of the "tiger" motive or the pentatonic scale of the "samurai" motive of the "Shore Leave" episode.

4. Greimas (1987: 106) uses the terms "actant" and "actor" to refine further the existent category. In Greimas's terminology, "actant" is a generic element of narrative syntax, while "actor" refers to a particular person in a particular story. The term "actant" can be defined also as a subcategory of "existent" because it refers to a person who helps propel (or is propelled by) the trajectory of the narrative. For example, Captain James Kirk as narrative hero is an actant, whereas William Shatner, who plays Captain Kirk, is an actor. Kirk is also actant versus the alien planet, which is an existent, that is, an inanimate object that is the part of the narrative. Once the planet is established as the setting of the narrative, it is no longer a meaningful part of the narrative syntax.

5. For a more in-depth discussion of types and tokens see Hatten 1994.

6. Propp's characters carry out 31 functions, beginning with an absence from a home/family setting and continuing on to the hero setting out for a quest and ending with the return of the hero and his (figurative or literal) marriage to the princess. For a full list of Propp's 31 functions, see appendix B. Propp's theory of the plot in the Russian folktale has been called a brilliant example of the Russian orthodox formalist method applied to the structural analysis of the fairy tale. In spite of this seeming orthodoxy, some functions may be omitted or circumvented in a given tale. As has been shown in this chapter, some of Propp's functions can be applied to the structure of a classic television narrative.

7. Chatman invokes Jean Pouillon's *Temps et roman* (Paris, 1946) definition of contiguity ("depending for its existence, occurrence, character, etc. on something yet uncertain," p. 47) to explain the modern author's rejection of causality as a requirement for narrative.

8. A similar structural theory of narrative to Chatman's was developed by Roland Barthes (1974, 1988), who developed categories of "functions" and "indices" that parallel Chatman's notions of kernels and satellites, functions being actions in a narrative that further the narrative story and indices being incidental actions that do not necessarily further the narrative but that may illuminate aspects or traits of the character or narrative situation.

9. Todorov reflects a Marxist ideology, emphasizing the social implications of events over the individual, as in Propp's model.

10. See also Lacey 2000: 29.

11. Feuer's perspective on the soap opera and other TV genres stems from Lacanian psychology and operates from the notion that the implied television audience does not comprise the pre-Oedipal individual described by Christian Metz, Jean-Louis Baudry, and others in their works on metapsychology for the cinema but, rather, is a post-Oedipal, fully socialized family member. In a twist on the notion of an audience member looking into the Lacanian mirror, a television viewer actually looks into a mirror of the family. Thus, to Feuer, the episodic television narrative consists week after week of establishing the status quo of the family followed by a threat to the family and an elimination of the threat that returns the family to normalcy. In some episodic series, such as *I Love Lucy* (1951–1957), *Father Knows Best* (1954–1960), and *Family Ties* (1982–1989), the series family is a kinship family, whereas in other series, such as the *Mary Tyler Moore Show*

(1970–1977) and *Cheers* (1982–1993), the idea of family extends beyond blood to friends and/or coworkers. In contrast, the serial narrative of a television soap opera deals with the continual dissolution of the family. There may be an implicit ideal of equilibrium within a seemingly happy family in a soap opera, but weekly (or daily) installments reveal continual disruptions to that family while, at the same time, any explicit resolution of disruption is nonexistent.

12. Among the vast amount of literature on musical representation, see particularly Peter Kivy's works, notably *Sound and Semblance* (1984), *Osmin's Rage* (1988), and *Sound Sentiment* (1989), the latter of which contains the complete text of an earlier work, *The Corded Shell* (1980).

13. Jerrold Levinson (2004: 429–431), among others, doubts that music, especially instrumental music, can be narrative at all because it lacks definite referential qualities as well as a narrative voice, point of view, or "true-to-lifeness" and cannot convey causal relations among states of affairs or events. While these points are arguable (at least to my mind), when correlated with images in a television narrative, the arguments for musical narrative, or at least narrative *traits* of music, are strengthened considerably. When correlated with images, music does have specific referential qualities, or at least references that are attached to music through the narrative images by the audience through verisimilitude.

14. Tarasti's statement seems to agree with Levinson, who sees music as having less narrative properties and more dramatic function (see Levinson 2004: 433; also see Maus 1997 and Newcomb 1987).

15. Tarasti's model of musical narrative has its historical antecedents, most notably in the theoretical work of A. B. Marx, who saw music as moving through states of *marche* (motion) and *repos* (rest/stasis).

16. In fact, Barthes himself acknowledged classical tonal music as following his five narrative codes. "What stands out, what flashes forth, what emphasizes and impresses are the semes, the cultural citations and the symbols, analogous in their heavy timbre, in the value of their discontinuity, to the brass and percussion. What sings, what flows smoothly, what moves by accidentals, arabesques, and controlled ritardandos through an intelligible progression (like the melody of ten given the woodwinds) is the series of enigmas, their suspended disclosure, their delayed resolution . . . . Finally, what sustains, flows in a regular way, brings everything together, lie the strings, are the proairetic sequences, the series of actions, the cadence of familiar gestures" (Barthes 1974: 29)

17. For such a list of musical functions, I adapt a list of formal functions of music listed by early-twentieth-century composer Arnold Schoenberg and further elaborated by William Caplin (1998) for classical music.

18. Four Star Productions was a small studio founded by Dick Powell, Ida Lupino, David Niven, and Charles Boyer, thus the name Four Star. The studio was noted for making TV westerns, but it also produced detective and police shows. The studio was sold to New World Pictures in 1989.

19. According to Trudy Gilbert, the composer's wife, Gilbert served as his own music editor, spotting all the cues for each episode. He worked closely with two associates, Al

Friede and Harry King, who are listed as music editors for the program, but it was Gilbert who supervised which cues were to be used for which spot.

20. In an early episode, McCain rescues Torrence, who portrays a washed-up peace officer who is now the town drunk. Just as McCain rescues Torrence from his life of alcoholism, Torrence saves McCain in a gunfight. Torrence's actions result in him becoming the town marshal.

21. Here I use the term "scene" for narrative segments and not necessarily in the more televisual sense of "shots." In my definition, a scene may have several shots, and even locations, such as walking from a hotel into the street and into the bank, etc.

22. Gilbert's sketch of this motif is labeled "Zwischenblatt 101" and is pitched in B minor, then transposed to E minor.

23. Musical examples for the episode are in Gilbert's manuscript obtained from the Gilbert Collection at the UCLA Music Library Special Collections.

24. This shift of signification of the leitmotif foreshadows the "migration of the signifier" mentioned in conjunction with *Twin Peaks* in chapter 9.

25. Although he was best known for his role in *The Rifleman*, Chuck Connors went on to star in the TV series *Branded* (1965–1966) and the film *The Poseidon Adventure* (1972) and made guest appearances on *Night Gallery* (1970–1973).

26. This fragment is taken from Gilbert's "stagecoach trouble" cue. It is the main theme played in the flute in D major.

27. Theorists have investigated how the traits of tonal music and narratives are similar. In particular, Patrick McCreless (1988) has adapted some of the tonal ideas of Schenker with Barthes's narrative theories as found in *S/Z*. McCreless (1988) refers to Schenker's syntactical *Ursatz* with its I–V–I bass arpeggiation and motion of scale degrees 3–2–1 in the upper part as a parallel with Barthes's idea of the hermeneutic sentence for narrative. In its simplest form, both the hermeneutic sentence and Schenker's fundamental structure have a beginning, middle, and end as well as a subject and predicate of being and doing, the subject being the tonic chord and the predicate being the motion from and to the tonic chord.

The legacy of tonality has carried into film scoring practices, first with silent film (and the use of preexisting music) and later with sound film and television. However, since film or television music is rarely continuous, as in art music, its ability to sustain narrative motion or trajectory may be called into question. While motion is indeed interrupted by the noncontinuous nature of the musical cues, the cues and the tonal areas in which they operate can be seen to exhibit the narrative functions listed by Barthes and interpreted for music by McCreless. While tonality in television music does not produce the tonal forms or tonal designs often found in a symphonic score, it may still carry the potential for pacing and cueing narrative in TV music scores. Tonal music on television can establish a sort of tonal narrative by establishing a tonic key, moving away from that key, and returning to it. Or the narrative may be frustrated, with no establishment of tonic, delayed return to tonic, or no return to tonic. The former situation can be seen as a proairectic code function; the latter, a hermeneutic code function. Both of these scenarios are found in Gilbert's score to the "Outlaw's Inheritance" episode.

28. For readers interested in learning more about Schenkerian analysis, I refer you to the source itself, *Free Composition* ([1935] 1979).

29. At this time there were usually three commercial breaks for a 30-minute program and six breaks for a 60-minute show. In this example, the breaks occur after the opening credits, between scenes 5 and 6, and between scene 8 and the epilogue (see Barnouw 1990: 280).

30. This delayed resolution of the "cadence" motif is reminiscent of Edward Cone's "promissory note" resolution in Schubert. See Cone 1982.

31. Think of John Williams's leitmotif for the shark in the film *Jaws*, for instance. The motif is played by cellos and basses in a very low register.

32. In fact, like many westerns at the time, *The Rifleman* could be quite violent, with several gunshot deaths occurring in an episode. Much of the violence is inherent to the genre at the time, but much of it can be attributed also to Peckinpah's direction.

33. This tonal motion is found in the "McCain's walk" cue (RD-119) of the composer's cue collection.

Chapter 6

1. Of course, I am oversimplifying Kant's notion of pleasure considerably, given the limited space devoted to it here. Kant regarded physical pleasure as the result of "sensation" while the higher pleasure of the mind derived from "imagination." A new account of Kant's philosophy of pleasure can be found in Rachel Zuckert's *Kant on Beauty and Biology* (2007), especially chapter 6.

2. In this regard, it is similar to the notion of *poeisis* and *esthesis* outlined by Jean-Jacques Nattiez (1990).

3. According to Kristeva, the *chora* is the earliest stage in psychosexual development. In this prelingual stage of development, humans are dominated by a chaotic mix of perceptions, feelings, and needs. They do not distinguish self from that of the mother or even the surrounding environment. Rather, humans spend their entire existence taking into themselves everything experienced as pleasurable without any acknowledgment of boundaries. This is the stage, then, when they are closest to the pure materiality of existence or what Lacan terms "the real." At this stage, humans are dominated entirely by drives of both life and death (see Kristeva 1984).

4. Peirce describes three types of interpretants: logical, emotional, and energetic.

5. There are notable exceptions, as many instrumentalists also have enjoyed success on television, including Doc Severinsen (on trumpet, leader of the NBC orchestra on *The Tonight Show Starring Johnny Carson*), Liberace (on piano, numerous guest appearances), Tommy and Jimmy Dorsey (mentioned above, though their program was short-lived), and of course, Lawrence Welk, whose longevity on television is legendary. Many of these programs, like *The Lawrence Welk Show*, also featured vocalists, and Liberace and renowned jazz trumpeter Louis Armstrong often sang as well as played while on television.

6. Barthes illustrates a less drastic example of these two types of pleasurable experiences in his famous comparison of two singers: the culturally impeccable classical singer Dietrich Fischer-Dieskau and folk singer Panzera. Barthes states that Fischer-Dieskau's voice induces a *plaisir* for the listener, that is, a Kantian form of mental pleasure based on cultural expectations, while Panzera's would instill *jouissance*, a pleasure of the body that extends beyond the realm of cultural expectation. To describe the difference, Barthes (1988: 182) borrows Kristeva's terms of phenotext and genotext and uses the terms "pheno-song" and "geno-song," pheno-song "covering all the features which belong to the structure of the language being sung, the rules of the genre, the coded form of the melisma, the composer's idiolect: in short everything in the performance which is in the service of communication, representation, expressions, everything which it values" and geno-song being "the volume of the singing and speaking voice, the space where significations germinate from within the language and its very materiality. It forms a signifying play having nothing to do with communication, representation (of feelings), expression; it is the apex (or that depth) of production where the melody really works at the language—not at what it says, but the voluptuousness of its sound-signifiers. It is where melody explores how the language works and identifies with that work."

7. This is not to say that several theatrical type singers did not have successful careers in television. Ethel Merman and Kate Smith, among others, made numerous appearances on television variety shows, despite (or perhaps because of) their big, theatrical voices. Nelson Eddy and Jeanette MacDonald, however, were less successful on television due to the operatic quality of their voices, which tended to translate poorly on the microphones of early TV.

8. According to Getty Images, the song being sung in this photo was "The Sun Shines on Andy," a tune unfamiliar to me and probably a parody of another song composed for this program.

9. The Internet Movie Database (www.imdb.com) reports a 1949 program, *The Sugarhill Times*, that was an all-black variety show that apparently had a one-year run, but I have not been able to trace its airing on any of the four networks at the time. The program featured as regulars composer-bandleader-singer Willie Bryant, singer Harry Belafonte, and singer-dancer Timmie Rogers.

10. According to Mary Ann Watson (n.d.), local sponsors were found but no sustaining national sponsors. This arrangement was not lucrative from the network's standpoint, and Cole praised NBC for their sustained efforts to find a national sponsor.

11. Uggams's show lasted only one season, but the next year black comedian Flip Wilson began a successful four-year tenure with his own show, *The Flip Wilson Show*, which ran through the 1975 season.

12. Sullivan actually was not hosting the show during Presley's first appearance because he was recovering from an automobile accident. Actor Charles Laughton served as guest host that evening.

13. See, among other sources, Brian Fairbanks, "Elvis: The Ed Sullivan Shows," www.angelfire.com/oh2/writer/Elvis_Sullivan.html (accessed Aug. 23, 2008).

313

14. "Supradiegetic" is Altman's (1987a: 69–70) term applied to music in film musicals in which actors lip-synch songs that are heard on the film.

15. See Kelly 1981 for more background on the show.

16. The hymn first appeared in Showalter's *The Glad Evangel, for Revival, Camp, and Evangelistic Meetings* (Dalton, Ga.: A. J. Showalter and Co., 1887). Elisha Hoffman contributed text for some of the stanzas. According to the NetHymnal Web site (http://www.cyberhymnal.org), the hymn was no stranger to Hollywood, as it was sung in the 1943 movie *The Human Comedy*, starring Mickey Rooney.

17. Altman (1987a) provides subgenres for film musicals, notably the show musical, the fairy-tale musical, and the folk musical, which Griffith's show emulates. The folk musical is noted for its use of ordinary characters often placed in rural settings. Notable folk musicals include *Oklahoma!*, *Carousel*, *State Fair*, and *The Music Man*.

18. In anthropology, the liminal is the transitional state between two phases of life, wherein individuals no longer belong to the society they previously were a part of and are not yet reincorporated into that society. In art, the liminal may be conceived as that which transcends normal practice into a new, ambiguous realm of performance. The liminoid becomes "superstructure" versus the liminal's "antistructure." Social examples of the liminoid are rituals that at one time had an ergic, or utilitarian, function but that today contain only ludic, or leisure, functions. Examples could include Christian confirmation or Jewish bar and bat mitzvah, historically rites of passage recognizing boys and girls as adults and functionally including them in mainstream society. Today, however, such rituals are viewed as largely symbolic, as opportunities for family reunions and the exchanging of gifts.

Chapter 7

1. *Twenty-One* (1956–1958) was a game show that began as an honest trivia contest between two players. Unfortunately, the first iterations of the program featured contestants who reportedly made a mockery of the format by demonstrating how little they really knew. Representatives of the show's sponsor, Geritol (a liquid iron and B-vitamin nutritional supplement), upon seeing the opening-night performance, reportedly became furious with the results and angrily ordered the rigging of *Twenty-One* so as to prevent a repeat of this incident. The result was contestants being fed answers to questions and ultimately deciding (with the consent of the participants) which contestants would win and lose. The rigged show came to light with the contest between Charles Van Doren, a popular college professor, and his opponent, the unpopular Herb Stempel, who was coached to take a dive and lose. Stempel answered a last question incorrectly but later threatened to blow the whistle on the show. The Federal Communications Commission caught wind of the scandal, and a congressional panel was convened with both Stempel and Van Doren testifying. The incident was the basis for the plot of the movie *Quiz Show* (1994).

2. Advertisers developed "a free-wheeling hipness of what finally began to live up to its name as the Creative Department" (Fink 2005: 128).

3. See chapter 3 of Himmelstein 1984 for a description of the process of finding psychographic groups for ads through marketing research techniques of the 1970s and 1980s.

4. Himmelstein (1984) identifies several individual commercial producers who enjoy reputations as creative artists and have also received awards for creative commercials, such as the Clio and Mobius awards.

5. As quoted on the Coca-Cola Web site: http://memory.loc.gov/ammem/ccmphtml/colaadv.html.

6. The demand for the song also is reported by Backer. At the same time, Pepsi Cola followed Coke's lead with its own pop song, "You've Got a Lot to Live, and Pepsi's Got a Lot to Give," in a campaign that was successful but never achieved the status of its counterpart.

7. The trend continues. See the Songtitle.Info: Music from TV Commercials Web site (www.songtitle.info) for 2002–2008 commercials that used pop tunes.

8. See chapter 1 of Frith 1997 for her three-stage model for advertising, which is similar to Fiske's "codes of meaning" model.

9. Coincidently, Nöth also uses the example of Coca-Cola, referring to the enameled Coca-Cola signs that bear the inscription "Drink Coca-Cola" instead of "Buy Coca-Cola."

10. These parameters are based on Jan LaRue's SHMeRG principle (sound, harmony, melody, rhythm, and growth). See LaRue 1992.

11. See Stefani's model of musical competencies (MMC) in appendix 2 of Stefani 1987a.

12. Quoted in an article in the *Village Voice*, May 17, 1992.

13. Roland Barthes regarded the quality or grain of the voice as essential in deriving pleasure from music (see chapter 6).

14. Nicole Biamonte (University of Iowa) calls this a "double plagal" progression, common in many rock tunes. "Pentatonic and Modal Systems in Rock Music," paper given at the 2008 Conference of Music Theory Midwest, Bowling Green State University, Bowling Green, Ohio, May16, 2008.

15. An interesting critique of the song can be found in the June 5, 1986, issue of *Rolling Stone*.

16. See Vermehren 1997: 199: "such cultural segregation is brought about when advertisers conceptualize people as consumers, and when they organize the 'market' into neatly distinct segments in accordance with class boundaries."

Chapter 8

1. Butler (1994: 296) also has acknowledged epistemological problems with defining genre: "The assumption underlying genre study is that television programs resemble one another and that grouping them together provides a context for understanding the meanings of a particular program." However, Butler sees no underlying definition of genre; rather, he relies on the viewer to define it based on experience, making his a sort

of audience-response model of genre. The problem becomes a chicken-or-the-egg issue as the viewer must be aware of a genre's characteristics in order to define a program within a particular genre, but in order to do that, the viewer must view many different types of television programs and somehow classify characteristics of similar programs without knowing what those characteristics are.

2. The first approach to genre is traced back to Claude Lévi-Strauss's notion of narrative as myth; the second, to articles on mass media by the Frankfurt School published in *Cahiers du cinéma*.

3. According to Butler, defining TV genre by style is rare. He uses the example of the musical (also a rare genre on TV) as a way of defining genre.

4. The postmodern attributes of TV and TV music are explored in more depth in chapter 9.

5. Reflecting the influence that nineteenth-century Romantic art music had on film composers, Dmitri Tiomkin, in accepting the Academy Award for his score to *The High and the Mighty* in 1955, said, "I'd like to thank Johannes Brahms, Johann Strauss, Richard Strauss, Richard Wagner..." (quoted in Flinn 1992: 3).

6. Mancini's score won the Grammy Award for best album of the year in 1958.

7. The use of jazz reflected a move by both television and film away from the classical Hollywood film style. During the 1950s, several films with jazz scores debuted, among them, *The Man with the Golden Arm* (1955). See Prendergast 1992, especially chapter 4, for an overview of film music in the 1950s and 1960s.

8. *Arrest and Trial* was brought back as a reprise series in 2000. It was produced by Dick Wolf, who, coincidentally, is executive producer of *Law and Order*.

9. For more on this topic, see Bloom 1997 and Straus 1990.

10. Hatten (1994: 291–292) has defined markedness as the "asymmetrical valuation of an opposition (in musical structure, language, culture). For musical meaning, markedness of structural oppositions correlates with markedness of (expressive or other) oppositions among cultural units. Marked entities have a greater (relative) specificity of meaning than do unmarked entities.... Stylistic meaning in music is systematically secured by correlations of oppositions between musical structures and cultural units, as mediated by markedness values." See also Hatten 2004.

11. The use of jazz in *M Squad* may not be considered marked when compared to films at the same time, however. Otto Preminger's film *The Man with the Golden Arm* (1955) featured a jazz score by Elmer Bernstein who utilized such artists as Shorty Rogers and drummer Shelly Manne. Although it was not technically a cop movie (the film did feature Emile Meyer as a police detective), the film was influential in showing that jazz could be used effectively in film and television dramas.

12. This marked versus unmarked process is tricky in television. In the 1970s, when the police drama was unmarked, so too was the detective series, especially programs involving characters who were former police officers who had become private detectives. These types of characters were undoubtedly intended to be marked, but because there were so many shows featuring such characters, they became unmarked, and finally, most of them became unmemorable.

13. The development of such products as TiVo, satellite and cable TV services, and online streaming is rapidly making this marker obsolete.

14. McCain's widower status may not be marked, however, as Yoggy (1995) cites several single-parent westerns that also aired at this time, including *Bonanza* (1959–1973), *The Big Valley* (1965–1969), and *The High Chaparral* (1967–1971), all mentioned in chapter 5.

15. Burlingame points out that Schumann's famous four-note motive was also the grounds for the first major lawsuit in television music. A similar motive occurs in the film score to *The Killers* (1946), by Miklós Rózsa. Robbins Music Corp. filed a lawsuit against Schumann for plagiarism; Schumann's lawyers contended that any plagiarism was unintentional, tracing similar motives to Dvořák's Cello Concerto and Brahms's Hungarian Dances. The suit was settled with both composers sharing royalties from the theme but with Schumann retaining screen credit. See Burlingame 1996: 16–17.

16. See Burlingame 1996 and "Mysteries of TV Music" on the ClassicThemes.com Web site, www.classicthemes.com/50sTVThemes/mysteriesOfTVM.html.

17. The score provided of course does not show the instrumentation that includes the drum parts of the TV theme. However, the inner parts of the score suggest the drum rhythms.

18. Instrumentation statistics are given in Burlingame 1996: 50.

19. Quincy Jones's theme to *Ironside* also is heavily jazz influenced, as is Earle Hagen's theme to *The Mod Squad*, both of which debuted at about the same time as *Hawaii Five-0*. The ambivalence about rock is evident in some of Hagen's comments about the show: "We used rock 'n' roll in the opening spots: chases, fights, and things like that, . . . but rock 'n' roll doesn't have any harmonic drive to it; it's rhythmic drive, which doesn't work well under dialogue. So when we got into scoring . . . we went to twelve-tone. With the exception of a theme that Shorty Rogers wrote that we used for an association with the kids . . . the rest of the scoring was always pretty tense" (as quoted in Burlingame 1996: 57–58). In fact, the theme to *Mod Squad* is not rock, but like *Hawaii Five-0* is big band—inspired jazz with a rock beat (though it features a 1960s Farfisa electronic organ, a very popular instrument with rock groups in the 1960s).

20. Parker's theme to the program was distinctive in that it featured the tuba, an iconic reference to actor Joseph Conrad's large girth.

21. Viewers are reminded of the multiple numbers of homicides by one of the show's visual leitmotifs, a white board in the squad room listing every homicide case in the city. Names listed in black are solved cases; names listed in red are unsolved. The names of the murder victims are in columns representing each homicide officer's list of cases.

Chapter 9

1. Theatrical speech is dialogue issuing from characters in a narrative and is by far the most common form of speech in film. In theatrical speech, the dialogue heard has a dramatic, psychological, informative, and affective function. Chion argues that theatrical

speech goes above mere dialogue but conditions not only the sound track but also the entire mise-en-scène of the film. Character speech is central to the action of a narrative, but at the same time it makes the viewer forget that it structures the film. Textual speech is found in voice-over commentaries of sound film and is viewed by Chion as descending from silent film intertitles. Textual speech is common in literature but doubly powerful in film. It controls the narrative and takes away a sense of the autonomous audiovisual scene. For that reason it is used sparingly in film, but often in television, from text overlays in early television commercials to text crawls in the videographic news and documentary programs of the 1980s and 1990s. Chion argues that textual speech also is powerful in that it details aspects of visual images in film and makes them more concrete to the viewer. Usually a voice-over will impose itself on a narrative just long enough to establish the film's narrative framework, setting, and so forth, and then disappear. Finally, emanation speech is that which is heard but not necessarily understood fully on the screen. It occurs in two situations: first, where the speech of a character is not understood fully (too soft, too many speakers, etc.), and, second, where other aspects of filming and editing make the speech unimportant to the narrative. Chion points out that emanation speech is perhaps the rarest of the three.

2. See "Here's the story... of the dying TV theme song" on the MSNBC Web site at www.msnbc.msn.com/id/15320031 (accessed July 2, 2008), and Pennington 1995.

3. According to program trivia found on the Internet Movie Database, between the shows *Cheers* and *Frasier*, Kelsey Grammer portrayed the character Frasier Crane for 20 years. James Arness portrayed Marshal Matt Dillon on the western *Gunsmoke* also for 20 years, making these two the longest-running fictional characters on American prime-time television to date.

4. Despite the show's rarefied musical score, Milan Records released a CD containing diegetic music from the program; it features music by Etta James, Louis Armstrong, Rosemary Clooney, Sarah Vaughan, Nat "King" Cole, and other jazz artists as well as Grammer's "Tossed Salad and Scrambled Eggs" song. Credit is given also to composer Bruce Miller for contributing music to 34 of the 263 episodes (see the Internet Movie Database at imbd.com). The rarefied music is consistent in employing the jazz style topic to connote urban sophistication.

5. I was told by Greg Haggerty, a musician who worked on the show, that all of the music was produced with only three synthesizers.

6. That particular music number (seen on YouTube) featured a cameo appearance by Lt. Howard Hunter (James Sikking), head of the SWAT team on *Hill Street Blues*, complete with his trademark pipe.

7. See "A Streetcar Named Marge" and "Marge vs. the Monorail," both from the fourth season, and "Simpsoncalifragilisticexpiala(d'OH!)cious" from season eight.

8. "Acousmatic" music is diegetic music in which the source of the music is not seen.

9. Bernard Herrmann's theme to *The Twilight Zone* (which could be considered a predecessor show) oscillates between only two chords before moving to a final cadence on a third chord. In sharp contrast is the *Twilight Zone's* second theme by Marius Constant,

an almost schizophrenic collage of harmonies and gestures. In fact, Constant's theme to *The Twilight Zone* is a series of independent compositional fragments spliced together for the show.

10. In the concert hall, the musical works of John Cage are usually cited as postmodern musical texts, but works by other composers, such as the minimalist composers, are frequently included. Luciano Berio's *Sinfonia* is cited as a quintessential postmodernist work in that much of it is a collage of various literary and musical texts, including excerpts of speeches by Martin Luther King and Claude Lévi-Strauss and poetry by Thomas Beckett, all set within a musical framework that quotes from other musical pieces by Berio and Boulez as well as the scherzo movement of Mahler's "Resurrection" Symphony. Using the analogy of music to architecture, Jane Piper Clendinning believes that a postmodern approach to music is through observing a diversity of styles, collages, and pastiches. Some argue, though, that collage is also a modernist form, especially in reference to visual art.

11. The progression in this case is the I–vi–IV–V7 progression, which in C major would involve the chords C–a minor–F–G7.

12. These cues can be found on the *Twin Peaks* CD (Warner Bros., ASIN: B000002LMM).

13. The migration of leitmotifs is not an innovation with *Twin Peaks*, as evident in a similar situation in the "Outlaw's Inheritance" episode of *The Rifleman*, where the "spur the horses" motif was applied to the villain Stafford at the beginning of the episode and, toward the end, to Mark. Practically speaking, recycling themes is necessary for economies of time and cost: time constraints on composers are too great for them to compose original works for each episode. However, the case made here is that this recycling can also be viewed artistically as an aspect of postmodernist thinking.

References

Abbate, Carolyn. 2004. "Music—Drastic or Gnostic." *Critical Inquiry* 30/3: 505–536.

Adorno, Theodor, and Hans Eisler. [1947] 1994. *Composing for the Films.* With a New Introduction by Graham McCann. London: Athlone.

Agawu, V. Kofi. 1991. *Playing with Signs: A Semiotic Interpretation of Classic Music.* Princeton, N.J.: Princeton University Press.

———. 1999. "The Challenge of Semiotics." In *Rethinking Music.* Edited by Nicolas Cook and Mark Everist, 138–160. Oxford: Oxford University Press.

Allen, Robert. 1992. "More Talk about TV." In *Channels of Discourse, Reassembled: Television and Contemporary Criticism.* 2nd ed. Edited by Robert C. Allen, 1–30. London: Routledge.

Altman, Rick. 1987a. *The American Film Musical.* Bloomington: Indiana University Press.

———. 1987b. "Television Sound." In *Television: The Critical View.* 4th ed. Edited by Horace Newcomb, 566–584. New York: Oxford University Press.

———. 1995. "A Semantic/Syntactic Approach to Film Genre." In *Film Genre Reader II.* Edited by Barry Keith Grant, 26–40. Austin: University of Texas Press.

Aswad, Jem. 2008. "Mark Snow: The X Factor." ASCAP Web site; http://www.ascap.com/filmtv/snow.html (accessed July 2, 2008).

Backer, Bill. 1993. *The Care and Feeding of Ideas.* New York: Times Books (Random House).

Barnes, Ken. 1988. "Top 40 Radio: A Fragment of the Imagination." In *Facing the Music: A Pantheon Guide to Popular Culture.* Edited by Simon Frith, 8–50. New York: Pantheon.

Barnouw, Erik. 1968. *A History of Broadcasting in the United States, Vol. 2: The Golden Web, 1933–1953.* New York: Oxford University Press.

———. 1978. *The Sponsor: Notes on a Modern Potentate.* Oxford: Oxford University Press.

———. 1990. *Tube of Plenty: The Evolution of American Television*, 2nd rev. ed. New York: Oxford University Press.

Barthes, Roland. 1972. *Mythologies*. Selected and translated from the French by Annette Lavers. New York: Hill and Wang. (Orig. pub. 1957.)

———. 1973. *Le Plaisir du texte*. Paris: Seuil. [English translation, *The Pleasure of the Text*, translated by Richard Miller. New York: Hill and Wang, 1975.]

———. 1974. *S/Z*. Translated by Richard Miller. Preface by Richard Howard. New York: Hill and Wang.

———. 1988. *Image-Music-Text*. New York: Hill and Wang. (Orig. pub. 1977.)

Bloom, Harold. 1997. *The Anxiety of Influence: A Theory of Poetry*. 2nd ed. New York: Oxford University Press.

Bond, Jeff. 1999. *The Music of Star Trek*. Los Angeles: Lone Eagle Press.

Booth, Mark. 1990. "Jingle: Pepsi Cola Hits the Spot." In *On Record: Rock, Pop, and the Written Word*. Edited by Simon Frith and Andrew Goodwin, 320–325. New York: Pantheon.

Bordwell, David. 1985. *Narration in the Fiction Film*. Madison: University of Wisconsin Press.

Bordwell, David, and Kristin Thompson. 1993. *Film Art: An Introduction*. 4th ed. New York: McGraw-Hill.

Bowman, Roger. 1949a. "Music for Films in Television." *Film Music Notes* 8/5: 20.

———. 1949b. "New Regulations Proposed for Music in T.V. Films." *Film Music Notes* 9/2: 6.

Bremond, Claude. 1970. "Morphology of the French Folktale." *Semiotica* 2: 247–276.

Briggs, John. 1959. "Aiding the Composer: Original Musical Scores Are Obtained for *Twentieth Century* Series." *New York Times*, April 12, 2:11.

Brown, Royal S. 1994. *Overtones and Undertones: Reading Film Music*. Berkeley: University of California Press.

Brumburgh, Gary. 2008. "Andy Williams." Internet Movie Database; http://www.imdb.com/name/nm0930023/bio (accessed Oct. 25, 2008).

Burkholder, J. Peter. 2006. "A Simple Model for Associative Musical Meaning." In *Approaches to Meaning in Music*. Edited by Byron Almèn and Edward Pearsall, 76–106. Bloomington: Indiana University Press.

Burlingame, Jon. 1996. *TV's Biggest Hits: The Story of Television Themes from "Dragnet" to "Friends."* New York: Schirmer.

Burnham, Scott G. 1995. *Beethoven Hero*. Princeton, N.J.: Princeton University Press.

Butler, Jeremy. 1994. *Television: Critical Methods and Applications*. Belmont, Calif.: Wadsworth.

———. 1997. "Police Shows." In *Encyclopedia of Television*, vol. 3. Edited by Horace Newcomb, Cary O'Dell, and Noelle Watson, 1779–1783. Chicago: Fitzroy.

Caldwell, John Thornton. 1995. *Televisuality: Style, Crisis, and Authority in American Television*. New Brunswick, N.J.: Rutgers University Press.

Caplin, William. 1998. *Classical Form: A Theory of Formal Functions for the Instrumental Music of Haydn, Mozart, and Beethoven*. New York: Oxford University Press.

Castleman, Harry, and Walter J. Podrazik. 1982. *Watching TV: Four Decades of American Television*. New York: McGraw-Hill.

Cawelti, John. 1971. *The Six-Gun Mystique*. Bowling Green, Ohio: Bowling Green University Popular Press.

————. 1999. *The Six-Gun Mystique Sequel*. Bowling Green, Ohio: Bowling Green University Popular Press.

Chandler, Daniel. 2002. *Semiotics: The Basics*. New York: Routledge.

Charaudeau, Patrick. 1983. *Langage et discourse: Elements de semiolinguistique*. Paris: Hatchette.

Chatman, Seymour. 1978. *Story and Discourse: Narrative Structure in Fiction and Film*. Ithaca, N.Y.: Cornell University Press.

————. 1990. *Coming to Terms: The Rhetoric of Narrative in Fiction and Film*. Ithaca, N.Y.: Cornell University Press.

Chion, Michel. 1994. *Audio-Vision: Sound on Screen*. Edited and translated by Claudia Gorbman. New York: Columbia University Press.

Chotzinoff, Samuel. 1949. "Music in Television." *Variety*, January 5, 170.

Clendinning, Jane Piper. 2002. "Postmodern Architecture/Postmodern Music." In *Postmodern Music/Postmodern Thought*. Edited by Judy Lochhead and Joseph Auner, 119–140. New York: Routledge.

Coe, Steve. 1991. "Quality TV: Hollywood's Elusive Illusions." *Broadcasting*, November 18, 3.

Collins, Jim. 1992. "Television and Postmodernism." In *Channels of Discourse Reassembled*, 2nd ed. Edited by Robert C. Allen, 327–353. London: Routledge.

Cone, Edward T. 1982. "Schubert's Promissory Note: An Exercise in Musical Hermeneutics." *19th-Century Music* 5: 233–241.

Connor, Steven. 1989. *Postmodernist Culture: An Introduction to Theories of the Contemporary*. Oxford: Blackwell.

Cook, Nicholas. 1998. *Analyzing Musical Multimedia*. New York: Oxford University Press.

————. 2006. "Uncanny Moments: Juxtaposition and the Collage Principle in Music." In *Approaches to Meaning in Music*. Edited by Byron Almèn and Edward Pearsall, 107–134. Bloomington: Indiana University Press.

Cooke, James Francis. 1949. "The New World of Television: A Conference with Paul Whiteman." *Etude* 67 (June): 341–342.

Covach, John, and Graeme Boone, eds. 1997. *Understanding Rock: Essays in Musical Analysis*. New York: Oxford University Press.

Cox, Christopher, and Daniel Warner. 2004. *Audio Culture: Readings in Modern Music*. New York: Continuum.

Creeber, Glen, ed. 2001. *The Television Genre Book*. London: British Film Institute.

Culler, Jonathan. 1975. *Structuralist Poetics: Structuralism, Linguistics, and the Study of Literature*. Ithaca, N.Y.: Cornell University Press.

————. 1981. *The Pursuit of Signs: Semiotics, Literature, Deconstruction*. Ithaca, N.Y.: Cornell University Press.

Donelly, K. J. [Kevin]. 2005. *The Spectre of Sound: Music in Film and Television*. London: British Film Institute.

Eaton, Mick. 1981. "Television Situation Comedy." In *Popular Television and Film*. Edited by Tony Bennett, Susan Boyd-Bowman, Colin Mercer, and Janet Woollacott, 26–52. London: British Film Institute.

Eco, Umberto. 1979. *A Theory of Semiotics*. Bloomington: Indiana University Press.

Elias, Albert. 1956. "TV Music by Contemporary Composers." *Etude* 74 (Nov.): 22.

Everett, Walter. 1999. *The Beatles as Musicians: Revolver through the Anthology*. New York: Oxford University Press.

———. 2001. *The Beatles as Musicians: The Quarry Men through Rubber Soul*. New York: Oxford University Press.

Fauconnier, Giles. 1997. *Mappings in Thought and Language*. Cambridge: Cambridge University Press.

Fauconnier, Giles, and Mark Turner. 2002. *The Way We Think: Conceptual Blending and the Mind's Hidden Complexities*. New York: Basic Books.

Faulkner, Robert. 2003. *Music on Demand: Composers and Careers in the Hollywood Film Industry*. New Brunswick, N.J.: Transaction. (Orig. pub. 1983.)

Feuer, Jane. 1984. "The MTM Style." In *MTM: Quality Television*. Edited by Jane Feuer, Paul Kerr, and Tise Vahimagi, 32–60. London: British Film Institute.

———. 1986 "Narrative Form in American Network Television." In *High Theory/Low Culture: Analyzing Popular Television and Film*. Edited by Colin MacCabe, 101–114. Manchester: Manchester University Press.

———. 1992. "Genre Study and Television." In *Channels of Discourse, Reassembled*. Edited by Robert C. Allen, 138–160. Chapel Hill: University of North Carolina Press.

———. 1994. "Melodrama, Serial Form, and Television Today." In *Television: The Critical View*. 5th ed. Edited by Horace Newcomb, 551–562. New York: Oxford University Press.

Fink, Robert. 2005. *Repeating Ourselves: American Minimal Music as Cultural Practice*. Berkeley: University of California Press.

Fiske, John. 1987. *Television Culture*. London: Routledge.

———. 1989. *Understanding Popular Culture*. Boston: Unwin Hyman.

———. 1990. *Introduction to Communication Studies*. London: Routledge.

Fiske, John, and John Hartley. 1978. *Reading Television*. London: Methuen.

Flinn, Caryl. 1992. *Strains of Utopia: Gender, Nostalgia, and Hollywood Film Music*. Princeton, N.J.: Princeton University Press.

Frith, Katherine Toland. 1997. "Undressing the Ad: Reading Culture in Advertising." In *Undressing the Ad: Reading Culture in Advertising*. Edited by Katherine Toland Frith, 1–17. New York: Peter Lang.

Geis, Michael. 1982. *The Language of Television Advertising*. New York: Academic Press.

Genette, Gérard. 1980. *Narrative Discourse: An Essay in Method*. Translated by Jane E. Lewin. Foreword by Jonathan Culler. Ithaca, N.Y.: Cornell University Press.

Genova, Tom, Webmaster. 2001. *Television History—The First 75 Years*; http://www.tvhistory.tv/1946%20QF.htm (launched April 9).

Goodwin, Andrew. 1992. *Dancing in the Distraction Factory: Music Television and Popular Culture*. Minneapolis: University of Minnesota Press.

Gorbman, Claudia. 1987. *Unheard Melodies: Narrative Film Music*. Bloomington: Indiana University Press.

———. 2004. "Aesthetics and Rhetoric." *American Music* 22 (Spring): 14–26.

Greenlee, Douglas. 1973. *Peirce's Concept of Sign.* The Hague: Mouton.

Greimas, Algirdas. 1987. *On Meaning: Selected Writings in Semiotic Theory.* Translation by Paul J. Perron and Frank H. Collins. Foreword by Fredric Jameson. Minneapolis: University of Minnesota Press.

Hall, Stuart. 1981. "Notes on Deconstructing 'the Popular'." In *People's History and Socialist Theory.* Edited by Raphael Samuel, 227–240. London: Routledge.

Harman, C. 1951. "Use of Music on Video: Ways in Which Programs Employ Live and Recorded Performances." *New York Times*, February 11, 2:7.

Hatten, Robert. 1994. *Musical Meaning in Beethoven: Markedness, Correlation, and Interpretation.* Bloomington: Indiana University Press.

———. 2004. *Interpreting Musical Gestures, Topics, and Tropes: Mozart, Beethoven, and Schubert.* Bloomington: Indiana University Press.

Hawes, William. 1986. *American Television Drama: The Experimental Years.* Birmingham: University of Alabama Press.

Hebdige, Dick. 1979. *Subculture, the Meaning of Style.* London: Methuen.

Herr, Norman. n.d. "Television and Health." *The Sourcebook for Teaching Science* Web site, http://www.csun.edu/science/health/docs/tv&health.html (accessed Oct. 1, 2008).

Heylbut, Rose. 1945. "The Background of Background Music: How NBC's Experts Fit Music to Dramatic Shows." *Etude* 63 (Sept.): 493–494.

Himmelstein, Hal. 1984. *Television Myth and the American Mind.* New York: Praeger.

Huron, David. 1989. "Music in Advertising: An Analytic Paradigm." *Musical Quarterly* 73: 557–574.

Jakobson, Roman. 1980. *The Framework of Language.* Ann Arbor: University of Michigan Press.

Jameson, Fredric. 1983. "Pleasure: A Political Issue." In *Formations of Pleasure.* Edited by Tony Bennett et al., 1–13. London: Routledge.

———. 1991. *Postmodernism, or the Cultural Logic of Late Capitalism.* Durham, N.C.: Duke University Press.

Jankélévitch, Vladimir. 2003. *Music and the Ineffable.* Translated by Carolyn Abbate. Princeton, N.J.: Princeton University Press.

Kalinak, Kathryn. 1992. *Settling the Score.* Madison: University of Wisconsin Press.

———. 1995. "Disturbing the Guests with This Racket: Music and *Twin Peaks.*" In *Full of Secrets: Critical Approaches to* Twin Peaks. Edited by David Lavery, 82–92. Detroit: Wayne State University Press.

Kaminsky, Stuart M. With Jeffrey H. Mahan. 1985. *American Television Genres.* Chicago: Nelson-Hall.

Kaplan, E. Ann 1987. *Rocking around the Clock: Music Television, Postmodernism, and Consumer Culture.* New York: Methuen.

Karlin, Fred, and Rayburn Wright. 1990. *On the Track: A Guide to Contemporary Film Scoring.* Foreword by John Williams. New York: Schirmer.

Karmen, Steve. 1989. *Through the Jingle Jungle.* New York: Billboard Books.

———. 2005. *Who Killed the Jingle? How a Unique American Art Form Disappeared.* Milwaukee, Wisc.: Hal Leonard Corp.

Kassabian, Anahid. 2001. *Hearing Film: Tracking Identifications in Contemporary Hollywood Film Music*. New York: Routledge.

Kellner, Douglas. 1999. "*The X-Files* and the Aesthetics and Politics of Postmodern Pop." *Journal of Aesthetics and Art Criticism* 57/2: 161–176.

Kelly, Richard. 1981. *The Andy Griffith Show*. Winston-Salem, N.C.: John Blair.

Kivy, Peter. 1980. *The Corded Shell: Reflections on Musical Expression*. Princeton, N.J.: Princeton University Press.

———. 1984. *Sound and Semblance: Reflections on Musical Representation*. Princeton, N.J.: Princeton University Press.

———. 1988. *Osmin's Rage: Philosophical Reflections on Opera, Drama, and Text*. Princeton, N.J.: Princeton University Press.

———. 1989. *Sound Sentiment: An Essay on the Musical Emotions*. Philadelphia: Temple University Press.

Klein, Michael. 2005. *Intertextuality in Western Art Music*. Bloomington: Indiana University Press.

Kozloff, Sarah. 1992. "Narrative Theory and Television." In *Channels of Discourse, Reassembled*. 2nd ed. Edited by Robert C. Allen, 67–100. Chapel Hill: University of North Carolina Press.

Kramer, Jonathan D. 2002. "The Nature and Origins of Musical Postmodernism." In *Postmodern Music/Postmodern Thought*. Edited by Judy Lochhead and Joseph Auner, 13–26. New York: Routledge.

Kramer, Lawrence. 1995. *Postmodern Music and Postmodern Knowledge*. Berkeley: University of California Press.

———. 2002. *Musical Meaning: Toward a Critical History*. Berkeley: University of California Press.

Kristeva, Julia. 1984. *Revolution in Poetic Language*. Introduction by Leon S. Roudiez. New York: Columbia University Press.

Lacey, Nick. 2000. *Narrative and Genre: Key Concepts in Media*. New York: St. Martin's.

LaRue, Jan. 1992. *Guidelines for Style Analysis*. Warren, Mich.: Harmonie Park Press.

Lavery David, Angela Hague, and Marla Cartwright. 1996. "Introduction: Generation X—*The X-Files* and the Cultural Moment." In *Deny All Knowledge: Reading* The X-Files. Edited by David Lavery, Angela Hague, and Marla Cartwright. Syracuse, N.Y.: Syracuse University Press.

Lerdahl, Fred. 2001. *Tonal Pitch Space*. New York: Oxford University Press.

Lerner, Neil. 2001. "Copland's Music of Wide Open Spaces: Surveying the Pastoral Trope in Hollywood." *Musical Quarterly* 85/3: 477–515.

Levinson, Jerrold. 1996a. "Film Music and Narrative Agency." In *Post Theory: Reconstructing Film Studies*. Edited by David Bordwell and Noël Carroll, 283–306. Madison: University of Wisconsin Press.

———. 1996b. *The Pleasures of Aesthetics*. Ithaca, N.Y.: Cornell University Press.

———. 2004. "Music as Narrative and Music as Drama." *Mind and Language* 19/4: 428–441.

Lévi-Strauss, Claude. 1970. *The Raw and the Cooked*. Translated from the French by John and Doreen Weightman. New York: Harper and Row.

Lewin, David. 1987. *Generalized Musical Intervals and Transformations.* New Haven:Yale University Press.

Lidov, David. 1980. "Musical and Verbal Semantics." *Semiotica* 31/3–4: 369–391.

———. 1999. *Elements of Semiotics.* New York: St. Martin's.

Littlefield, Richard. 1998. "The Silence of the Frames." In *Music/Ideology: Resisting the Aesthetic.* Edited by Adam Krims, 213–232. Amsterdam: G + B Arts International.

Littlefield, Richard, and David Neumeyer. 1992. "Rewriting Schenker: Narrative–History–Ideology." *Music Theory Spectrum* 14/1: 38–65.

London, Justin. 2000. "Leitmotivs and Musical Reference in the Classical Score." In *Music and Cinema.* Edited by James Buhler, Caryl Flinn, and David Neumeyer, 85–98. Hanover, N.H.: Wesleyan University Press.

Lotman, Juri. 1976. *Semiotics of Cinema.* Translated from Russian, with foreword, by Mark E. Suino. Ann Arbor: Department of Slavic Languages and Literature, University of Michigan.

Lull, James. 1992. *Popular Music as Communication.* London: Sage.

MacDonald, J. Fred. 1979. *Don't Touch That Dial: Radio Programming in American Life from 1920 to 1960.* Chicago: Nelson-Hall.

Martinez, José Luiz. 1997. *Semiosis in Hindustani Music.* Helsinki: Acta Semiotica Fennica.

Maus, Fred. 1991. "Music as Narrative." *Indiana Theory Review* 12: 1–34.

———. 1997. "Music as Drama." In *Music and Meaning.* Edited by Jenefer Robinson, 105–130. Ithaca, N.Y.: Cornell University Press.

McClary, Susan. 1991. *Feminine Endings: Music, Gender, and Sexuality.* Minneapolis: University of Minnesota Press.

McCreless, Patrick. 1988. "Roland Barthes's *S/Z* from a Musical Point of View." *In Theory Only* 10/7: 1–29.

———. 1991. "The Hermenuetic Sentence and Other Literary Models for Tonal Closure." *Indiana Theory Review* 12: 35–73.

McKibben, Gordon. 1998. *Cutting Edge: Gillette's Journey to Global Leadership.* Boston: Harvard Business School Press.

McQuail, Denis. 1984. *Mass Communication Theory: An Introduction.* London: Sage.

McQuail, Denis, and Sven Windhal. 1993. *Communication Models for the Study of Mass Communications.* 2nd ed. London: Longham.

McQueen, David. 1998. *Television: A Media Student's Guide.* London: Arnold.

Mellencamp, Patricia. 1977. "Sound and Spectator." *Cin e-tracts* 1/2: 28–35.

Mercer, Colin. 1983. "A Poverty of Desire: Pleasure and Popular Politics." In *Formations of Pleasure.* Edited by Tony Bennett et al., 84–100. London: Routledge.

Metz, Christian. 1974a. *Film Language: A Semiotics of the Cinema.* New York: Oxford University Press.

———. 1974b. *Language and Cinema.* The Hague: Mouton.

Meyer, Leonard. 1989. *Style and Music.* Philadelphia: University of Pennsylvania Press.

Middleton, Richard. 1990. *Studying Popular Music.* Maidenhead, Berkshire, U.K.: Open University Press.

Mills, Bob. 1998. "Everything I Know about Selling I Learned from Bob Hope." *Judy Vorfeld's Webgrammar's Ezine*; http://www.webgrammar.com/article-mills.html (accessed June 7, 2007).

Mittell, Jason. 2004. "A Cultural Approach to Television Genre Theory." In *The Television Studies Reader*. Edited by Robert C. Allen and Annette Hill, 171–181. London: Routledge.

Molino, Jean. 1975. "Fait musical et sémiologie de la musique." *Musique en jeu* 17: 37–62.

Monelle, Raymond. 2000. *The Sense of Music*. Princeton, N.J.: Princeton University Press.

———. 2006. *The Musical Topic: Hunt, Military and Pastoral*. Bloomington: Indiana University Press.

Morris, Charles W. 1946. *Signs, Language, and Behavior*. New York: Prentice-Hall.

Mundy, John. 1999. *Popular Music on Screen*. Manchester: Manchester University Press.

Nalle, Billy. 1962. "Music for Television Drama." *Music Journal* 20/1: 120–121.

Nattiez, Jean-Jacques. 1990. *Music and Discourse: Toward a Semiology of Music*. Translated by Carolyn Abbate. Princeton, N.J.: Princeton University Press, 1990.

Neale, Stephen. 2000. *Genre and Hollywood*. London: Routledge, 2000.

Newcomb, Anthony. 1987. "Schumann and Late Eighteenth Century Narrative Strategies." *19th Century Music* 11: 164–174.

Noske, Frits. 1977. *The Signifier and the Signified: Studies in the Operas of Mozart and Verdi*. The Hague: Martinus Nijhoff.

Nöth, Winfried. 1987. "Advertising: The Frame Message." In *Marketing and Semiotics*. Edited by Jean Umiker-Sebeok, 279–294. Berlin: Mouton de Gruyter.

———. 1990. *Handbook of Semiotics*. Bloomington: Indiana University Press.

Paulin, Scott D. 2000. "Richard Wagner and the Fantasy of Cinematic Unity: The Idea of the Gesamtkunstwerk in the History and Theory of Film Music." In *Music and Cinema*. Edited by James Buhler, Caryl Flinn, and David Neumeyer, 58–84. Hanover, N.H.: Wesleyan University Press.

Peirce, Charles S. 1931–1958. *Collected Papers of Charles Sanders Peirce*. 8 vols. Edited by Charles Hartshorne, Paul Weiss, and Arthur Burks. Cambridge: Harvard University Press.

Pennington, Gail. 1995. "Have TV Songs Sung Their Last?" *St Louis Post Dispatch*, July 27, 44.

Perry, David. 1967. *The Concept of Pleasure*. The Hague: Mouton.

Prendergast, Roy. 1992. *Film Music: A Neglected Art*. 2nd ed. New York: W. W. Norton.

Propp, Vladimir. 1968. *Morphology of the Folktale*. 2nd ed. Translated by Laurence Scott. Introduction by Svatava Pirkova-Jakobson. Austin: University of Texas Press. (Orig. pub. 1958.)

Rapée, Ernö. 1924. *Motion Picture Moods: For Pianists and Organists*. New York: Schirmer.

———. 1925. *Encyclopaedia of Music for Motion Pictures*. New York: Belwin.

Ratner, Leonard. 1980. *Classic Music: Expression, Form, and Style*. New York: Schirmer.

References

Reeves, Jimmie, Mark Rodgers, and Michael Epstein. 1996. "Rewriting Popularity: The Cult Files." In *Deny All Knowledge: Reading* The X-Files. Edited by David Lavery, Angela Hague, and Marla Cartwright. Syracuse, N.Y.: Syracuse University Press.

Reeves, Rosser. 1950. "Memo to Copy Department." Unpublished manuscript (Sept. 11). Madison: Wisconsin Institute for Film and Television Research.

————. 1961. *Reality in Advertising*. London: MacGibbon and Kee.

Reiss, Steve, and Neil Feineman. 2000. *Thirty Frames per Second: The Visionary Art of the Music Video*. New York: Harry N. Abrams.

Ricoeur, Paul. 1980. "Narrative Time." *Critical Inquiry* 7: 169–190.

Rodman, Ronald. 1997. "And Now an Ideology from Our Sponsor: Musical Style and Semiosis in American Television Commercials." *College Music Symposium* 37: 29–48.

Rothenbuhler, Eric, and Tom McCourt. 1992. "Commercial Radio and Popular Music: Processes of Selection and Factors of Influence." In *Popular Music and Communication*. Edited by James Lull, 101–115. Newbury Park, Calif: Sage.

Rubiner, Joanna. n.d. "Lawrence Welk Biography." Index of Musician Biographies Web site; http://www.musicianguide.com/biographies/1608000917/Lawrence-Welk.html (accessed May 28, 2008).

Samuels, Robert. 1995. *Mahler's Sixth Symphony: A Study in Semiotics*. Cambridge: Cambridge University Press.

Sanders, Coyne, and Tom Gilbert. 1993. *Desilu: The Story of Lucille Ball and Desi Arnaz*. New York: Quill William Morrow.

Saussure, Ferdinand de. 1959. *Course in General Linguistics*. Edited by Charles Bally and Albert Sechehaye, in collaboration with Albert Reidlinger. Translated, with an introduction and notes, by Wade Baskin. New York: McGraw-Hill Book Co.

Schenker, Heinrich. [1935] 1979. *Free Composition*; vol. 3 of *New Musical Theories and Fantasies*. Translated and edited by Ernst Oster. New York: Longman.

Scodari, Christine. n.d. "Northern Exposure: U.S. Dramedy." Museum of Broadcast Communications Web site; http://www.museum.tv/archives/etv/N/htmlN/northernexpo/nothernexpo.htm (accessed March 28, 2005).

Sconce, Jeffrey. n.d. "Twin Peaks: U.S. Serial Drama." Museum of Broadcast Communications Web site; http://www.museum.tv/archives/etv/T/htmlT/twinpeaks/twinpeaks.htm (accessed April 15, 2007).

Scott, Linda M. 1990. "Understanding Jingles and Needledrop: A Rhetorical Approach to Music in Advertising." *Journal of Consumer Research* 17/2: 223–236.

Scott, Tom. 1956. "Music for Television." *Film Music* 15/5: 19–23.

Seiter, Ellen. 1992. "Semiotics, Structuralism, and Television. In *Channels of Discourse, Reassembled*. Edited by Robert C. Allen, 31–66. Chapel Hill: University of North Carolina Press.

Shields, David Jackson. 2002. "The History of Production Music" (as updated on July 10, 2006). ClassicThemes.com; http://www.classicthemes.com/50sTVThemes/prodMusHistory.html.

Skiles, Marlin. 1976. *Music Scoring for TV and Motion Pictures*. Blue Ridge Summit, Pa.: Tab Books.

329

Sosnik, Harry. 1949. "Scoring for Television." *Variety*, January 5, 95.

————. 1963. "Songwriting." Unpublished manuscript (Oct. 6). Madison: Wisconsin Institute for Film and Television.

————. 1982. "The Rise (Radio) and the Fall (TV) in the Importance of Composers." *Variety*, January 20, 100.

Spadoni, Mike. 2004. *Cop Rock* (review). Television Heaven Web site; http://www.televisionheaven.co.uk (accessed Nov. 23, 2007).

Stefani, Gino. 1987a. "A Theory of Musical Competence." *Semiotica* 66/1–3: 7–22.

————. 1987b. "Melody: A Popular Perspective." *Popular Music* 6/1: 21–35.

Steiner, Fred. 1989. "What Were Musicians Saying about Movie Music during the First Decade of Sound?" In *Film Music 1*. Edited by Clifford McCarty, 81–107. New York: Garland.

Straus, Joseph. 1990. *Remaking the Past: Musical Modernism and the Influence of the Tonal.* Cambridge, Mass.: Harvard University Press.

Tagg, Philip. 1982. "Nature as a Musical Mood Category." Philip Tagg Web site; http://tagg.org/articles/nature.html (accessed Aug. 29, 2008).

————. 2000. *Kojak: Fifty Seconds of Television Music; Toward the Analysis of Affect in Popular Music.* New York: Mass Media Music Scholars' Press. (Orig. pub. 1979.)

Tarasti, Eero. 1994. *A Theory of Musical Semiotics.* Bloomington: Indiana University Press.

Tedlow, Richard. 1990. *New and Improved: The Story of Mass Marketing in America.* New York: Basic Book Publishers.

Todorov, Tzvetan. 1977. *The Poetics of Prose.* Translated from the French by Richard Howard. New foreword by Jonathan Culler. Ithaca, N.Y.: Cornell University Press.

Turino, Thomas. 1999. "Signs of Imagination, Identity, and Experience: A Peircian Semiotic Theory for Music." *Ethnomusicology* 43/2: 221–255.

Turner, Victor. 1982. *From Ritual to Theater: The Human Seriousness of Play.* New York: PAJ Publications.

————. 1986. *The Anthropology of Performance.* New York: PAJ Publications.

Ulanoff, Stanley M. 1977. *Advertising in America: An Introduction to Persuasive Communication.* New York: Hastings House.

van Baest, Arjan, and Hans van Driel. 1995. *The Semiotics of C.S. Peirce Applied to Music: A Matter of Belief.* Tilburg, the Netherlands: Tilburg University Press.

Vermehren, Christian. 1997. "Cultural Capital: The Cultural Economy of U.S. Advertising." In *Undressing the Ad: Reading Culture in Advertising.* Edited by Katherine Toland Frith, 197–224. New York: Peter Lang.

Vernallis, Carol. 2004. *Experiencing Music Video: Aesthetics and Cultural Context.* New York: Columbia University Press.

Wagner, Richard. 1900. *Opera and Drama*; vol. 2 of *Richard Wagner's Prose Works.* 2nd ed. Translated by William Ashton Ellis. London: Kegan Paul, Trench, Trübner and Co., Ltd. (Orig. pub. 1849.)

Watney, Simon. 1983. "The Connoisseur as Gourmet: The Aesthetics of Roger Fry and Clive Bell." In *Formations of Pleasure.* Edited by Tony Bennett et al., 66–83. London: Routledge.

Watson, Mary Ann. n.d. "The Nat 'King' Cole Show: U.S. Musical Variety." The Museum of Broadcast Communications Web site; http://www.museum.tv/archives/etv/N/htmlN/natkingcole/natkingcole.htm (accessed Nov. 21, 2008).

Weingarten, Marc. 2000. *Station to Station: The History of Rock 'n' Roll on Television.* New York: Pocket Books.

Westcott, Steven. 1985. *A Comprehensive Bibliography of Music for Film and TV.* Detroit Studies in Music Bibliography No. 54. Detroit: Information Coordinators.

White, Armond. 1988. "The Pop Solution: Commercials Move from Jingles to Singles." *Millimeter* 16: 89–90.

Wilk, Max. 1976. *The Golden Age of Television: Notes from the Survivors.* New York: Dell.

Williams, Betsy. 1994. "'North to the Future': *Northern Exposure* and Quality Television." In *Television: The Critical View.* 5th ed. New York: Oxford University Press.

Williams, Raymond. [1974] 1992. *Television: Technology and Cultural Form.* Introduction by Lynn Spiegel. Middletown, Conn., and Hanover, N.H.: Wesleyan University Press and University Press of New England.

Wiseman, Mary Bittner 1989. *The Ecstasies of Roland Barthes.* London: Routledge.

Woodward, Walt. 1982. *An Insider's Guide to Advertising Music.* New York: Art Direction Book Co.

Wyman, Bill. 2002. "Seinfeld." Salon.com; http://dir.salon.com/story/ent/masterpiece/2002/01/07/seinfeld/index.html? (accessed Nov. 27, 2007).

Yoggy, Gary. 1995. *Riding the Video Range: The Rise and Fall of the Western on Television.* Jefferson, N.C.: McFarland and Co.

Zbikowski, Lawrence. 2002. *Conceptualizing Music: Cognitive Structure, Theory, and Analysis.* New York: Oxford University Press.

Zicree, Marc Scott. 1982. *The Twilight Zone Companion.* New York: Bantam.

Zuckert, Rachel. 2007. *Kant on Beauty and Biology: An Interpretation of the Critique of Judgment.* Cambridge: Cambridge University Press.

Index

Page numbers in bold indicate illustrations and musical examples.